We Shall Return!

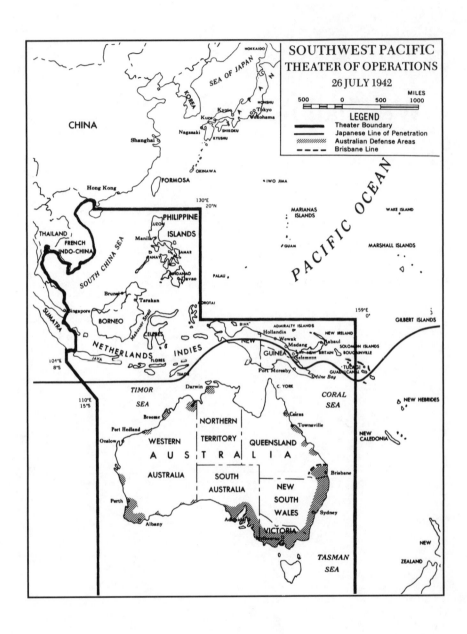

SOUTHWEST PACIFIC
THEATER OF OPERATIONS
26 JULY 1942

MILES

500   0   500   1000

LEGEND
Theater Boundary
Japanese Line of Penetration
Australian Defense Areas
Brisbane Line

We Shall Return!

MacArthur's Commanders and the Defeat of Japan 1942-1945

WILLIAM M. LEARY, Editor

THE UNIVERSITY PRESS OF KENTUCKY

Frontispiece: Southwest Pacific Theater of Operations, July 26, 1942.
Source: Hugh J. Casey, ed., *Engineers of the Southwest Pacific, 1941-1945*,
vol. 6 (Washington, D.C., 1951).

Photos on chapter opening pages courtesy of the following: MacArthur, Krueger,
U.S. Army; Blamey, Australian War Memorial; Kenney, Whitehead, U.S. Air
Force; Kinkaid, U.S. Navy; Eichelberger, Duke University Library; Barbey,
U.S. Naval Institute.

Copyright © 1988 by the University Press of Kentucky

Scholarly publisher for the Commonwealth,
serving Bellarmine College, Berea College, Centre
College of Kentucky, Eastern Kentucky University,
The Filson Club, Georgetown College, Kentucky
Historical Society, Kentucky State University,
Morehead State University, Murray State University,
Northern Kentucky University, Transylvania University,
University of Kentucky, University of Louisville,
and Western Kentucky University.

Editorial and Sales Offices: Lexington, Kentucky 40506-0024

Cataloging-in-Publication Data appear on p. 306

CONTENTS

MAPS

ACKNOWLEDGMENTS

When John Garraty asked me to do a biographical sketch of General Walter Krueger for the *Dictionary of American Biography*, I had no idea that the task would lead to a volume of essays on MacArthur's senior field commanders in World War II. Krueger proved an intriguing topic, however. During the course of my research, I was surprised to learn that so little had been written about him or about his associates in the Southwest Pacific. I decided that a more extended treatment of their contributions to MacArthur's triumphant return to the Philippines would fill a significant gap in the literature of the war.

D. Clayton James of Mississippi State University, MacArthur's foremost biographer, generously encouraged me and advised me at the inception of the project, while Stanley L. Falk came to my rescue at several crucial points along the way. This volume would not have been possible without their support. Alvin D. Coox of San Diego State University, a source of wise counsel over two decades, made several helpful suggestions. Lester D. Stephens, head of the history department at the University of Georgia, provided his usual full measure of sympathetic understanding. I am indeed fortunate to count them both as friends. My wife Margaret suggested the title; I am grateful to her for that—and for a lot more.

I have dedicated this book to the memory of a man whom I never met but whose letters over the years gave me great insight into the nature of war.

TO THE MEMORY OF

Lieutenant Colonel Raymond C. Mullen, Jr.
(1926-1986)

PREFACE

General Douglas MacArthur reached the end of what sometimes seemed a personal crusade on September 2, 1945. Standing on the deck of the battleship *Missouri* in the calm waters of Tokyo Bay, he watched with deep satisfaction as representatives of the Japanese government signed the instrument of surrender that ended World War II. "Today the guns are silent," MacArthur announced to the world on radio at the conclusion of the ceremony. He spoke about the winning of a great victory, the end of a great tragedy, and he recalled the "long, tortuous trail from those grim days of Bataan and Corregidor."[1]

The road to Tokyo Bay had begun in March 1942, when MacArthur reached Australia tired and frustrated after suffering a series of bitter defeats in the Philippines. The president of the United States, he told reporters at Adelaide, had ordered him to leave Corregidor, but this departure did not signal an end of the battle for the islands. He intended to lead a relief force back to the Philippines. "I came through," he announced, "and I shall return."[2]

MacArthur made good on his promise, if not as quickly as he had hoped. He had good reason to be proud of his triumph, and he deserved the acclaim that it brought him, but he had a lot of help.

In many ways, MacArthur's subordinates were the forgotten men of World War II. While European battlefield commanders such as Bradley and Patton became familiar names to the American people, Krueger and Eichelberger were relatively unknown. MacArthur dominated press releases from his theater. "Like everyone else in the Southwest Pacific," amphibious commander Vice Admiral Daniel E. Barbey later recalled, "I soon found myself fully into the habit of referring to 'MacArthur's troops,' 'MacArthur's planes,' and 'MacArthur's ships.' "[3] When General Eichelberger did receive favorable notice following the Battle of Buna, he incurred the wrath of his superior. Eichelberger quickly learned that MacArthur was not about to allow anyone to "rise up between him and his place in history."[4] Thereafter he maintained a low profile. On the eve of the planned invasion of Japan, a war correspondent felt able to write about

Krueger—a four-star general and MacArthur's senior field commander—
as "the mystery man of the Pacific."[5]

Several of MacArthur's subordinates published postwar accounts of
their service, but the public paid little notice. Historians also neglected
them, and not a single biography appeared in the four decades following
V-J Day.

This volume is intended to address a serious shortcoming in the literature of World War II in the Pacific. Stanley L. Falk begins with a critical
overview of MacArthur as strategist, calling into question his emphasis on
an advance through the Philippines as the best road to Tokyo. D.M. Horner then explores General Blamey's relationship with the theater commander, making clear that MacArthur lacked the diplomatic skills that
Dwight D. Eisenhower displayed in Europe. I write about Walter Krueger, the tough old professional soldier who was MacArthur's senior combat commander, defending him against charges of excessive timidity on
Leyte and Luzon. Herman Wolk demonstrates that command of the air
was essential to victory in the Southwest Pacific and that George Kenney
was one of the foremost air strategists of the war. As Gerald Wheeler
shows, MacArthur was often at loggerheads with the navy, but Thomas
Kinkaid earned his respect and admiration. Jay Luvaas and John Shortal
emphasize that MacArthur turned to the brilliant and temperamental
Robert Eichelberger when the going got toughest and that Eichelberger
always rose to the challenge. Donald Goldstein celebrates the tactical
leadership of Ennis Whitehead, an aggressive airman who deserves more
recognition than he has received. Finally, Paolo Coletta explains how
Daniel Barbey's mastery of amphibious warfare greatly contributed to victory in the Southwest Pacific.

MacArthur, to his great credit, was open to the ideas of his subordinates. Although he was not known at the beginning of the war for a keen
appreciation of air power or enthusiasm for amphibious operations, he became the foremost practitioner of both by war's end. MacArthur may have
come to believe that he had originated both concepts, but these essays
make clear that he had been educated by others. MacArthur's flexibility
and capacity for growth enabled him to seize upon innovations, employing them with vigor.

More detailed studies are needed before the role of MacArthur's subordinates can be fully understood, especially where his staff is concerned.
Richard K. Sutherland, as chief of staff, was closest to MacArthur at GHQ,
and the two men spent long hours together discussing strategy.[6] Sutherland did not hesitate to make major decisions in MacArthur's name, even
changing the timing of the assault on Leyte.[7] Still, how does one evaluate
his later claim that he, and not MacArthur, made practically *all* the major
strategic decisions in the Southwest Pacific theater?[8] Other key members
of MacArthur's staff who merit attention include Richard J. Marshall, the

quiet and methodical officer who served as Sutherland's deputy and helped to temper his superior's abrasiveness; Stephen J. Chamberlin, an accomplished professional who as G-3 (operations) worked closely and effectively with MacArthur's combat commanders; Charles A. Willoughby, MacArthur's temperamental intelligence officer; and Hugh J. Casey, the theater's often overlooked chief engineer.

This volume, then, represents only a beginning. We hope that its essays will provide both a point of departure and incentive for future scholarship.

ABBREVIATIONS

AEF	Allied Expeditionary Force
AAF	army air forces
ADS	aide-de-camp
AIF	Australian Imperial force
AK	large cargo ship
AP	armor piercing
APA	large amphibious transport
APD	high speed transport
ATC	amphibious training center
CINC	commander in chief
CNO	chief of naval operations
COMINCH	commander in chief (U.S. Navy)
CTF	commander, task force
CVE	aircraft carrier, escort
DUKW	amphibian truck
ESB	engineer special brigade
FEAF	Far East air forces
GHQ	general headquarters
HQ	headquarters
Landops	land operations
LCI	landing craft, infantry
LCI (Rs)	landing craft, infantry (with rocket launcher)
LCM	landing ship, medium
LCT	landing craft, tank
LCVP	landing craft, vehicle, personnel
LHQ	Allied land force headquarters
LSD	landing ship, dock
LSM	landing ship, medium
LST	landing ship, tank
LVT	landing vehicle, tractor

MP	military police
MTB	motor torpedo boat
PAC	Pacific area command
PBY	Consolidated patrol bomber
PC	patrol craft
POA	Pacific Ocean Areas
PT	patrol torpedo boat
RAAF	Royal Australian Air Force
RCT	regimental combat team
SC	subchaser
SOPAC	South Pacific
SWPA	Southwest Pacific area
TBS	talk-between-ships (radio)
TF	task force
TG	task group
TU	task unit
WAC	Women's Army Corps

Douglas MacArthur and the War against Japan

STANLEY L. FALK

More than any other American commander in World War II, Douglas MacArthur symbolized this country's fears, hopes, and expectations about the war. In the early, dark days of that conflict, he was the lonely hero in a desperate fight, boldly and firmly withstanding the onslaught of an evil foe. In his dramatic escape from siege to sanctuary, he epitomized the faith that victory lay even within defeat and that Japan's initial conquests were neither decisive nor permanent. In his pledge to return to the Philippines, he proclaimed the moral basis of America's cause and, in his forceful advance north from Australia, the increasing certainty of ultimate triumph.

No matter that his initial defeat was worse than it might have been or his subsequent victories less glorious and decisive than they appeared, MacArthur became for an admiring American public the heroic symbol of our military success. As such, he was practically immune to criticism, his detractors being apparently limited to jealous rivals in or out of uniform, uninformed skeptics, and other frustrated enemies. The theme of his greatness was reflected in the wartime press and in the early postwar writings of both journalists and historians. Only in recent decades have careful scholars exposed the general's weaknesses and failings and offered a more balanced view of his role as commander. Even then, some still insist on his genius.

MacArthur's intense and striking personality made him perhaps the most dramatic, exciting, and controversial general of World War II. A brave and distinguished soldier, he was at once imaginative, articulate, arrogant, theatrical, emotional, ambitious, energetic, contradictory, political, and charismatic. He combined a reckless desire for success with an unseemly paranoia, a blatant contempt for authority, and a fierce appeal for recognition and approval. His brilliant leadership and innovation on the battlefield were manifest, but they were often marred by questionable strategic judgments or unfortunate tactical decisions. Endowed with obvious courage, he wore distinctive uniforms, disdained to carry arms or protective equipment, and took extraordinary personal risks. Often his displays of valor seemed less spontaneous than staged, as if he were an actor carefully plotting each movement for effect. Gifted with an almost instinctive ability to handle the press, he enhanced his popular image or strengthened his demands on authority by skillful public appearances, dramatic interviews, and carefully worded announcements. But his fustian oratory and penchant for hyperbole frequently undermined his most impassioned arguments. His impressive military career, spanning half a century of battlefield triumphs in Europe, Mexico, and the Far East, sparkled with good fortune and grand achievements. Yet it was dominated by an almost psychological obsession with the Philippine Islands, which shaped his thoughts and deeds and in almost every sense dictated his actions in World War II.[1]

Douglas MacArthur was born in 1880, the son of the successful and flamboyant General Arthur MacArthur and of a determined and domineering mother who did much to influence his life and career. Entering the U.S. Military Academy in 1899, he graduated four years later at the top of his class. He served briefly in the Philippines and elsewhere in the Far East and in Washington and participated in the 1914 Mexican expedition, distinguishing himself in action at Vera Cruz. He fought in France during World War I, where he displayed outstanding bravery and leadership: he was decorated nine times, won his general's stars at the age of thirty-eight and ended the war in command of a division. Over the next decade, he left his mark as an innovative and progressive superintendent of the Military Academy, sat on the court-martial of the contentious General "Billy" Mitchell, and served two tours of duty in the Philippines.

In 1930 MacArthur became chief of staff of the army, holding this post for five years under Presidents Hoover and Roosevelt. He was probably best known for his controversial action in suppressing the 1932 Bonus March, but he made his major contribution in vigorously fighting off reductions in the military budget and in opposing other attempts to reduce the size and quality of the army. In 1935 he returned once again to the Philippines as military adviser to the Commonwealth, to organize and develop the Philippine armed forces in preparation for the planned 1946 independence of the islands. He retired from the army in 1937. By now MacArthur had become field marshal of the Philippine army, a post in which he continued until July 1941, when President Roosevelt recalled him to active duty to command all American and Philippine forces in the Far East.

In his new assignment, MacArthur's immediate responsibility was the defense of the Philippines against the Japanese invasion that seemed almost sure to come. American military planning, however, had conceded the impossibility of thwarting a Japanese assault. The Philippines lay thousands of miles from the nearest other American base, surrounded by waters sure to be dominated by a powerful Japanese fleet and air force and certain to be cut off from support. The most that could be hoped for was that the defenders could somehow hold out for six months, by which time the American Pacific Fleet might be able to fight its way through with a relief force.

But by the eve of World War II, no one in Washington believed that this was possible. The Japanese were obviously too strong and controlled too large an area of the Pacific to allow for ready American access to the Philippines. And the Anglo-American decision to make the primary war effort against Germany, the more dangerous enemy, meant that there was little hope of saving the Philippines. They would be lost to the Japanese, perhaps for several years, until sufficient American strength could be amassed in the Pacific to support a successful counteroffensive.

MacArthur, however, did not agree. For nearly four decades he had believed firmly in the importance of the Philippines to Pacific strategy and in their critical value to the United States in any war with Japan. He had derived this assessment from the views of his father, the general, who had served in the islands both as a senior commander and as military governor, as well as from his own warm links to the Philippines, developed during four tours of duty there. He had thus always questioned the approved American strategy for the islands, which he regarded as overly passive and essentially defeatist. Indeed, the Philippine National Defense Plan that he had prepared for President Manuel Quezon in 1935 envisioned an active defense based on local military forces so strong and well supported by the United States that they could deter any attack and, if necessary, defeat it.

For half a dozen years now, MacArthur had been working to build and train a Philippine army capable of defending the islands. He faced budgetary limitations, equipment shortages, inadequate facilities, poor communications, and the problem of mobilizing and training thousands of raw recruits, many of whom were illiterate and not all of whom even spoke the same language. Nevertheless, MacArthur expressed only confidence in his command. Although most of the Philippine army was barely capable of minimal operations, let alone defeating a seasoned foe, his reports to Washington spoke only of progress and increasing strength.

MacArthur's optimism and persuasive arguments soon found sympathetic ears. During the latter half of 1941, some American reinforcements, including an impressive force of new B-17 heavy bombers, began moving into the Philippines. By April 1942, predicted MacArthur, he would be able to defeat any Japanese invasion, and although Japan's decision to begin the war in December 1941 gave him less time than he needed, he remained supremely confident.

The crippling of the American fleet at Pearl Harbor and the overwhelming tide of Japanese victories in the opening weeks of the war cut off any hope of early rescue or reinforcement of the Philippines. MacArthur's own strongest weapon, his large force of B-17s and fighter planes, was itself quickly destroyed by the Japanese in an action that still remains controversial. The devastating air raid on Clark Field, which caught American planes on the ground many hours after MacArthur had been informed of the attack on Hawaii, was all but ignored in the public dismay over Pearl Harbor and other Japanese successes. It thus received little attention and has never been satisfactorily explained.

MacArthur blamed his air commander, Major General Lewis H. Brereton. Brereton blamed MacArthur. Both were probably at fault, with the greater share of culpability probably going to MacArthur for his failure to make a decision about how and when to use his air force. For several hours he apparently hesitated, vacillated, and perhaps remained frozen with shock at the impact of sudden war. There is little comfort in the fact that the Japanese would almost certainly have destroyed most of Brereton's planes in a few days anyway. MacArthur's inability to face reality on the morning of December 8 illustrates the sort of self-delusion that frequently marred his career.[2]

In early December 1941, MacArthur was thus left to face the Japanese with only the newly mobilized Philippine army—still relatively untrained and poorly equipped—and a small force of American troops. Prewar plans for defending the Philippines had taken into account the impossibility of preventing Japanese landings in the islands and had aimed instead at defending only the vital harbor of Manila, denying it to the Japanese and retaining it as a future base for the American fleet. War Plan ORANGE, as it was called, directed that in the face of Japanese landings American and Filipino forces on the main island of Luzon would fall back to the shelter of Bataan, a small, mountainous, jungle-covered peninsula that juts out into the mouth of Manila Bay. On Bataan, and the island fortress of Corregidor at the entrance to the bay, the defenders would withstand Japanese assaults until the arrival of the fleet or, in the light of more realistic assessments, until starvation or an overwhelming enemy force brought their inevitable collapse.

MacArthur, however, viewed this course of action with disdain. He felt confident that Japanese invaders could be halted on the beaches of Luzon and made little effort to prepare Bataan for defense. Nor did the loss of the fleet at Pearl Harbor or of his own air force at Clark Field deter him from this view. He held fast to it despite successful early Japanese landings on Luzon followed by a major two-pronged invasion of the island that he was powerless to thwart. Only when faced with impressive Japanese strength ashore did he finally give the order to withdraw to Bataan.

The withdrawal was executed skillfully and effectively—not without some help from the Japanese, who misjudged MacArthur's intentions—but the decision had come far too late. Not only had Bataan been inadequately stocked for a long siege, but vital supplies had been moved forward to oppose the enemy landings and now had to be hastily retrieved and rushed back to the rear. This shift proved impossible in most cases, and the troops on Bataan, who held out stubbornly for more than three months, fell victim as much to starvation and disease as to the overwhelming pressure of the enemy.

MacArthur, of course, pressed Washington constantly for supplies and reinforcements. But despite strong efforts to assist the Philippines, the Japanese clearly controlled all routes to the islands, and Bataan and Corregidor had to hold out as best and as long as they could on their own. Yet MacArthur was unwilling to accept the inevitability of defeat. He called for an immediate offensive strategy in the Far East, warning that the fall of the Philippines could lead to the loss of the entire Pacific and Asia. To forestall this outcome, he urged a complete reversal of Allied strategy, shifting from a "Germany first" priority to a concentration of resources in the Far East to defeat Japan. Early offensive action in the Pacific was imperative, he argued, starting with a strong air attack against the Japanese home islands from the north, presumably from Soviet Far East territory. The "second front" should be in the Pacific, Where it would not only protect Allied positions in the Far East, according to MacArthur, but would also free Soviet forces for use in Europe or to join the offensive against Japan.

But Washington remained firm in its commitment to "Germany first." The greatest danger to the Allied cause was clearly in Europe. No matter what early victories Japan might win, the Japanese would eventually be halted and could be dealt with later. The defeat of Germany was a far more pressing and difficult task, and it remained the key to final Allied victory throughout the world. Nor could the Soviet Union spare resources to attack Japan and undertake a two-front war. The Philippines, it seemed clear, were doomed.

MacArthur continued to believe otherwise. Despite Washington's inability to deliver any significant amount of supplies through the Japanese blockade, he constantly exhorted his men to fight on. Help was coming, he declared repeatedly. If only the Philippine defenders held out, reinforcements would surely arrive to ensure their victory. Yet strangely enough, he denied his beleaguered forces the personal leadership that would have meant so much to them. While there is no question of his own bravery—an almost foolhardy courage that he displayed frequently in the face of enemy fire—he was unwilling to visit his troops on Bataan. After an

initial inspection of the peninsula in early January 1942, MacArthur remained on Corregidor until he left the Philippines, never again encourag-
ing the Bataan defenders with his presence. Perhaps his helplessness to
improve their situation, the gradual realization that victory was impossible, inhibited him from facing his men. Perhaps he sought to disassociate
himself from their defeat. Whatever the reason, the troops called him
"Dugout Doug," implying that he was afraid to leave the shelter of his
protective bunker, a nickname completely unjustified but one which
would remain with him throughout the war.

MacArthur's dealings with Philippine President Quezon are also
somewhat curious. The two men had been associated for nearly forty
years. At times the relationship had been fairly close, although not always
without friction. Now both had an interest in the postwar Philippines,
Quezon because he hoped to continue as president and MacArthur because he wanted to resume his well-paid job as Philippine field marshal.
On several occasions, the general deferred to Quezon on matters favoring
the Filipino population at the expense of the desperately needy troops
fighting the Japanese. During the withdrawal to Bataan, he heeded Quezon's request that rice and other food stocks, even those in warehouses of
Japanese-owned firms, not be removed to Bataan (since, presumably, the
food might later be used by Filipino civilians). MacArthur also acceded to
Quezon's wishes when he failed to take over operations of a key railroad
needed to carry supplies to Bataan and when he delayed returning damaging enemy artillery fire because of the possible presence of Filipino civilians near the Japanese guns.

Nevertheless, with the withdrawal to Bataan completed, when Washington urged MacArthur on January 1 to evacuate Quezon to safety, the
general argued strongly that the Philippine president had to remain in the
islands to prevent the collapse of Filipino will. Two days later, President
Quezon issued an executive order awarding half a million American dol-
lars to MacArthur for "distinguished service" from 1935 through December 1941.

It would be a month and a half before the general actually received
this money, during which time Quezon remained in the Philippines. In
January, however, the military situation grew increasingly desperate as
the Japanese made strong advances on Bataan. On February 8, Mac-
Arthur forwarded to Washington, with what amounted to his own strong
endorsement, a proposal by Quezon that the United States grant the Philippines immediate independence and that the islands be neutralized by
the withdrawal of American and Japanese forces and the disbanding of the
Philippine army. The proposal was emphatically rejected by President
Roosevelt. But in his reply to MacArthur, the president again urged that
Quezon be evacuated. Two days later, on February 11, MacArthur re-

plied that he was now willing to let Quezon leave when it seemed safe to do so.

On February 15 MacArthur notified the War Department of his half million dollar award and requested approval of the transfer of the corresponding amount of Philippine funds in a New York bank to the general's personal account. By February 19 the transfer had been approved and carried out. The next day, President Quezon left Corregidor by submarine.

While MacArthur's acceptance of this money was then probably legal—and he had the approval of President Roosevelt—the events surrounding it raise obvious questions of propriety. The general himself must have been aware of this difficulty, for in his published memoirs, in which he carefully itemized every medal and award he ever received, no mention of Quezon's executive order can be found. Not until 1979, when a diligent historian published the documentary evidence from newly opened materials in the National Archives, did the world learn of these strange and unusual events.[3]

Less than three weeks after Quezon's departure from Corregidor, MacArthur and his family, at the express order of President Roosevelt, left the Philippines for Australia. He also took with him his entire staff, depriving his successor on Corregidor, Lieutenant General Jonathan N. Wainwright, of the support of an established and experienced staff that he badly needed to help direct the fight against the Japanese. MacArthur in fact intended to run the Philippine campaign from Australia, as if he had never left the islands. Astonishingly enough, he did not inform Washington of this arrangement, and more than a week passed before the War Department discovered what had happened and could take steps to correct the situation.

It made little difference. Bataan fell in early April and Corregidor and the rest of the Philippines a month later. The defenders had delayed Japanese seizure of Manila Bay for five months, an impressive example of bold resistance far beyond the achievements of Allied forces elsewhere in the Far East. In later years, MacArthur supporters would claim that the general's prolonged defense of the Philippines had upset the Japanese timetable for conquest throughout the southwest Pacific. Yet this was hardly the case. With the exception of the Philippines, the Japanese achieved their initial war aims well ahead of schedule—in part because, once MacArthur had been cooped up on Bataan, they simply transferred forces from the Philippines for use elsewhere. Later on, the forces were shifted back to finish off the Philippines. The American surrender there came much later than the Japanese had hoped, but it was within their overall timetable for the first phase of the war.

MacArthur, meanwhile, had reached Australia in mid-March, where he made his classic "I shall return" statement, expressing his determination to liberate the Philippines. He also announced that he had been chosen to head "the American offensive against Japan."[4]

MacArthur's statement was not based on any directive from Washington. Nor did it reflect American command arrangements for the Pacific, on which no decisions had yet been reached. But in a way it made sense. It would be most practical to fight the war by placing the American effort against Japan under a single commander. This approach would avoid the problems and difficulties of a divided command and of coordinating rival campaigns, with their inevitable competition for resources. It would not, to be sure, eliminate interservice disputes, but neither would establishing separate service or area commands. Surely a single Pacific command, headed by an officer of sufficient stature and reputation to inspire the respect and loyalty of both services, would be the most logical solution. If so, MacArthur was easily the senior American officer in the Pacific, with broad experience both in military operations and in dealing with civilian leaders. He would also clearly be a very popular choice with the American public. And of course his appointment would satisfy the strong army opposition to turning the vast Pacific theater over to the navy.

Yet the waters of the Pacific had always belonged to the navy. And American prewar strategy against Japan had stipulated a naval offensive across the central Pacific to recapture bases in the Philippines, destroy the Japanese fleet, and reduce the enemy home islands by blockade and bombardment. Direction of this effort was clearly a job for a naval officer. The navy, moreover, would never agree to turn control of the fleet over to MacArthur.

Still, what should be done with the general? By rescuing him from Corregidor, Roosevelt had satisfied an admiring public badly in need of a hero and had muted to a degree the criticisms of the political right. But for the same reason he could hardly leave MacArthur without a job. In fact, however, the general already had a mission, one that had little to do with either the fleet or the projected counteroffensive through the central Pacific. MacArthur's immediate task was to halt the Japanese advance toward Australia, which appeared to be increasingly threatened. To do so he would command a considerable force of Australians and a small but growing number of American ground and air units. But he would have his hands full defending Australia, much less mounting any major offensive aimed at Japan.

The solution worked out for the problem of the Pacific command was a compromise that divided the ocean and the fight against Japan into two commands. General MacArthur was given what was called the Southwest Pacific area, essentially Australia and the islands north of it to the Philippines. The rest of the Pacific, designated the Pacific Ocean areas, was under the command of Admiral Chester W. Nimitz. This arrangement remained substantially unchanged until the final stages of the war. But it solved neither the problem of divided command nor that of interservice rivalries in the Pacific. And given the nature and public impact of Mac-Arthur himself, it exerted a major effect on the course of Pacific strategy.

More than a year would pass after these decisions were made before the buildup of American naval forces would enable Admiral Nimitz to begin his major drive across the central Pacific. Now, in the late spring of 1942, attention focused on General MacArthur and the need to halt the southward thrust of Japanese conquest. The victorious Japanese held an area from southeast Burma through Malaya, the Indies, parts of New Guinea, and the Bismarck Archipelago to the Solomon Islands and were continuing to press forward. A repulse in May in the naval and air battle of the Coral Sea and a punishing defeat at Midway a month later failed to halt them. Intelligence gave ample warning of Japanese plans to land on the north coast of Papua, in eastern New Guinea, but MacArthur was slow in reacting, and the Japanese were ashore before he could stop them. By midsummer they were driving across the rugged mountainous Papuan spine toward Port Moresby, a small Allied base on the southern coast just three hundred miles from Australia.

Whatever MacArthur's intention to launch a major counteroffensive to retake the Philippines, the Japanese had preempted him in Papua. The danger to Australia now seemed greater than ever. Before any offensive could be started, the handful of Australian militiamen defending the approaches to Port Moresby would have to be reinforced and the enemy advance brought to a halt. Only then could MacArthur's determination to return to the Philippines begin to take on tangible form.

In August, even as the first Australian reinforcements were reaching Papua, marines from Nimitz's command invaded Guadalcanal, in the southern Solomons, forcing the Japanese to divert troops and supplies from New Guinea. A month later the enemy advance in Papua ground to a halt, just twenty miles from Port Moresby. The diversion of Japanese resources to Guadalcanal, the relentless attacks of MacArthur's air units on their supply lines, the difficult New Guinea terrain, and the tough defense of the small force of Australians proved too much for them. Exhausted, with their stores of food and ammunition almost depleted, the Japanese in Papua began to fall back. MacArthur now went over to the offensive.

The Papuan campaign that followed in the fall and winter of 1942-1943 was bitter, hard fought, and extremely bloody on both sides. The Australians did most of the fighting, but enough Americans entered the action to claim their share of the victory and, unfortunately, the casualties. MacArthur used his superior air strength skillfully, both to attack the enemy and to transport his own troops and supplies. But aside from one hasty trip forward in early October, the general again showed a remarkable reluctance to visit the front and learn for himself something about the rugged terrain, the stubborn Japanese defenses, and the debilitating nature of the battle. To make matters worse, he lacked the greater intelligence resources he would later enjoy and failed to realize that there were far more Japanese opposing him than he supposed. MacArthur thus underestimated the difficulties faced by his troops and time and time again made impossible demands on them.

Perhaps he felt the need for an early victory after his defeat in the Philippines, or he was driven to win in Papua before the marines could conquer Guadalcanal. But whatever the reason, his repeated orders to frontline commanders to take objectives "regardless of losses" or "at all costs" led to needlessly heavy casualties and did not significantly hasten the Japanese defeat. The Papuan campaign was one of the costliest Allied victories of the Pacific war in terms of casualties per troops committed. It was far bloodier than Guadalcanal, where larger forces were involved, and it allegedly caused MacArthur to resolve that he would never again order his soldiers into such grinding, head-on confrontations.[5]

Two-thirds of the casualties in Papua were sustained by Australian troops, who for another year were to constitute the bulk of the ground forces under MacArthur's command. This point was hardly understood in the United States, and the general did little to publicize it. Indeed, although Australia and the United States were supposedly equal partners in the fight against Japan, and although the Southwest Pacific headquarters was ostensibly an Allied organization, MacArthur allowed Australia practically no voice in the development of strategy or military policy and no effective command or staff role. The Australian general Sir Thomas Blamey, who theoretically commanded all Allied land forces in the Southwest Pacific area, controlled for the most part only Australian troops and not always even those. MacArthur steadily reduced Blamey's role while at the same time systematically excluding Australian officers from key positions on his staff, which thus operated as an American body rather than as an Allied one. At one point, indeed, as Blamey complained to Australian prime minister John Curtin, it was "obvious" that MacArthur intended "to treat my Headquarters as a purely liaison element," a reasonably accurate observation.[6]

MacArthur's ability to control matters to such an extent stemmed not only from America's obvious position as the senior and greater ally but also from his forceful personality, his great popularity with the Australian public, and his ease in handling Curtin. While the two men worked well together, MacArthur was clearly dominant, especially in military matters. He praised the prime minister publicly and to his face, but in private conversations with others made no effort to hide their true relationship. From the point of view of advancing American interests, as MacArthur saw them, Curtin's subservience was a definite asset. But Blamey was not the only Australian to be unhappy or to complain about it.

If the Australian war effort was only slightly acknowledged by Mac-Arthur, it was nonetheless vital to his early success in New Guinea and opened the way for further advances. The twin victories in Papua and on Guadalcanal at the beginning of 1943 were the first moves in a step-by-step American strategy aimed at the great enemy stronghold of Rabaul, on the island of New Britain, that the Japanese had seized in the early months of the war. The next phase, under MacArthur's strategic direction, would involve advances by Admiral Nimitz's forces up the Solomons from Guadalcanal and a simultaneous drive from Papua by the general along the northern coast of New Guinea. In the final stage, also under MacArthur, both offensives would converge on Rabaul. This strategy was aimed at defeating the Japanese threat to Australia and to the vital line of communications between that continent and the United States. It was, of course, a change from the prewar plan for a central Pacific drive, and it foreshadowed the two-pronged strategic form that the American Pacific counteroffensive would soon take.

MacArthur's role in the development of the strategy against Rabaul is illuminating. In late May 1942, on the eve of the battle of Midway, when Admiral Nimitz proposed to take advantage of Japanese preoccupation with that operation and seize a base in the southern Solomons, MacArthur vetoed the idea as too risky. After Midway, however, despite the Japanese threat in New Guinea, the general proposed that he himself be given additional naval and assault forces to launch a full-scale invasion of New Britain and the Bismarck Archipelago to seize Rabaul. This would have been a far more dangerous and costly operation, risking the few precious carriers and amphibious forces then available in close, poorly charted, and reef-strewn waters dominated by enemy air bases.

Fortunately, the more feasible step-by-step approach to Rabaul was adopted instead, with Guadalcanal as the initial target. But again Mac-Arthur objected. Barely a month after he had claimed he could strike directly at Rabaul, he now insisted that invading Guadalcanal would be too risky. Still, once that island had been occupied, he willingly directed the subsequent advance up the Solomons toward Rabaul, whose capture he still intended to undertake in what he claimed could well be "the decisive action of the Pacific war."[7]

By the summer of 1943, however, the successful Allied advance and the heavy losses inflicted on the Japanese had ended the need to take Rabaul. It was no longer required as an American base, and neutralizing it through air and naval pressure seemed to make more sense than attempting a frontal assault against 100,000 well-prepared Japanese defenders.

Once more, MacArthur protested. Apparently forgetting the bloody

lesson of Papua, he continued to urge an attack on Rabaul. To bypass the
Japanese stronghold, MacArthur charged, "would go down in history as
one of time's greatest military mistakes."[8] In fact, it was one of the wisest
decisions of the war, and even MacArthur eventually came to agree. A decade later he claimed that it had been his own decision to bypass Rabaul
and that this had been part of his overall strategy of "hit 'em where they
ain't."[9]

Behind MacArthur's fixation with Rabaul lay his growing concern
about the projected central Pacific drive and the shift of emphasis and resources to Admiral Nimitz that was sure to come once those operations
had begun. In his mind, they were a costly diversion from the best route
to defeat Japan: through the Southwest Pacific to the Philippines. This
view reflected not only the usual "localitis" of any area commander but
also MacArthur's continued obsession with the Philippines—reinforced
perhaps by a desire to redeem himself for his failure to hold them initially
as well as by his hopes for a postwar life and career in the islands.

MacArthur's strategic parochialism was perhaps best shown by his
constant complaints about lack of support and resources for his operations. Denied his wish that the Pacific be given priority over Europe, and
denied overall command in the Pacific, he constantly argued for a concentration of men, ships, planes, and supplies in his own Southwest Pacific
theater. "No commander in American history has so failed of support as
here," he protested.[10] Yet in fact the Pacific took a far greater proportion
of Allied resources than is commonly understood, and MacArthur certainly received his share.[11] Nevertheless, he complained steadily about
logistical priorities and Washington's failure to understand the importance of the southwest Pacific offensive.

Underlying these complaints was the general's persistent and oft-
stated belief that resource allocations and strategic decisions derived
essentially from prejudices against him and from conspiracies by jealous
rivals or superiors. Two of the main villains in this scenario were Army
Chief of Staff General George C. Marshall and the entire U.S. Navy. The
alleged Marshall-MacArthur feud supposedly started during World War I
and remained unresolved until Marshall's senior position in World War II
purportedly gave him the opportunity to revenge himself. Yet there is no
convincing evidence to uphold this contention, and Marshall's patient
support of his difficult subordinate probably assured the continuation of
Southwest Pacific operations when many others would have seen them
sharply restricted.[12]

MacArthur's other bête noire was the navy. Certainly his fight for Pacific priority was in no way diminished by his long-held antipathy toward
that service. The navy, he told Secretary of War Stimson, "fails to understand the strategy of the Pacific."[13] Worse, he charged, naval leaders were
seeking to assume command of "all operations in the Pacific," an out-

growth of an old scheme to take over the entire American defense system and limit the army to training and supply functions.[14]

The navy might well have replied in kind. MacArthur's repeated efforts to gain control of the navy's aircraft carriers, the striking heart of the Pacific Fleet, were not the least bit inhibited by his frequently stated preference for land-based air support or his admonitions on the limitations of carrier warfare. Operating carriers in the central Pacific, he argued, was dangerous, costly, and short-sighted, and they could be more effectively employed under his command. Their absence "affected and hampered the Southwest Pacific operations most seriously," he wrote later. "I know of no other area and no other theater where they could have been used to such advantage."[15] Yet carrier operations in the Southwest Pacific posed definite risks. Most of the waters there were narrow, inadequately charted, and dangerously exposed to enemy land-based air attack. They were far less suited to the free and wide-ranging movements of fast aircraft carriers and large amphibious and support fleets than the broad, relatively empty expanses of the central Pacific.

What MacArthur could not accept was that the central Pacific offered the shortest and most direct route to bring early and decisive naval and air pressure to bear on the heart of Japan. Once they were available, the highly mobile carrier and amphibious forces, cruising freely across the open Pacific with their great floating logistical bases, would be able to advance further and faster and bypass enemy strong points far more readily than MacArthur's land-bound units. Their success in the central Pacific would in fact facilitate MacArthur's own offensive, even as his step-by-step approach through the Southwest Pacific would divert Japanese attention and resources from the danger further north. The dual approach—twin supporting drives—that American Pacific strategy embraced would keep the Japanese off balance, unable to concentrate against either American offensive and incapable of stopping both.

It was November 1943 before Admiral Nimitz could amass sufficient naval and amphibious strength to launch his central Pacific campaign. By then MacArthur's forces had reached the northern Solomons and had made equally impressive gains along the north coast of New Guinea. Other advances in the months that followed completed the isolation of Rabaul and brought MacArthur to the western end of New Guinea.

These successes were characterized by imaginative and aggressive use of air power to lift troops and supplies over difficult or dangerous areas, to bomb, strafe, and observe enemy positions and movements, and to cut Japanese supply lines. Indeed, successful aerial interdiction of enemy convoys in early 1943 forced the Japanese to give up further major attempts to resupply or reinforce their troops in New Guinea. Japanese forces there would hold out stubbornly, but they were no longer a significant factor in the war.

Perhaps the greatest advantage enjoyed by MacArthur was an intelligence capability far exceeding that of the enemy. Aerial reconnaissance, a flood of captured documents, and a few prisoners offered some important information, but his greatest intelligence asset was the interception and deciphering of Japanese radio messages in a remarkable program called Ultra. Beginning in 1943 and especially after January 1944, Ultra provided MacArthur with detailed knowledge of enemy strengths, dispositions, and, most important, intentions. Thanks to Ultra, the general was able to bypass enemy strongholds and strike where the Japanese were weak, to anticipate Japanese attacks and defeat them, and to blast enemy convoys from the sea before they could deliver badly needed supplies. While he occasionally failed to use his intelligence to the utmost, for the most part MacArthur exploited it with devastating effect. Two of the best cases in point are the March 1943 battle of the Bismarck Sea, when Ultra allowed MacArthur's bombers to destroy a huge Japanese reinforcement convoy, and the advance to Hollandia a year later, when MacArthur jumped his forces over hundreds of miles of strong Japanese positions along the New Guinea coast to a point that Ultra had told him was only weakly defended.[16]

The dramatic vault to Hollandia was perhaps the best example of the leapfrogging or bypassing technique so often associated with MacArthur's successes. It was a technique for which he claimed authorship but which was hardly his own invention. Indeed, he came to it reluctantly. Once convinced, however, he quickly grasped the advantages of amphibious operations and the varied applications of air power. Well informed by Ultra, he used both weapons to strike where the Japanese were weakest and to bypass their strong points. But he was certainly not the first or the only one to employ this technique, and he did so as much because of circumstances and the urgings of his naval and air commanders as from his own initiative. Certainly his stubborn insistence on attacking Rabaul is hardly consistent with the picture of MacArthur as a practitioner of "hit 'em where they ain't."

Bypassing, as MacArthur himself has pointed out, is "as old as warfare itself"[17] and a concept long understood by the military forces of most countries. Certainly this statement was true of the Japanese, who had bypassed Bataan and Corregidor in order to accelerate their advance elsewhere. The Americans had returned the favor little more than a year later in recapturing the Aleutians. Admiral Nimitz's forces invading the island of Attu in May 1943 purposely bypassed the more heavily defended Kiska, causing the Japanese to evacuate that island without a fight. Three months later, Nimitz's forces introduced this technique to the South Pacific, when they began leapfrogging Japanese-held islands in the central Solomons. And the Allied decision, at about the same time, to bypass Rabaul established the maneuver as a basic practice of Pacific strategy. That Mac-

Arthur, too, now adopted it reflected neither innovation nor initiative; it was simply a sound tactical move made possible by the preponderance of military strength newly available to him.

The most obvious example of bypassing was, of course, the island-hopping campaign across the central Pacific initiated by Nimitz in late 1943. Starting with the seizure of the Gilbert Islands in November of that year, his amphibious forces jumped two thousand miles to the Marshalls in February 1944 and four months later were in the Marianas, another thousand miles farther west and practically on the doorstep of Japan. In the process, Nimitz had bypassed scores of Japanese islands and their garrisons, leaving them isolated and cut off from supply, reinforcement, or escape. He had leaped forward roughly twice as far in eight months as MacArthur had in nearly two years.

The general, to be sure, had been limited in his advances by the range of land-based aircraft that covered his operations. Nevertheless, he had been moving peripherally along the outer edge of the Japanese strategic perimeter, against enemy forces essentially written off by Tokyo. While his victories clearly weakened the Japanese and made Nimitz's task far easier, the central Pacific drive had pierced the center of the enemy's defenses and posed the greatest threat to Japan. The newly captured bases in the Marianas would allow American B-29's to drop their lethal cargoes on the heart of that nation itself and, in another year, to bring the war to a close. The Philippines, meanwhile, were still in Japanese hands and would remain so for many months to come. In any event, the Philippine bases would not be as close to Tokyo as were those already seized in the Marianas. Nor were they as well suited for blockading the Japanese home islands.

American strategy in mid-1944 called for MacArthur and Nimitz to push forward aggressively along their respective axes of advance. While the central Pacific drive continued, MacArthur planned to seize islands northwest of New Guinea and then leap the final five hundred miles to the Philippines where, in November, he would invade the huge southern island of Mindanao. This much was clear. The next objective remained uncertain.

MacArthur himself hoped to move from Mindanao to Leyte, in the central Philippines, and then on to Luzon. This maneuver would cut Japanese lines of communication to the south, provide a base for final action against Japan itself, and fulfill his pledge to liberate the Philippine people. The navy, however, preferred to invade the great island of Formosa rather than Luzon, since it offered better bases for interdicting Japanese lines of communication and for mounting operations against Japan. There were, however, some negative aspects to the Formosa option, and on balance the arguments in favor of Luzon were probably stronger, especially since bypassing that important island would leave hundreds of thousands

MacArthur and Nimitz discuss strategy at GHQ, Brisbane, March 27, 1944.
U.S. Army photo.

MacArthur, Roosevelt, Nimitz, and Admiral William D. Leahy in Honolulu,
July 1944. Courtesy National Archives.

of Filipinos in Japanese hands. But there were not enough resources in the Pacific to invade both Luzon and Formosa, so a choice obviously had to be made.

President Roosevelt, MacArthur, and Nimitz were unable to resolve the issue when they met at Pearl Harbor in July. Despite claims that MacArthur's eloquence swayed the president in his favor, no decision was actually made. MacArthur would invade Mindanao and then Leyte, but the Luzon/Formosa controversy would remain unresolved.[18]

In early September, a carrier task force under the aggressive Admiral William F. "Bull" Halsey struck the Philippines and other Japanese-held islands and encountered surprisingly weak resistance. Halsey therefore recommended that operations scheduled by Admiral Nimitz as preliminaries to the Mindanao invasion be canceled and that Mindanao itself be bypassed in favor of an immediate invasion of Leyte.

Swift approval of this bold recommendation meant that MacArthur could attack Leyte in October, two months earlier than scheduled, and that, if he wanted to do so, he could then jump much more quickly to Luzon. This move would take place well before Nimitz could possibly be ready to invade Formosa. Along with other military considerations, it made Luzon the obvious choice and ended the Luzon/Formosa controversy. MacArthur would advance to Luzon from bases on Leyte, while Nimitz turned his attention northward toward targets closer to the Japanese home islands.

The Leyte operation would be a hard-fought one, primarily because cancellation of the Mindanao invasion had deprived MacArthur of a crucial element of support. The key to all of his previous campaigns had been the availability of land-based air power to cover each major advance. Mindanao would have provided vital air bases to protect the Leyte invasion, even as Leyte would do so for operations in the northern Philippines. Without Mindanao, MacArthur would have to depend for air support on navy carrier-based planes until he could gain a foothold on Leyte and build airfields there for his own planes to use. But the carriers could remain on station for only a limited amount of time, and the terrain and weather on Leyte would make it extremely difficult to carve out the necessary airstrips as quickly as they would be needed.

There was yet another problem. MacArthur's forces landed on Leyte in late October and within a few days had secured a considerable lodgment against relatively weak Japanese opposition. The main enemy counterblow came in the form of a major naval effort to destroy the American invasion fleet and the newly established beachhead. The air and naval battle of Leyte Gulf that followed was the crucial point of the invasion, and the American victory in that fight ensured MacArthur's success and eliminated the Japanese fleet as a factor in the war.

But for a few hours on the final day of battle, the outcome hung in doubt. Admiral Halsey's fast carrier forces supporting MacArthur were under Nimitz's command, so the general did not control their operations and was unable to prevent them from moving away from Leyte to intercept part of the enemy fleet. Halsey's departure left the beachhead open to attack by other Japanese naval units, which were turned back only by the gallant stand of a handful of small American warships still on station off Leyte. This brush with disaster—a perfect example of the problems of divided command—was a legacy of the 1942 decision not to appoint a single overall American Pacific commander. It was an important lesson and nearly a very costly one.

Nor was it the end of MacArthur's difficulties. As anticipated, continuous heavy rains and the soft and spongy nature of the ground on Leyte delayed airfield construction for many weeks. The problem badly hampered American air operations, while Japanese aircraft, flying from dryer bases elsewhere in the Philippines, struck again and again at the beachhead area. And to make matters worse, with American air operations severely limited, the Japanese were able to bring in strong reinforcements and greatly extend the fighting on Leyte. Securing the island took longer than expected and exacted a much heavier toll in American casualties than MacArthur had predicted. Indeed, Leyte turned out to be far bloodier than several other operations in the central Pacific that MacArthur had

MacArthur returns to the Philippines, October 20, 1944. President Osmeña is on his right and General Sutherland on his left. U.S. Army photo.

criticized as "frontal attacks by the Navy" involving "tragic and unnecessary massacres of American lives."[19]

The assault on Luzon was delayed for a few weeks by the difficulties on Leyte. But in January 1945, MacArthur's forces landed practically unopposed on Luzon and in two months captured almost all important areas. Fighting was hard but, with some notable exceptions, not prolonged, since the Japanese had previously transferred their strongest units to Leyte. The battle for Manila, however, was a difficult one, with heavy casualties on both sides. Indeed, it involved the same type of costly "frontal assault" that MacArthur had ascribed to "mediocre commanders"[20] and the same bitter sacrifices. There would also be long, bloody struggles in the mountains east of the capital and in western and northern Luzon before enemy opposition was finally crushed. The half a year required for this struggle was considerably longer than the six weeks or less that, MacArthur had previously asserted, was all he would need for the campaign.[21]

Roughly 200,000 Japanese died on Luzon, but American losses were hardly light: nearly 47,000 battle casualties and almost twice as many nonbattle casualties, the latter constituting an extraordinarily and inexplicably high toll. At Pearl Harbor in July 1944, MacArthur had confidently predicted that he could recapture Luzon at relatively low cost. "Good commanders," he had told President Roosevelt, did "not turn in heavy losses."[22] Yet in this largest of all campaigns in the Pacific war, involving more American troops than any other World War II operation except the drive through northern France, the number of dead and wounded was as great as might have been expected in any such massive campaign against a difficult and stubborn foe. Luzon was a magnificent victory but hardly a cheap one.

MacArthur's heavy losses on Leyte and Luzon underline the fact that casualties sustained by his forces were comparable to those taken by other American commanders. The myth that the general's "brilliant maneuvering would produce the war's shortest casualty lists"[23] does not hold up under analysis. When MacArthur commanded relatively small forces, or when geography allowed him to leapfrog enemy strong points, his losses were low. But when forced to come to grips with a stubborn foe, he paid the usual bloody price: as he did in Papua and in the Philippines, and, had he been allowed to have his way, as he most certainly would have at Rabaul.

During the first half of 1945, even as he was subduing Luzon, MacArthur was also liberating the rest of the Philippines. From February through July, his troops made some fifty amphibious landings throughout the Philippine archipelago, fulfilling the general's pledge to free the islands. American casualties during these operations were not heavy but, as was so often the case with anything involving MacArthur, there arose another controversy.

While eventual liberation of all of the Philippines was undoubtedly a long-term American war objective, Washington had had no intention of committing American troops to this mission, preferring to leave it to Filipino guerrilla forces and other units raised within the Philippines. This approach would have been consistent with the successful bypassing strategy that had brought American military power so close to Japan. It would also have freed five American divisions for operations elsewhere; certainly those divisions might have been better used to help reduce the bitterly defended Japanese positions on Luzon.

But American forces could liberate the Philippines far more quickly than the Filipinos themselves could, and American naval and air support would be required in any event. By pushing ahead rapidly with American divisions, MacArthur could make good his promise by an early date, secure air bases to support operations he planned in Borneo and elsewhere in the Indies, and, incidentally, lend support to certain Filipino political factions.

So MacArthur pressed onward. And Washington, which had never authorized operations beyond Luzon, raised no objections. In April, finally, by which time most of these operations had been completed, MacArthur received retroactive authority to liberate all of the Philippines and, in response to his continued requests, grudging permission to initiate operations with Australian troops against Borneo.

The Borneo landings, from May through July 1945, were the final amphibious assaults of the war. They were undertaken somewhat reluctantly by the Australians, who were already engaged in clearing out or compressing Japanese pockets of resistance long since bypassed by the Americans and who viewed many of these operations as unnecessary expenditures of lives and resources.

MacArthur, however, was looking forward to using Borneo as a base from which to invade the rest of the Netherlands Indies. It was again a plan of which Washington disapproved and which, if carried out, would have exacted a heavy toll in casualties and diverted Allied resources from the scheduled November invasion of Japan. Only the sudden end of the war in August prevented this problem from coming to a head.

MacArthur's staff, meanwhile, was also developing plans to invade Japan, an operation which both he and the army staff in Washington fully believed was necessary. Others might argue that blockade and bombardment, or strategic bombing alone, might force a Japanese surrender. But as MacArthur asserted unhesitatingly in June 1945, he was convinced that "bombing can do [a]lot to end [the] war but in [the] final analysis doughboys will have to march into Tokyo."[24] And there was no question in his mind who should be leading the parade.

MacArthur was also certain, along with many others, of the necessity of securing Soviet entry into the war before American forces attempted to invade Japan. Although he denied having done so in his postwar memoirs, in 1945 he "emphatically stated that we must not invade Japan proper unless the Russian army is previously committed to action in Manchuria." This strategy, he argued, would tie down a large number of enemy divisions and was "essential" for saving American lives and hastening the end of the war.[25]

A major change in command arrangements in April 1945 had given MacArthur control of almost all army ground and tactical air units in the Pacific while turning nearly all naval resources over to Admiral Nimitz. The general would command all land operations and Nimitz all those at sea. For the invasion of Japan, MacArthur had overall responsibility, although Nimitz's command of the naval aspects of the operation gave him control until the landings were actually under way.

It was an awkward arrangement, continuing the divided command that had bedeviled American Pacific strategy and operations from the very start of the war. It reflected the long-standing army-navy rivalry as well as the continuing struggle for resources between MacArthur and Nimitz. Fortunately, two atomic bombs and Soviet entry into the war forced the Japanese to surrender before these command arrangements could be tested.

The conflict in the Pacific thus ended on a note similar to that on which it had begun: the problem of interservice rivalry and divided command. But for the towering presence of MacArthur this problem might have been solved in early 1942. That it was not remains one of the more disturbing aspects of the Pacific war.

What can be said in summary regarding General MacArthur and the war he fought? Despite his reputation for military genius, it is not at all clear that he displayed the attributes of a great commander. During most of his campaigns, he controlled resources far more extensive than those of the enemy he faced. He enjoyed a much greater overall proportion of ground, air, and sea strength; an overwhelmlng intelligence capability; a watchful high command in Washington that prevented him from embarking on excessively wild or dangerous operations; and a national economy and industrial base that gave him the wherewithal to carry on an expensive and extravagant war with little thought for the cost. To his credit, he used these resources ably and effectively, with skill and imagination, and his great persuasive powers won for him many a prerogative and asset that lesser commanders would have been denied.

Yet on those occasions when the Japanese faced him with equal or greater strength, he was unable to defeat them or to react swiftly or adequately to their initiatives. His deft use of air and sea power enabled him to bypass heavily defended enemy strongholds, which saved the lives of thousands of American troops. But when a bypass proved impossible, he resorted to the same sort of frontal assaults for which he ridiculed others, and he took commensurately heavy casualties. Above all, he displayed a strategic parochialism and an inflated sense of the value of his own operations that failed to acknowledge the validity of other strategies, the competence of other commanders, and the sincerity and honor of anyone who disagreed with him.

MacArthur's successes in World War II are manifest. But in the final analysis, his contributions toward ultimate victory were no greater than those of other major commanders. His axis of advance from Australia to the Philippines supported the decisive central Pacific offensive and was never the primary military avenue to the heart of Japan. The Japanese armies he destroyed would have had no greater effect on the outcome of the war had they simply been bypassed, isolated, and contained.

It is interesting to speculate on what might have happened in the Pacific had General MacArthur been left to surrender on Corregidor, unable to participate further in the great war against Japan.

Blamey and MacArthur

The Problem of Coalition Warfare

D.M. HORNER

Of General Douglas MacArthur's subordinate commanders during his campaigns in the Southwest Pacific, none faced as wide a range of problems and challenges as the commander of Allied land forces, General Sir Thomas Albert Blamey. Equally, none of MacArthur's subordinates presented him with as tough an opponent as the controversial Australian general, his only foreign senior subordinate. MacArthur and Blamey were a formidable pair, and an examination of their adversarial relationship throws valuable light upon MacArthur's methods of command, on Australian strategic policy making, and on the problems of coalition warfare.

Blamey was burdened with three major tasks during the war with Japan. First, as commander, Allied land forces, under MacArthur, he was responsible for the land defense of Australia and then for offensive land operations planned by MacArthur. Second, as commander in chief of the Australian military forces, he was responsible for the training, development, and administration of an army soon to exceed twelve divisions, plus a multitude of training and base establishments. Third, as the Australian government's chief military adviser, he was responsible for counseling the prime minister on high-level defense policy. He also undertook a further, self-imposed task of ensuring that Australian interests were safeguarded against the wider interests of Australia's more powerful allies, particularly the United States.

In pursuing these tasks Blamey soon found himself at odds with MacArthur, who, having no wish to place American troops under a foreign general, decided to conduct his land operations through task force commanders rather than through his land force commander. Considering the joint nature of these operations and MacArthur's desire to retain control, perhaps task forces were the best organizational structure anyway, but the issue was never resolved through open discussion. In his desire to obtain a greater share of Allied resources for his command, MacArthur tried to persuade the Joint Chiefs of Staff of the importance of his theater. In these attempts he sought and received the assistance of the Australian government. The Australian prime minister, John Curtin, who lacked experience in military affairs, looked to MacArthur for advice on strategic matters. Thus when Blamey had a contrary view on strategic policy, he found himself challenging not only MacArthur but also his own prime minister. Inevitably a time came when MacArthur's personal and American-oriented policies were not necessarily the best for Australia, and Blamey understood this point earlier than his political masters.

To the various tasks, which in their complexity and importance to Australia overshadowed those presented to any military leader in Australia's earlier history, including Lieutenant General Sir John Monash, Australia's outstanding commander in World War I, Blamey brought wide experience and knowledge, although his career had not been without difficulties. He had begun his working life as a schoolteacher but in 1906 at the age of twenty-two had gained a permanent commission in the embryo Australian army, then a force consisting mainly of militia, with only a small cadre of regular soldiers. Six years later he attended the Staff College at Quetta in India and graduated in December 1913. With the outbreak of World War I he joined the staff of the First Australian Division, serving at Gallipoli, and by the time the division reached France in the following year he was the chief operational staff officer. To his great disappointment he served only short periods in command of a battalion and a brigade, but in May 1918, at the age of thirty-four, he was promoted to brigadier general as chief of staff of the Australian Corps under Monash, and he served in that appointment during the corps's great victories in August and September. The demanding corps commander wrote that Blamey "possessed a mind cultured far above the average, widely informed, alert and prehensile. He had an infinite capacity for taking pains." The commander of the Australian Imperial Force in World War I, General Sir William Birdwood, described Blamey as "an exceedingly able little man, though by no means a pleasing personality."[1]

After the war Blamey was appointed second (deputy) chief of the General Staff before his retirement in 1925 to become chief commissioner of the Victoria police. In 1936, following several earlier controversies, he was forced to resign after he had issued an untrue statement in an attempt to protect the reputation of the police. The next year he relinquished command of the Third Division (militia), which he had held for the previous six years, and went on the unattached list, his career apparently over. Then, on a suggestion from Frederick Shedden, the secretary (public service permanent head) of the Department of Defense, in 1938 he was appointed chairman of a recently established Manpower Committee and controller-general of recruiting. Shedden later explained: "The aim was twofold. His military experience and organizing ability would be most valuable to the Committee, and he would be brought back into the Defence Organization as the most probable Army Commander in the event of war."[2]

Blamey's quickness of mind and force of personality more than any scarcity of other suitable officers caused the Australian prime minister, Robert Menzies, to appoint him to command the Sixth Division, the first division of the Second Australian Imperial Force, which was raised following the outbreak of war in September 1939.[3] The previous prime minister, J.A. Lyons, who felt that Blamey lacked the moral qualities to lead Australian soldiers in battle, had to agree after meeting him that he was "really somebody." When in early 1940 it was decided to form an Australian corps by raising another division, Blamey received the corps command. Major General L.E. Beavis, Blamey's chief ordnance officer throughout the war, has written that he "had his shortcomings, such as aspects of his personality which affected some of the personal clashes in which he became involved, evidenced in a degree of ruthlessness when he felt sure he was right," but Beavis "had the greatest admiration and respect for him as a commander." The Australian official historian, Gavin Long, wrote: "He had a mind which comprehended the largest military and politico-military problems with singular clarity, and by experience and temperament was well-equipped to cope with the special difficulties which face the commander of a national contingent which is part of a coalition army in a foreign theatre of war."[4]

Yet at the outbreak of World War II he was out of touch with recent developments in military technology. Although he had an excellent grasp of the command and staff techniques being used at the corps level at the end of World War I, he had had no opportunity to study the problems of joint warfare, particularly the coordination of air and armored units which became the hallmark not only of the German blitzkrieg but also of the Japanese advance in China and Malaya. As World War II approached, he had concerned himself with world affairs by delivering a weekly radio broadcast, and his work with the Manpower Committee had given him insight into policy making at the senior level of the Department of Defense and the government, but this background prepared him more for high command appointments, such as command of the AIF in the Middle East, or of the army, than for a battlefield command, such as command of a division or a corps.

This experience at the policy-making level stood him in good stead during the eighteen months he spent in the Middle East as commander of the AIF. In particular, he fought long and hard to maintain the integrity of the AIF, against both General Archibald Wavell in 1940 and 1941 and General Claude Auchinleck later in 1941. Blamey's performance during this time was uneven. His most obvious error was his failure to inform the

Australian government early enough that he had strong doubts about the wisdom of the Greek campaign. He learned this lesson well and never again failed to let the government know his views. He commanded the Australian Corps (renamed the ANZAC Corps, as it included the New Zealand division) during its skillful withdrawal down the Greek peninsula and evacuation from beaches reconnoitered earlier by him in expectation of just such an eventuality.

At the beginning of the campaign, Blamey erred in placing his headquarters in an obvious location which was inevitably bombed by the German air force. Furthermore, his chief of staff, Brigadier S.F. Rowell, has claimed that at the height of the withdrawal Blamey was "physically and mentally broken." While this accusation has been supported by some other officers, it has been strongly refuted by a number of senior officers, and his ADC recalled that in Greece he never saw him "fearful or abnormally troubled." Whatever the truth regarding Blamey's performance as commander, and Wavell was certainly impressed with his performance, he lost much support among some of his senior staff when he chose his son to fill the one remaining seat on the plane carrying him out of Greece.[5]

At the end of the campaign, Blamey was appointed deputy commander in chief in the Middle East and reluctantly gave up the corps command, but he still made his presence felt. He intervened in the Syrian campaign in June 1941 to alter Lieutenant General Sir Henry Wilson's strategy when he believed that the latter was not exercising strong enough control, and he successfully demanded that the Ninth Australian Division in Tobruk be relieved in August and September 1941 because he thought that it was being used to the point of exhaustion by the British high command.

In September 1941, now aged fifty-seven, Blamey was promoted to the rank of general and became the only active service Australian general holding that rank at the time. No other Australian general was to reach that rank in the next twenty-five years. Blamey never had the classical physique of an active commander in the field. Short, rotund, and with a white moustache, he was perhaps the archetypal Colonel Blimp. But both Generals Wavell and Auchinleck had quickly learned not to underestimate his determination or energy.

In many quarters Blamey enhanced his reputation in the Middle East, but he failed to win the unanimous support of a small but influential group of senior officers. There were many tensions in the upper echelons of the AIF as ambitious, and at times disloyal, regular and militia officers vied for commands. Perhaps Blamey could never have won the support of them all. Admirably, it was not his style to curry favor with subordinates, but at times he seems to have fueled the antipathy toward himself rather than trying to dissipate it. Rarely able to inspire complete loyalty and trust among soldiers, he enjoyed life to the full in a manner which soldiers understood but which they did not expect to find in their commanders. He was sensitive to criticism and relentless in his pursuit of personal enemies. Perhaps his greatest failing was his failure to understand the importance of public relations. He was determined to fight for Australia, and his approach was blunt, even tactless, although effective.

On March 26, 1942, five days after General MacArthur had been given an enthusiastic welcome in Melbourne, Blamey reached that city on his way back from the Middle East to take up his new appointment as commander in chief of the Australian military forces. He was faced with a number of demanding tasks: he had to resolve the command arrangements with the Americans, he had to defend Australia with the forces then available, and he had to build and train an army for future battles. By March 1942 the army and indeed the nation were in deep crisis. In the four months from the outbreak of war in the Far East, Japanese forces had overrun Southeast Asia; had defeated and captured Australian forces in Singapore, Java, Ambon, New Ireland, and New Britain; and had landed on Timor and New Guinea. Darwin and Broome had been bombed, and an assault against the mainland was expected any day. The inexperienced Labor government, led by John Curtin, had been in power for barely two months before the Japanese had entered the war. Nevertheless, although the country was largely defenseless, the Seventh Division and one brigade of the Sixth Division were returning from the Middle East. Militia divisions were mobilizing and undergoing training, and a number of senior commanders had been recalled from the Middle East. MacArthur's appointment as commander in chief of the Southwest Pacific area seemed to promise American help, but until this help materialized, and until the troops could be trained and equipped, the Japanese threat would continue to grow.

Initially there was a little delay while the terms of MacArthur's directive were agreed upon by the Australian and American governments, but eventually, at midnight on April 18, all combat units of the Australian defense forces were assigned to MacArthur's command. MacArthur was adamant that he should deal directly and alone with the Australian prime minister and vice versa. Thus MacArthur became the government's principal strategic adviser when Curtin set up the Prime Minister's War Conference, consisting of himself, MacArthur, and anyone else he wished to invite, as the senior body for the high direction of the war. The third member of this body was inevitably Frederick Shedden, the secretary of the Department of Defense, who acted as secretary of the conference and for the remainder of the war as liaison between the other two members. Blamey resented this exclusion from strategic policy making, but after he offered his resignation to Curtin, it was made clear that as commander in chief of the Australian military forces he would also have direct access to the prime minister on matters of broad military policy. Nevertheless, while the Prime Minister's War Conference included other members at times, it generally consisted of MacArthur, Curtin, and Shedden.

In his capacity as commander of the Allied land forces, Blamey had his main dealings with MacArthur, who had been informed by U.S. Chief of Staff General George C. Marshall that he would not be eligible to retain direct command of any national force. Vice Admiral Herbert F. Leary was given command of the Allied naval forces and Lieutenant General George H. Brett the Allied air forces. Blamey's appointment was made against the wishes of MacArthur, who, as early as March 21, told Marshall that for the land forces he planned to create task forces "to meet tactical requirements." Marshall replied that, since Australians formed the majority of his land forces, an Australian should command both American and Australian forces. But events were to show that MacArthur never intended Blamey to exercise command over American forces. MacArthur resisted Marshall's efforts to ensure that general headquarters for the Southwest Pacific area in Melbourne was a truly Allied headquarters, and his only concession was the appointment of an Australian liaison officer. Similarly, MacArthur resisted Blamey's efforts to provide Allied land force headquarters with an Allied staff. Blamey wrote later that his "requests for American officers to establish a joint staff were met with face-saving acceptance that was completely ineffective."[6] In contrast, the headquarters of the Allied air forces included both American and Australian officers.

Brett, who had his own problems with MacArthur, recorded his impression of Blamey and his role in the new command structure:

General Blamey is a well-met man of broad experience and, I believe, of considerable force if occasion arose. In spite of his short stocky build and rather indifferent appearance, I believe the man has a lot of brains. He has been very friendly to me, but has closed up like a clam very recently. He and I have discussed many features of the Allied command and I believe back of his attitude lies the fact that he feels MacArthur intends sloughing-off the Australians if he possibly can. He is a typical Australian. . . .

I believe that if MacArthur had taken Blamey into his full confidence and used him to the fullest extent, and if they both brought pressure to bear on the Federal Government a great deal more would have been accomplished. MacArthur has built a wall around himself which has excluded Blamey, Leary and myself in such a way that he has not secured whole-hearted cooperation in the prosecution of the war. Blamey as an Australian, has probably not understood this attitude and undoubtedly holds it against all Americans.[7]

American feeling was shown when Major General Robert C. Richardson visited Australia in June 1942 and reported to Marshall that placing American soldiers under Blamey "was an affront to national pride and to the dignity of the American Army." Although Richardson reported that there "was no resentment of the Australians themselves, but merely of the system of control," elsewhere he described Blamey as "a non-professional Australian drunk." As a result Washington advised MacArthur that the American troops should be placed under a corps commander whom they were sending out and that in due course the corps should be assigned to an American task force for operations—the very scheme originally proposed by MacArthur. Blamey and the Australian government were not informed of this proposal to circumvent the original agreement. As for Blamey's suitability, the new American corps commander, Lieutenant General Robert L. Eichelberger, found him to be "a very fair commander and I would have taken his judgement at any time above the three characters who were behind me in the chain of command—I refer to Mac-Arthur, [General Walter] Krueger and [Lieutenant General Richard K.] Sutherland."[8]

Despite these underlying tensions, from the beginning Blamey and MacArthur cooperated closely in organizing the defense of Australia. MacArthur later claimed that, when he arrived, the Australians had a "largely defeatist conception" of defending their country from the "Brisbane Line." However, events of the period and MacArthur's own plans showed his contention that it was he who after his appointment decided to take the fight to the Japanese in New Guinea, and that it was never his "intention to defend Australia on the mainland of Australia," to have been oversimplified.[9]

When Blamey became commander in chief of the Australian military forces, the Military Board was abolished, and LHQ was established with five principal staff officers: the chief of the general staff, Lieutenant General Vernon Sturdee, who retained his position, plus a lieutenant general in charge of administration, an adjutant general, a quartermaster general, and a master general of the ordnance. The day-to-day control of operations was in the hands of the deputy chief of the general staff, Major General George A. Vasey. The old state-based geographic command system was disbanded, and the army was divided into the First Army (responsible for the defense of New South Wales and Queensland), the Second Army (Victoria, South Australia, and Tasmania), the Third Corps (Western Australia), Northern Territory Force, the forces in New Guinea, and LHQ units. The old military districts became line-of-communication areas supporting the field forces in their areas. Sturdee had earlier recommended these changes.

In his memoirs Blamey recalled: "From the outset it had been decided between General MacArthur and myself that as soon as possible we would move to the offensive against Japan as far north as we could proceed. But it was essential first to ensure that the defence of vital areas should be secure." Blamey's deployments, which had been begun by his predecessors and which were endorsed by MacArthur, kept most of the troops in southeast Australia, but soon the headquarters of the First Army was moved to Queensland and the Second Army to Sydney. One division was sent to Western Australia, where the Third Corps was being formed, and an AIF brigade was ordered to Darwin to join the two militia brigades already there. In addition, U.S. antiaircraft and engineer troops were sent to Darwin, a squadron of heavy bombers and a U.S. antiaircraft regiment were ordered to Perth, a U.S. antiaircraft regiment and an additional Australian infantry brigade went to Townsville in northern Queensland, and the remainder of the U.S. antiaircraft troops were grouped in Brisbane. The air force concentrated most of its striking force in the Townsville-Cloncurry area where airfields were becoming available.

Both MacArthur and Blamey wanted to move troops to the north as quickly as possible, but initially most of the formations, including the two U.S. divisions in Australia, were only partly trained, and accommodation and training facilities were more plentiful in the south. The key position of Port Moresby in Papua was not reinforced substantially because lack of naval and air resources made it difficult to maintain and support more than the one brigade already there. During April a light antiaircraft battery, U.S. engineers and antiaircraft units, and an Australian independent company were deployed to Port Moresby, but until the Battle of the Coral Sea in early May 1942, the Australian army stood on the defensive. Indeed, the Australian official historian noted: "So hesitant had General MacArthur and General Blamey been to send reinforcements to New Guinea that on 10th May, the day on which the Japanese planned to land round Port Moresby, the defending garrison was not materially stronger than the one which General Sturdee had established there early in January."[10]

During this time Blamey, and the other senior officers who had returned from the Middle East, had worked with great drive and determination to train and organize the forces, initially for the defense of Australia and then for offensive operations. The differences between the compulsorily enlisted former part-time soldiers of the militia and the voluntary AIF were never completely resolved, but progress was made. The commander of the Seventh (militia) Brigade at Milne Bay at the eastern tip of Papua remembered meeting Blamey at Port Moresby in mid-1942. Blamey asked the brigadier what his officer position was, and the brigadier replied that it was fair but that he would like some AIF captains. Blamey said "very well," and the next day four captains from the Seventh Division arrived. Blamey ordered, "Promote corporals to lieutenants if necessary," but these measures needed time to take effect. The expansion and training of the Australian army in mid-1942 was an impressive feat facilitated by the rapid decisions from LHQ.[11]

After the Battle of the Coral Sea, MacArthur decided to reinforce Port Moresby with another brigade. In executing this order Blamey has been criticized for his decision to send a militia rather than a better-trained and battle-experienced AIF brigade. This error was compounded by his decision to send the Seventh (militia) Brigade to Milne Bay. In reply to a question from the government, Blamey's chief of the general staff said that the Seventh AIF Division had to be kept for overseas operations contemplated later. In a report for the prime minister, Defense Secretary Frederick G. Shedden observed that, "though this may have fitted in with projected offensive plans, the security of such a vital place should have had priority." MacArthur supported this view and later claimed that he had asked Blamey to send his best troops to New Guinea. He did not think that the militia were adequately trained. Shedden concluded that Blamey had not sent the AIF because he and the Australian chiefs of staff had decided that two militia brigades would be sufficient to repel a seaborne attack and that there was no chance of an overland advance on the town. Shedden added that it was "probably not an unfair surmise that the Owen Stanley Range and the difficulties of communications on the southern side induced a 'Maginot Line' complex that there was an easily defensible barrier to a Japanese advance beyond Kokoda." As events were to show, Shedden's criticism could just be easily been leveled at MacArthur. [12]

Not until after the decisive defeat of the Japanese fleet at Midway on June 4 did MacArthur realize that his dreams of an offensive could become reality. He told Curtin that "the security of Australia had been assured" and persuaded the Joint Chiefs of Staff to endorse a grandiose and fanciful plan to leave a small garrison in Papua and to capture Rabaul with amphibious forces. In anticipation of this offensive, on July 20 GHQ moved to Brisbane. But MacArthur was beaten to the punch; on the night of July 21 the Japanese landed at Buna on the north coast of Papua.

During the four months from the time he arrived in Melbourne on March 26 until the opening of GHQ in Brisbane on July 20, Blamey had worked effectively and cordially with MacArthur. Although the Japanese had landed on New Britain in January 1942 and in New Guinea in March, since then small Australian army units had conducted only limited land operations in New Guinea, and neither Blamey nor MacArthur had been closely involved. Blamey's responsibilities for command of both the Australian military forces and the Allied land forces did not conflict, and he found himself in general agreement with MacArthur's strategic advice to the prime minister. However, after the move of GHQ to Brisbane, Blamey had to follow suit, and on August 1 Advanced Land Headquarters (Landops) opened at St. Lucia, a suburb of Brisbane. General Vasey moved north to run the operational headquarters, while the principal staff officers and the main administrative headquarters remained in Melbourne. Sturdee explained the new arrangements: Blamey "combines the functions of operational commander with the head of the housekeeping side and will therefore spend a considerable period of time in Melbourne in addition to traveling about Australia generally." Indeed, between August

1 and September 23, when he moved forward to Port Moresby, Blamey spent barely half his time in Brisbane, and this absence contributed to the command problems in the early stages of the Papuan campaign.[13]

The fiction that Blamey had full authority as commander, Allied land forces, lasted until there was the likelihood that American troops would be committed to battle. On August 1, with the Japanese beginning their advance over the rugged Kokoda Trail, MacArthur suggested that the Thirty-second U.S. Division be sent to New Guinea to operate directly under the control of GHQ. This move would have produced an impossible command structure, with two separate superior headquarters in Australia controlling separate national forces in one operational area. Apparently Blamey talked MacArthur out of that folly, and instead the commander of the First Australian Corps, Lieutenant General S.F. Rowell (who had been Blamey's chief of staff in Greece) and the Seventh Australian Division were ordered to New Guinea. One brigade of the division was to go to Milne Bay, bringing Milne force to two brigades, while another brigade was to go to Port Moresby, bringing the force there and on the Kokoda Trail to three brigades.

Despite intelligence from radio intercepts that the Japanese intended to march over the forbidding Owen Stanley Range toward Port Moresby, MacArthur remained confident throughout August that the Japanese were no great threat. Then, on August 26, the Japanese mounted sustained attacks both on Milne Bay and along the Kokoda Trail. MacArthur's headquarters reacted with anxiety and despite ignorance of the situation issued instructions for quick results. Blamey was absent from Brisbane, and Vasey bore the brunt of the demands. On August 28 he wrote to Rowell in Port Moresby: "You possibly do not realize that for GHQ this is their first battle and they are therefore, like many others, nervous and dwelling on the receipt of frequent messages. . . . It boils down to the question of who is commanding the army—MacArthur or T.A.B. [Blamey], and it seems the sooner that is settled the better."[14]

Meanwhile, in signals to Washington, MacArthur was beginning to blame the Australian reverses not on his faulty strategy or on the superior numbers of the Japanese but on the poor quality of the Australian troops and commanders. Also, he told General H.H. Arnold, then visiting Brisbane, that the Australians "were not good in the field, they were not good in the jungle, and they came from the slums of the cities in Australia and they had no fighting spirit." Naturally Rowell resented these criticisms, and wrote to Vasey: "I do hope that there is a showdown [between Blamey and MacArthur]. Taking it by and large, we do know something about war after three small campaigns." By early September the Australians had won the battle at Milne Bay, and Vasey summed up the feeling in Brisbane: "GHQ is like a bloody barometer in a cyclone—up and down every two minutes. When C-in-C [Blamey] returned from there yesterday, he said one would have thought they had just won the battle of Waterloo.[15]

On the Kokoda Trail, information was now coming in that the Japanese were driving the Australians back, and MacArthur appealed to Washington for reinforcements, claiming that "the Australians have proven themselves unable to match the enemy in jungle fighting." Blamey had ordered two more brigades to Port Moresby but remained confident that Rowell would succeed in holding the Japanese advance. He reaffirmed this view when he visited Port Moresby on September 12. MacArthur, however, had been listening to the advice of his new air commander, Major General George C. Kenney, who had visited Port Moresby but had not visited Rowell.[16] Preferring to believe Kenney's report that the Australians would not fight, he toyed again with the idea of sending the Thirty-second U.S. Division as a separate task force under General Eichelberger. Then on September 15 came the news that a newly arrived Australian brigade on the Kokoda Trail had withdrawn to within twenty-five air miles from Port Moresby. Afraid of his reputation in Washington, MacArthur had to act, and the Australian prime minister had to decide who to believe.[17]

From the time of his return from the Middle East, Blamey would have been aware that in some quarters he was being criticized as unsuitable. There had been proposals from a few senior officers that all generals over the age of fifty be retired, and at least three other generals had coveted his position. But for a while Blamey's position seemed secure, and before the operations in New Guinea, MacArthur was lavish in his praise. For example, in response to a letter criticizing Blamey, at the Prime Minister's War Conference on July 17, 1942, MacArthur said that he considered Blamey

to be the best of all the Australian Generals. He was above the average military ability of Generals. In his considered professional opinion, General Blamey was a first class Army Commander. . . . MacArthur added that . . . he was not concerned with any personal idosyncrasies which General Blamey might possess. He judged him by results, and he considered that he had effected great improvements in the Australian Army since his return to Australia. Furthermore, he had the confidence and respect of the United States Army Staff.

After the conference, Curtin confidentially told newspapermen that MacArthur had commended Blamey: "He praised his organization of the evacuation of Greece as one of the most outstanding events of the war, greater even than Dunkirk where the evacuating troops had the protection of almost unlimited aeroplanes." Curtin added that Blamey's private life had nothing to do with his military office: "He said when Blamey was appointed the Government was seeking a military leader not a Sunday School teacher." General Kenney described Blamey as "a short, ruddy-faced, heavy-set man with a good-natured friendly smile and a world of self-confidence. No matter what happened, I didn't believe Blamey would ever get panicky. He appealed to me as a rather solid citizen and a good rock to cling to in time of trouble." Looking back over these early months, Blamey observed later that a good relationship was established with MacArthur "which ripened into a deep regard and friendship."[18]

Despite these comments, there is plentiful evidence that, as the crisis in New Guinea deepened, Blamey's position became increasingly precarious. On MacArthur's part, Blamey could provide a convenient scapegoat if Port Moresby fell. After all, MacArthur knew that, if he suffered another defeat, following the fall of the Philippines, his own position would be unsteady; hence the reports to Washington of the poor quality of the Australians. When Marshall suggested that MacArthur visit New Caledonia, MacArthur replied that Blamey's "entire methods and conception differ so materially from ours that his actions during my absence would be unpredictable." Perhaps this message prompted the comment in William Frye's *Marshall: Citizen Soldier* that Blamey was a commander "in whose capacity the Americans found themselves able to place less than complete faith." At this time MacArthur privately described Blamey as possessing a "sensual, slothful and doubtful character but [as being] a tough commander likely to shine like a power-light in an emergency. The best of the local bunch."[19]

That some Australian politicians shared MacArthur's doubts about Blamey became clear when Blamey reported on September 17 to the Advisory War Council, the top-level all-party committee overseeing the conduct of the war. Fresh from his visit to Port Moresby, he expressed confidence in Rowell, but one minister was heard to comment: "Moresby's going to fall. Send Blamey up there and let him fall with it!" That evening MacArthur telephoned Curtin and told him that Blamey should go to Moresby to take personal command. Not only did MacArthur consider this a military necessity for Blamey, "he thought it was a personal necessity since, if the situation really became serious, it would be difficult for the Australian leader to meet his responsibility to the Australian public." This consideration may have decided Curtin, for he confessed later that, "in my ignorance (of military matters), I thought that the Commander-in-Chief should be in New Guinea." Curtin therefore agreed with MacArthur and spoke to Blamey.[20]

Aware of the government's decreasing confidence in his ability, Blamey "raised no question." William Dunstan, the general manager of the *Melbourne Herald*, wrote soon afterward to Rowell that, at two background conferences for senior newspapermen, Curtin had discussed Blamey's position "more or less freely—off the record, of course":

"They are not satisfied with him. . . . His every move is watched. . . . He was sent to New Guinea for no other reason than to give him one final chance. . . . To this extent we must sympathize with him. . . . He has had to submit to the MacArthur holiness. Just how much do we know of what he has suffered under the set-up? Granted he is GOC [General Officer Commanding] Land Forces, just how much does it mean if he took strong directive over US Forces? Would he have to go cap in hand to MacArthur?" Dunstan added that there had been a canvass of names to find a replacement.[21]

If some observers, such as Rowell, were able to accuse Blamey of a lack of moral courage in not challenging the government at this time, others might have seen it as the pragmatic approach of an experienced soldier convinced that he was the only man for the job. Rowell, of course, failed to appreciate the merit of this view and regarded Blamey's arrival as reflecting a lack of confidence in his ability. After an unfortunate dispute, in one of the most controversial episodes in Australian military history, on September 28 Rowell was relieved of his command. Blamey probably had no alternative, but the decision polarized feeling for and against him among senior Australian officers.[22]

On October 1 Lieutenant General E.F. Herring arrived to assume command of the corps, but Blamey remained in Port Moresby. Ironically, before Blamey had arrived, the Japanese commander had already found himself overstretched. As a result of Rowell's careful planning, the Australians were now poised for the counteroffensive. In effect, Blamey had assumed the role of commander of New Guinea force, and thus MacArthur had achieved his desire to conduct the operations through a task force. But there was one problem: when the Thirty-second Division, then arriving in New Guinea, was finally committed to battle, Blamey would, in fact, resume his position as commander, Allied land forces.

General Herring was to prove a more amenable, if no less able, subordinate than Rowell, and he worked effectively with Blamey. Although Blamey tried to let Herring conduct the operations, there is no doubt that MacArthur in Brisbane considered Blamey to be in charge. On October 2 MacArthur visited New Guinea for the first time, to mark the beginning of the counteroffensive. With Blamey he visited Owers' Corner at the beginning of the Kokoda Trail and saw in the distance the country over which their soldiers had toiled for the previous months. Soon the Seventh Division was advancing back over the Kokoda Trail, a regiment of the Thirty-second Division was crossing the mountains by another trail, and troops from Milne Bay were creeping along the northern coast of Papua.

Meanwhile the American naval forces in the Solomons were under severe pressure, and MacArthur reacted by demanding that the Seventh Division move faster across the Kokoda Trail. Major General Arthur S. Allen, commanding the Seventh Division, was faced with great difficulties:

Blamey, MacArthur, and Prime Minister Curtin; *below*, Blamey and Mac-Arthur with Australian troops at Port Moresby, October 2, 1942. Courtesy Australian War Memorial.

the Japanese were defending stubbornly, the terrain and vegetation made it hard to use artillery or air support, his own resupply system was precarious, and his arrangements for evacuating casualties were primitive. Supplies were brought forward and casualties carried back by native porters along steep, muddy tracks which clung to mountainsides in mist and rain and then descended to deep valleys and rushing streams. Neither MacArthur in Brisbane nor Blamey in Port Moresby could appreciate these difficulties, but even if he had some idea, Blamey believed that he was in no position to resist MacArthur. Finally, on October 27 Blamey sent a signal to Allen, telling him that he was to be relieved by Vasey, who somewhat earlier had moved from Brisbane to Port Moresby. Few divisional commanders in history have been replaced by their army commander without having been visited by either the army or the corps commander or indeed by anyone above the rank of lieutenant colonel. The night before Vasey took command, the Japanese abandoned their main defensive position in the mountains, and on November 2 his troops entered Kokoda.

As the Allies began to close in on the Japanese positions on the north Papuan coast, it was clear that the Thirty-second U.S. Division, with one regiment marching over the mountains in what a sergeant called "one green hell" and another regiment flying into a remote airfield, would soon be in action. MacArthur again began to fret about the command arrangements. On October 19 he commented to his British liaison officer, Colonel G.H. Wilkinson, that it "would not do to leave [Blamey] in Supreme Command." Wilkinson suggested that another American commander would "have to be put in over" Blamey. MacArthur was not sure how that "should be handled" but added that he "could handle Blamey." A few days later MacArthur discussed the operations with Shedden in Brisbane, and with the exception of Blamey, "whom he considered to be a good offensive commander," he criticized the lack of offensive spirit of the Australian officers. He "said that Australian permanent officers were too greatly concerned about their personal interest for the good of the country." With respect to the command setup, MacArthur said that "it would be necessary for General Blamey sooner or later to make a decision as to whether he was going forward in command of the advanced forces in any offensive operations, or was remaining in Australia to command the forces left there for the defense of the base."[23]

With the Australian Seventh and U.S. Thirty-second divisions closing in on the Japanese beachheads, Blamey indicated that he intended allowing Herring to assume his role as corps commander and to control the operations on the north coast. General Kenney, however, was worried that these command arrangements "might get complicated especially if [MacArthur's chief of staff, Major General Richard K.] Sutherland gets to giving much advice." He thought that Sutherland lacked confidence in the Australians. "Every time I talk to him he tries to impress on me the

terrible consequences if we should have a reverse. He says that any reverse would result in MacArthur being sent home."[24]

On November 6, a little over a week before the main attack on the
Japanese beachheads was due to begin, MacArthur moved his own advanced headquarters to Port Moresby, thus ending Blamey's period of six
weeks as an independent commander in New Guinea. During that time
the Seventh Division had fought back across the Kokoda Trail and the
Thirty-second U.S. Division had been brought across the mountains. The
Allied position had been consolidated, but neither Blamey nor Mac-
Arthur had fully appreciated the fierce determination of the Japanese in
defense or the problems of the terrain.

The Allied offensive against the Japanese beachheads on November
16 began in an atmosphere of extreme optimism; indeed, the commander
of the Thirty-second Division, Major General Edwin F. Harding, doubt-
ed that the Japanese would defend Buna strongly and thought that he
"might find it easy pickings." It therefore came as a severe shock to the inexperienced National Guard division when its assault on Buna was repulsed on November 19, prompting MacArthur to bypass the chain of
command to order Harding to "take Buna today at all costs." But a week
later the Americans had still not advanced, and the Australians were now
beginning to complain that the Americans would not fight. Vasey at Sanananda, six miles west of Buna, wrote to Blamey that the Americans had
"maintained a masterly inactivity."[25]

Blamey used such information to give MacArthur back some of the
medicine which Blamey had been forced to swallow in August and September, when the Australians were being driven back along the Kokoda
Trail. Blamey's chief of staff, Major General Frank H. Berryman, told Eichelberger: "The jokes of the American officers in Australia, making fun of
the Australian Army, were told all over Australia. . . . Therefore . . .
when we've got the least thing on the American troops fighting in the
Buna sector, our high command has gone to General MacArthur and
rubbed salt in his wounds." He added that MacArthur, his chief of staff,
Sutherland, and Kenney were "not guiltless" among those who made dis-
paraging remarks about the Australians. Blamey's attitude was neither
dignified nor diplomatic, but in view of MacArthur's strictures on the AIF,
it can be understood. Thus when on November 25 MacArthur suggested
bringing the Forty-first U.S. Division up from Australia to reinforce the
Seventh Division, Blamey objected. Kenney, who was present, observed:
"Blamey frankly said he would rather put in more Australians, as he knew
they would fight. . . . I think it was a bitter pill for General MacArthur to
swallow."[26]

Upset and humiliated by reports that American soldiers had dropped
their weapons and run, MacArthur not surprisingly called his American
corps commander, Eichelberger, to Port Moresby and on November 30

told him "to take Buna, or not come back alive." Eichelberger later wrote: "At the time I did not realize General MacArthur was being gloated over by the Australian High Command who had been criticized by him previously."[27]

Meanwhile Herring had moved over the mountains to establish his corps headquarters at Dobodura to control the operations of Vasey's Seventh Division and the Thirty-second U.S. Division, soon to be commanded by Eichelberger, who had relieved Harding.[28] But Blamey was now faced with a rapidly dwindling reservoir of troops, and MacArthur was applying pressure for quick results. An American attack at Buna supported by Australian Bren gun carriers failed, and for a last attempt Blamey ordered the Eighteenth Brigade and some tanks to move from Milne Bay to Buna. The Eighteenth Brigade's attack was successful, but at Sanananda and Buna the Japanese still resisted strongly.

MacArthur's concern for quick results was shown by his constant exhortations to Eichelberger to attack and by his meddling in operations. On December 26 he told Herring: "This situation is becoming serious. If we can't clear this up quickly I'll be finished and so will your General Blamey." The next day MacArthur ordered the first regiment of the Forty-first U.S. Division (163rd) to be sent to Eichelberger's command. Herring had intended to send the regiment to Vasey's command in the Sanananda area. Blamey felt that this was a matter of principle and that he was now in a strong enough position to stand up to MacArthur. In a forthright letter to MacArthur he stated that there were sound military reasons for sending the regiment to Vasey; the Eighteenth Brigade in Eichelberger's area was still relatively strong, while some of Vasey's battalions numbered fewer than one hundred men. He continued: "I regret still more that you should have personally taken control of a single phase of the action. . . . I do not for one moment question the right of the Commander-in-Chief to give such orders as he may think fit, but believe that nothing is more contrary to sound principles of command than that the Commander-in-Chief or the Commander, Allied Land Forces, should take over the personal direction of portion of the battle. This can only result in disturbing the confidence of the inferior commanders."[29]

MacArthur disagreed with Blamey and replied that the Buna area was the most important and that the Japanese force at Sanananda was less than that imagined by the local commanders. However, he concluded: "You have mistaken my advice as an arbitrary order. . . . My verbal discussions are advisory only"—a fine distinction indeed when the advice comes from the commander in chief. Blamey informed Herring that, although there had been "a keen difference of opinion" between himself and MacArthur, the regiment would go to Vasey's area. As it turned out, by January 2 Eichelberger had defeated the Japanese in his area, while, contrary to MacArthur's beliefs, Vasey was still facing significant enemy forces in the Sanananda area. The incident well illustrated the extent to which Blamey believed that his position had strengthened since he had given in to MacArthur in the previous September and October.[30]

In the wake of the American success at Buna, MacArthur announced that the Japanese army had been annihilated, and on January 9 he returned to Australia. Blamey returned to Australia soon afterward, as he had no intention of allowing MacArthur to confer with Curtin without being able to present his own point of view. Herring became commander of New Guinea force and Eichelberger the corps commander. The campaign was far from over, and it took a further two weeks of hard fighting before the Japanese at Sanananda were wiped out on January 22. The Papuan campaign had lasted exactly six months. According to the Australian official history, the Japanese committed a little over 20,000 troops to the Papuan campaign, of whom about 13,000 were killed. The Australians and Americans suffered 8,546 battle casualties. Casualties from malaria exceeded 27,000; those suffering from tropical disease numbered over 37,000. Eight Australian brigades and four American infantry regiments from five Allied divisions had been deployed.

Although the successful conclusion of the campaign was considered a triumph for Blamey, his performance had not been flawless. Like MacArthur, he had initially made a faulty strategic appreciation and he had failed to familiarize himself with the terrain. However, unlike MacArthur, on January 5 and 6 he belatedly visited the battlefields at Buna and Sanananda. At Buna he told Eichelberger "that a miracle had been performed." Blamey made a strong impression on the Americans and after an inspection the commander of an American battalion said: "He's the commander all right. I'd know him for the top man without any badges of rank. I'd know the sonofabitch in his pyjamas. He descended on us like a cartload of tigers." At Sanananda he moved forward to gain firsthand knowledge of the fighting still in progress.[31]

Although his decision to use Bren carriers at Buna was unwise, he followed it with the correct decision to send in the Eighteenth Brigade with tanks. Simultaneously handling the administrative problems of the Australian army and commanding operations, he had demonstrated patience, wisdom, strength, and a generally unappreciated humanity. The campaign had been marked by constant and at times damaging interference from MacArthur, interference that Blamey had not been able to resist until the closing stages. His dismissal of Rowell in September, his relief of Allen by Vasey, and his criticism of some of the troops who had fought on the Kokoda Trail confirms the view of some officers that Blamey had been fighting for his political life when he had gone to New Guinea. By the conclusion of the campaign he had reinstated his authority with the government, MacArthur, and his subordinates.

Between January 16 and 20, 1943, Shedden discussed the recent operations with MacArthur and began by asking why the campaign had taken so long. MacArthur replied by criticizing the Australian commanders: "He regretted to state that his criticism of slowness in exploiting advantages and following up opportunities applied to all Australian commanders including General Blamey." MacArthur did not mention that the commander and senior officers of the Thirty-second U.S. Division had been replaced or that he himself might have erred in not sending troops to New Guinea earlier than he did. But he did acknowledge that, "of the nine campaigns in which he had fought, he had not seen one where the conditions were more punishing on the soldier than this one." Expanding on this general criticism of the Australian commanders, he observed that "Blamey had had quite an easy time in New Guinea." He described Blamey "as a good, courageous commander in the field, but not a very sound tactician" and noted that Blamey did "not command the fullest support of all in the Australian Army and that he had political ambitions." MacArthur concluded by stating that Blamey should become commander in chief of the Home Defence Forces in Australia and that Lieutenant General Sir Leslie Morshead, then returning from commanding the Ninth Division in North Africa, should command the Australian part of an Allied Expeditionary Force.[32]

MacArthur was already acting to remove Blamey from command of American troops. Indeed, on January 11 he had asked Marshall to send Lieutenant General Walter Krueger from America "to give the U.S. Army the next ranking officer below General Blamey in the Allied Land Forces which is not now the case and is most necessary." Soon after Krueger's arrival MacArthur formed Alamo Force to conduct the operations of the Sixth Army, which was to be commanded by Krueger. There were not yet enough troops to form a U.S. army in Australia, but Krueger, who also commanded Alamo Force, "realized that this arrangement would obviate placing Sixth Army under the operational control of the Allied Land Forces." Krueger's deputy chief of staff commented later that Alamo Force was created "to keep the control of Sixth Army units away from General Blamey."[33]

This new command system was, in the words of the Australian official historian Gavin Long, achieved "by stealth and by the employment of subterfuges that were undignified, and at times absurd." These subterfuges revealed a lack of consideration by MacArthur toward a subordinate who, to date, had shown outstanding loyalty. Indeed, on May 17, 1943, MacArthur's chief public relations officer, Colonel LeGrande A. Diller, wrote to MacArthur from Melbourne: "I found no question from any source of General Blamey's loyalty and fidelity." F.M. Forde, the minister for the army, commented later that Blamey "worked very hard in order to give satisfaction to MacArthur." Yet it was to be almost two more years before Blamey lodged a formal complaint with Curtin over MacArthur's degradation of the role of commander, Allied land forces.[34]

There is no evidence that, at this stage, Blamey lost any sleep over MacArthur's machinations; rather he was concerned with completing the reorganization of the army for the Pacific offensive. With the Ninth Division then returning from the Middle East, Blamey grouped the Sixth and Seventh divisions on the Atherton Tableland in northern Queensland to form the First Australian Corps under General Morshead. These three AIF divisions were to be his main striking force for the advance through the islands.

Meanwhile the Australians in New Guinea had fought grim battles around Wau and were now advancing slowly through rugged country toward Salamaua. For a while Herring had remained in command of New Guinea force, but he had been relieved by Lieutenant General Sir Iven Mackay, who had commanded the Sixth Division in the Middle East in 1941. After a rest, Herring was to resume command of New Guinea force. On May 6, MacArthur issued his orders for Operation CARTWHEEL to advance his forces toward Rabaul. Against Blamey's advice, on June 30, Alamo Force was scheduled to capture the unoccupied islands of Woodlark and Kiriwina while at the same time Admiral William F. Halsey's forces would begin landing on New Georgia. Blamey was given responsibility only for the operations of New Guinea force. Supported by Allied air and naval forces, New Guinea force was ordered to accomplish two objectives:

1. By airborne and overland operations through the Markham Valley and shore-to-shore operations westward along the north coast of New Guinea, seize Lae and Salamaua and secure in the Huon Peninsula-Markham Valley area, airdromes required for subsequent operations.

2. By similar operations, seize the north coast of New Guinea to include Madang; defend Madang in order to protect the northwest flank of subsequent operations to the eastward.[35]

It soon became apparent to Blamey and his planners that a further operation would be needed. Since the maximum range of the landing craft carrying troops for the assault on Lae was sixty miles, it was necessary to establish a shore base within that distance, and Blamey suggested Nassau Bay. Furthermore, its capture would ease the supply difficulties for the Third Australian Division advancing overland from Wau to Salamaua. MacArthur readily agreed to this plan, which would involve the use of an American regiment, and it was to begin with the other operations on June 30. Despite the fact that he had been specifically charged with responsibility for the operations, Blamey preferred to work through Herring, who as commander, New Guinea force, was to act as his deputy during the planning, and Blamey instructed him that the operations against Salamaua were "to act as a magnet drawing reinforcements from Lae to that area."[36]

After the success of the Nassau Bay landings, however, MacArthur and some of his staff became carried away with the possibility of capturing Salamaua quickly. Indeed, General Kenney criticized Australian tardiness, claiming that Blamey was loath to employ additional troops to attack Salamaua, as it would involve the use of the Seventh and Ninth divisions, which were to capture Lae; the Americans would then have to undertake the Lae operation. This criticism was clearly not correct, and on both July 15 and July 28, Blamey put the case to MacArthur that he wanted to keep the Japanese at Salamaua. After the success of the landing at Lae in early September, MacArthur claimed that it had been his idea to delay the capture of Salamaua, but Blamey's chief of staff, Major General Frank H. Berryman, saw things differently and wrote in his diary: "the landing [at Lae] was a surprise and effected without opposition—a vindication of C-in-C [Blamey's] and my judgment in adhering to plan to bypass Salamaua. Herring and [Fifth Air Force] wanted to alter plan and take out Salamaua — that would have ruined surprise and spoilt the manoeuvre." Blamey summed up the incident another way: "The greatest pressure was put on me to force the Salamaua position but I was lucky enough to stick to my plan to bypass Salamaua" before the capture of Lae. In this case he can properly claim to have exerted an important influence on Allied strategy.[37]

On August 20, Blamey arrived in Port Mosesby to assume command, allowing Herring to command the assault divisions for the Lae operations. But before the operation, on September 3, Blamey discussed the coming operations with MacArthur and recommended that after the Lae landing he should advance with airborne forces up the Markham Valley into the Ramu Valley, thus securing airfields to provide Kenney with a base to give air cover for Alamo Force's simultaneous operations against Saidor and Cape Gloucester. Despite objections from the U. S. Navy, which wanted an advance along the New Guinea coast before the landing at Cape Gloucester, MacArthur accepted Blamey's plan, but it was to be the last time that Blamey exercised any influence as commander of the Allied land force.[38]

On September 4, in the largest amphibious operation hitherto undertaken in the Southwest Pacific area, the Ninth Division went ashore near Lae, and the next day the Seventh Division began landing by air to the north of the town. Salamaua was captured on September 11 and Lae on September 16. It was a brilliant orchestration of sea, air, and land resources. Herring immediately began planning for a seaborne attack on Finschhafen along the coast to the east. MacArthur and Blamey disagreed about the expected enemy strength at Finschhafen, with Blamey's intelligence officer anticipating double the number claimed by MacArthur's in-

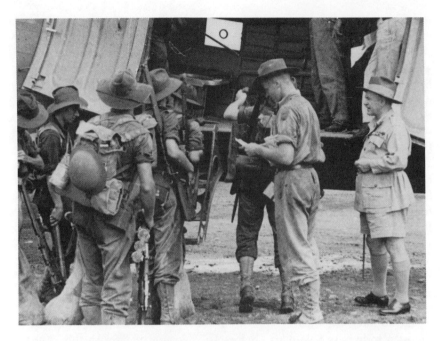

Blamey watches troops of the Seventh Australian Division board a plane at Port Moresby, September 6, 1943. Bound for Nadzab, they will take part on the advance to Lae. Courtesy Australian War Memorial.

telligence officer. Thus although MacArthur wanted to use only one brigade, Blamey urged a landing with two brigades. Eventually it was agreed to land with one brigade, but Herring was warned to be prepared to land a second brigade if necessary. Indeed, on September 22, the day the first brigade landed at Finschhafen, Blamey ordered Herring to send in the additional brigade. Blamey then followed MacArthur south to Brisbane, leaving Lieutenant General Sir Iven Mackay in command of New Guinea force. Rear Admiral Daniel E. Barbey hesitated to react to Herring's request to carry the second brigade ashore, and a bitter dispute ensued which Mackay was unable to resolve. Eventually Herring signaled Blamey, who contacted MacArthur, and on September 30 he ordered the brigade to be landed. As it turned out, the Japanese were in greater numbers than even the Australians had anticipated, and as Herring observed, "We damn nearly lost Finschhafen."[39]

Although the naval and land commanders in New Guinea must bear some responsibility for the incident, the underlying cause was the absence of MacArthur and particularly Blamey from New Guinea. After all, Blamey was MacArthur's nominated commander of the task force, and the Americans claimed that he should not have delegated that responsibility

to Mackay. If he had been in New Guinea, perhaps Blamey could have resolved the problem with Barbey, who later wrote that Blamey "went out
of his way to be helpful, including the assignment to my staff of some excellent liaison officers." But as commander, Allied land forces, Blamey
believed that his position was in Brisbane, and he had his responsibilities
as commander in chief of the Australian military forces. The incident provided further evidence of the problems of Allied cooperation. Already
MacArthur was planning to reduce the Australian involvement in offensive operations. On October 7 he spoke of creating two commands in the
Southwest Pacific. One command would consist of Australian land, naval,
and air forces and would be responsible for an area south of Madang. The
other, all-American command would advance along the north coast of
New Guinea to the Philippines. Nothing came of this plan, but on October 20, GHQ issued RENO III, the plan for the operations culminating in
the capture of the southern Philippines. In five phases of operations beginning on February 1, 1944, and ending with an attack on Mindanao on
February 1, 1945, the Australians were allocated an offensive role in part
of only one phase, namely the occupation of islands in the Arafura Sea in
June 1944. That operation never come to pass.[40]

After the landing at Finschhafen, the Ninth Division advanced along
the coast and, after a difficult fight against strong Japanese counterattacks,
captured Satelberg. Meanwhile the Seventh Division moved up the
Markham Valley and into the Ramu Valley to seize forward airfields. Soon
troops were moving into the rugged Finisterre Range. General Morshead
replaced Herring as the forward corps commander, and when Mackay returned to Australia, Morshead took over as commander of New Guinea
force, with Berryman commanding the corps responsible for the operations along the coast.

The campaign which began with the defense of Wau in March 1943
and ended a year later with Australian forces advancing along the coast to
Madang was an outstanding achievement by the Australian army, supported by the Australian and American air forces and the U.S. Navy.
Blamey rotated commanders and formations as troops became exhausted
from battle, terrain, and sickness. Relentless pressure was maintained on
the enemy by five divisions, three of which were militia. All divisions
were well trained for jungle warfare—a tribute to Blamey's foresight in
establishing training areas in Queensland, particularly on the Atherton
Tableland, and to his organizational ability and unparalleled knowledge of
how an army should be formed and put to work. Even more than the
Papuan campaign, the campaigns of 1943 were a tribute to Blamey's ability, but at the moment of his triumph it was clear that Australia's involvement in MacArthur's offensive was to be curtailed.

While the Lae-Finschhafen campaign had been progressing, the Australian government had been considering how best to balance its war ef-

fort. In particular, Blamey had been concerned that the provision of administrative support to the American forces was imposing a heavy burden on Australian manpower. The best that Prime Minister Curtin could do about this problem was to seek the advice of MacArthur, who was adamant that Australia should continue to supply him with administrative support. These discussions continued for some months until October 1, when the war cabinet approved a new policy on manpower and the allocation of the Australian war effort. It was agreed that it was "of vital importance to the future of Australia" that her "military effort should be on a scale to guarantee her an effective voice in the peace settlement." But it was also agreed to release twenty thousand men from the services and a further ten thousand from munitions industries by June 1944.[41]

MacArthur disagreed with these proposals and argued for a major Australian effort. Advised by Blamey, Curtin asked MacArthur for advice on his plans for the use of the Australian army. But in discussions in Brisbane in November 1943, MacArthur was unable to provide detailed plans. When the question of Blamey's performance as commander of the Allied land forces was raised, MacArthur said that he now saw little of Blamey "because the latter was trying to do too many things," and he only went to New Guinea as "a Task Commander when special operations were afoot." As a result, MacArthur said that he himself had had to take personal command of all major operations. He added that Blamey had originated the suggestion for the appointment of task force commanders for operations by the land forces.[42]

It is difficult to believe that MacArthur was completely sincere in responding to this question; since his arrival in Australia he had worked assiduously to separate the Australian and American forces. If Blamey had mentioned the advantage of using task forces, he would have envisaged their use under his command as land forces commander. In the discussions MacArthur described General Blamey as "an able operational commander with a good strategical mind which quickly appreciated the facts of a situation and reached a sound conclusion." However, he thought that Blamey was trying "to cover too wide a field." For future operations MacArthur planned to use the Australian forces under a task force commander.[43]

Blamey had not yet expressed to the government his dissatisfaction with MacArthur's treatment of him as commander, Allied land forces; he suspected that Curtin would be afraid to act, and if he did so, a damaging political row would ensue. Nonetheless, his response to another question shows that his attitude was hardening. In the correspondence over the government's manpower proposals, MacArthur had stated that it had never been his intention to defend Australia on the mainland of Australia. Curtin referred the matter to Blamey, who replied that there was "no justification" for MacArthur's statement. As Blamey's biographer noted,

"Even in a letter to his Prime Minister a serving soldier can hardly call his superior officer a liar. Blamey could not have gone closer to it than he did."[44]

It was already clear to Blamey that the operational role of the Australian army was to be assumed by American forces. Indeed, in the early months of 1944, all but two of the six Australian divisions in New Guinea were returned to Australia for "training and rehabilitation." Meanwhile, in February in a daring operation MacArthur had seized the Admiralty Islands and was preparing to leap forward four hundred miles to capture Hollandia in April. Faced with this possible exclusion from MacArthur's operations, Blamey had been attracted by a proposal then being discussed by the British chiefs of staff for an advance from Darwin into the Netherlands East Indies.[45] He intended to raise this scheme when he visited London in April with Curtin, who was traveling to Washington and London to seek approval from the Combined Chiefs of Staff for his readjustment of the Australian war effort.

Before leaving Australia, Curtin and Shedden discussed future operations with MacArthur, who explained his plans to capture the Philippines. Despite the fact that his own RENO plans made no mention of Australian formations, he told Curtin that the spearhead of his advance would be three AIF divisions and an American paratroop division. He assumed that the Australian Corps would be commanded by Morshead or Berryman and that Blamey would exercise somewhat less of a command than he had previously. MacArthur also emphasized the necessity that the overall command organization in the Southwest Pacific area remain unchanged. Now was the time for Curtin to complain if he thought that Blamey should remain an effective commander of the Allied land forces. Given these changing circumstances, Blamey's desire to find an independent role for the Australian can be understood. Nonetheless, if MacArthur was to be believed, the Australian Corps was committed to the Philippines.[46]

For two years Blamey had worked comfortably with Curtin on a strictly business relationship, and indeed throughout the war Curtin maintained his loyalty to Blamey, prompting Blamey to write later that he had "no need to bother about rear armour." But as they traveled overseas together, Curtin was forced to deal with Blamey on a personal basis. As a teetotaller who in earlier years had had a drinking problem, Curtin was not impressed by Blamey's rowdy parties on board the U.S.S. *Lurline*, which was supposed to be a "dry ship." These and other incidents led Shedden to comment about Blamey: "Though good as a Commander-in-Chief, he is not suitable as a member of a Prime Minister's party." It may be postulated that the overseas trip led to Blamey's estrangement from Curtin, and this directly affected Australian strategy later in the year.[47]

When the party arrived in London at the end of April 1944, Blamey was greeted with a cable from his chief of the general staff in Australia, stating that MacArthur intended to use the Australian troops on garrison duties. Blamey was therefore particularly interested in a proposal from the British chiefs of staff for an advance from Darwin to Ambon and then on to the Celebes, Borneo, and Saigon. This proposal was later changed to the so-called modified middle strategy, an advance from the American-occupied north coast of New Guinea to Borneo. There were two problems. First, Prime Minister Winston Churchill opposed the strategy, preferring to move from India directly into Sumatra, but eventually the British chiefs of staff believed that they had persuaded their prime minister to drop that scheme. Second, although Curtin was happy to see the British involved in the Southwest Pacific, he was unwilling to alter the command arrangements with MacArthur. The British had proposed that the Southwest Pacific area, then under the U.S. Joint Chiefs of Staff, should come under the Combined Chiefs of Staff.[48]

An important aspect of the British proposal was that Blamey might be given command of the joint British and Australian force involved in the advance into the Netherlands East Indies and that, although this force should operate under MacArthur, "this arrangement should be left open for reconsideration at a later date." This provision meant that the commander of the force could eventually become an Allied supreme commander on a par with General Dwight D. Eisenhower, Lord Louis Mountbatten, General Harold Alexander, MacArthur, and Admiral Chester W. Nimitz. Such a command, when linked with his role as commander in chief of the Australian army, might have been sufficient to warrant Blamey's promotion to field marshal—a possibility which was apparently discussed in London.[49]

When Blamey and Curtin left London on May 29, the final commitment of British troops to Australia had not been resolved. Churchill, however, had agreed to the allocation of the Australian war effort proposed by Curtin, and the two men had also agreed to the establishment of a joint British-Australian planning staff in Australia. Nevertheless, Blamey was under the impression that there was a strong possibility that the British-Australian offensive would eventually occur, and as soon as he reached Australia, he began tentative preparations for the new command. He even briefly mentioned the proposals to MacArthur.[50]

As might be expected, MacArthur was far from enthusiastic about the proposals. When he met Curtin and Shedden in Brisbane in June, he expressed concern that the Australian divisions would not be ready in time for him to use them in the Philippines. MacArthur said that it was evident that Blamey, in his discussions in London, had been disloyal to him and to the command organization in the Southwest Pacific area and, since Curtin supported the command organization, also disloyal to the prime minister. MacArthur said "that the position of Commander of the Allied Land Forces had now become a fiction—Blamey had refused to associate himself closely with MacArthur in the same manner as the Commanders of the Allied Naval and Air Forces, and because of his duties as Commander-in-Chief of the Australian Military Forces, he was rarely available when required." MacArthur believed that Blamey was holding back from providing Australian troops to use them in the new command, and as a consequence he had begun planning to recapture the Philippines using American troops only. At about the same time, MacArthur told his British liaison officer, Lieutenant General Herbert Lumsden, that, despite the fact that Blamey was "the most able soldier in the Australian Army, Mr. Curtin would be well advised to make a change." Thus, through his over-enthusiastic advocacy of the use of Commonwealth forces on a separate axis, Blamey provided MacArthur with a ready-made excuse for not using Australian troops in the assault on the Philippines. In the case of Blamey, whom Lumsden described as being the "vital force" of the Australian services, with "a better strategical and military technical knowledge" and the capability of "taking a wider view militarily and politically, than any other Australian high commander," reliance on the militarily unsound "middle strategy" must be seen as a serious miscalculation.[51]

On July 12, 1944, MacArthur issued a directive for the employment of Australian forces. He wanted the Australians to assume responsibility for neutralizing the Japanese in the Solomons, New Britain, and Australian New Guinea and be prepared to provide one division for the Philippines operations in November 1944 and another in January 1945. Blamey replied that the proposal to employ the Australian divisions was unacceptable; rather he wanted the two Australian divisions to operate together as an Australian corps. MacArthur would not accept this plan, as "he did not consider that public opinion in America would countenance the first landing on the Philippines being shared with the Australians." As a result the Australian divisions were removed from the plan for the landings at Leyte and Lingayen.[52]

Meanwhile Blamey had produced plans to relieve the American divisions in the Solomons and New Guinea with a total of seven Australian brigades, but MacArthur considered such forces "totally inadequate" and directed that Blamey use twelve brigades. Gavin Long has observed that, since American staff doctrine stated that, once given a mission, a commander should be free to decide how to carry it out, "the question arises whether considerations of *amour-propre* were involved: whether GHQ did not wish it to be recorded that six American divisions had been relieved by six Australian brigades (taking into account that one of the seven Australian brigades already had a role in new Guinea and was not part of the relieving force)." Another explanation is that MacArthur wanted to keep the Australians occupied in New Guinea, providing fewer AIF divisions for the Philippines and also fewer AIF divisions for any new command which might be set up.[53]

MacArthur's first formal directive for the Philippines landings, issued on August 31, indicated that he had concocted a plan for a landing by a corps of two Australian divisions at Aparri on the north coast of Luzon on January 31, 1945, as a preliminary to the landing at Lingayen Gulf on February 20, but after many changes this operation never took place. Then in late September came news from Quebec that the Combined Chiefs of Staff had agreed that the British would contribute their main fleet to the Pacific in 1945 and that the plans for a British-Australian command had been terminated. In October 1944 the Americans landed at Leyte. The only Australian involvement was a small naval force. Australian forces were not employed in the Philippines but were to wait until February 1945, when MacArthur completely dismissed the possibility of their being used.[54]

On September 25, MacArthur had destroyed the myth that Blamey had any role as commander, Allied land forces, when Alamo Force was dissolved and orders were given directly from GHQ to HQ Sixth Army. Also, the first Australian Corps was to come under the Sixth U.S. Army if it was involved in the Philippines. Already New Guinea force had changed its title to First Australian Army, nominally under GHQ, not Allied land forces. With the elimination of land headquarters from an operational role, Blamey's influence in 1945 appeared likely to be severely curtailed. Throughout 1944 he had made strenuous efforts to influence Allied strategy. His miscalculation in pressing for the use of British forces might have given MacArthur an excuse for excluding the Australians from the Philippines, but evidence shows that MacArthur's staff were determined to exclude the Australian anyway. While MacArthur's views are more difficult to pin down, it seems that he misdirected Curtin with his promises to use the Australians. Blamey too was misinformed, and he said later: "General MacArthur said to both myself and Mr. Curtin, 'I will go into the Philippines and take the First Australian Corps with me.' That never eventuated, and there were many good reasons why it didn't. The Americans didn't wish anyone else to take part."[55]

The incident reveals something of the decision-making machinery in Australia, for Curtin and Blamey were shown to have been working at cross-purposes. Blamey attempted to play a lone hand in controlling strategic policy, keeping his plans to himself and telling few of his senior staff. While both Curtin and Blamey were concerned to preserve Australian national interests, they differed markedly in how this aim was to be pursued. Lacking military experience, Curtin placed his faith in MacArthur and was determined to maintain the command relationship established in early 1942. Blamey saw clearly that MacArthur was less concerned with Australia and more concerned with American and his own interests. These trends became even more obvious during the campaigns of 1945.

During the latter months of 1944 and early 1945, Blamey was becoming increasingly concerned by the nature of Australia's involvement in the Pacific war. He observed in February 1945 that a "feeling that we are being side-tracked is growing throughout the country." Lieutenant General Berryman, Blamey's representative at MacArthur's headquarters, constantly sought information as to how the First Australian Corps was to be employed but was increasingly frustrated by the lack of an answer. MacArthur appeared to want to keep the Australian divisions earmarked for the Philippines without actually using them. Finally, at Blamey's instigation, Curtin wrote to MacArthur on February 15 that he was now faced with the problem of maintaining a large army most of which was not being involved in operations. In a covering note Shedden told MacArthur: "There is a tendency in Government quarters to ask why the AIF Divisions were not used earlier. Australian opinion considered it a point of honour to be associated with operations in the Philippines as an acknowledgement of American assistance to Australia." MacArthur had already planned to use the Australians in the Borneo-Java area, and Curtin's letter gave him more ammunition to use with the Joint Chiefs of Staff. Indeed he told General Marshall that the Australians were "becoming restive because of the inactivity of their troops."[56]

As part of these plans MacArthur now issued instructions for the employment of the Sixth Australian Division in an invasion of Java. MacArthur's instructions involved reducing the twelve brigades employed in the Solomons and New Guinea areas to nine—a curious development, considering MacArthur's instructions to Blamey in July 1944 that he had to use twelve rather than seven brigades.[57]

MacArthur also stated that the operations would be controlled by the Eighth U.S. Army. When Blamey complained, MacArthur decided that Morshead's First Australian Corps would act as a task force directly under GHQ. But this elimination of the AIF from his operational control was the last straw for Blamey, and on February 19 he wrote to the prime minister. He pointed out that from the beginning MacArthur had taken upon himself the functions of commander, Allied land forces, and that his own command had been limited to that of the Australian forces:

It is my view, unless the authority of the Australian command over Australian national forces is effectively asserted, an undesirable position will rise as far as the Australian troops are concerned, by which they will be distributed under American control and Australian national control of its forces will be greatly weakened. The insinuation of American control and the elimination of Australian control has been gradual, but I think the time has come when the matter should be faced quite squarely, if the Australian High Command are not to become ciphers in the control of the Australian Military Forces.[58]

Curtin felt unable to adjudicate on this matter. As on previous occasions, he sought MacArthur's advice. First, he told MacArthur that the

Sixth Division would not be available for the Java operation, and then he discussed the principle according to which Australian troops should operate under Australian commanders. He asked MacArthur how this principle was to be applied in future operations. On March 5 MacArthur replied, asking Curtin to reconsider the availability of the Sixth Division. He then stated that since the Lae operation he had followed a fixed pattern of using task force commanders. He intended to do so in the future and said that it was essential for the task force commander to remain in the field with his troops. Blamey's position as commander, Allied land forces, was not mentioned at all in MacArthur's three-page letter. Nevertheless, he told Lieutenant General Sir Charles Gairdner, his British liaison officer, that "Blamey's dual position was an intolerable situation." On the one hand Blamey was under his orders, and on the other he was quite independent. Unless Blamey was assigned to MacArthur's command, the latter "was not prepared to take him as commander of the Australian forces for any future operations which might arise."[59]

Curtin should not have been surprised by MacArthur's reply. After all, MacArthur had described his concept when he had met Shedden and Curtin in June 1944. While Blamey had exercised command over the Australian forces in action during early 1944, by late 1944 MacArthur had eliminated advanced LHQ from the chain of command. Consequently, when Curtin replied to MacArthur on March 23, he promised to consult Blamey about the employment of the Sixth Division but merely noted the statement that the First Australian Corps would report directly to GHQ. Blamey had been correct. The Australian government had acquiesced in a situation which he believed was intolerable. Unable to argue with Blamey, Curtin and the government had been equally unable to be firm with MacArthur. Blamey's influence would depend on the outcome of a personal approach to MacArthur.[60]

On March 13, Blamey flew to MacArthur's new headquarters in Manila. In discussions with MacArthur it was agreed that, while GHQ would deal directly with the First Australian Corps, "the necessary administrative functions would be performed by Advanced LHQ," which was now being established on Morotai. The forward echelon of LHQ, located in Manila and commanded by Lieutenant General Berryman, would keep Blamey informed. Blamey questioned MacArthur about the Java operation and observed that, if the Sixth Division were taken away from mopping up operations in New Guinea, it would have to return to complete the job later. These operations, which MacArthur considered unnecessary, were of the same nature as those he considered necessary in the Philippines. As a result Blamey recommended to Curtin that MacArthur be denied the use of the Sixth Division. Although other factors might have prevented MacArthur from carrying out the plan, one historian has noted that "it was fortunate for the lives of the soldiers of the Australian I Corps" that MacArthur did not get "his way on the Java plan, for that two-division invasion could have produced the most tragic blood bath of the Pacific war."[61]

Meanwhile MacArthur continued with his plans to advance into Borneo. Blamey approved of the operations to capture Tarakan, Brunei, and Labuan, and thus on May 1 troops from the Ninth Division started landing on Tarakan, while the rest of the division landed at Brunei Bay on June 10. But later research has shown that MacArthur's, and the U.S. Joint Chiefs', arguments that the British wanted a naval base at Brunei were hardly truthful. The airfield on Tarakan could not be repaired in time for use in further operations.[62]

Although Blamey had supported these operations, he was less enthusiastic about MacArthur's plan to land the Seventh Division at Balikpapan on July 1, and his concerns were shared by the corps and divisional commanders and by the navy and air commanders. With the American invasion on Okinawa on April 1, the Japanese were cut off from the Netherlands East Indies, and the capture of Balikpapan would hardly contribute to their defeat. On Blamey's advice, the acting prime minister, J.B. Chifley, suggested to MacArthur that the operations be canceled. MacArthur replied that the operation had to proceed because it had been ordered by the Joint Chiefs of Staff, and if the Australian government withdrew the Seventh Division, he would "make the necessary representations to Washington and London." Yet it will be recalled that the Joint Chiefs had agreed to the operation only because MacArthur had said that not to carry it out would "produce grave repercussions with the Australian government and people." His threat to make representations was pure bluff. Nevertheless, in his last administrative act from his hospital bed, Curtin remained loyal to MacArthur and agreed to the operation. When it took place, 229 Australians were killed and 634 were wounded. Japan did not surrender one minute earlier as a result of this action.[63]

While Blamey had been discussing the role of the First Australian Corps in the Borneo operations, during the early months of 1945 he had been subjected to severe criticism in Parliament and the press. Some of the criticism concerned his administration of the army and reflected the heavy burden the large army was placing on Australian manpower resources. Other criticism was personal: he was accused of sidetracking his military rivals to maintain his position of authority. Party politics were being played more keenly as the end of the war approached, and Blamey was a ready target. His readiness to retaliate and his contempt for the press only fueled the criticism. But one area of criticism brought him into further dispute with MacArthur and concerned a matter of high strategic policy.

From October 1944 until July 1945, the First Australian Army fought a series of grim and unrewarding campaigns against large formations of enemy cut off on Bougainville in the Solomon Islands and in New Guinea. Blamey's critics claimed that the campaigns were unnecessary and wasteful of Australian lives and had been conducted to further Blamey's own ambitions. Although the First Army was nominally under MacArthur's direct command, Blamey had exercised control over the commander of the First Army because he believed that MacArthur had shown a complete lack of interest in the affairs of that army, and MacArthur seemed happy for this unofficial command arrangement to continue. MacArthur claimed later that from the beginning he had expressed reservations about the offensive nature of the operations, stating that "if he was doing the job himself, he wouldn't jeopardize a single Australian life in an offensive in these back areas." Indeed at his last meeting with Curtin in Canberra on September 30, 1944, he had told Curtin that the "Australian local commanders would possibly find the garrison duties irksome and might desire to undertake some active operations, but this would be a matter for direction by the Australian authorities." For the present, the correct policy was "to garrison the islands and leave the Japanese gradually to waste away."[64]

Having been directed by MacArthur to use more brigades than he considered necessary, Blamey decided that the offensives should be conducted for at least four reasons. First, he believed that it would be bad for morale and health to keep so many troops relatively inactive in the presence of large groups of enemy. Second, he thought that the best way to reduce the manpower requirement and to provide troops for MacArthur's invasion of Japan was to defeat the Japanese forces and thus eliminate the need for garrison troops. He could not know that the war would end abruptly in August 1945. Third, he believed that Australia had a moral responsibility to liberate the native population under Japanese control; the natives in Australian Mandated Territories were after all an Australian responsibility. Fourth, some leading American politicians and military men had mentioned the possibility of a postwar policy that would allow the United States to retain the Pacific islands that U.S. forces had liberated; it might be wise if Australia was seen as liberating its own territories. It was, of course, government policy for Australia to win recognition at the peace table for the important role played by troops. It was really up to the Australian government to decide whether to conduct an offensive for these sorts of reasons, but the Australian government had shown itself singularly unable to tackle strategic issues, and Blamey merely informed the government of what he was doing.[65]

Perplexed by criticism of the operations, Curtin wrote to MacArthur to inquire whether they were in accordance with his directive to the First Army. MacArthur ducked the question but on April 18 observed that, while the operations had been conducted with skill, a more passive policy might have been better. Blamey quickly replied that, since MacArthur had provided the necessary landing craft for the Sixth Division operations, he must have approved of them. By now Curtin had become ill, and acting prime minister Chifley passed on Blamey's views. MacArthur retorted that, although he had met a request for support, the operations were "unnecessary and wasteful of lives and resources." On May 22 the members of the Australian war cabinet considered a detailed written statement from Blamey and concluded that they had "made a very sound case in justification of the operations."[66]

Clearly Chifley did not know quite what to do. Perhaps he was hampered by the fact that he was only acting prime minister. Eventually, on July 21, after Curtin had died and he had become prime minister, he replied to MacArthur. The letter, which expressed the views of the late prime minister, began by reminding MacArthur that as commander in chief he was responsible for the operations of the forces assigned to him. The only right possessed by Australia was to withhold forces. Thus the government had proceeded on the assumption that, "even within the limits of discretion allowed subordinate commanders, their plans would be subject to your approval." Chifley pointed out that since MacArthur had left Australia in October 1944 the government had "not been fully and continuously in touch with all variations in your plans." For example, MacArthur's letter of March 5 in response to Curtin's query about command arrangements provided the government with its first knowledge that the Australian forces were not to be used in the Philippines.

When the Australian Forces became more active against the Japanese in New Guinea, New Britain and the Solomon Islands, it appeared reasonable and logical to the Government for it to assume that there must have been some variation in the views expressed by you to the Prime Minister in Canberra, and that the exercise of the freedom of action of a local Commander referred to you in your reply of 19th [actually 18 but received 19] April would be vetoed by you . . . if the operations undertaken by him did not meet with your approval. I regret to say that the Government is greatly embarrassed by your reply. It has publicly defended the wisdom of these operations.

Thus in the strongest letter written by an Australian prime minister to MacArthur, Chifley acknowledged that the Australian government had abdicated strategic responsibility. Ten days later the government informed Blamey that the objectives he had spelled out for the operations of the First Army had been approved, but by then the war was almost over. No reply was received from MacArthur.[67]

During the last months of the war, Blamey's relationship with MacArthur had grown more distant, but with the end of hostilities he was sent by the Australian government to represent Australia at the main surrender ceremony on board the U.S.S. *Missouri* in Tokyo Bay. It was a fitting recognition for a general whose contribution to the Japanese defeat had been surpassed by few others and for a nation which per head of popula-

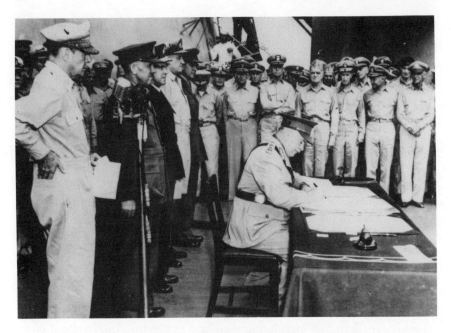

Blamey signs the instrument of surrender on the deck of the U.S.S. *Missouri*,
Tokyo Bay, September 2, 1945. Courtesy Australian War Memorial.

tion had borne an unsurpassed burden. One week later Blamey himself
accepted the surrender of the commander of the Japanese Second Army
on Morotai. His comments reflected his approach even if they represented the views of many Australians.

In receiving your surrender I do not recognize you as an honourable foe, but you
will be treated with due but severe courtesy in all matters. I recall the treacherous
attack upon our ally China . . . I recall the treacherous attack made upon the
British Empire and upon the United States of America. . . . I recall the atrocities
inflicted upon the persons of our nations as prisoners of war and internees, designed to reduce them by punishment and starvation to slavery. In the light of
these evils, I will enforce most rigorously all orders I issued to you, so let there by
no delay or hesitation in their fulfilment at your peril.[68]

While Blamey had little opportunity to display his ability as a field
commander in the Pacific war, he quickly grasped the nature of the war.
the need for the use of sea and air resources, the debilitating effect of the
climate and the terrain, the need for thorough training and fitness as well
as frequent reliefs of commanders and soldiers, the importance of logistics, and the value of accurate intelligence. He did not immerse himself in
detail, preferring to leave it to his first-rate chief of staff, Lieutenant Gen-

eral Berryman, yet he had a clear grasp of details. Importantly, he was not wasteful of Australian lives (apart from his miscalculation regarding the use of Bren carriers at Buna) and always protected Australian interests. Brigadier Sir Kenneth Wills, controller of the Allied Intelligence Bureau, wrote after the war: "Few people realize how much of the credit of the successful Australian operations, both in the Middle East and in New Guinea, was due to the Chief's personal control and planning." Wills thought that Blamey was ahead of Mackay, Lieutenant General Sir John Lavarack, Morshead, and Herring in "brainpower, leadership and drive."[69]

In 1942 Blamey had made it clear that he would resign as commander in chief at the end of the war. In September 1945, after the surrender ceremony in Tokyo, he offered to resign. For a while the government chose to retain him as commander in chief, informing him in early November that the complexity of problems confronting the army made it desirable for him to remain on the job. Then suddenly, in mid-November, the minister for the army, Francis M. Forde, advised Blamey that Lieutenant General Vernon Sturdee, the commander of the First Army, was to become acting commander in chief from December 1 until the Military Board could be reformed. This peremptory dismissal of the government's top military adviser without any recognition or reward for his service shows the depth of feeling against him in some quarters of the Labor party. Clearly many members of the government were anxious to dismantle the wartime high command organization, and the first step was to remove Blamey. Other advisers, such as Shedden, were keen to strengthen the role of the Department of Defence, and Blamey had some unacceptable ideas. He had to await the election of a Liberal government before he received any reward. In 1950 he was appointed field marshal, becoming the only Australian to reach that rank. He died the following year.

As commander, Allied land forces, and as the government's chief military adviser, Blamey suffered serious frustrations and disappointments that would have broken most men. His strength of personality and determination showed that he was well equipped for the task of safeguarding Australian interests. He had strong views on the need to maintain Australian sovereignty and, unlike some Australian generals, understood that wars are fought for political purposes. As one of the most controversial figures in Australian military history, Blamey has inspired such passions that for some forty years his detractors have tended to discount automatically the admiration in which he has been held by a score of senior officers. As one writer observed, these detractors seemed to believe that "by some mysterious power the senior officers still dance to the beat of the dead field marshal's baton."[70]

Blamey's critics have assigned personal motives to all of his actions. To them he was a self-seeking, devious manipulator who cared little for Australian lives and who struggled to retain his powerful position and to fuel his own ego. But to many others he was Australia's greatest general. To them he revealed a deep experience of military and political affairs and proved a wise and forceful administrator. He fought relentlessly to maintain Australian independence in military matters, and he had a genuine concern for the welfare of his troops. Without his efforts MacArthur would have found it easier to disregard Australia's wishes.

The most credible evaluation of Blamey's character lies somewhere between these two views, probably closer to the second view than to the first. Once, when asked his opinion of MacArthur, Blamey replied that "the best and the worst things you hear about him are both true."[71] The same could have been said about Blamey himself. He walked a tightrope, both maintaining his own position and protecting Australian interests, risking loss of his own position and also risking the distrust of his subordinates. He made few concessions to his critics. He advanced his own point of view ruthlessly—advocating a course which, like MacArthur, he believed coincided with the best interest of his army and nation.

Although MacArthur might privately fulminate against Blamey, particularly with regard to his insistence on retaining his two appointments as commander of Allied land forces and commander in chief of the Australian Military Forces, his real complaint against Blamey was that he was not entirely under his command. Although Blamey's position was precarious in September and October 1942, he was never really afraid of MacArthur in a personal sense. Any fear that Blamey might have felt related to the maintenance of Australian sovereignty, and unlike MacArthur's other subordinates, he had an experience of war greater than that of his American superior. There was no lasting animosity between them, and in 1948 MacArthur invited him for a visit in Tokyo. MacArthur sent his own plane to fly Blamey from the British Commonwealth Occupation Force base at Iwakuni to Tokyo, and he met Blamey at Haneda airport when it landed. As Blamey's biographer wrote, "There was a great warmth in the meeting of the two old comrades. Now that the wartime national rivalries were dead and buried, they could talk and walk and laugh together without reserve or pretence, and they drew closer, perhaps, than they had ever been before."[72]

Blamey's record contains no outstanding peak. Rather it is marked by year upon year of wise decisions, stubborn determination to further the interests of Australia, and a deep concern for the well-being of his soldiers. He had many weaknesses but greater strengths. He was Australia's senior soldier for the full period of World War II, during which time the army fought with skill and bravery in a score of campaigns. After the war

MacArthur wrote that Blamey was "a veteran soldier of highest quality" who deserved his high reputation and his appointment as field marshal. A greater testimony of Blamey's achievement, however, was the outstanding performance of the Australian army in the Allied campaigns of the Pacific war.[73]

Walter Krueger

MacArthur's Fighting General

WILLIAM M. LEARY

Had it not been for a family tragedy, Walter Krueger might well have become a senior *Wehrmacht* commander during World War II. He was born in 1881 on the large crown estate of Flatow, West Prussia (Zlotow, Poland, after World War II), which had been leased by his father, a former officer in the Prussian army who had fought in the Franco-Prussian War. The father, Julius O.H. Krüger, died in 1885. Four years later, his mother brought Walter and two younger children to the United States to live with her maternal uncle, Edward Nixdorff, a prominent brewer in St. Louis, Missouri. Shortly after her arrival, Anne Hasse Krüger married Emil Carl Schmidt, a German-born Lutheran minister.[1]

Walter Krueger grew up near Madison, Indiana. He was educated in local schools, and his most valuable training came at home. His mother taught him to play the piano, inculcating in him a lifelong love of classical music. His stepfather—once characterized as "brilliant but inexorable and very severe"—tutored him in mathematics and languages. Krueger also developed a strong sense of discipline and an impatience with careless mistakes and laziness. In other respects we know little about his childhood, although there are indications that the Schmidt home was not an especially happy one.[2]

In 1898 Krueger was attending Cincinnati Technical School, planning to go to college and study engineering, when the Spanish-American War broke out. It changed his life. Watching as the Sixth Infantry marched out of Cincinnati on its way to Cuba, he became caught up in the patriotic fervor that was sweeping the nation and enlisted in the Second Volunteer Infantry. The young soldier reached Santiago in August, shortly after the Battle of San Juan Hill. He remained in Cuba until he was mustered out with the rank of sergeant in February 1899.

Krueger enjoyed his brief taste of military life. Within a short time, he began to find the prospects of a career as a civil engineer pale in comparison to the adventure of fighting in the Philippines. In June he enlisted as a private in the Twelfth Infantry. He was sent to the Philippines three months later and saw action at Angeles, Mabalacat, and Bamban and during the advance on Tarlac. An outstanding soldier, he rose to the rank of sergeant before receiving a commission as second lieutenant of infantry in 1901.

A variety of assignments over the next fifteen years taught Krueger the trade of a professional soldier. He attended the Infantry and Cavalry School at Fort Leavenworth, commanded a company, and served a second tour in the Philippines, during which he was in charge of mapping northern Luzon. He gained considerable attention by translating Colonel William Balck's *Tactics* (2 vols., Fort Leavenworth, Kans., 1911, 1914; reprinted, Westport, Conn., 1977), a highly regarded study of tactical principles by a German authority that was adopted by the Army service schools.

After commanding a regiment of the Pennsylvania National Guard on the Mexican border in 1916, Krueger rejoined the regular army during World War I and served in France as assistant chief of staff for operations with the Twenty-sixth Division and, at the end of the war, as chief of staff of the AEF tank corps. Promoted to the temporary rank of colonel following the Armistice, he held staff positions with the Sixth and Fourth Army Corps before returning to the United States in the summer of 1919 and reassuming his permanent rank of captain.

Krueger graduated from the Army War College in 1922, after which he had a three-year staff assignment with the War Department. Frustrated by the apparent lack of prospects with the infantry, Krueger decided to transfer to the air corps. In 1927, at the age of forty-five, he went to Brooks Field at San Antonio for flight training, an experience that proved bittersweet. The personnel at Brooks, he reported, "welcomed me literally with open arms and I have been shown a courtesy and spirit that I really did not know existed anywhere." They were more than willing to make concessions because of his age, but their superiors in Washington insisted that he meet all the requirements of a demanding flying curriculum. Krueger could not. "I learned a great deal," he wrote to a friend; however, "my failure to make the grade in the air corps . . . sticks in my bones. I'll probably never get over it entirely."[3]

In the wake of this disappointing flirtation with the air corps, Krueger spent four happy years on the faculty of the Naval War College. He loved history, enjoyed teaching, and found the work "both interesting and, I think profitable." The academic hiatus ended in 1932 when Krueger took command of the Sixth Infantry at Jefferson Barracks, Missouri, a choice assignment. "Naturally," he observed, "I was delighted to get this fine command."[4]

Krueger flourished at Jefferson Barracks. A spit-and-polish soldier, hardworking and intense, he set out to make the Sixth Infantry the finest unit in the U.S. Army. His inspections were constant and rigorous. Kitchens had to be spotless, correspondence letter perfect, and troops brought to the highest state of training. "He was a strict constructionist," his adjutant recalled, "but NEVER for the purpose of being mean. When he cracked the whip it was for a good reason and one never forgot the lesson. I have received it and I have watched others get it, and I know."[5]

After duty with the War Plans Division of the General Staff, which brought a brigadier's star, Krueger moved rapidly through important field assignments. Within the space of three years, as the army began to respond to a threatening international situation, he led, in turn, a brigade, division, and corps.

In April 1941 Army Chief of Staff George C. Marshall recommended Krueger for promotion to lieutenant general and command of the Third Army. At the same time, Marshall called to Krueger's attention several personal shortcomings that he found troubling. After praising Krueger's "mental ability" and "tremendous capacity and willingness for hard work," the chief of staff expressed his concern about "the fact that you are very sensitive to criticism, to suggestions, and to anything that you think might not reflect to the best advantage for you personally. You are a man of decided opinions, along with great ability cultivated through many years of hard work, and as a partial result of this there has grown up the impression that you have a hard time hearing other people's views and adapting them to your own use—and that you are evidently unaware of this reaction of yours." Marshall expressed his hope that Krueger would accept this criticism as "sincere and friendly" in purpose. The sole reason for the remarks, he stressed, was to facilitate "the development of this new army of ours, on which so many may depend."[6]

Krueger responded like a good soldier. "I offer neither explanation nor excuse", he wrote to Marshall, "but accept your comments without reservation, in the same spirit in which they are offered, and will profit by them." He pledged his full effort to the creation of the new army. "You shall have no cause hereafter", he assured Marshall, "for anxiety on my account in this connection."[7]

Krueger made good on his promise when he took command of the Third Army and Southern Defense Command, with headquarters at San Antonio, in May. Units throughout the southwestern United States soon found that "pretty good is not good enough." Krueger was constantly on the move, conducting rigorous inspections and lecturing officers on the importance of looking after the welfare of their enlisted men. Commanding men, Krueger believed, was "the holy duty of an officer." Officers had to know "a soldier's heart and what makes him tick." Over and over again, he stressed: "We will have an army only if we take care of the enlisted men."[8]

William H. ("Bill") Mauldin, who was destined to gain considerable fame for his wartime "Willie and Joe" cartoons, which well expressed the sentiments of enlisted men, had firsthand experience with Krueger—"a tough old bird who liked to sneak up on his troops"—during the summer of 1941. As he later recalled:

Twice in the same month I encountered him while my company was doing field exercises. It is an awesome experience when a man with three stars on each shoulder steps out of the bushes and demands to see your bare feet. As we sat on the ground and peeled off footgear, Krueger picked up our socks, inspected them for holes, and ran his hands inside our shoes to check for nails. Then he had us spread our toes as he peered between them, his august nose not six inches away. . . . When Krueger found an infantryman with untreated blisters, athlete's foot, or leaky socks, the soldier's noncoms lost their stripes and his officers got official reprimands. We in the lower echelons sort of loved the crusty old boy, were delighted to learn that he had enlisted as a private and risen through the ranks, and were not surprised when later he turned out to be one of the most distinguished generals in the Pacific.[9]

Training intensified as the summer wore on and the United States edged closer to war. September brought the Louisiana maneuvers, the largest and most realistic peacetime military exercises ever conducted by the army. Lieutenant General Ben Lear's Second Army clashed with Krueger's Third Army on the banks of the Red River, south of Shreveport. Lear had the advantage of an experimental armored corps under George S. Patton, but Krueger's skillful employment of his supporting air force checked the Second Army's initial assault. While Innis P. Swift's First Cavalry Division attacked the Second Army's rear area, Krueger's main force pinned it against the Red River. By the time the first phase of the maneuvers had ended, Krueger clearly held the upper hand. Lear fared no better in a second phase, held later in the month.

The Louisiana maneuvers paid rich dividends. Talented officers were identified, including Krueger's chief of staff, Dwight D. Eisenhower. Troops gained experience in withdrawals, river crossings, and antitank tactics. Commanders of large units and their staff coordinated infantry, armor, and air, and learned valuable lessons in logistics. Weaknesses in personnel and training were identified, and corrective action was initiated.[10]

Krueger's first experience of commanding an army in the field had been marked by success. An officer who observed him in action during the maneuvers has written a graphic description of his style of leadership:

Louisiana Maneuvers, 1941: Brigadier General Mark Clark and Colonel Dwight
D. Eisenhower in back; in front, unidentified man with Lieutenant Generals
Ben Lear, Krueger, and Leslie J. McNair. Courtesy Walter Krueger, Jr.

The General emphasized the coordination and teamwork within and between all
units and by staff at all levels. He showed the way by long hours of visiting and inspecting all types of units—squads to regiments. He talked to scouting patrols,
bridge guards, gun crews, and officer and non-commissioned officers of all ranks.
Beware to the Company Commander whose soldier showed the General a hole in
the sole of his combat boot, or told the General that he had not had a hot meal for
two days, or could not explain how his weapon functioned. Gen. Krueger knew
the tactical principles from the infantry squad and artillery gun crew to his Army
headquarters, and all the tactical and logistics operations necessary to success. He
constantly emphasized his theme that his Army headquarters was "to serve the
troops" and that staff officers were acceptable only if they had the faculty of working effectively as a team.[11]

While he was pleased with the conduct of his troops, Krueger believed that the maneuvers had revealed serious shortcomings in the training of junior infantry officers. He immediately established the Junior
Officers' Training Camp at Camp Bullis, outside San Antonio, under
Colonel John W. ("Iron Mike") O'Daniel. Students at "Krueger Tech"
underwent six weeks of rigorous physical conditioning and intensive training in infantry weapons and small unit tactics under simulated combat

conditions. They also received instruction in what Krueger called the "vulgar part of soldiering"— housekeeping, kitchen management, sanitation, care of weapons, supplies, transport, and so forth.[12]

Krueger often visited Camp Bullis, and he usually came away pleased. O' Daniel worked the men hard, ignoring the peacetime amenities that characterized most army training prior to Pearl Harbor. A staff officer later recalled the smile on Krueger's face when he returned from a rainy day visit to the camp. He had asked Colonel O'Daniel if there was a rainy day schedule for the troops. "Yes," O'Daniel had replied. "Raincoats."[13]

When the United States entered World War II in December 1941, Krueger was approaching his sixty-first birthday. He may have hoped at first for overseas duty, but it quickly became clear that combat assignments were going to younger officers. No matter how he may have felt about this turn of events, no one ever heard him complain about his fate. Instead, Krueger devoted all his considerable energy to transforming a flood of volunteers and draftees into an effective military force.

While Krueger trained troops in the United States, General Douglas MacArthur struggled to stem the Japanese advance in the Southwest Pacific. The Imperial Army captured Rabaul on New Britain in January 1942, then established bases on the northern coast of New Guinea. Deterred from a seaborne assault on Port Moresby by the naval battle of Coral Sea, the Japanese launched an overland drive across the Owen Stanley Mountains. Advance elements of Major General Horii Tomitaro's forces reached Imita Ridge in mid-September, only twenty miles from Port Moresby, before disease, lack of supplies, and Australian resistance stopped the offensive.

MacArthur ordered an immediate counterattack. Australian and American troops chased the exhausted Japanese back across the mountains, occupied Kokoda on November 2, and attacked the main enemy positions at Buna, Gona, and Sanananda. Weeks of repeated frontal assaults took a heavy toll on Allied forces. Unhappy with the performance of the U.S. Thirty-second Infantry Division, MacArthur sent Lieutenant General Robert L. Eichelberger, commander of the First Corps, to relieve the division's commanding officer, Major General Edwin F. Harding, and take charge of the fighting. Eichelberger's more aggressive leadership, coupled with the arrival of reinforcements, brought success. Buna fell on January 2, 1943, followed by Sanananda on the twenty-second.[14]

Experience with the campaign on New Guinea convinced MacArthur that the tactical organization of an American army was an "imperative necessity" for operations in 1943. Unhappy with his relationship to Australian forces, he wanted an American as the next ranking officer under Australian General Thomas Blamey in the chain of command. Eichelberger lacked the necessary experience for such a position. "I recommend that the Third Army [Headquarters] under General Krueger be transferred to Australia," MacArthur radioed Washington on January 11, 1943. Not only would this give the theater "an able commander and an efficient operating organization," but it would also place an American officer in the desired position in the command structure. "I am especially anxious to have Krueger," he emphasized, "because of my long and intimate association with him."[15]

In characteristic fashion, MacArthur overstated his past relationship with Krueger. The two had first met, briefly, in 1903 at the Army and Navy Club in Manila, shortly after MacArthur arrived in the Philippines from West Point. Their paths next crossed in 1909, when they served together on the faculty of the General Service Schools at Fort Leavenworth. "But," Krueger recalled, "I saw little of him then." They did not meet again until the 1930s. Assigned to the War Plans Division, Krueger reported to Chief of Staff MacArthur; however, their relationship could hardly be described as intimate. "That he should have remembered me well and favorably enough to ask for my services in SWPA," Krueger observed, "was as remarkable as it was flattering."[16]

Krueger was inspecting the Eighty-ninth Infantry Division at Camp Carson, Colorado, when he received word that he would be transferred to the Southwest Pacific theater. He was delighted. "My assignment came as a complete surprise to me," he wrote to a friend, "because I had about concluded that I would not get to see active [overseas] service during this war. While I was inclined to accept that philosophically, I must admit that I was greatly pleased to be mistaken."[17]

Krueger flew to Washington on January 14 and spent a week conferring with officials in the War Department. He was disappointed to learn that MacArthur's request for headquarters, Third Army, had been refused. Instead, Krueger was directed to organize and activate headquarters of a new Sixth Army. Given the demands of other theaters, and the low priority attached to SWPA, he had to settle for half the commissioned officers authorized by the table of organization for an army headquarters. However, he did receive permission to retain his key staff officers.[18]

Krueger left San Antonio with the advance party on February 2 for the long air journey to Australia via California, Oahu, Canton Island, Fiji, and New Caledonia. He landed at Brisbane's Amberly Field on February 7, was met by a senior SWPA staff officer, and was escorted to quarters at Lennon's Hotel. Reporting to MacArthur the next day, Krueger learned that he would be conducting operations under the designation of Alamo Force. Although the theater commander offered no explanation, it was obvious to Krueger that this was an organizational ploy to prevent the Sixth Army from coming under the operational command of General Blamey.

MacArthur then outlined Krueger's area of responsibilities. Although

MacArthur commanded all Allied forces in the theater, he did not exercise personal control over any units. "He formulated all strategic plans," Krueger noted, "issued directives designating the operations to be undertaken, the commanders to conduct them, the forces and means to be used, the objectives, and the missions to be accomplished. But in conformity with the principle of unity of command, he did not prescribe the tactical measures or methods to be employed." That would be Krueger's job, along with coordinating the plans of supporting air and naval forces.

MacArthur went on to brief Krueger on the current situation in the theater and future plans. The Japanese held positions along the northern coast of New Guinea from Hansa Bay to the Huon Peninsula, then through New Britain and the main naval and air base at Rabaul, to Munda in the Solomon Islands. The Combined Chiefs of Staff, meeting at Casablanca in January, had designated Rabaul as the primary SWPA objective for 1943. MacArthur fully agreed with the decision, but he was troubled by the meager resources allocated for the campaign. He was nevertheless developing appropriate plans to defeat the enemy on New Britain.[19]

Whatever MacArthur decided, Krueger would have to fight under difficult conditions with meager resources. His units stretched over two thousand miles, from Melbourne to New Guinea. The major elements of his command—the Thirty-second Infantry Division at Brisbane and the Forty-first Infantry Division on New Guinea—were ravaged by disease, inadequately supplied, and demoralized. Nor did conditions in the theater give much cause for optimism. Australia suffered from inadequate port facilities and a poor rail infrastructure; New Guinea offered inhospitable terrain, some of the world's worst weather, and a bewildering variety of debilitating diseases. Krueger certainly had his work cut out for him.[20]

Krueger spent his first week in Brisbane calling on high SWPA officials. He met with General Blamey, had dinner with Lieutenant General Eichelberger ("He was most friendly in every way," Eichelberger wrote to his wife, "and really quite amusing."), and conferred with Lieutenant General Richard K. Sutherland, MacArthur's chief of staff, for whom he developed a deep distaste that was shared by many others. In the midst of this introduction, Krueger received the sad news that one of five planes carrying the rest of Sixth Army's advance echelon had crashed on Canton Island, killing thirteen key members of his staff.[21]

Krueger moved out of Lennon's Hotel on February 16 and established his headquarters at Camp Columbia, ten miles west of Brisbane. Among the many problems he faced over the next few months, improving logistical support for subordinate units held a high priority. He made it clear that he would not tolerate a situation that forced members of the Forty-first Division to patch their uniforms with material from captured Japanese uniforms because they could not secure replacement clothing. Requisitions would be filled promptly; deficiencies would be corrected immediately. "It was not long," one of Krueger's subordinates recalled, "until logistic agencies jumped into action when they saw a Sixth Army staff officer approaching."[22]

The malaria situation also demanded immediate attention. Distressed to learn that so little was being done to improve the health of his men, Krueger sent to the United States for experts on tropical diseases to staff a new malaria treatment center at Rockhampton. He activated malaria survey and controls units, and he stressed preventive measures, such as the wearing of proper clothing. Prevention of malaria became a command responsibility.[23]

While Krueger took action to restore the fighting efficiency of his troops, MacArthur worked on plans for the forthcoming campaign. In late March the Joint Chiefs of Staff had issued new objectives for 1943, ones more closely tied to the theater's limited resources. After establishing airfields on islands north of the southeastern tip of New Guinea, SWPA forces would advance northwestward along the coast and seize the Lae-Salamaua-Finschhafen-Madang area, together with the western portion of New Britain. Also, operations would be directed against Japanese positions in the Solomon Islands as far as southern Bougainville. Rabaul would be squeezed in a double envelopment, preparatory to a direct assault in 1944.[24]

To achieve these objectives, MacArthur developed a flexible general plan of operations that involved thirteen amphibious landings over a six-month period, beginning in June. In early May Krueger received orders to occupy the islands of Kiriwina and Woodlark. After conferring with supporting naval and air commanders, Krueger's staff prepared a detailed operational plan that GHQ approved on May 28.[25]

Operation CHRONICLE, SWPA's first amphibious operation, went off smoothly. The main landings took place on June 30 and July 1. Krueger's forces encountered no Japanese, and airstrips became operational by the end of July. This bloodless exercise provided valuable training for Sixth Army/Alamo Force. Krueger's staff gained needed experience in concentrating and staging troops that were scattered over long distances; they learned how to allot shipping, arrange for escort and air coverage for convoys, make loading diagrams for ships, and cope with the thousand and one details that often spell the difference between the success and failure of complex amphibious operations. As noted in the army's official history, the thorough and comprehensive planning for CHRONICLE "became standing operating procedure for future invasions."[26]

As Krueger prepared to execute the next phase of MacArthur's plan to "pinch off Rabaul"—the seizure of western New Britain, with landings at Arawe and Cape Gloucester—he became increasingly concerned with the lack of adequate ground intelligence on terrain and enemy dispositions. In October he asked Major General Innis P. Swift, commander of the First Cavalry Division, to select a "most highly qualified officer" as director of a new camp to train reconnaissance teams. "He should be highly intelligent," Krueger wrote, "enthusiastic, resourceful, and have a natural knack of teaching. In addition he must be hard as nails, tough . . . and capable of getting things done." Krueger planned to name the outfit "Alamo Scouts," although he was reconciled to the notion that some wag would doubtless dub them "Krueger's Apaches."[27]

Alamo Training Center on Ferguson Island, just off the southeastern tip of New Guinea, was launched in November. Colonel Frederick W. Bradshaw directed a six-week training program that included instruction in map reading, scouting and patrolling, weapons, message writing, field communications, use of rubber boats for night landings, and other essential techniques. Between December 1943 and September 1945, the ten teams that graduated from the center conducted over seventy missions. The Alamo Scouts, Krueger later wrote, "proved of inestimable value to the Sixth Army. Their daring exploits, sometimes even behind the Japanese lines . . . bear eloquent testimony of their courage, fortitude, skill and teamwork."[28]

Sixth Army units came ashore at Arawe on December 15; the First Marine Division, under Krueger's operational control, assaulted Cape Gloucester eleven days later. At MacArthur's instructions, Krueger also landed a task force on the New Guinea coast at Saidor on January 2, 1944, in an effort to cut off Japanese troops retreating from the Huon Peninsula. Although the amphibious operation, conducted on short notice, was a success, Krueger's concern about his supply lines and enemy strength in the area, combined with rugged country and torrential rains, allowed the Japanese to slip around the American force. Some of the enemy reached Madang, but many died en route of illness and starvation.[29]

The pace of operations accelerated in 1944. In February the Sixth Army attacked enemy positions in the Admiralty Islands, completing the encirclement of Rabaul. As it was now clear that the Japanese fortress could be left "to die on the vine," MacArthur directed his attention toward his primary goal: the return to the Philippines. The Sixth Army led the drive along the northern coast of New Guinea, conducting a series of amphibious assaults. The names are obscure, but the fighting was real enough at Hollandia-Atape (April 22), Wakde (May 17), Biak (May 27), Noemfoor (July 2), and Sanspor (July 30). By the end of the summer, the Japanese had been defeated on New Guinea, and American preparations to invade the Philippines had commenced.[30]

Krueger matured as a combat commander during the New Guinea campaign. Although he was hesitant at Saidor, his confidence grew with each successful amphibious assault. He admired the courage and fortitude of the men who were called upon to fight against a tenacious enemy in one of the world's most difficult climates, and he insisted that all officers "give

Krueger comes ashore at Los Negros, 1944, followed by Major General Innis P.
Swift. Courtesy U.S. Military Academy Library.

close personal attention to the health, food, and comfort of my troops."
When an inspection of a forward area revealed that the men were being
fed a monotonous diet of corned beef hash, he arranged for six aircraft to
carry perishable items from Australia. On another trip, he noticed a hulk-
ing barefoot soldier. He wore a very big shoe, his commander explained,
and replacement footware could not be obtained through logistic channels. New shoes came by air within days.[31]

Officers had to lead. Bruce Palmer, Jr., recalled how Krueger had
once made this point. Chief of staff of the Sixth Infantry Division, Palmer
encountered Krueger at Maffin Bay, New Guinea, shortly after the Twentieth Infantry had fought the bloody Battle of Lone Tree Hill. "How many
officer casualties?" Krueger wanted to know. Palmer said that they had
been heavy. "Good," Krueger responded. No doubt noticing the surprised look on Palmer's face, Krueger explained that the high toll indicated to him a fighting outfit with good leadership.[32]

One of the most explicit statements of Krueger's approach to leadership came in September 1944. The Infantry School was marking the
graduation of 50,000 enlisted men as second lieutenants, and Krueger had
been asked to say a few words on the NBC Army Radio Hour. The subject
was close to Krueger's heart, and he spoke with feeling: "Your men will
follow where you lead, if you have their confidence and respect. Look to
their welfare always, share their hardships, be fair in all things, and they
will never let you down. No matter how small any task assigned to you

may be, do it well; there is no greater pleasure than the satisfaction of a job well done. Your reward will be the good will and approbation of your comrades. Set your standards high; place duty above all else, and remember always that only he who has learned to obey is fit to exercise command."[33]

Krueger's staff shared at least some of the hardships of the troops. Everyone lived in tents or huts, and all messes used the same rations. Krueger allowed his subordinates a good deal of autonomy. "General Krueger was one who would tell a person what he wanted done," a staff officer recalled. "He wouldn't tell them how to do it, but he would insist on performance."[34] Brigadier General George H. Decker (destined for four stars and the post of U.S. Army chief of staff) had replaced Brigadier General Edwin D. Patrick as chief of staff in May 1944. This had been a good move. Although he was able, Patrick failed to soften the blows that came down from Krueger, causing resentment among the staff. The intelligent and hardworking Decker had a better personal relationship with Krueger; he served as a buffer between the commander and his staff, and he could often arrange for the modification of orders. "He's the only one who could handle General Krueger," a staff officer commented.[35]

Krueger also placed great confidence in Colonel Clyde D. Eddleman, Sixth Army's G-3. The future four-star general served as chairman of the army-navy-air planning group that translated GHQ's general directives into tactical plans of operation. "In order to permit the fullest and freest discussion by the Joint Planning Group," Krueger explained, "I never injected myself into its deliberations, but kept unobtrusively in the background, though in close touch with Colonel Eddleman, to whom I made such suggestions from time to time as I deemed necessary." The joint plan received final approval at a commanders' conference.[36]

Major General Stephen J. Chamberlin, MacArthur's G-3, was the key point of contact between GHQ and the Sixth Army. Chamberlin usually discussed proposed operations with Krueger, Decker, and Eddleman. He would later secure MacArthur's approval for Sixth Army's plan of action. Decker and Chamberlin got along especially well. Chamberlin was "a very fine staff officer," Decker believed, "and a very fine operator." In the rare event of a major disagreement, Krueger would see MacArthur, bypassing the detested Sutherland.[37]

In July 1944, as the fighting on New Guinea continued, GHQ issued a broad strategic plan for liberating the Philippines. MacArthur wanted to land on Mindanao in mid-November, invade Leyte on December 20, then attack the main Japanese positions on Luzon early in 1945. While MacArthur was in Honolulu attempting to persuade President Roosevelt not to support the navy's proposal to bypass the Philippines in favor of a landing on Formosa, Eddleman and a group of Sixth Army staff officers were in Brisbane for discussions about the forthcoming campaign. One engineering officer, Colonel William J. Ely, was not at all happy with

GHQ's optimistic approach to airfield construction on Leyte. He viewed as impossible the plans to build airfields for two fighter groups, one bomber group, and seven additional squadrons within five days after landing. The invasion, he pointed out, would take place during the rainy season; typhoons could be expected; the soil at likely construction sites would be unstable; the road system would likely disintegrate under constant heavy rain. Ignored in Brisbane, Ely sent a protesting memorandum to his superior, Colonel Samuel D. Sturgis, Jr., chief engineer of Sixth Army. Sturgis supported Ely, but GHQ decided to proceed as planned.[38]

Early September brought a series of devastating air attacks on Japanese positions in the Philippines by Admiral William F. Halsey's Third Fleet. Surprised by the lack of opposition, Halsey recommended the immediate invasion of Leyte, bypassing Mindanao. This move would place Sixth Army for the first time beyond the support of land-based air; it would have to depend on naval air until fields could be built on Leyte. MacArthur decided to take the gamble. "I had no illusions about the operation," he recalled. "I knew it was to be the crucial battle of the war in the Pacific. On its outcome would depend the fate of the Philippines and the future of the war against Japan."[39]

Krueger received word on September 15 that Mindanao had been canceled and the target date for Leyte advanced to October 20. This gave the Sixth Army only thirty-five days to alter its complex scenario for the movement of men and supplies. Although at times the task seemed impossible, Krueger's staff performed a minor miracle. Working with VIII Amphibious Force and Fifth Air Force, Decker and his associates made the necessary revisions, and the required forces were ready on schedule.[40]

GHQ assigned two corps to Krueger for the invasion: the Tenth Corps (First Cavalry and Twenty-fourth Infantry divisions) and the Twenty-fourth Corps (Seventh and Ninety-sixth Infantry divisions). The Thirty-second and Seventy-seventh Infantry divisions would form the Sixth Army's reserve. Krueger planned to land the two corps abreast on the east coast of Leyte. The Tenth Corps would come ashore on the right, capture Tacloban and its airfield, then advance toward Carigara. The Twenty-fourth Corps on the left would seize Dulag, then continue on toward Burauen. Krueger expected the heaviest resistance in the north, but he had great confidence in the commander of the Tenth Corps, Major General Franklin C. Sibert. "He is cool and very aggressive," Krueger informed MacArthur, "and his troops reflect that spirit."[41]

Krueger sailed from Humboldt Bay the night of October 14, 1944, bound for Leyte. During the next five days, the Sixth Army's commander often paced the deck of U.S.S. *Wasatch*, flagship of naval attack force commander Vice Admiral Thomas C. Kinkaid, but more for exercise than to relieve tension. "Assured of strong naval and naval air support", Krueger reflected, "I was confident that our main assault landing would be successful."[42]

The great naval armada reached Leyte on October 20. Beginning at 0600 in the south and 0700 in the north, battleships from the naval attack force began pounding Japanese positions from Dulag to Tacloban. At 0900, as the assault waves of the Tenth and Twenty-fourth Corps approached the landing area, cruisers and destroyers moved close to shore to pour their fire on flank and rear areas. Minutes before the landing, rocket and mortar barrages from landing craft combined with air strikes from escort carriers to add to the violence.[43]

The timing and location of the landing caught the Japanese by surprise, and the Sixth Army (no longer using its Alamo Force designation) met little resistance. MacArthur splashed ashore in the afternoon and announced: "People of the Philippines, I have returned!" By evening, Krueger's forces had achieved all their initial objectives, including capture of Tacloban airfield. As Krueger remarked, the landing phase had been accomplished "more easily than we had anticipated," but the real battle for Leyte remained to be fought.[44]

Japanese resistance was not long in developing. Both the army and the navy decided that the time had come to fight a decisive battle in the Southwest Pacific. The Imperial Navy set in motion an elaborate plan to destroy the American beachhead—and it nearly succeeded. At one point during the naval engagement of October 23-26, only Rear Admiral Clifton Sprague's escort carrier force stood between the Japanese and their main objective. The courageous action of this small force—which put up "one of the most gallant, heroic defenses in naval annals"—averted a major disaster.[45]

Meanwhile, the Imperial Army had begun to reinforce its small garrison (twenty-six thousand men) on Leyte. The first troops landed at Ormoc on the west coast on October 23. Over the next two weeks, the Japanese managed to put ashore over forty-five thousand troops, including the veteran First Division. "This was one of the four best divisions in the Japanese Army," Krueger noted, "and it did more than any other enemy unit to prolong the Leyte operation."[46]

Krueger was unable to stop these reinforcements because he lacked air support. Colonel Ely has been right about the construction difficulties. Three typhoons swept the east coast of Leyte between October 20 and 28, washing out roads and making airfield construction nearly impossible. Engineers reported that all proposed airfield sites were unfit for use during the rainy season. Only Tacloban remained, and it was no prize. Short, uneven, and poorly drained, the field had to be reshaped, lengthened, and covered with steel matting. "Life during those early days on Leyte," engineers would recall, "was brutal." They soon came to look back on New Guinea "as being downright hospitable."[47]

Deprived of air superiority and unable to exploit the Sixth Army's mechanized strength, Krueger had to rely on his infantry to defeat the Japanese. His first objective was to secure Leyte Valley. While the Twenty-fourth Corps in the south advanced from Dulag to Burauen, the Tenth Corps split into two forces after landing. The Twenty-fourth Infantry Division headed south to seize Palo, then attacked along Highway 2 toward San Miguel and Barugo. At the same time, the First Cavalry Division proceeded along the north coast, joining with the Twenty-fourth Division at Barugo for the assault on Carigara. The second phase of Krueger's plan would see the Twenty-fourth and the Tenth Corps converge on Ormoc and bring an end to Japanese resistance on the island.[48]

Krueger opened his command post at San Jose on October 24. Despite the constant rain and frequent enemy air attacks on the beachhead, the Sixth Army made good progress at first, capturing Carigara on November 2, then advancing toward Pinampoan. As the Tenth Corps prepared to attack southwest across mountainous terrain toward Limon at the head of the Ormoc Valley, the Japanese First Division began to move north from Ormoc. On the morning of November 3, the Sixth Army received word that a column ten miles long, containing trucks, tanks, and artillery, extended from Ormoc to Valencia. That evening, the Tenth Corps G-2 reported on possible Japanese courses of action. The enemy could defend the Pinampoan-Ormoc road at any place he chooses, Colonel W. J. Verbeck estimated, or he could launch a coordinated attack from this area. Above all, Verbeck warned: "He can make an amphibious attack in CARIGARA BAY area."[49]

The possibility that a Japanese assault on Carigara Bay could cut off the Tenth Corps worried Krueger. In the absence of American air cover, the Japanese certainly had the capability for such a move, as they had demonstrated by landing the First Division at Ormoc. Also, Krueger fretted over the supply situation at Pinampoan. The road from Carigara had been washed out, and units at Pinampoan were being supplied by sea. "Although I was anxious to gain early possession of the hills north of Limon which controlled access to Ormoc Valley," Krueger later noted, "I could not ignore the possibility of such a landing." Lacking sufficient forces to prepare Carigara Bay against enemy attack *and* attack south, Krueger chose the prudent course. At 1350, November 4, he ordered the Tenth Corps to break off its attack at the end of the day and spend forty-eight hours securing Carigara Bay against an amphibious assault.[50]

The Tenth Corps resumed its offensive on November 7. The next two weeks saw the bloodiest fighting of the campaign, as American infantry struggled to dislodge a tenacious enemy from their mountain positions between Pinampoan and Limon. Historians later would question Krueger's decision to delay the advance of the Tenth Corps. As Stanley Falk has written: "A more aggressive general might have ignored the seaward threat to Carigara, shifted some of Hodge's forces [the Twenty-fourth Corps] north, and thrown everything into seizing the crucial ridges and hills before the Japanese could secure them. But Krueger was not by nature inclined to take such a gamble. A careful, deliberate commander, he was not adverse to taking risks when necessary. Yet he was more cautious than others might have been, and in this situation his instinct prescribed the conservative course."[51]

More recently, Professor Ronald Spector has offered a much more critical interpretation of Krueger's conduct, labeling "a mystery" the "disastrous decision" to delay the Tenth Corps and allow the Japanese to turn the mountainous terrain between Pinampoan and Limon "into a veritable fortress." According to Spector, intercepted Japanese messages (Ultra) had failed to indicate any plans for an amphibious landing at Carigara. "It would appear," he argues, "that Krueger and his staff, rather than basing their estimates on cryptographic intelligence, disregarded it in favor of their own surmises."[52]

Was Krueger's conduct on Leyte in early November a case of excessive caution? Certainly the Japanese were capable of launching an amphibious assault at Carigara Bay. In fact, General Yamashita Tomoyuki, Japanese commander in the Philippines, later stated that at one point he had planned to make such a landing. To rely on cryptographic intelligence to predict enemy intentions—especially the absence of information about an attack—would have been foolish in the extreme. "Ultra," G-3 Eddleman later commented, "was of little value to the Sixth Army directly. It gave some indication of Japanese morale but little else." Krueger preferred to see his actions as prudent rather than cautious. "A commander cannot afford to be rash," he once commented. "I don't mean that he must be cautious. I certainly am not cautious. But rashness must be tempered with reasonable prudence"[53]

Furthermore, the results of the Tenth Corps's two-day delay have probably been exaggerated. By November 3, strong Japanese forces—including the Forty-first Infantry Regiment, Tempei Battalion, and 171st Independent Infantry Battalion—already held the approaches to the heavily wooded range of mountains that blocked the entrance to Ormoc Valley. Continuation of the offensive without delay would likely have produced only limited gains. The Tenth Corps, short of supplies, did not have the strength to break through to Limon. Also, as one of Krueger's staff officers has emphasized: "Certainly a commander is obligated to seize a key locality when the advantage that will accrue outweighs the risks, but this principle applies to features such as the Remagen Bridge which opened up Germany east of the Rhine, or on the Golan Heights from which it is downhill all the way to Damascus. It certainly doesn't apply to thirty miles of mountains, every inch of it defensible."[54]

One can speculate on the consequences for the Tenth Corps—and for

Krueger's reputation—if the Sixth Army's commander had decided to neglect Carigara Bay in favor of pushing the offensive and the Japanese *had* landed. It seems reasonable to believe that Krueger would have been condemned for failing to take the most elementary precautions, and MacArthur would have looked elsewhere for a general to lead the assault on Luzon.

With Japanese reinforcements pouring into Ormoc, Krueger grew increasingly concerned about the Sixth Army's personnel shortages. His request for 10 percent overstrength for the start of the campaign had been denied; his attempt to secure nineteen thousand trained replacements to make up losses during the first month of combat had also failed. On October 29, without consulting Krueger, GHQ had ordered the Seventy-seventh Infantry Division (part of the Sixth Army's reserve) to proceed from Guam to the Solomons for rest and rehabilitation instead of sailing for Leyte. By early November, the Sixth Army was about twelve thousand officers and men short of authorized strength, with the worst shortages occurring in the heavily engaged rifle companies.

Krueger brought this situation to MacArthur's personal attention during a visit to Sixth Army headquarters on November 8. MacArthur gave Krueger all replacements in SWPA, but his amounted to only five thousand men. After the Japanese landed the Twenty-sixth Division at Ormoc on November 9, Krueger told MacArthur that additional combat units would be required to bring the campaign to a speedy conclusion. MacArthur agreed. The Thirty-second Infantry Division and the 112th Cavalry Regimental Combat Team arrived on November 14. They were welcomed by the Tenth Corps, which had suffered greatly during the battle for the northern approaches to Ormoc Valley. The Eleventh Airborne Division reached Leyte four days later; Krueger sent it to the Twenty-fourth Corps to relieve the combat-weary Seventh Infantry Division.[55]

Krueger had special plans for the Seventy-seventh Division, which MacArthur diverted from the Solomons to Leyte. He wanted to use the division to make an amphibious landing on the west coast, just south of Ormoc. Not only would this ploy close Ormoc to reinforcements and cut Japanese supply lines, but also it "would form the jaws of a giant pincher to crush the enemy forces in the Ormoc Valley." The navy, however, opposed the operation. Inadequate air cover, Rear Admiral Arthur D. Struble feared, would result in heavy losses to enemy air attack, making the assault on Mindoro, which was scheduled for December 5, impossible. "Although these objections were weighty ones," Krueger acknowledged, "my disappointment was naturally keen."

On December 1, after MacArthur delayed the Mindoro operation to December 15, Krueger again pressed for the amphibious attack. This time the navy agreed, albeit reluctantly. Despite intense enemy air opposition, the Seventy-seventh Division landed safely at Despito on December 7. Ormoc fell four days later. The Seventy-seventh then fought its way north, linking up with the Tenth Corps at Valencia on December 16. By Christmas, the Sixth Army had defeated most major Japanese units on Leyte. "The Ormoc Operation was a complete success," Krueger noted, "contributed materially to crushing organized resistance in the Ormoc Valley and formed a fitting climax to the Leyte campaign."[56]

MacArthur sent his congratulations on Christmas Day. The campaign, he rejoiced, had "few counterparts in the utter destruction of the enemy's forces with a maximum conservation of our own. It has been a magnificent performance on the part of all concerned." The bloody toll of combat certainly was impressive: by midnight, December 25, 56,263 Japanese had been killed (by actual count of bodies); the Sixth Army had losses of 2,888 killed and 9,858 wounded.[57]

The Sixth Army had fought well. Deprived of friendly air support and plagued by the constant rain that often turned the battlefield into a sea of mud, American infantry had faced the best troops that Japan had to offer. The Japanese gave no quarter—and asked for none. Their field commander, Lieutenant General Suzuki Sosaku, expressed this sentiment in a poem written shortly before his death:

> Every soldier must expect to sacrifice his life in war,
> Only then has his duty been done;
> Be thankful that you can die at the front,
> Rather than an inglorious death at home.[58]

In a memorandum on mistakes made and lessons learned, written while the battle for Leyte was still underway, Krueger stressed the need for "aggressive leadership" to defeat a determined enemy. The Japanese were tenacious fighters; they could be dug out of their entrenched and concealed positions only by small infantry units. "Infantry is the arm of *close combat*," he emphasized. "It is the arm of *final* combat." The American soldier had demonstrated that he could do the job, "but he must be aggressively led. There can be no hesitation on the part of his leaders." He urged unit commanders to look after their troops, to provide shelter and hot meals whenever possible. The American infantryman would fight best if he believed that everything possible was being done for his well-being and comfort. "It must never be forgotten," Krueger concluded, "that the individual soldier is the most important single factor in this war".[59]

While Lieutenant General Eichelberger's Eighth Army took over responsibility for "mopping up" the Japanese troops remaining on Leyte (an operation that involved a good deal of hard fighting), Krueger turned his attention to the invasion of Luzon. GHQ had issued operations instructions on October 12, directing the Sixth Army to land in the Damortis–San Fernando area of Lingayen Gulf. Although MacArthur's planners had selected the best beaches in the area (the ones that the Japanese had used in 1941), Krueger had reservations. The Sixth Army had intelligence reports indicating that the area would be heavily defended. Krueger sought and obtained MacArthur's approval for a landing at Lingayen-Dagupan-Mabilao. This was a gamble. The beaches were subject to high winds that could make landing difficult, and beyond lay a zone of streams, ponds, and swamps. If the Japanese blocked the limited egress routes inland, the Sixth Army would be extremely vulnerable.[60]

Krueger envisioned a three-phase operation. First, the Fourteenth Corps (Thirty-seventh and Fortieth Infantry divisions) and First Corps (Sixth and Forty-third Infantry divisions) would land abreast and secure the beachhead, permitting the construction of airfields and logistical bases. In phase two, the Sixth Army would engage and destroy the enemy north of the Agno River. The final phase called for the defeat of Japanese forces in the central plains and the capture of Manila.[61]

Krueger sailed from Leyte Gulf on U.S.S. *Wasatch* on January 6. It turned out to be a rough voyage. Japanese air attacks, especially kamikaze, inflicted painful losses on the invasion forces, sinking three ships and heavily damaging fourteen others. The troops that went ashore on January 9 had an easier time. Within a week, the beachhead was twenty miles deep and thirty miles wide. Krueger's bold gamble had paid off. Although the Japanese had known that a landing was imminent, his choice of beaches had caught them by surprise."[62]

The Sixth Army's initial success pleased MacArthur, but he quickly became impatient with its pace of advance toward Manila. On January 12 he told Krueger that he did not expect the Japanese to defend the port city. He could not understand why the Sixth Army had not made greater progress in its drive southward. Krueger pointed out that the First Corps had to protect the beachhead and guard the left flank of the advance against strong Japanese forces in the northeast. As a result there were only the two divisions of the Fourteenth Corps left to cover the 120 miles to Manila. "I considered that a precipitate advance on its part toward Manila," Krueger explained, "would probably expose it to a reverse and would in any case cause it to outrun its supply—a serious matter, since all bridges had been destroyed. . . . General MacArthur did not seem to be impressed with my arguments. He did not appear to take very seriously the danger that the enemy might well take advantage of any overextension of our forces to attack them in the flank as we moved south." However, while MacArthur obviously did not share Krueger's view of the situation on Luzon, "he did not direct me to change my dispositions or my plans."[63]

MacArthur may have been reluctant to issue new orders to Krueger, but he was not at all averse to applying unremitting pressure. On January 17, as the Fourteenth Corps began crossing the Agno River, MacArthur sent Krueger a radio message, urging him to speed south and capture Clark Field. A radio message the following day informed Krueger that MacArthur had recommended him for four-star rank. MacArthur followed up with a visit to Krueger's command post on January 19, where the two men had a private talk. On the way back to his headquarters, MacArthur told an aide: "Walter's pretty stubborn. Maybe I'll have to try something else."[64]

"Something else" came on January 25. In "a blatant effort to prod Krueger into more aggressive action," Professor D. Clayton James notes, MacArthur moved his headquarters to Hacienda Lusita, far ahead of the Sixth Army headquarters at Calasiao. The ploy did not work. Krueger realized that MacArthur wanted to be in Manila for his birthday (January 26), but he could not ignore the strong Japanese forces on his left flank. On the twenty-sixth he visited MacArthur at Hacienda Lusita, and the two old warriors exchanged greetings on their shared birthday (MacArthur, at sixty-five, was one year older than Krueger). "General MacArthur was undoubtedly greatly disappointed that Manila would not be secured as early as he had desired," Krueger observed. "But he refrained from directing me, as he might well have done, to take a risk that I considered unjustifiable with the forces available to me at the time." Krueger waited for the arrival of reinforcements before launching the assault on Manila.[65]

No doubt to MacArthur's relief, the Sixth Army began its two-pronged drive on Manila on February 1. On the left, Krueger organized the newly arrived First Cavalry Division (reinforced by the Forty-fourth Tank Battalion) into a fast flying column. This force, its flanks protected by patrolling fighters from the Fifth Air Force, headed south from Guimba along Highway 5. The head of the column reached Grace Park on the outskirts of Manila on February 3, having covered nearly one hundred miles in two days. Meanwhile, the Thirty-seventh Infantry Division attacked on the right, entering the northern suburbs of Manila on February 4.[66]

MacArthur was not satisfied. On February 5 he again stressed to Krueger the importance of securing Manila at the earliest possible moment. But twenty thousand Japanese troops had turned the city into a fortress. Despite the gallantry of his infantrymen, Krueger emphasized, "it took time to crush Japanese resistance for they defended every substantial building in the city and fought savagely until they were killed." As MacArthur planned his victory parade, the Thirty-seventh Infantry Division battled its way across the Pasig River barrier on February 7, followed by the First Cavalry Division three days later. At the same time, the Eleventh Airborne Division attacked from the south. The end of the fight was in sight by February 18, but it took another week to crush all enemy resistance. The city—what was left of it—was secured on March 4.[67]

MacArthur played a more direct role in the drive on Manila than he had in any previous SWPA campaign. Ever since landing at Lingayen, biographer D. Clayton James observes, "He had dashed from one sector to another, obviously in personal command of operations, impatiently and sometimes antagonistically prodding Krueger and his commanders, and even participating in a regimental engagement." Anxious to enter Manila by his birthday, and having assured the Joint Chiefs of Staff that he could secure the city within four to six weeks after the initial landing, MacArthur chafed at Krueger's methodical advance. Major General Charles A. Willoughby, MacArthur's intelligence chief, had assured him that only 152,000 Japanese troops defended Luzon, with no more than half in the north, facing Krueger. "Given Willoughby's estimates," the army's official history notes, "it is smalll wonder that MacArthur was unworried about Sixth Army's left and felt that Krueger would have little difficulty occupying Manila."

Krueger took a different approach. Colonel Horton V. White, Sixth Army's G-2, put Japanese strength on Luzon at 234,000, with most concentrated in the north. This was a far more accurate estimate than Willoughby's. General Yamashita Tomoyuki had divided his forces into three main groups. One group (30,000 men) occupied the mountainous area on the west side of the central plains, overlooking Clark Field; another (80,000 men) was centered in the mountains east and northeast of Manila. The third and largest group (152,000 men), under Yamashita's personal command, held the Caraballo Mountains on the left flank of Krueger's advance. Unable to ignore this threat, and convinced that the Japanese intended to defend Manila, Krueger saw no good *military* reason for a headlong dash to the south. If MacArthur had an overriding priority for such a move, then he would have to issue the necessary orders. He never did. And whereas other generals might have succumbed to MacArthur's pressure, Krueger was made of sterner stuff.[68]

The fall of Manila did not signal an end to the Luzon campaign. Indeed, the Sixth Army had yet to engage the main Japanese forces on the island, strongly entrenched in the mountainous terrain east and north of the capital. MacArthur showed little interest in this part of the fighting. He transferred units from the Sixth Army to Eichelberger's Eighth Army, which was engaged in what one authority has labeled "highly questionable" operations in the central and southern Philippines. In the months ahead, MacArthur would heap praise on Eichelberger, but he would say little to Krueger and visited Sixth Army headquarters only once.[69]

The publicity that Krueger began to receive no doubt added to the tension between the Sixth Army's commander and his superior; it certainly roused the jealousy and ire of General Eichelberger. After *Time* magazine put Krueger on its cover, and the *New York Times* hailed him as a "master of amphibious warfare," Eichelberger wrote to his wife: "If he is a great general or has any of the elements of greatness then I am no judge of my fellow man. Beyond a certain meanness, which scares those under

Krueger confers with Eichelberger (Colonel Harry Reichelderfer, Sixth Army's signal officer, on left). Courtesy Walter Krueger, Jr.

him, and a willingness to work, he has little to offer. He doesn't even radiate courage, which is one thing we like to think a soldier has." These comments, which say more about Eichelberger than about Krueger, demonstrated the hazards of publicity in SWPA. Little wonder that, when asked to supply a biographical sketch for a radio program, Krueger responded: "I should much prefer to have you drop the matter."[70]

Handicapped by dwindling resources and facing a resolute enemy dug into strong defensive positions, Krueger did what he did best: he fought superbly. His routine varied little during this difficult campaign. He usually woke at 0645 to orange juice and hot tea. G-3 Eddleman would brief him on the night's developments. A staff meeting followed. Should current operations proceed on course? Was a change of plans needed? Which units required additional ammunition and logistical support? "Each day," Chief of Staff Decker recalled, "each staff member that attended this meeting knew what was going on, knew what his part in it should be, and in that way everybody seemed to be pulling together toward the proper objective."[71]

Krueger then set out with an aide and representative from G-3 to inspect units, usually traveling in company with two MP Jeeps, one in front and one behind. "To cover his schedule," one staff officer recalled, "we had to travel fast with sirens going most of the way, pebbles and dust flying in all directions and chickens scurrying for cover." The roads were

often rough. While Krueger had special holds in his Jeep, accompanying
junior officers had to grab at anything, including each other, to stay inside
the vehicle. During one of these hectic rides, Krueger pointed to a distant
range of mountains and asked the G-3 representative, "Where is the Villa
Verde Trail?" As the young officer tried to orient his maps, Krueger commented: "You've heard of it, haven't you?" "Of course, I had," David W.
Gray later recalled. "U.S. troops were fighting hard on the trail, one of the
approaches to Baguio, but I knew General Krueger had a good idea where
it was so I wasn't about to make a wild guess. It was his way of saying that a
good officer studies the terrain and knows where he is all the time. From
then on I paid less attention to hanging on and more attention to my
map."[72]

John J. Tolson, who went on to three-star rank and high command in
Vietnam, often traveled with Krueger as G-3 representative. "I learned
more of the art of soldiering from being with General Krueger on those
trips than from anything else in my entire career," he reflected. "He
was out in the field himself, seeing what the troops were doing and what
their commanders at all echelons were doing to take care of their
troops. . . . He knew what was taking place on the battlefield by personally seeing himself, not by only verbal and written reports to his C. P."[73]

Arthur S. Collins, Jr., a regimental commander on Luzon, recalled a
visit from Krueger on the morning following a night attack. "We walked
around a churchyard where my mobile command post was located, and he
asked questions about the operation. As we talked, it was obvious to me
that he was taking everything in, sizing everything up—vehicles, wire,
weapons positions, the condition of the men and the equipment. He
headed for a mortar position and asked a few of the questions that, I was
soon to learn, he asked all soldiers—when they last had had a hot meal,
how often they were resupplied with clean fatigues, and other ones that
showed him whether their commanders were taking proper care of
them."

On another inspection, at a time when Sixth Army was short of artillery ammunition, Krueger gave Collins a lesson in resource conservation.
"He told me how many artillery tubes there were in the Sixth Army; how
many rounds would be fired if all the artillery pieces were fired once, five
times, or ten times a day; how much tonnage each rate of fire added up to;
and how many ships would have to ply the Pacific to get that amount of
ammunition to all the different places where Sixth Army troops were
fighting. It was a graphic presentation of the tremendous effort needed to
keep my cannon company and supporting artillery firing." Collins never
forgot the lesson. "Because of it, more than twenty years later when I
arrived in Vietnam [as commander of the Fourth Infantry Division]
and observed the waste of artillery ammunition on unobserved harrassing

and interdiction firing, I would not allow it by the units under my command."[74]

Krueger usually returned to his Spartan headquarters in the late afternoon and discussed the results of his inspection with Decker, often "letting down his hair" to appraise the strengths and weaknesses of subordinate commanders. At the same time, the G-3 representative, who had been taking careful notes during the inspection, passed Krueger's comments to Eddleman for action. Dinner, often shared with Decker, Eddleman, and a few close staff members, was served promptly at 1800. Krueger ate little, although he used tremendous amounts of salt on his food. He finished in a hurry, then had a cup of coffee without sugar or cream. He smoked a great deal: Camel cigarettes, Antonio & Cleopatra cigars, and pipes ordered from Bertram's in Washington.[75]

Krueger enjoyed movies in the evening, but his main relaxation came from reading. Prior to Luzon, he preferred history (he ordered a volume of Douglas Southall Freeman's *Lee's Lieutenants* during the fighting on Leyte), but during the spring of 1945 his tastes ran to detective stories and novels. In the midst of the hardest fighting of his career, Krueger doubtless needed the diversion.[76]

The Sixth Army conducted two campaigns simultaneously, one against Lieutenant General Yokoyama Shizuo's 80,000-man Shimbu Group, which controlled the dams and reservoirs in the mountains east and northeast of Manila, and the other against General Yamashita's 152,000-man Shobu Group, with headquarters at Baguio. The fighting was fierce on both fronts. In late February, the First Cavalry and Sixth Infantry Division attacked Japanese positions guarding the Wawa Dam, east of Manila. During this battle, Japanese machine gun fire killed Major General Edwin D. Patrick, commander of the Sixth Division and Krueger's former chief of staff, and an enemy grenade severely wounded First Cavalry commander Major General Verne D. Mudge. It took until late June to shatter General Yokoyama's defenses. "If Krueger had had the Sixth Army force that MacArthur had given to the Eighth," Professor James has observed, "his troops east of Manila could have brought the Shimbu Group to that shattered status much earlier."[77]

The First Corps under General Swift faced the even more difficult task of assaulting General Yamashita's mountainous stronghold in northern Luzon, which was shaped like a triangle (Baguio-Bontoc-Bambang). Krueger began this campaign in early March with only three divisions—the Twenty-fifth Thirty-second, and Thirty-third—and Colonel Russell W. Volckmann's U.S. Army Force in the Philippines, an eighteen-thousand-man guerrilla unit. He had hoped to apply pressure on Yamashita by driving on Baguio and Bambang, but after MacArthur sent Sixth Army units to support the Eighth Army in the southern Philippines,

Krueger had had to revise his plans. He identified the Cagayan Valley, a rich farmland extending two hundred miles from Bambang to Aparri on the north coast, as the key to Yamashita's defenses. Seizing this valley would deprive the Japanese of vital food supplies and cut communication with enemy forces to the west. Yamashita's destruction would then be inevitable.[78]

While the Thirty-third Division contained the Japanese at Baguio and Colonel Volckmann's guerrillas harassed the enemy at Bontoc, the Twenty-fifth and Thirty-second divisions launched a converging attack in the Balete Pass-Santa Fe area, south of Bambang, gateway to the Cagayan Valley. Plans called for the Twenty-fifth Division, commanded by Major General Charles L. Mullin, Jr., to drive north on Highway 5 and clear Balete Pass, while the Thirty-second Division, headed by Major General William H. Gill, attacked from the west along the Villa Verde Trail toward Santa Fe, three miles north of Balete Pass.[79]

The terrain favored the enemy. The Villa Verde Trail was a narrow, twisting mountain track that provided ample opportunity for defense. And the Japanese exploited all possibilities. As noted in the army's official history: "Every knoll and hillock on or near the trail was the site of at least one machine gun emplacement; every wooded draw providing a route for outflanking was zeroed in for artillery or mortars." The battle for the trail came down to a series of frontal assaults, and Gill's infantry units suffered grievous losses, including the death of a regimental commander.[80]

By mid-April, as battle and nonbattle casualties mounted, it was clear that the exhausted Thirty-second Division had major problems of morale. Although Krueger usually came down hard on subordinate commanders when an attack stalled, he realized that Gill could not get any more out of his tired men. When Gill expressed concern over the lack of progress, Krueger assured him "that I was fully satisfied that his division had done and was doing all that was humanly possible under the incredibly difficult terrain conditions and resistance facing it." In any event, Krueger had no reserves to relieve the battered division. He had to fight with what he had.[81]

Pressure on the Villa Verde Trail facilitated the task of the Twenty-fifth Division, but progress still came slowly along Highway 5. The enemy resisted bitterly, and Japanese positions had to be reduced one by one. Short of artillery ammunition, Krueger found that 90-millimeter antiaircraft guns, for which there was an abundant supply of high-velocity ammunition, had a devastating effect on Japanese strong points, especially in caves. On May 13, after two months of fierce fighting, the division finally broke through Balete Pass. It captured Santa Fe on May 27, then drove westward to link up with the Thirty-second Division at Imugan.[82]

Krueger brought in the Thirty-seventh Division, earlier released from occupation duty in Manila, to exploit the breakthrough. Having lost his best troops, Yamashita could offer only limited resistance. Bambang and Bagabag fell in early June, and American troops poured into the Cagayan Valley. By the end of the month, the Sixth Army had gained effective control of the region. Although twenty-five thousand Japanese troops remained in the north, they were doomed to be hunted down by American and guerrilla forces or die of starvation and disease. "One thing was certain," Krueger emphasized: "General Yamashita—the 'Tiger of Malaya'—and his army had been decisively defeated by the United States Sixth Army."

Victory over the largest Japanese army encountered by American forces in the Pacific war had not come cheaply. The Luzon campaign cost the Sixth Army 8,140 killed and 29,557 wounded. The Japanese lost nearly a quarter of a million men in defending their lost empire.[83]

Krueger may have caused MacArthur to become impatient from time to time during the fighting in the Philippines, but there is no question that he retained the confidence of his superior. In December 1944 General Eichelberger wrote in his diary that MacArthur had become so dissatisfied with "Molasses in January" during the Leyte campaign that he intended to relieve Krueger. Instead, MacArthur selected the Sixth Army's commander to lead the assault on Luzon. "The tough old veteran was MacArthur's top soldier," historian Stanley Falk has pointed out. "For what had originally promised to be the roughest battle of them all . . . MacArthur wanted the best." Again in February and March 1945, Eichelberger recorded MacArthur's complaints against Krueger—and again MacArthur turned to Krueger. Faced with the certainty of hard fighting for the Japanese home islands, he picked the Sixth Army to invade Kyushu. MacArthur, in short, trusted Krueger. Aware of his own tendency toward impetuosity, he prized his experienced field commander for his prudence.[84]

By summer 1945 the Sixth Army was a mighty force of 650,000 battle-hardened veterans. Krueger planned to assault Kyushu on November 1, employing nine army and three marine divisions. But the final battle proved unnecessary: Japan surrendered in August, and the Sixth Army was able to land peacefully as an occupation force. In September Krueger established Sixth Army headquarters in Kyoto, where he administered occupation policy until the end of the year. Ordered to deactivate, the Sixth Army turned over its occupation duties to the Eighth Army on December 31, 1945.[85]

Krueger left his headquarters at the Daiken Building for the last time on January 25, 1946. Following a special reception for his staff at the Miyako Hotel, he left for the Kyoto railroad station. Despite a light afternoon rain, American soldiers and Japanese civilians jammed the flag-draped route. Fifteen armored cars, three abreast in five files, preceded Krueger's car as a guard of honor. MP Jeeps flanked the automobile, followed by seventeen sedans with corps, division, and other senior commanders. A military escort awaited at the station: the Thirty-third Division band, fifteen hundred men from the Twenty-fifth, Thirty-third, and Ninety-eighth divisions, and a platoon each from the Second Marine and Twenty-fourth and Thirty-second Infantry divisions. Krueger stepped out of the car and took his place in front of the commander of troops. Behind him, in line, stood his two corps commanders, followed by division commanders and other general officers and a final line of staff officers.

Krueger bid farewell to his beloved Sixth Army. "My association with you," he said, "will always be the most precious recollection of my military career. I am proud indeed to have been one of you." The old soldier then boarded his special train—the "Alamo Special"—for the journey to Tokyo. He called on General MacArthur the next day. In a brief ceremony at his headquarters in the Dai Ichi Building, MacArthur awarded Krueger the Distinguished Service Cross and attached a second oak leaf cluster to his Distinguished Service Medal. Three days later Krueger sailed out of Tokyo Bay on the U.S.S. *New Jersey* for the long voyage home.[86]

In June 1945, war correspondent Gordon Walker published an article in the *Christian Science Weekly Magazine* under the title "General Walter Krueger: Mystery Man of the Pacific." Although Krueger had recently been promoted to four-star rank, Walker pointed out, his name "never garnished the official communiques, and to many he is still something of a mystery man in the Pacific." Walker then quoted Socrates on the characteristics of the ideal general: " ' He must be observant, untiring, shrewd; kindly and cruel; simple and crafty; a watchman and a robber; lavish and miserable; generous and stingy; rash and conservative.' " Walker concluded: "Of all the military commanders with whom I have served during two and a half years as a war correspondent, no one more closely fulfills these qualifications than this kindly-faced, yet 'hard-boiled,' German born American."[87]

Tough and aggressive junior combat officers who served with Sixth Army and went on to senior commands later reached similar judgments about Krueger. Lieutenant General Tolson, who led the First Cavalry Division (Airmobile) in Vietnam, has written: "I consider him one of the great Army combat commanders of all time." Lieutenant General Arthur Collins, the outspoken commander of the Fourth Infantry Division in Vietnam, shares this view: "He impressed me always as the finest general around. . . . He was, for many of us, the ideal of a soldier and leader."[88]

Krueger has fared less well with historians in recent years. After examining the Aitape campaign on New Guinea in detail, Edward J. Drea faulted Krueger for acting too aggressively ("out of keeping with his otherwise plodding and methodical generalship") and for failing to make optimum use of Ultra intelligence. Ronald H. Spector's survey of the Pacific war, as noted earlier, singled out the Sixth Army's commander for especially harsh criticism. Even D. Clayton James, who offers a balanced and not unfavorable treatment of Krueger in his biography of MacArthur, compared him to George McClellan ("painstakingly in his preparations and extremely cautious in his moves")—not exactly a high compliment.[89]

MacArthur once said of Krueger: "The mantle of Stonewall Jackson rests upon his shoulders." Yet it seems in many ways as inappropriate to compare him with Jackson as with McClellan. Krueger in fact most resembles George H. Thomas. Known during the Civil War as "Slow Trot," Thomas was meticulous in his preparations for battle and refused to be rushed—as Grant discovered at Nashville. He took great care with the appearance and welfare of his troops, making sure they were well fed, clothed, and sheltered. Above all, he husbanded the lives of his men. He was unlike Grant, Sherman, or Lee, as historians Martin Blumenson and James L. Stokesbury have noted, in that "there is no instance in which he ever threw away the lives of his men, expending them in useless battle." In words that might apply to Krueger, they conclude: "Steady and even-tempered, courteous and gentlemanly, Thomas never departed from the highest standards of personal and public conduct. Unswerving in his devotion to his country and his duty, unsurpassed in his professional performance, Thomas was the personification of generalship in a period in United States military history that is notably distinguished for the quality of its leaders."[90]

Uninterested in publicity and without political ambition, Krueger may have lacked the charisma of his peers, but "Molasses in January"—like "Slow Trot"—served his country with high distinction. As one experienced soldier commented at the end of the Pacific war, "If I had a campaign to direct in circumstances that called for the greatest prudence, the largest skill and the utmost employment of all resources of a single army, I would put it in Krueger's hands." Douglas Southall Freeman, another admirer, had no reservations about his place in history. "Krueger," he wrote, "is one of the great American soldiers of all time."[91]

George C. Kenney

MacArthur's Premier Airman

HERMAN S. WOLK

The U.S. Army Air Forces produced a number of great operational air commanders in World War II. Although such leaders as Spaatz, Eaker, LeMay, and Doolittle richly deserve the acclaim that they have received, some historians and airmen would rank George Churchill Kenney first among equals for his ability to overcome severe organizational, logistical, personnel, technical, and strategical difficulties.

In the Southwest Pacific area during World War II, as commander of the Allied air forces and the Fifth Air Force of the U.S. Army Air Forces, General Kenney became the complete airman. He inherited a terrible situation, and he moved quickly to rectify it. He scrapped what he considered to be a chaotic organization and created clear lines of authority. Faced with severe shortages of planes and equipment, he instituted new supply and maintenance programs. Confident without being cocky, he commanded with authority and won the respect and admiration of his men. Perhaps the most daring and innovative air commander of the war, Kenney gained General Douglas MacArthur's confidence because he knew how to run a combat air force and produced results quickly.

Kenney was five feet six inches tall, with closely cropped hair and full lips. He was almost fifty-three years old in July 1942 when he arrived in the Southwest Pacific to take command of the Allied air forces under General MacArthur, who headed the Southwest Pacific area command. Kenney inherited a disparate organization distinguished by personal animosities. His predecessor, Lieutenant General George H. Brett (a former acting chief of the air corps), failed to develop a satisfactory communicative relationship with MacArthur, who he thought knew little of what air operations might do to help support his forces. Brett's relations with MacArthur's chief of staff, Major General Richard K. Sutherland, bordered on openly antagonistic. Brett considered Sutherland egotistical and arbitrary, with a genius for alienating most of the people with whom he had to deal.

Thus General Kenney found himself called upon to turn around an unstable, tense situation. Moreover, in 1942 Japanese forces had marched through the southern Philippines, most of New Guinea, and the islands northeast of Australia. Japan controlled the Pacific west of Midway. To Allied commanders, invasion of Australia seemed possible. However, prior to Kenney's arrival, in May and June 1942, the Japanese had taken heavy losses in the battles of the Coral Sea and Midway. They lost major warships, including carriers, and several hundred planes. At Midway, twelve hundred miles west of Pearl Harbor, naval air power sent four Japanese attack carriers to the bottom, leaving Japan with only three heavy aircraft carriers. Meanwhile, Japanese troops secured positions on Guadalcanal and other points in the Solomon Islands and continued to advance from the north coast of New Guinea across the Owen Stanley Mountains toward Port Moresby.

MacArthur was extremely fortunate to be able to secure a man of Kenney's ability and experience. Kenney proved to be an extraordinarily able air commander. Bold and innovative, he was skilled in logistics, strategy, and tactics and knew how to organize air forces. He also possessed the ability to select effective subordinate commanders.

Born on August 6, 1889, in Yarmouth, Nova Scotia, where his parents were visiting, Kenney came from an old Massachusetts family, grew up in Brookline, Massachusetts, and attended the Massachusetts Institute of Technology (MIT). He worked as an engineer, was attracted to flying, and in the summer of 1917 enlisted in the army. He trained at Mineola, Long Island, under Bert Acosta, a noted early flyer. "I landed dead stick my first landing," Kenney recalled. Acosta said: "What's the idea coming in there dead stick?" Kenney replied: "Any damned fool can land it if the motor is running. I just wanted to see what would happen in case the motor quit."[1]

Kenney distinguished himself in World War I, commanding the Ninety-first Squadron and undertaking special missions for Brigadier General Billy Mitchell. He flew seventy-five missions, downed two German planes, and received the Distinguished Service Cross and Silver Star. Promoted to captain, he decided to make army aviation a career. Little did he realize that he was fated to remain a captain for seventeen years, except for one year when he reverted to first lieutenant.

Kenney's experience in the army air corps between the wars gave him the kind of exceptional background that enabled him to command air forces with such success during World War II. He was the quintessential air corps officer in the sense that his experience in the relatively small air corps encompassed a broad range of functions, from maintenance, supply and production to strategy, tactics, and operations.[2] During these years, he gained a reputation as a technical and tactical innovator.

After World War I, the strength of the air service plummeted from 195,000 officers and men to an approximate average of 10,000 in the 1920s. Kenney built on his MIT background and in 1921 graduated from the Air Service Engineering School, McCook Field, Ohio. According to Kenney, "it was a hell of a stiff course. I worked like a dog and finished first in the class."[3] Appointed air service representative and test pilot at the Curtiss Aircraft factory, Garden City, Long Island, he worked with the MB-1 bomber, originally produced by the Martin Company.

Assigned in 1923-1925 to the inspection and contract sections of production engineering at the Air Service Engineering Division at McCook Field, Kenney mastered the important lessons connected with scheduling and production quality control. He was learning and gaining a reputation in the air corps for innovation. For example, in World War I guns had been fixed to a plane's fuselage and fired through the propeller, which required complex synchronization lest the propeller be torn. Kenney conceived the idea of mounting machine guns on the aircraft's wings instead of the engine cowling. This amounted to a considerable technological breakthrough—requiring strengthening of the wings and consideration of flight characteristics—and Kenney immediately demonstrated its feasibility by mounting two .30-caliber machine guns to the wings of a DH-4. However, his idea was ahead of its time, and before World War II, the Curtiss P-40 fighter still mounted two (.50-caliber) machine guns on the cowling.

Like all air corps officers moving through career patterns, pointing toward command, Captain Kenney in the 1920s attended the leading interwar schools, the Air Corps Tactical School at Langley Field and the Command and General Staff School at Fort Leavenworth. In 1927-1929 he served as an instructor at the tactical school, the laboratory for the evolution of air doctrine, strategy, and tactics. Here he met Major Frank M. Andrews, who was impressed with Kenney's imagination and his grasp of technical problems. At the tactical school, Kenney continued to develop his ideas about "attack aviation," teaching doctrine and tactics and revising the basic attack aviation textbook. Flying at treetop level during World War I, it had dawned upon him that very low altitude flying might well be safer and more effective than high-altitude tactics.[4]

In the late 1920s and early 1930s, pursuit doctrine and tactics were being challenged by advocates of bombardment aviation. Development of the Boeing B-9 and B-10 bombers spurred evolution of bombardment doctrine and strategy within the air corps. An all-metal monoplane with a speed of two hundred miles per hour, a ceiling of twenty-one thousand feet, and a nine-hundred-mile range, the B-10 gave impetus to plans for a bomber aircraft that could fly faster at greater altitudes with heavier payloads. Together with the appearance of the Norden and Sperry bombsights in the early 1930s, these breakthroughs presaged the arrival in 1935 of the XB-17 long-range bomber.[5]

Kenney was gaining a varied background, melding the practical and conceptual. After serving in 1933-1935 in the Plans Division of the chief of the air corps, under Major General Benjamin D. Foulois, he was appointed by Brigadier General Frank Andrews to the key post of chief of operations and training, headquarters, GHQ Air Force, Langley Field. Working with Hugh Knerr, Follett Bradley, and Joseph McNarney, he became increasingly convinced of the need for an independent air arm.

Kenney played a leading role in honing the general headquarters air force into a mobile, effective unit. Now a lieutenant colonel, Kenney described his work at GHQ as "building this show and putting it together," writing tables of organization and planning maneuvers throughout the country. Instrument and night flying received special attention. Because he continued to badger the War Department general staff about the need for B-17s, in 1936 Kenney was ordered into a kind of exile at Fort Benning, where he taught in the Infantry School.[6]

Two years later, Major General Henry H. (Hap) Arnold became chief of the air corps, following the death (in an air crash) of Major General Oscar Westover. An aviation pioneer who had commanded one of the three wings of the GHQ Air Force, Arnold knew Kenney and appreciated his varied talents. He plucked the outspoken airman from Fort Benning and made him chief of the production engineering section of the air corps Materiel Division at Wright Field, Ohio. In retrospect Kenney thought that from this point forward Arnold always considered him a trouble-shooter. "Every time he got something going wrong," observed Kenney, "he would say, 'send George Kenney out there; he is a lucky son of a bitch. He will straighten it out.' I never was supposed to have any brains; I was just lucky."[7]

Nazi Germany's attack on Poland, France, and the Low Countries galvanized President Franklin D. Roosevelt into ordering a large aircraft production program. Kenney returned to the United States following a brief tour as assistant military attaché for air in Paris full of ideas for important aircraft modifications, including installation of power turrets in bombers, use of bullet-proof glass, and plans for a demand oxygen system, an idea he borrowed from the Luftwaffe. He supervised aircraft modifications at Wright Field until the Japanese attacked Pearl Harbor in December 1941. General Arnold then ordered Kenney, with the temporary rank of major general, to command the Fourth Air Force in San Francisco. Responsible for the air defense of California, Oregon, and Washington, the Fourth Air Force also trained units for overseas assignment. When Kenney took command, he found that the Fourth was having difficulty with

P-38s and A-29 Lockheed Hudson bombers. He personally showed pilots how to fly the P-38 on one engine and how to land the A-29 properly without a ground loop.[8]

Kenney did not remain long with the Fourth Air Force. On July 12, 1942, General George C. Marshall, army chief of staff, and Arnold, informed Kenney that he was to replace Brett as MacArthur's air commander. MacArthur had been offered Major General James H. Doolittle but turned him down because he wanted someone less flamboyant. Marshall and Arnold then turned to Andrews. However, the former GHQ Air Force commander was appalled at Arnold's idea, since his antipathy for MacArthur went back to the early 1930s and the disagreements between the air corps and the War Department.

Kenney's meeting in July 1942 with Marshall and Arnold was something less than pleasant. Marshall emphasized that the command situation in the Pacific had been marked by tense personality clashes. Kenney replied that he intended "to get rid of a lot of the Air Corps deadwood as no one could get anything done with the collection of generals" that Brett had under him.[9] Arnold and Marshall were "a bit peeved," according to Kenney, but agreed to go along if it was all right with MacArthur. The "dead wood" that Kenney wanted to return to the States included Generals Edwin S. Perrin, Ralph Royce, Albert L. Sneed, Martin F. Scanlon, and Rush B. Lincoln. He looked forward to working with Generals Ennis Whitehead and Kenneth Walker.[10]

Lieutenant General John DeWitt, commanding the Fourth Army on the west coast, warmly endorsed Kenney's appointment. He cabled MacArthur that Kenney was "a practical, experienced flyer with initiative, highly qualified professionally, good head, good judgment and common sense. High leadership qualities, clear conception of organization and ability to apply it. Cooperative, loyal, dependable with fine personality. Best general officer in the Air Force I know qualified for high command."[11] MacArthur replied that Kenney "would have every opportunity here for the complete application of the highest qualities of generalship."[12]

Kenney confronted numerous problems in his new assignment. The first related to basic Allied strategy. As Marshall and Arnold made clear in Washington, Germany was the main enemy and had top priority. The major offensive drive in the western Pacific must await Germany's defeat. Allied Pacific strategy posited a holding operation or, as Arnold expressed it to Kenney, defensive operations with intermittent offensive strokes. Kenney noted: "I am supposed to help MacArthur hold the south part of Australia until the European show is cleared up."[13]

Additional difficulties related to logistics, maintenance, personnel, and equipment. Kenney described the overall situation as "a mess." Most fighters and bombers were out of commission. The logistics network was a shambles. Personality clashes were rampant. As to supply in the South-west Pacific theater, he noted that "a lot of stuff has gone out there but no one knows what has happened to it."[14]

Nothing was more important than clear lines of command, and Kenney moved quickly to solidify his own authority and to create a sound organization. He had talked with Brett, the departing air commander, and concluded that Sutherland, General MacArthur's chief of staff, although brilliant and conscientious, was egotistical, interfered in the planning of air operations, and was overly protective of MacArthur. MacArthur himself had lost confidence in the ability of the air forces, believing that they had contributed little.

Kenney met with MacArthur for the first time on July 29, 1942. "I listened to a lecture," Kenney recalled, "for approximately an hour on the shortcomings of the Air Force in general and the Allied Air Force in the Southwest Pacific in particular." The air forces had done nothing at all, and most air generals should never have held such high rank in the first place. Kenney finally interrupted and told MacArthur candidly that he intended to run air operations. As for loyalty, "if for any reason I found that I could not work with him or be loyal to him I would tell him so and do everything in my power to get relieved." He grinned and put his hand on my shoulder and said, 'I think we are going to get along all right.' "[15] Kenney would deal directly with MacArthur; Sutherland's role in air operations had ended.

Having resolved the question of direct access to MacArthur, or as Kenney put it, "the fact that I would run the air show," he turned his attention to solving issues of command and organization. He immediately got rid of the dead wood—several generals (Royce, Sneed, and Scanlon) and about forty colonels and lieutenant colonels.[16] He replaced the inflexible "directorate" system with an organization that could meet the peculiar demands of the theater. On August 7, 1942, the Fifth Air Force was formally established, with Brigadier General Kenneth Walker heading the Fifth Bomber Command and Brigadier General Paul B. Wurtsmith (whom Kenney called "a thief" and "a reformed bad boy") heading the Fifth Fighter Command. The traditional group-and-squadron organization worked best.[17] With Kenney as commander of the Fifth Air Force and the Allied air forces, headquartered in Brisbane, one thousand miles south of the New Guinea front, an obvious command problem existed. Kenney attempted to resolve this difficulty by making Brigadier General Ennis C. Whitehead commander of the advanced echelon of the Fifth Air Force, at Port Moresby.

Kenney had great confidence in Whitehead. He knew "Whitey" as a rough, aggressive commander of the air corps of interwar years—exactly the kind of "operator" he wanted. Kenney would forward general operational directives from Brisbane, allowing his subordinate great flexibility in carrying out the assigned mission. The two men communicated with each other practically on a daily basis to work out operational details. They would maintain a strong, close personal and professional relationship throughout the war.

Kenney received MacArthur's approval for these organizational moves and also for his basic outline of air strategy to be pursued in the New Guinea campaign. It will be recalled that the overall mission of the Southwest Pacific theater was to keep Australia in Allied hands and to establish control over eastern New Guinea (Papua). At the same time, MacArthur's forces were to contribute to the neutralization of the major Japanese base at Rabaul, New Britain, the fulcrum of enemy operations. Also, as part of the major Allied strategy, Southwest Pacific theater forces would drive west along New Guinea's north coast and ultimately north to the Philippines.

The primary air mission was to gain air superiority over the Japanese. Kenney made clear to MacArthur that the Allied air forces needed to "own the air over New Guinea. . . . there was no use talking about playing across the street until we got the Nips off our front lawn."[18] Japanese shipping and airdromes should be struck at every opportunity, but first it would be necessary to get the Fifth's B-17s, B-25s, and B-26s in proper shape to conduct these operations. According to Kenney, "the effort against the New Guinea airdromes should be continuous until the Jap air power in New Guinea is destroyed and the runways so badly damaged that they even stop filling up the holes."[19] All of this was in keeping with an air strategy that Kenney had evolved since his days as an instructor at the air corps tactical school. He refined his ideas under Frank Andrews at GHQ Air Force and also as commander of the Fourth Air Force just prior to his arrival in the Pacific. Ironically, while he was at the Fourth Air Force he spelled out his operational precepts to General Arnold. Now Kenney had a grand opportunity to put them into practice.

The immediate problem was aircraft maintenance and supply. Kenney had a total of 517 aircraft. About two-thirds of these planes were not ready to fly operational missions. They were awaiting parts, undergoing overhaul, needing gun installation, or awaiting salvage. The aircraft of the Fifth Air Force broke down as follows (P-400s were the export model of the P-39):[20]

Fighters		
P-39s	27	
P-40s	115	
P-400s	103	
Total		245
Light bombers		
A-20s	38	

A-24s	15	
Total		53
Medium bombers		
B-25s	15	
B-26s	55	
Total		70
Heavy bombers		
B-17s		62
Transports		
(all types)		36
Total tactical aircraft		466
Miscellaneous aircraft		51
Grand total		517

Kenney noted that the Royal Australian Air Force had a total of seventy planes, most of them P-40s, plus a few Hudsons, Catalinas, Beauforts, and Beaufighters.[21]

In addition to the need to keep his aircraft in commission, Kenney immediately informed MacArthur, and also Arnold in Washington, of the need for replacement crews. Many of the personnel inherited from Brett were tired veterans of the Java campaign. One of Kenney's top priorities was to send these battle-weary troops home, along with most of their commanders. This goal was accomplished.

Kenney also moved to straighten out the supply "mess." He knew that the rear supply area was holding back equipment, figuring that New Guinea would be lost anyway, and that the supplies would eventually be required for the defense of Australia: "Bombers were in New Guinea with no tail wheels, no props, and needing new engines, and fighters with tail feathers gone and shot up and nothing to replace them, tanks leaking. It was a hell of a mess."[22]

Not only did the rear supply area, fifteen hundred miles from the New Guinea battlefront, lack knowledge of combat conditions, but even when orders for parts arrived, supply headquarters frequently failed to fill them, noting that the requisition forms were improperly made out. Kenney ordered this practice immediately terminated, observing that orders were to be filled upon receipt whether or not forms were properly completed. Wars, he emphasized, were "not won by file cabinets."[23]

Kenney needed more planes of all kinds—fighters, bombers, reconnaissance, and transports. He also required a large infusion of 150-gallon droppable fuel tanks and racks for parachute fragmentation bombs that he had ordered. He directed Major Paul I. (Pappy) Gunn, who had a brilliant reputation as an innovator, to design and install these fragmentation bombs on the Fifth's A-20 light bombers. Gunn had developed a package of four .50-caliber machine guns (five hundred rounds per gun) for the nose of the A-20. Kenney ultimately directed Gunn to install the same cluster on the B-25 medium bomber.[24]

As MacArthur and Kenney in the late summer of 1942 made preparations to stem the Japanese advance toward Port Moresby, and ultimately to mount some offensive actions in Papua, the fact remained that the Allied strategy was to defeat Germany prior to concentrating heavy offensive forces against Japan. The Pacific command was fragmented in that three theaters had been established: the central Pacific, under Admiral Chester W. Nimitz, to conduct offensive operations toward the Japanese home islands; the South Pacific theater, under Vice Admiral Robert L. Ghormley (subsequently under Admiral William F. Halsey), whose main objective was the great Japanese base at Rabaul; and the Southwest Pacific theater, under MacArthur.

Although the basic Allied stance in the Southwest Pacific was defensive in nature, once the Japanese drives in the southern Solomon Islands and New Guinea had been stopped, Allied forces planned to mount a limited offensive. The U.S. Joint Chiefs of Staff, first convened in 1942, and the Pacific commanders, agreed that, prior to a counteroffensive, forces had to be built up. The Battle of Midway, as noted, was a turning point. After this defeat, the Japanese in fact had lost the ability to mount a sustained offensive. Japan's so-called lengthy oil line, stretching from the home islands southwest to the Netherlands East Indies, was vulnerable to Allied offensive strikes.

The American military high command disagreed as to the primary strategy to adopt in the Pacific. MacArthur advocated the so-called southern Pacific strategy, a series of thrusts from New Guinea, through the Bismarck Islands, to the Philippines. This would be mainly an army drive, with MacArthur in control. Admiral Chester W. Nimitz, commander of the central Pacific theater, and Admiral Ernest J. King, chief of naval operations, emphasized to President Roosevelt that MacArthur's plan would prove to be prohibitive in terms of the high cost of personnel involved. The naval hierarchy proposed strikes across the central Pacific, through the Marshall Islands, to the Marianas, and then to the Philippines, using fast carrier task forces, air power, and amphibious assault groups. An island-hopping strategy could be adopted, bypassing Japanese strong points. The Joint Chiefs of Staff compromised. They adopted both strategies.

With the overall strategic compromise in place, and having persuaded MacArthur, at least initially, of the soundness of his tactical approach, Kenney began the task of achieving air superiority. His air forces would strike Japanese airdromes, smash the enemy's air force on the ground and in the air, support Allied ground troops, attack Japanese shipping and supply lines, and rip enemy troop concentrations. In early August 1942

Kenney's forces helped in the invasion of Guadalcanal in the Solomons by attacking the Japanese airdrome at Vunakanau, near Rabaul. MacArthur was pleased as Kenney sent his bombers against the shipping and airfields at Rabaul and also hit the Japanese forces attempting to reinforce Buna. However, this was only a bare start. MacArthur recognized that Kenney must build up his forces, shake down his new organization, and generally contend in the Pacific with the "Europe-first" approach.

The attack at Vunakanau in August 1942 was the first under Kenney and to that point the heaviest air attack of the Southwest Pacific war. Eighteen B-17s of the Nineteenth Bombardment Group, under Colonel Harold Carmichael, took off for Rabaul and fifteen arrived over Vunakanau.[25] Kenney estimated that seventy-five Japanese planes were destroyed and about twenty Japanese Zeros encountered. Eleven were shot down. Seventeen tons of bombs were dropped on Vunakanau (five-hundred-pound, instantaneous-fuse bombs), where enemy bomber planes were "lined up wing tip to wing tip on both sides of the strip."[26]

Kenney's plan was to solidify air superiority over New Guinea and to support the Allied ground drive westward along the north coast of New Guinea by airlifting Australian troops from Port Moresby to Wanigela Mission and then up the coast to Buna, where the Japanese had landed in July 1942. Kenney would also fly in supplies to support the ground operations of these troops. The Fifth Air Force would continually strike the enemy airdromes at Lae and Salamaua, shipping between these two points, and also the area around Rabaul, supporting the drive in the Solomons, including Guadalcanal and Bougainville.

MacArthur's staff opposed Kenney's airlift and supply plan as audacious and uncertain, but MacArthur liked it. During the first week of October 1942, natives cut a strip around Wanigela Mission, and Kenney's C-47 transports landed a battalion of Australian troops and engineers. No Japanese opposition materialized either on the ground or in the air. Kenney described this first airlift and supply operation as having "turned the corner in the New Guinea war."[27] In September 1943 the same kind of airlift operation would result in the capture of Nadzab by seventeen hundred paratroops. MacArthur was extraordinarily enthusiastic about the airlift.

By September 1942 Kenney had received P-38s, but they were not operational with serviceable fuel tanks until December. They would be available for escort of bombers, for strafing, and also to carry two five-hundred-pound bombs under the wings, designed to put holes in runways. In the meantime, A-20s, B-25s, B-26s, and Beaufighters, flying from Dobodura, hit the Japanese in Buna. Kenney's bombers and fighters supported the Seventh Australian Division and the American Thirty-second Division in pushing toward Buna, the key base in the planned, intensified Allied drive along the north coast of New Guinea. Kenney's transports played a key role, hauling equipment and supplies from Port

Moresby "over the hump" of the Owen Stanley Mountains, to keep the Buna-bound troops supplied.

MacArthur's staff was again reluctant to base the Buna campaign upon aerial resupply of the main force. Although MacArthur himself had doubts, Kenney managed to convince him. Kenney later noted that MacArthur had said: "The Fifth Air Force hasn't failed me yet and I'll never doubt them again. I believe they can work themselves out of any trouble they run into."[28]

General Arnold in Washington was not always as certain about the effectiveness of Kenney's operations. In late November 1942 he wanted to know why four days had passed without "all out" bombing attacks on Japanese shipping reinforcing Buna and also at Rabaul. Kenney replied with "some of the facts of life": combat crews arriving in the theater poorly trained; extremely adverse weather; planes grounded because proper equipment was lacking; and a dearth of maintenance personnel. Despite these conditions, Kenney informed Arnold that the Fifth Bomber Command had sunk or damaged more than 200,000 tons of shipping over a six-week period, "operating under extremely difficult conditions at a pace which cannot be sustained without an increased replacement rate for both personnel and equipment." The Fifth Air Force, Kenney emphasized, was solving these problems "with the means available and under conditions existing at the time."[29] Kenney wanted more and better trained crews and more planes with a 20 percent replacement rate per month by type. He noted in his diary, "Some day I'll lose patience over some of these damn messages his [Arnold's] staff cooks up at their desks in Washington."[30]

Kenney pointed out that during November 1942 the Fifth Air Force had lost sixty planes from both combat and operational causes but had received only twenty replacements. "If I cannot keep on owning the air over New Guinea," he stressed, "the whole show here will collapse."[31] Arnold, as usual, was basically understanding of Kenney's situation while transmitting the "large picture." The army air forces commander appreciated Kenney's "enthusiasm for expansion." However, it was not possible to consider each theater from an offensive point of view: "Our main effort must continue to be the hammerhead upon which we depend for a quick and complete victory and to divert sufficient forces from it to maintain every theater at offensive strength would result in such a dispersed effort as to invite disaster. My aim is to keep your forces at sufficient strength to enable you to support yourself defensively and to carry out a limited offensive against the Japanese."[33] In Arnold's judgment, Kenney's forces were sufficient to accomplish this objective. Moreover, President Roosevelt had given the highest priority to aircraft production, and Arnold had scheduled deliveries of planes and crews to the Southwest Pacific theater in November and December 1942. These shipments included fifty-six

Four of Kenney's P-38s in formation. U.S. Air Force photo.

P-38s, a plane Kenney especially liked because of its range, and twenty-six B-24 heavy bombers. Crews would also be on the way for these aircraft as well as for the P-39 squadrons.[33]

Kenney, however, did not always appreciate Arnold's reference to the Southwest Pacific as a "defensive" theater. He pointed out that the Japanese failed to understand this argument: "He attacks all the time and persists in acting that way. To defend against him you not only have to attack him but to beat him to the punch."[34]

As much as Kenney required fighters and bombers, his concept of the role of air resupply, and its demonstrated success in supplying the Australian Seventh Division and the American Thirty-second Division in the Buna campaign, persuaded him that transport aircraft would be in critical demand. The Fifth Air Force lost nineteen transports during August-November 1942 to combat and noncombat causes. Transports continued to fly the hump over the Owen Stanley Mountains to forward landing strips at Wanigela, Dobodura, and Popendetta; large quantities of supplies were also dropped free and by parachute in places where landing strips were not available. Among the equipment resupplied were 105 millimeter howitzers, complete with tractors, flown from Australia to Port Moresby by B-17s and then by C-47s to forward positions on New Guinea's north coast. Kenney emphasized to Arnold that, until the Japanese were forced out of the Solomons and Bismarcks, ground and air forces in forward areas must be resupplied by Fifth Air Force transports. Mac-Arthur's plans to move air and ground forces northwest along the northern coast of New Guinea toward the Markham Valley and Finschhafen depended upon air supplies. This included materiel such as steel mat and Jeeps to build airdromes.[35] As of the end of 1942, an average of twenty C-47s at Port Moresby delivered a weekly average of more than 2 million pounds to Papuan locations.[36]

Kenney had sold MacArthur on aerial resupply. It was part of his

inventing new ways to win a war on a shoe string. We are doing things nearly every day that were never in the books. It really is remarkable what you can do with an airplane if you really try. Any time I can't think of something screwy enough I have a flock of people out here to help me. . . . We carry troops to war, feed them, supply them with ammunition, artillery, clothes, shoes, and evacuate their wounded from fields cut out of jungle. . . . We have just started a new stunt of dropping food and ammunition through the overcast to a fogged-in jungle strip where the troops can pick it up and carry it forward by jeep or on their backs. Just a simple radio homing proposition that actually puts the stuff down in a seventy-five yard diameter circle.[37]

Thus, by the close of 1942, MacArthur had gained confidence in Kenney's strategy, tactics, and operations. The theater commander and his top airman frequently met to talk and plan their strategy and operations. According to Kenney, "it is a lot of fun to talk to General MacArthur. He thinks clearly, does not have preconceived ideas, weighs every factor and plays the winning game for all it's worth. As soon as air power could show him anything he bought it."[38]

The strategy they agreed upon was in effect to place an air blockade around the enemy to prevent him from reinforcing his positions; to strike Japanese troops and installations continually; to cover and assist Allied troops in driving the Japanese out; and then to occupy territory, build airdomes, and advance the bomber line northwest up the coast of New Guinea. As MacArthur's island-hopping strategy was keyed to the radius of the Fifth Air Force's planes, Kenney informed Arnold that he would take all the long-range P-38 fighters and B-24 bombers that he could get.

By the end of 1942, with Kenney's airmen in command of the air, it had become clear to MacArthur and Kenney that the Japanese had all but lost Papua. The Fifth Air Force continued to strike Lae and Salamaua, as well as the enemy's supply line from Rabaul to these two bases. January 1943 was a turning point as Buna fell to the Allies, and Kenney's aircraft pounded the big base at Rabaul. General Walker disobeyed Kenney's orders and on January 5 personally led the attack on the Japanese bastion, the fulcrum of the enemy position in the Southwest Pacific. Six B-17s and six B-24s sank fifty thousand tons of Japanese shipping, but it cost the

Fifth Air Force Bomber Command its leader: Walker was lost when his plane was shot down. (He was posthumously awarded the Medal of Honor.) His replacement, Brigadier General Howard Ramey, increased the intensity of attacks on Rabaul with the help of B-25 "commerce destroyers" equipped with eight .50-caliber machine guns.

During the first week of March 1943, the Japanese suffered a crushing blow in the Battle of the Bismarck Sea. Signal intelligence had determined that a large Japanese convoy was present at Rabaul, undoubtedly destined for the north coast of New Guinea. Reconnaissance planes located it fifty miles north of Cape Gloucester. Bad weather ensued, but Fifth Air Force reconnaissance planes again sighted the augmented convoy, including eight cruisers or destroyers along with merchant ships, heading south through the Vitiaz Straits. Fifty miles southeast of Finschhafen, eighteen heavy bombers and twenty medium bombers jumped the convoy. Thirteen Australian Beaufighters, twelve B-25 commerce destroyers, and twelve A-20 light bombers also attacked, covered by sixteen P-38 fighters. The skip-bombing B-25s were especially effective. Their delayed-action bombs, released from masthead height, skipped off the water and penetrated the ship's hull before exploding. When the carnage was over, the Japanese had lost four destroyers, eight transports, approximately thirty aircraft in aerial action, and some twenty-nine hundred personnel. Allied losses were four aircraft shot down and two damaged in crash landings; thirteen personnel had been killed and twelve injured.[39]

The victory in the Bismarck Sea resulted from one of the most important applications of signal intelligence in the Southwest Pacific theater. It should be noted that MacArthur's intelligence bureau—the Central Bureau—had been organized at Brisbane in August 1942. However, headquarters, Fifth Air Force, relied primarily upon its own signal intelligence squadron rather than the Ultra intercepts forwarded by the Central Bureau.

Despite the success of his air operations and his knowledge that MacArthur trusted him "to run the air show," Kenney continued to agonize over the question of replacement aircraft. In March 1943 he made the first of several trips to Washington to participate in war planning and to attempt to squeeze more planes out of Arnold. Kenney and Sutherland presented to the Joint Chiefs (Marshall, King, Arnold, and Leahy) MacArthur's plan to take Lae and Salamaua. Kenney noted: "Neither the War nor Navy Departments however, appreciate what can be done with air supply despite the demonstration we have just given them in the Papuan campaign."[40]

Kenney talked with Secretary of War Henry L. Stimson, Assistant Secretary of War Robert P. Patterson, and Assistant Secretary of War for Air Robert A. Lovett. Patterson offered to present Kenney's request for more planes to President Roosevelt, but the air commander "asked him not to as I don't want to go over Arnold's head unless I can't get anything any other way."[41]

Kenney, however, pressed his case in Washington at the highest levels. To the Joint Chiefs, he emphasized the need to replace his losses and to maintain air superiority over New Guinea. He wanted 10 percent of the aircraft factory production but could elicit no commitment. Kenney wondered about planes being used for training in the States: "I will bet if they flew them half as much in training as my kids are doing in combat, there would be plenty left over to send me. I am willing to take anything that will fly. I am not particular like the British and Russians."[41]

In talks with Arnold, Kenney persuaded the AAF commander to modify the B-25 commerce destroyers at the factory. Although representatives of the AAF Materiel Division disagreed, arguing that guns in the nose would make the plane almost impossible to fly, Kenney reported that "Arnold practically threw them out of the office and told them to do the job and quit arguing." Kenney lost a long-standing argument with Arnold over renaming the Third Light Bomber Group "Attack Group"; Kenney contended that this group applied attack tactics and that such a designation would greatly improve morale. Arnold refused. Kenney concluded that he would say nothing and "let the kids call themselves whatever they please."[42]

Kenney met with the president before he left Washington. He told Roosevelt that the average B-17 in training was doing only about twenty flying hours each month while flying three or four times that per month in theater combat. "Be reasonable about it," Roosevelt replied, "and I shall see what I can do even if I have to argue with the whole British Empire about it."[44] Kenney was convinced that the president would get him some airplanes.

Two weeks later, Arnold informed Kenney that the Joint Chiefs had decided to send him, during the remainder of 1943, several bomb groups (heavy, medium, and light), several fighter groups, and also one transport, one photo, and one observation group. Arnold emphasized that he planned to furnish a 25 percent reserve for all units as soon as possible but that these planes were to be used as reserves and not under any circumstances to increase the strength of existing groups or to equip proposed new units. Arnold concluded that his analysis of Kenney's requirements and the enemy's situation indicated to him that "you are no longer the forgotten man."[45]

Beginning in the summer of 1943, Kenney pressed Arnold on the question of the B-29 very long-range bomber. "It is the plane with which we are to win the war," Kenney had heard. He wanted to try it out, not "to drop bombs on Tokyo," but to see what detailed preparations had to be made if the big bomber was to be based in Australia and employed in the Southwest Pacific theater.[46] Arnold was noncommittal, stressing that if

B-29s should be sent to the Southwest Pacific, Kenney would be notified sufficiently in advance to make preparations.[47] Kenney planned to have airfields built in northwest Australia, supplied by an air depot in Darwin. He wanted the B-29s to strike the oil refineries at Palembang, Sumatra, and Balikpapan, Borneo. Oil was the single essential commodity Japan needed to continue the war, Kenney reasoned. "If you want the B-29 used efficiently and effectively where it will do the most good in the shortest time," he emphasized to Arnold, "the Southwest Pacific Area is the place and the Fifth Air Force can do the job. . . . Japan may easily collapse back to her original empire by that time (1944), due to her oil shortage alone."[48]

However, Kenney would not win this battle over the B-29s. Arnold had never wavered in his conviction that use of the big bomber directly against Japan would be most effective, the ultimate expression of the army air forces' strategic bombing doctrine of high-altitude, precision bombing against the enemy's industrial fabric. By the end of 1943, at the Cairo conference, President Roosevelt approved a plan to base B-29s in India and China by May 1944 and to begin operating them from the Marianas by the end of 1944. Major General Laurence S. Kuter, on orders from Arnold, visited Kenney in Australia in March 1944 to inform him of the decision to send the bombers first to India, staging through China ("Matterhorn"), and then base them in the Marianas by October 1944.

The B-29 decision by Arnold was part of the overall JCS strategy of twin Pacific drives, including the central Pacific, bypassing Truk, to take the Marianas, then moving through the Carolines and Palaus to join MacArthur's drive northwest to the Philippines. Arnold himself stressed the central Pacific drive so as to secure bases for the B-29 offensive against the Japanese homeland. Kenney thought that B-29 attacks from the Marianas against Japan would accomplish little; "nuisance raids," he termed them.

However, Arnold was concerned about control, determined to have command of the B-29 units rather than assign them to the theater commander. In April 1944, the Joint Chiefs of Staff approved establishment of the Twentieth Air Force, directly under Arnold, as executive agent of the Joint Chiefs. Headquarters, Twentieth Air Force, would be located under Arnold in Washington.

The crushing defeat of the large Japanese convoy in the Bismarck Sea—actually, the decisive action occurred in the Solomon Sea—terminated the enemy's attempts to reinforce Lae by convoy. Subsequently, the Japanese had to rely on barge traffic. In the spring of 1943, as marine and army forces continued to drive through the Solomons, MacArthur and Kenney made plans to advance along the north coast of New Guinea, with Salamaua and Lae as the objectives. Simultaneously, the Allied command had to be concerned about Rabaul, but the more immediate threat was the Japanese air strength at Wewak, about five hundred miles north-west of the Allied airdrome at Dobodura. To Kenney, Wewak was "a primary target to take out."[49] However, before the Allies could strike Wewak in strength, fighters had to be based further forward. Bombers from Port Moresby or Dobodura were within range of Wewak, but they required fighter escort in daylight.

To solve this problem, Kenney established an airdrome at Marilinin (originally named Tsili Tsili; Kenney did not like the connotation), near a native village sixty miles west of Lae. Natives and engineers hacked out a runway before the end of July 1943. On August 17-18, 1943, bombers of the Fifth Air Force, covered by P-38s, struck the airdromes at Wewak, But, Borum, and Dagua with devastating results. About 175 enemy planes were destroyed on the ground, most of the Japanese air force in the Wewak area. Kenney's losses were light, and although the Japanese reinforced Wewak and challenged the Fifth Air Force again, Allied air superiority was established from Marilinin to Wewak.[50] Whitehead emphasized to Kenney: "Unless we get instructions to the contrary, we intend to keep on returning to Wewak, weather permitting, until the Nips no longer come up to fight."[51]

The shattering attacks on the Wewak airdromes supported the successful Huon Gulf campaign which forced the Japanese to base their forces in New Guinea far in the rear, preventing effective support of their troops in the Salamaua and Lae areas. In addition to the strikes on Wewak, the Fifth Air Force in August attacked the Alexishafen and Madang areas, bases supporting enemy operations in the Ramu Valley, and major targets in the locale of Hansa Bay.

By the first week in September 1943, Salamaua and Lae had been isolated by Allied forces in a coordinated ground, air, and naval operation. Amphibious troops landed northeast of Lae, cutting the enemy's communications to Finschhafen. This offensive was aided by a spectacular airborne operation, when Kenney's transport planes dropped seventeen hundred troops of the 503rd Parachute Regiment and an Australian artillery battery at Nadzab, approximately nineteen miles northwest of Lae. Fighters based at Marilinin provided cover for the Nadzab operation. Nadzab became a primary fighter base subsequently used for operations against Wewak, Hollandia, and Rabaul.[52]

Salamaua and Lae fell to the Allies in September 1943, followed by the occupation of Finschhafen, on October 2, on the tip of the Huon Peninsula, sealing control of the Huon Gulf. Simultaneously, an air and ground drive, spearheaded by the Australians, advanced up the Markham Valley, through the center of New Guinea, giving MacArthur's forces control of the entire Huon Peninsula. These operations delighted Arnold, who wrote Kenney: "I want to tell you that I don't believe the units could possibly perform the missions in the manner that they are doing without the most sympathetic support from General MacArthur. It requires a complete understanding between General MacArthur and you. In this respect, our Air Forces are very, very fortunate."[53]

In October 1943 Kenney again turned his attention to the big Japanese base at Rabaul. The Rabaul harbor and nearby airfields at Vunakanau, Papopo, and Lakunai had been bombed since the start of the Papuan campaign in 1942. The Allied air offensive against Rabaul in the winter of 1943-1944 virtually nullified its usefulness. Additional enemy installations in the area, including Gasmata, Arawe, and Cape Gloucester on New Britain, the Admiralty Islands, and Kavieng, New Ireland, were also attacked, so that the enemy could not use these bases for the concentration and movement of forces to bases in New Guinea and the Solomons. The way was thus open for Allied moves against the Bismarck Archipelago.

This strategy followed the main lines of the agreement reached in Washington in March 1943, and in conferences in September 1943 in which MacArthur, Sutherland, and representatives of the other services operating in the Southwest and Southern Pacific theaters had participated. Simultaneously, Halsey was to drive northward through the Solomons, into Bougainville Island. Supporting Halsey, Kenney's Allied air forces would increase its attacks on Rabaul while at the same time supporting the New Guinea campaign. After Halsey established airdromes on Bougainville, his aircraft could take over the major responsibility for pounding Rabaul.[54]

Beginning in October 1943, the Fifth Air Force and the Thirteenth Air Force (based in the Solomons) intensified their attacks on Rabaul, almost daily dropping record bomb loads. Kenney informed Arnold that this air offensive against Rabaul would be "the most decisive action initiated so far in this theater. We are out not only to gain control of the air over New Britain and New Ireland but to make Rabaul untenable for Jap shipping and to set up an air blockade of all the Jap forces in that area."[55]

The strike of November 2, 1943, was one of the most spectacular of the Pacific war. More Japanese tonnage was sent to the bottom in thirty minutes than was sunk in the entire Bismarck Sea operation. In addition, about eight-five enemy aircraft were shot down or destroyed on the ground, with an additional 300,000 tons of supplies destroyed. Of Kenney's forces, six bombers were shot down, three bombers were missing, and nine P-38 fighters were lost.[56]

Japanese air strength at Rabaul on November 2 was estimated at about forty bombers and one hundred fighters. Seventy-five B-25 commerce destroyers, covered by eighty P-38s, struck Japanese shipping. Two squadrons of B-25s began the attack by dropping one-hundred-pound phosphorus bombs around the northern half of the Rabaul harbor to nullify the antiaircraft defense. This attack was extremely successful.

Seven squadrons of B-25s then came in at low altitude, decimating the enemy shipping. Fifth Air Force losses were primarily caused by about 125 Japanese fighters that broke through the P-38s to hit the B-25s during their strafing and skipbombing of the shipping.[57]

Reflecting immediately after this mission, Kenney emphasized to Arnold that the first priority continued to be the enemy air force, followed by shipping, and finally bombing strikes "to destroy the accumulated stores and supplies and reduce the town itself to the state of a city dump."[58] Even when attacks were directed against shipping, the primary objective remained the destruction of enemy fighters that took to the air. As Kenney noted, "we are actually using the Jap Navy and Merchant Marine as bait."[59]

These heavy strikes on Rabaul were coordinated between Mac-Arthur's forces and the navy's. For example, MacArthur received a radio message from Halsey informing him that carrier strikes would be made on a specific date and requesting an "all out effort" to neutralize the enemy air. MacArthur replied that, weather permitting, the Rabaul airdromes would be bombed. This message was passed on to Kenney, who would then inform Whitehead at the Fifth's advanced echelon headquarters in New Guinea, recommending certain tactics and timing. To Whitehead, in November 1943, Kenney observed: "Don't ever worry about your authority for sufficient latitude in dealing with an actual situation. I still have plenty of confidence in your judgment and expect you to use it regardless of seemingly stereotyped orders which you may get from me from time to time."[60]

Returning again to one of his favorite subjects, Kenney stressed to Arnold that such spectacular operations as the November 2 strike on Rabaul were possible only because he had been able to keep six P-38 squadrons at full strength. "The P-38," Kenney observed, "is the best offensive fighter in the world today." He needed more of them. Losses were running at between twenty to twenty-five per month. Assigned squadron strength had been cut to eighteen and if necessary Kenney would cut it to fifteen or even lower in order to keep the organizations in business. Beginning in January 1944, Kenney wanted a sufficient flow of P-38s to put his six squadrons back at full strength.[61]

Kenney made his second trip to Washington in early January 1944 to participate in discussions with Arnold and the air staff as well as the Joint Chiefs. The next Allied thrusts in New Britain, the Admiralty Islands, and New Guinea, toward Wewak and Hollandia, were weighed. As he had planned, Kenney wrestled again with Arnold over airplanes and crews and persuaded Arnold to send more B-24s, A-20s, and P-38s. Marshall, along with Arnold, also accepted Kenney's recommendation that the Thirteenth Air Force, from the South Pacific theater, should be turned over to Kenney in the near future. Major General St. Clair Street would take command of the Thirteenth. Subsequently, Kenney could then move two heavy bombardment groups into the Admiralties, keep up the pressure on New Britain and New Ireland, support the central Pacific forces driving westward, and also add two fighter groups and one medium bomber group to his forces operating on the north coast of New Guinea. [62]

In late January at Pearl Harbor, Kenney, Vice Admiral Thomas C. Kinkaid, Sutherland, and other Southwest Pacific representatives discussed future strategic moves with Admirals Nimitz, Halsey, and Carney and their staffs. Agreement seemed to be reached on pooling forces in the Pacific for a drive along the north coast of New Guinea to the Philippines, followed by an attack on Formosa as a preliminary to the final assault on Japan. This strategy meant that the Marianas and Carolines would be bypassed. However, as noted, the Joint Chiefs approved the central Pacific strategy, favored by Admiral King, chief of naval operations, and Arnold, who was determined to base the B-29s in the Marianas, positioned for a knockout blow against Japan. MacArthur and Kenney were disappointed that, in effect, the Southwest Pacific had lost out to the central Pacific. [63]

Along with navy and marine forces, the two commanders turned their attention to finishing off Rabaul, gaining a foothold on western New Britain, occupying the Admiralties, and establishing a position farther west on the north coast of Dutch New Guinea. Prior to the close of 1943, the Fifth and Thirteenth air forces, and navy planes from the Solomons, had crushed Japanese air strength on New Britain and neutralized Rabaul. In mid-December, the Allies invaded New Britain. After sustained attacks by planes of the Fifth Bomber Command, the Cape Gloucester airfield fell to the marines. Aircraft from the Solomons finished off Rabaul, leaving it in ruins. When the Admiralties were invaded at the end of February 1944, possession of airdromes on these islands completed the blockade of Kavieng, Rabaul, and the northeast coast of New Guinea. By the middle of March, all crucial areas in the Admiralties had been taken by the Allies, all enemy bases in the Bismarck Archipelago had been isolated, and the Fifth Air Force had been positioned within striking range of the big Japanese supply base at Truk, in the Carolines.

In New Guinea by early 1944, MacArthur had made the decision to bypass the Japanese Eighteenth Army at Wewak and to strike instead at the enemy's base at Hollandia. Kenney's B-24s, B-25s, and A-20s, with P-38s equipped with new wing tanks to extend their range to 650 miles, mounted a sustained campaign in March 1944 to deal the final, crushing blow to Wewak. The B-24s dropped one-thousand and two-thousand pound bombs, blasting runways and planes on the ground. The B-25s and A-20s came in at low altitude, raking planes, personnel, and installations. Between March 11 and 27, 1944, the B-24s mounted 1,543 sorties, the B-25s flew 488, and the A-20's mounted 555. [64]

As previously planned in discussions with Arnold, the Thirteenth Air

Force transferred to the command of the Southwest Pacific area on March 25, 1944. Air Northern Solomons was established to include navy, Royal New Zealand Air Force, and U.S. Marine Corps planes, with the primary objective of keeping Rabaul neutralized. In the middle of June 1944, the Far East air forces, under Kenney, was created to control the Fifth and Thirteenth air forces and the Royal Australian Air Force and Dutch units based at Darwin. Under this organization, Whitehead took command of the Fifth Air Force. From the Admiralties, the Thirteenth's B-24 Liberator bombers supported the central Pacific drive, enabling the Fifth to concentrate upon Hollandia. On March 29, 1944, B-24s of the Thirteenth made their first attack on Truk, key enemy bastion in the Carolines.[65]

Kenney, meanwhile, readied his newly equipped long-range P-38s to accompany his heavies from Gusap to Hollandia. On March 30 the B-24s started plastering enemy planes on the ground at Hollandia. These attacks intensified, and on April 22, 1944, Hollandia and Aitape were assaulted, covered by Navy Task Force 58. This campaign featured more than seventeen hundred sorties flown by the Fifth, dropping 1,450 tons of bombs on Dutch New Guinea airfields, including Wewak, Hansa Bay, Aitape, and the coast northwest of Alexishafen.[66]

By July 1944, after the occupation of Hollandia and its airfields, Allied forces took Wakde, Biak, Owi, Woendi, and Noemfoor islands, off the north coast of New Guinea, important for their airstrips. Here, as before, strategy had been evolved between MacArthur and the naval forces. The Fifth Air Force mounted heavy strikes, and then naval forces bombarded the enemy positions prior to troop landings. During MacArthur's island-hopping campaign, landings were virtually unopposed, although heavy fighting usually took place inland. These actions culminated a brilliant three-month campaign in which MacArthur's forces, along with navy and marine units, controlled the air, leaped over enemy concentrations, and left them "to die on the vine." Huge numbers of Japanese forces were left behind in New Guinea, New Britain, New Ireland, and the Solomons. By September, Sansapor and Morotai, southeast of Mindanao, had been taken. The Allies now turned their attention to the Philippines.

In late September and early October, as MacArthur and Kenney began preparations for the return to the Philippines at Leyte and coordinated plans with the navy and the Joint Chiefs, Kenney returned to what he considered unfinished business. The commander of the Far East air forces had lost his case for the B-29s, which were about to arrive in the Marianas to begin the strategic bombing campaign against the Japanese home islands, but he had not forgotten the oil refineries at Balikpapan, Netherlands Borneo, first attacked in 1943. In September 1944 it was estimated that the Balikpapan refineries were processing approximately five and a quarter million barrels of crude oil annually. The Leyte landing, originally set for December, had been moved up by the JCS to October.

In view of the accelerated planning and movements now required to position FEAF for the Philippine invasion, Whitehead wanted to scrub the attack on Balikpapan. Kenney, long convinced that the oil refineries were critical to Japan's effort, especially the aviation fuel, insisted that the strikes be mounted.[67]

In September and October, Street's Thirteenth Air Force and Whitehead's Fifth struck a series of four blows against the Pandasari and Edelanu refineries at the Balikpapan complex. These raids were heavily contested by the enemy. Two groups of B-24s from the Thirteenth, and three groups from the Fifth, scored heavily with one-thousand pound bombs. The bombers were covered by P-38s from Sansapor and P-47s from Morotai, both types of planes extending their range barely enough with wing tanks. Although both the Pandasari and Edelanu refineries appeared to be damaged—a total of 280 B-24s hit the refineries and adjacent complexes between September 30 and October 18—the Japanese soon had them going again. However, before long the Allies had the entire Netherlands East Indies blockaded.[68]

The decision of the Joint Chiefs of Staff to move up the Leyte invasion from December to October was based upon a number of factors, including the capture and development of advanced bases, especially Morotai, southeast of Mindanao, and also the success of the navy's fast carrier task forces that had ravaged the Japanese throughout the central Pacific and were now operating with equal effectiveness in the Philippines. Coordinated planning between the services targeted a first landing on Mindanao, and the Fifth Air Force concentrated upon bombing and reconnaissance in the Mindanao area for this operation. Because of these operations, the Japanese appeared to expect a thrust at Mindanao (or the Taluad Islands), and MacArthur's intelligence, based on the reports of Philippine partisans, confirmed this point as well as the assumption that Leyte was more lightly defended, perhaps by about twenty-five thousand enemy troops.[69]

The U.S. Sixth Army, commanded by General Walter Krueger, landed on the east coast of Leyte Gulf near Tacloban airstrip on October 20, 1944, covered by a large naval task force, including Kinkaid's Seventh Fleet and Halsey's Third Fleet. MacArthur, Kenney, and Sutherland watched the operations aboard the cruiser *Nashville*. After a foothold had been gained and airstrips matted down, the approved plan called for Kenney's air elements to take over coverage of the shipping and support of the ground troops from the navy's air units. While Krueger's forces encountered stiffening enemy resistance, Japanese naval forces attacked the U.S. task force but were dealt a heavy blow by Kinkaid and Halsey in the Battle of Leyte Gulf.

The Japanese fleet had decoyed Halsey's fast carriers to the north on October 24, leaving the beachhead exposed. Halsey believed that the enemy fleet that he had repulsed had turned back instead of attempting to pass through the San Bernardino Straits. However, the Japanese had not turned back but instead negotiated the straits in force. Only a determined, brilliant effort by Kinkaid's escort carriers had saved the shipping in Leyte Gulf.

Kenney summed up the action for Arnold: "The Jap missed an opportunity to give us a bloody nose. His naval dumbness, his wretched gunnery, his stupid handling of his air forces and his incredibly inaccurate bombing more than compensated for Halsey being out of position when the Jap Central Group slipped through San Bernardino Strait and headed for our almost helpless shipping in Leyte Gulf." Kenney thought that the Japanese had lost a chance to sink about "one million or so tons of shipping" which would "have given our planning sections a few headaches figuring how long we would postpone our future operations while we also figured how we would feed and supply 150,000 or more troops that we had just dumped ashore."[70]

Only slowly did the Fifth Air Force gain control of the air over the battlefield, as constant rain delayed airfield construction. For a time, Kenney's airmen had to rely on a single steel-matted fighter strip at Tacloban—and that was not ready until October 27. Nevertheless, the Fifth Fighter Command made the Japanese pay a heavy price. Between October 27 and December 31, American pilots shot down 314 enemy aircraft, losing only 16 of their own aircraft in aerial combat. (The Fifth Fighter Command, however, lost 203 aircraft from accidents, enemy bombing, and other causes.)[71]

The Leyte operation, Kenney explained to Arnold, was a singular event, no signpost for future action. As long as the enemy had the means to resist, amphibious operations should be made only after enemy air had been defeated. Shore defenses should be bombed out of commission; this objective could not be accomplished by naval gunfire alone. Kenney noted that, on the afternoon the troops landed, he was "astonished and considerably disappointed at the lack of evidence of destruction from naval gunfire."[72]

According to Kenney, coordination, control, and communications between naval, air, and surface forces, and the ground forces being supported, could easily be worked out. "We have never," he stressed, "had any troubles on that score in this theater that could not be and have not been solved in a conference or two." The major lesson to be drawn from Leyte was that reliance should be placed on land-based air support whenever amphibious operations were being launched against a hostile shore. For the Luzon operation, Kenney noted that aircraft based on Leyte and Mindoro could accomplish the main mission. Halsey's carriers would provide support by contesting enemy aircraft from Formosa and the islands to

Kenney talks to Sutherland while MacArthur gazes at Leyte, October 20, 1944; *below*, Kenney and Arnold, 1945. U.S. Air Force photos.

the north. Kinkaid's escort carriers could provide cover for themselves and for the troop and supply vessels. [73]

Prior to the invasion of Luzon, a landing on Mindoro was made in the middle of December 1944. Japanese suicide planes (kamikazes) struck at convoys bound for Lingayen Gulf, but the landings in January 1945 and the campaign on Luzon were unopposed by enemy planes. The Japanese air forces had been defeated. Hundreds of enemy planes were destroyed on the ground by the Far East air forces under Kenney and by navy aircraft. Corregidor, which had fallen to the Japanese in 1942, was retaken by paratroops in February. By early March 1945, Manila had fallen. Krueger was pleased with the support his forces received in the Luzon campaign from the Fifth Air Force. Similarly, Lieutenant General Robert L. Eichelberger praised Wurtsmith's Thirteenth Air Force for its outstanding support in the southern Philippines.

In March 1945 Kenney made another trip to Washington and found out directly from President Roosevelt that he was being promoted to four-star rank. He also learned from Roosevelt that MacArthur would be placed in command of OLYMPIC, the planned invasion of Kyushu in November 1945. In April the Joint Chiefs approved new command arrangements for the Pacific. MacArthur was to command all army forces in the Pacific, including the Southwest Pacific and the Pacific Ocean areas. Nimitz would command all navy forces in the Pacific theaters. The Twentieth Air Force would continue under Arnold's command, taking its directives from the Joint Chiefs. Disappointed at not receiving B-29s, Kenney pressed Arnold to send him B-32s, comparable to the B-29. Arnold agreed to ship him the first of these planes off the production lines. [74]

Following the capture of Iwo Jima in mid-March, Nimitz's forces invaded Okinawa on April 1, 1945. The Japanese resisted ferociously, especially with kamikaze attacks, which took a heavy toll of U.S. naval forces, and the island was not captured until well into June. The Fifth Air Force subsequently used Okinawa as a base of operations against Kyushu, southernmost of the Japanese home islands. In July Brigadier General Thomas D. White's Seventh Air Force joined Kenney's Far East air forces and teamed up with the Fifth to hit Kyushu and Japanese shipping in the Yellow Sea, along the China coast, and the Tsushima Straits between Japan and Korea. White's fighter groups at Iwo Jima also covered the B-29s striking Japan from the Marianas.

Also in July the U.S. Army Strategic Air Forces in the Pacific were established under General Carl A. Spaatz, with headquarters at Guam. Kenney was somewhat ambivalent about this move, but MacArthur thought that Arnold was "muddying the waters" and directly told Arnold (who was on tour in the Pacific) that there was no room for two four-star AAF generals in the Pacific. [75]

By this time, President Harry S. Truman had approved the JCS plan for an invasion of Kyushu on November 1, 1945. It was to prove unnecessary. Japan was being strangled by blockade and pounded into ruins by the B-29 campaign from the Marianas. On the way back from the Potsdam conference, Truman ordered that the atomic bomb be used. On August 6 1945, it was dropped on Hiroshima, and on August 9 a second A-bomb was dropped on Nagasaki. Japan sued for peace the next day. The Pacific war was over.

On August 19, 1945, Arnold cabled Kenney: "It may truthfully be said that no air commander ever did so much with so little."[76] And MacArthur wrote: "Of all the commanders of our major Air Forces engaged in World War II, none surpassed General Kenney in those three great essentials of successful combat leadership: aggressive vision, mastery over air strategy and tactics, and the ability to exact the maximum in fighting qualities from both men and equipment."

In a sense, prior to World War II, George C. Kenney was one of Arnold's best-kept secrets. Although he had seen combat in World War I, made an impressive record between the wars articulating attack aviation doctrine and in materiel production and engineering, and in the mid-1930s served General Frank Andrews as director of operations at the headquarters of GHQ Air Force, Kenney was not widely known outside the inner circle of the relatively small prewar army air corps. He had not made his mark as an operational commander, such as Andrews, nor had he set aviation records and won trophies, like Doolittle or Arnold. Unlike Carl Spaatz, he was not considered a confidant and a protégé of Hap Arnold. When Arnold became chief of the army air corps in 1938, he considered Kenney a master fixer, a troubleshooter. He relied on Kenney, for example, to straighten out severe production problems at Wright Field and to teach fledging pilots how to avoid ground loops with their planes. It was not until immediately prior to Kenney's joining MacArthur that Arnold gave him an important command as head of the Fourth Air Force on the west coast.

Kenny was a brilliant, innovative airman under MacArthur because there was little he did not know about flying and maintaining airplanes. He had learned and practiced the important details of airmanship for all the years between the wars. And there remained one last ingredient, which he demonstrated in his brief tenure at Fourth Air Force—leadership of men. Under MacArthur, in the Southwest Pacific during World War II, Kenney turned in a stunning performance of air leadership, gaining the trust, respect, and admiration of those who served under him and with him.

When Kenney arrived in the Southwest Pacific in the summer of 1942, MacArthur's air forces were a shambles. The theater commander had no confidence in General Brett and little communication with him.

Kenney changed this situation. He made the air setup comprehensible; he brought in "operators," such as Whitehead and Wurtsmith, who knew how to run combat air forces; and he straightened out the entire logistical swamp, making supply and maintenance supportive of air operations.

Moreover, from the start he was sympatico with "the old man." Kenney exuded confidence, know-how, and leadership. He and MacArthur communicated and remained in step on strategy and tactics. Kenney and his air forces abetted the island-hopping strategy. Kenney's ideas were perfectly tailored to MacArthur's philosophy and strategy. Kenney supplied the air strategy, logistics, and operational competence that MacArthur desperately needed. Nothing impressed MacArthur more, for example, than Kenney's demonstration of the value of transport and resupply in the Buna campaigns.

Kenney got results early. MacArthur immediately grasped the potential for his grand strategy. The Fifth Air Force would gain air superiority; support the ground forces and resupply them; strike Japanese shipping and troop concentrations; and the line of advance would be moved forward on the ground and in the air along New Guinea's north coast. The enemy would be kept off balance and the war would be won by leaps, by island hopping.

Flexible, innovative, and daring, Kenney modified his planes and tactics to fit the situation. He knew how to lead air forces in combat. He knew how to win and how to work for a "big man" like Douglas MacArthur. He got results and proved himself the consummate airman in the kind of war we shall never see again.

Thomas C. Kinkaid

MacArthur's Master
of Naval Warfare

GERALD E. WHEELER

On October 26, 1943, Secretary of the Navy Frank Knox announced that
Vice Admiral Thomas C. Kinkaid would replace Vice Admiral Arthur S.
Carpender as commander, Seventh Fleet ("MacArthur's Navy").[1] To
those who read the war news closely, Kinkaid was not a total stranger.
Though he was rarely mentioned throughout 1942, he had earned six battle stars on his Asiatic-Pacific campaign ribbon as a cruiser group commander in such engagements as the Battle of the Coral Sea and the Battle
of Midway and as the *Enterprise* task force commander in three major engagements in the Guadalcanal area. Detached from his carrier task force
command on November 24, 1942, Kinkaid went to Kodiak, Alaska, where
he assumed command of the North Pacific force and its Task Force 8. During the ten months that he commanded American naval forces in Alaska
and the Aleutian Islands, the admiral directed the seizure of Amchitka in
January 1943, the capture of Attu against fanatical Japanese resistance in
May, and the occupation of Kiska in August. For his management of the
Attu campaign, he was awarded his third Distinguished Service Medal
and promoted to vice admiral. He also received considerable press recognition for the first time in his naval career.

By the time commander in chief Admiral Ernest J. King and Pacific
commander Admiral Chester W. Nimitz met for their quarterly conference in San Francisco in September 1943, Kinkaid was already on their
agenda. Because of Carpender's inability to please General MacArthur,
King had come to the conclusion that his Seventh Fleet commander
would have to be replaced.[2] He needed an aggressive, battle-experienced
admiral who had demonstrated ability to work with the army. Tom Kinkaid seemed to fill the bill quite nicely. Where his predecessor in Alaska,
Rear Admiral Robert A. Theobald, had been ineffective in preventing the
Japanese from occupying Attu and Kiska, and had failed miserably in rela-

tions with the Alaskan army commander Major General Simon Bolivar Buckner, Kinkaid had been a total success. The Japanese had been driven out of Alaska; and he had earned the full confidence and friendship of General Buckner.[3] As Kinkaid's direct superior, Nimitz knew his work and reliability quite well. Having had MacArthur twice ask that his naval commander be relieved, King knew what he needed. So the decision was made to move Kinkaid from Alaska to Australia.

Following briefings in Washington, where King made sure that his new Seventh Fleet commander understood his views on strategy in the Pacific for the year ahead, Kinkaid flew to San Francisco and then Pearl Harbor. There he was again briefed thoroughly, this time on problems, as seen by CINCPAC, that had existed between the navy and MacArthur. Kinkaid flew to Admiral William F. Halsey's South Pacific command headquarters in Noumea, New Caledonia, where he heard the admiral's views on MacArthur's command and the news that Halsey was to visit Brisbane and would be pleased to make the introductions. Kinkaid was not shy about meeting his new boss, but he wondered how he would be received, for Secretary Knox had announced his appointment without MacArthur's blessing.[4]

While the Australian press cheered the appointment of a "fighting admiral,"[5] MacArthur told General George C. Marshall that neither he nor the Australian government of Prime Minister John Curtin had been consulted. As Australian forces would be included in his command, prior consultation had been expected. King provided the formula to smooth the general's feathers: it was the Navy Department's intention to replace Vice Admiral Carpender with Vice Admiral Kinkaid, but the latter had received no orders as yet. Would he be acceptable?[6] The *amende honorable* having been proffered and accepted, Kinkaid's passage to the realm of commander in chief, Southwest Pacific area, was now clear. But it was probably lucky that he had the legendary "Bull" Halsey for an escort.

While the expulsion of the Japanese from the Aleutians had brought a spate of articles concerning Kinkaid in the newspapers and weekly magazines, his name was still not quite a household word. Born on April 3, 1888, in Hanover, New Hampshire, he had spent his early years in a variety of areas, as his family followed his father, a naval officer, from one duty station to another. He entered the U.S. Naval Academy in 1904 and graduated in the Class of 1908. He stood in the lower half of his class; there was little in his record to suggest that "Tommy" Kinkaid would achieve great distinction. As a junior officer, he had two years of postgraduate education in ordnance, most of it consisting of on-site training in factories and ordnance testing grounds. He did most of his sea duty between 1908 and 1919, including the World War years, in battleships. Between the wars he had an interesting mix of shore and sea duty, including a year at the Naval War College in 1929-1930. From June 1930 until January 1933, though detailed to the General Board of the navy in Washington, he was assigned to the State Department for service with the American delegation to the World Disarmament Conference. Following this duty, which took him several times to Europe as a naval adviser, he completed tours as executive officer of the battleship *Colorado* (BB-45) and eventually as commanding officer of the heavy cruiser *Indianapolis* (CA-35). He returned to Europe in 1938 as naval attaché to Italy and Yugoslavia. At the completion of this service, he took command of Destroyer Squadron 8 in the Atlantic Fleet; he left this duty in November 1941, following selection as rear admiral. He had meanwhile, in 1911, married Helen Sherbourne Ross of Philadelphia; they had no children. His two sisters married into the navy: Helen, the older, married a doctor; Dorothy married Husband E. Kimmel, commander in chief, U.S. Fleet, at the time of the Pearl Harbor attack.[7]

Kinkaid arrived in Brisbane on November 23 and quickly began the process of settling in, meeting his staff and General MacArthur's, arranging to make official calls on Australian and American civilian officials he needed to know. Because of the press of Halsey's business, he met only briefly with MacArthur. He did, though, have a chance to visit with Rear Admiral R.W. Christie, his submarine force commander, who normally operated from the naval base on the other side of the continent at Perth-Fremantle. Carpender had felt it important that Christie be in Brisbane to meet his new boss.[8]

MacArthur and Kinkaid finally had a serious meeting the day after he formally relieved Carpender, Friday, November 26. He described this first session to Helen, his wife: "This morning I had a long talk with the General and he was extremely cordial. He told me all of his troubles in detail and we discussed the situation here. He asked for suggestions from me not only regarding the Navy but concerning any other phases of operations in this area. He said that his door is always open to me and that he would like me to come to see him often and keep him informed. I could not have asked for a more cordial reception." This was Saturday. The next day he again wrote Helen about the general. "This morning I transacted my first business with the General and I must say I could not ask for greater consideration."[9] He found, of course, that MacArthur worked every day, including most weekends. He also expected his senior staff—and the navy—to maintain the same pace.

Kinkaid knew when he arrived in Brisbane that he would be "wearing two hats." One hat would be that of MacArthur's naval commander, formally: commander, Allied naval forces, Southwest Pacific area. As such he commanded all U.S. naval forces in SWPA, plus those of Australia and the Netherlands that were operating in the area. Except for operations involving selected individual units, each of the non-American naval forces was commanded by its own nation's officers. As a vice admiral, Kinkaid was senior to all naval officers in SWPA with the exception of Admiral Sir Guy Royle, R. N., who commanded Australia's naval forces, and Vice Admiral C. E. L. Helfrich, commander in chief, Netherlands East Indies navy. By agreement among all concerned, Kinkaid was granted the authority to command, though he may have lacked a fourth star on his collar or a fourth stripe on his dress blues.[10]

By design, Kinkaid's headquarters were located in Brisbane's AMP Insurance Building, the same place that MacArthur had chosen for GHQ. Consequently the general could see personally, and on a daily basis if he so desired, the commanders of the Allied naval forces (Kinkaid) and the Allied air forces (Lieutenant General George C. Kenney). The commander of the Allied land forces, General Sir Thomas Blamey, an Australian, was not so favored. With headquarters in another location, he lacked the daily contact with MacArthur that might have led to significantly different relations between the Australian and American fighting forces. The result of these physical arrangements was the development of an American GHQ, dominated by the general and the army, with little meaningful participation in planning or control of operations by non-American military leaders.[11]

While MacArthur alleged that his GHQ had no service bias, the navy saw things differently. In fact, interservice rivalry had grown to epidemic proportions by the time Kinkaid was ordered to SWPA. Accustomed to joint planning, joint operations, and unity of command at sea and ashore, he was astounded by the lack of such practices in MacArthur's command. Rear Admiral Daniel E. Barbey, commander, Seventh Amphibious Force, recognized this problem and noted that in 1943 and most of 1944 operations were carried out by "mutual cooperation" rather than "unity of command" practices.[12] Kinkaid and Barbey both chafed at their lack of input when GHQ was working up an operation.

Another source of what Kinkaid called chronic "belly-aching" among the services was traceable to the "Bataan Gang." Headed by Lieutenant General Richard K. Sutherland, chief of staff, this praetorian guard protected MacArthur from outsiders (nonarmy types) and controlled public knowledge of affairs in the SWPA by censoring all news reporting.[13]

In 1943 and early 1944 there were few American flag officers in the Seventh Fleet. Among these, Admiral Barbey was clearly the most important after Kinkaid himself. As the commander of Seventh Fleet Amphibious Force, designated Task Force 76 for operational purposes, Barbey had spent almost all of 1943 organizing, equipping, and training the naval forces that would carry SWPA land forces into battle. In closest contact with MacArthur's troop commanders, he unfortunately left the impression that his was the fighting part of Seventh Fleet and that Kinkaid and his staff were simply rear echelon people whose jobs were to keep TF 76 fighting.[14]

The navy in Australia, as Kinkaid later analyzed the situation, had serious problems with its organization and command relationships that tended to exacerbate relations with the army. MacArthur's Navy was a good-sized command for a vice admiral,[15] but Kinkaid had two bosses. His operational orders came from MacArthur, who was close at hand to see that they were carried out. But Seventh Fleet's personnel and materiel, including ships, came from Admiral King in Washington. When he created the Seventh Fleet in February 1943, he kept it under his personal command, as COMINCH, rather than adding it to Admiral Nimitz's Pacific fleet. It is significant that King wrote Kinkaid's fitness reports, not MacArthur or Nimitz. It is also significant that all admirals were assigned to their commands by King.

While his first contacts with MacArthur were pleasant and reassuring, there was an underlying tension that Kinkaid could do little to lessen. Anxious to get his "show on the road," MacArthur needed more navy than was currently at hand. Along with a new fleet commander, he had hoped that he would soon receive additional carriers, cruisers, and possibly some battleships. Kinkaid quickly set him straight. There would be no carriers except what CINCPAC would lend for specific SWPA operations. He even let the general know that he did not believe these larger units should be given to the Seventh Fleet. Operating in SWPA they would not be facing the Japanese Combined Fleet, and they would definitely be at risk from all of the land-based bombers that would be thrown at them. Cruisers, carriers, and battleships held in Sydney, Melbourne, or Brisbane for future use would be offering very little return on the heavy investment in their construction.[16]

As MacArthur's naval commander, Kinkaid also suffered from the fact that the general was deeply frustrated about his relationships with the navy. By the time Kinkaid arrived in Brisbane, it had become clear to his new boss that he had little chance of being able to change the basic strategy of the war against Japan; and the navy appeared to be the principal source of resistance to change. In its simplest form, current strategy called for an approach to the Philippines and the China coast along two lines of advance. One axis had already been established with MacArthur's operations in New Guinea and Halsey's in the Solomon Islands. These were expected to eliminate the Japanese from Rabaul and Kavieng in the Bismarck Archipelago, take control of New Guinea, then push on to Mindanao and eventually Luzon in the Philippines. The second axis of advance would be a drive through the central Pacific, which required seizing the heavily fortified islands that Japan had occupied since the end of World War I. As seen by King, and Nimitz somewhat concurred, the island bases were an ongoing threat to the right flank of MacArthur and Halsey and must be removed.[17]

What galled MacArthur was the obvious primacy of the central Pacific drive over his own line of advance. American shipyards were sending out a steady stream of new heavy and light aircraft carriers, fast battleships, and equally fast cruisers that were going to Nimitz, not to him. MacArthur's operations had been built on the premise that his forces would be covered by Kenney's land-based Fifth Air Force whenever they grappled with the enemy. Plans for Nimitz's central Pacific drive required that the invasion forces be protected by carrier task forces until airfields could be seized or constructed, after which marine or air corps squadrons could be brought in. Because of planned operations in the Pacific, Mediterranean, and Atlantic during 1943-1944, there were simply not enough combat vessels constructed to supply everyone, so MacArthur's Navy came last.

By the time that Kinkaid took command of the Seventh Fleet, preliminary planning for the opening operations in MacArthur's campaign to eliminate Rabaul, the most important Japanese bastion in the Southwest Pacific area, had been completed. The first assault on "Festung Rabaul" would be an invasion of southwestern New Britain at two points, Arawe on December 15, 1943, and Cape Gloucester eleven days later. Barbey's Seventh Amphibious Force, of course, would do the lifting. [18]

Though the planning for these assaults was well advanced, Kinkaid found plenty of opportunities to add his own ideas and to seek modifications of existing decisions. Probably the most serious problem that was brought to the admiral came from amphibious commander Barbey. On the basis of past experience, he was concerned that Kenney's airmen would not provide air coverage when it was most needed—while the assault vessels were in restricted waters, unable to maneuver, or when they were beached. With a series of operations facing them, the Seventh Amphibs could not afford to lose ships. Kinkaid explained the problem to MacArthur forthrightly. The latter understood and promised that Barbey would receive more fighter coverage than he had ever seen before. As it turned out, Kenney's fighters filled MacArthur's promise admirably but were unable to prevent the loss of *Brownson* (DD-518) and damage to three destroyers and two LSTs at Cape Gloucester. [19]

Kinkaid also brought about another change. General Krueger and his troop leaders insisted that army officers command amphibious landings. The navy needed only to see that the troops reached their destination. Kinkaid proposed to MacArthur that the naval attack force commander remain in charge until the troops were ashore and command posts had been established. At that point the troop commander ashore would take charge and the amphibious commander would be concerned only with his ships. Seeing the point, MacArthur directed that all operational plans, starting with Arawe's (Operating Plan 3A-43), contain a transfer-of-command paragraph. [20]

During the first days of the Cape Gloucester operation, Krueger said that the schedule for amphibious shipping was too tight and proposed that the follow-on Saidor landing not be carried out on January 2, 1944, as planned. The assault area, about 110 miles west of Finschhafen, was important to MacArthur because he hoped to trap a large number of Japanese troops who were retreating toward Saidor from Finschhafen. A delay would probably allow the Japanese to escape. Kinkaid joined MacArthur in the argument against Krueger. The navy would see that his supplies and troops arrived safely and on schedule, he promised the Sixth Army commander. Like MacArthur, Kinkaid believed that SWPA forces were developing momentum, and he did not want to see it lost. In the end, Krueger's troops hit Saidor on schedule, and the navy delivered the supplies as promised.[21]

During the invasion of New Britain and Saidor on New Guinea, Kinkaid remained at the advanced base headquarters in Port Moresby. He had accompanied the general north from Brisbane on December 12 and remained with him until their return on January 4. This was the second time that he had moved up "to the front." Earlier, in the first week of December, he had briefly visited Barbey's headquarters at Milne Bay, more or less on a get-acquainted trip. His assistant chief of staff, Captain R.C. Hudson, had felt that Admiral Carpender had not spent enough time personally visiting his forces in New Guinea and had urged his new boss to leave Brisbane and become known to his troops in the field. During his second trip to the New Guinea area, Kinkaid several times dropped in at Goodenough Island, where Krueger's soldiers were preparing for the landings at Arawe and Cape Gloucester.[22]

Kinkaid's letters to his wife make it plain that Kinkaid preferred to be closer to the action than Brisbane. In Australia he was perpetually spending time that he felt he could ill afford on matters that contributed little to defeating the enemy. Though Port Moresby was 250 miles from Milne Bay or Goodenough Island, or an hour and a half flight time in his R5D (C-54), he told Helen he still preferred "to stay here with plenty of forces at my disposal and move on to the northwestward." He summed up his view of Brisbane when he wrote: "This business of living in a hotel in a city and at the same time being mixed up in war operations is incongruous. On my mud flat at Adak everything seemed to fit into the picture. I would rather be farther forward pushing this war towards its end."[23]

Planning and operations in SWPA did not always move ahead in an orderly manner. There always existed a certain degree of flexibility that permitted MacArthur to seize fresh opportunities when they became available.[24] This flexibility became apparent in mid-February, when reconnaissance photographs convinced General Kenney that the Japanese had evacuated the Admiralties or had at least removed most of their troops. On February 23 he recommended to MacArthur and Kinkaid that Los Negros be seized immediately and then Manus. MacArthur and Kinkaid decided to use about eight hundred troops from the First Cavalry Division for a landing on February 29 and to call it a "reconnaissance in force." If resistance was too great, the assault force would be withdrawn. Kinkaid agreed to the operation, and the planning was accomplished "in just four days." By the time the "reconnaissance in force" had left Oro Bay, the number of troops had grown to 1,026. Because MacArthur wanted to observe the operation, Kinkaid brought in the light cruisers *Phoenix* (CL-46) and *Nashville* (CL-43), plus another division of destroyers. He and the general rode *Phoenix* to the scene of action, and MacArthur had the opportunity to experience at close quarters his first naval bombardment in support of an assault. [25]

In the afternoon of the first day of the Los Negros operation, MacArthur, Kinkaid, and several of the general's staff went ashore to observe the action at first hand. The general was apparently unconcerned about his personal safety. He was doing what he had always believed a military leader should do: let his troops see him in the presence of the enemy. Along with Krueger, who felt quite strongly that MacArthur should not even have been present on board *Phoenix*, Kinkaid probably deplored this whole exercise in military bravado. He had told MacArthur that he did not believe Krueger had any business being present at several of the landings. For Kinkaid, the rule was that the senior commanders should be close to their communications, and the scene of action fighting should be in the hands of less senior flag officers. [26]

MacArthur's presence at Los Negros, and Kinkaid's as well, was probably necessary. The general had stuck his neck out in ordering the early seizure of the island. As he stated candidly, "I was relying almost entirely upon surprise for success and, because of the delicate nature of the operation and the immediate decision required, I accompanied the force aboard Admiral Kinkaid's flagship." The decision was to stay, and the general directed Kinkaid to have the reinforcements brought up. [27] Given the fact that there were actually more that four thousand Japanese troops on Los Negros, though somewhat bomb-happy from the pounding they had received in the past month, it required some desperate fighting by General Chase's cavalrymen to turn a shoestring operation into a complete success. [28]

During the period that Manus was being cleared of its defenders, and the Joint Chiefs were planning the next moves for Nimitz and MacArthur, the general provoked a crisis in army-navy relations in SWPA. He had received from Nimitz a copy of the latter's proposal to the JCS to have Halsey's construction battalions (Seabees) build a great naval base in Seeadler Harbor (Manus) for the use of the Seventh Fleet and Nimitz's forces. The storm was prompted by his further proposal that Halsey and his Seabees do this work under his direction. MacArthur was furious, seeing Nimitz's move as a back-door means of taking control of a base within SWPA and of reasserting command over an admiral (Halsey) who worked for him. The

Kinkaid and MacArthur on Los Negros, February 29, 1944. Courtesy National Archives.

general would have none of it; in fact, he threatened to close Seeadler Harbor to all but the Seventh Fleet and other ships under his command. Recognizing the foolish nature of the issue, Kinkaid got MacArthur to invite Halsey to Brisbane to thrash out the problem. During three sessions on March 3 and 4, the general expostulated at length on these attacks on his authority, leadership, even honor. In the end, Kinkaid, Halsey, and others won agreement to let Nimitz and the Joint Chiefs know that they believed the naval base should be under SWPA control but open to use by all naval forces.[29]

To Kinkaid, the Manus incident was another example of army paranoia over naval proposals. "Working in an Army organization is extremely difficult," he wrote to his wife. "I try to fit in with their methods and organization but they are a bunch of horse traders and horse thieves and don't know the meaning of cooperation. They do not cooperate among themselves and therefore cannot be expected to cooperate with others." He believed that during five months of "fast talking" he had convinced MacArthur that he was not "trying to steal the Army's shirt every time I make a suggestion. At least he claims he is convinced. But the small boys all the way down the line are suspicious of everything. I often wonder if they spend more time on studying how to put something over on the Navy than how to lick the Japs."[30]

The opportunist venture against the Admiralty Islands led MacArthur to propose other alterations to the Joint Chiefs' schedule of future operations in the SWPA. On March 4 he requested permission to bypass the Wewak-Hansa Bay region and make Humboldt Bay-Hollandia-Tanamerah Bay the next target for April 15. This operation would include a simultaneous landing at Aitape, about 120 miles east of Hollandia. Because landings at Tanamerah Bay and Humboldt Bay would be beyond the reach of Kenney's fighters, MacArthur insisted that to defend the beachheads he would need carrier aircraft support from the Pacific Fleet. The Joint Chiefs approved this proposal and somewhat simplified the operations by canceling the mid-April assault on Kavieng. It was felt that aircraft from Los Negros, Emirau (in the St. Matthias Islands), and the Green Islands could prevent any aerial interference at Hollandia from Japanese in Rabaul or Kavieng.[31]

Planning for the four landings was left to Barbey and Krueger, but naval aid from Nimitz had to be negotiated. Dissatisfied with Nimitz's proposals, Kinkaid suggested that MacArthur invite him to Brisbane for consultations. MacArthur agreed, and Nimitz accepted immediately.[32]

The admiral and his retinue arrived on March 25. MacArthur and Kinkaid were at the seaplane dock to greet them. Nimitz came bearing gifts: orchids for Mrs. MacArthur, candy and a playsuit for young Arthur. The general laid on a grand dinner at Lennon's, with some forty-eight of the highest-ranking officers in the area in attendance. The second evening Kinkaid's stewards prepared a Chinese dinner for the general and his wife, Nimitz, and four others. Both dinners went well, as did the small dinner that the general gave in his apartment on the third evening. By the end of the visit, Kinkaid had had his fill of conferences, but he had to admit that much had been accomplished.[33]

There was no hesitancy on the part of CINCPAC about furnishing carrier support; the problem was how long the ships could stay. Until the Hollandia area airfields could be seized and put into operation, land-based fighter planes would find it difficult to protect the beaches and the ships because their bases were too far to the east. Task Force 58, which then included a dozen of the Pacific Fleet's fast carriers, would raid the Palau Islands three weeks before the Hollandia operation and eliminate any Japanese aircraft that might move down to western New Guinea and then against Hollandia. Vice Admiral Mitscher would then bring TF 58 to the New Guinea coast, sweep the area of Japanese planes, and assist in whatever ways were possible. But Nimitz did not want his fast carriers being held in a static situation for too many days, as they would be sure to attract Japanese land-based bombers and torpedo-carrying aircraft. Although Mitscher would be pulled out after only one day, two "Jeep carrier" groups (eight CVEs) would remain in the area for at least another week. To provide a margin of safety, the landing at Aitape was designed to capture an airfield that could be used by Kenney's fighters one or two days thereafter.[34]

As the date of the Hollandia operation approached, MacArthur left Brisbane on April 18 for Port Moresby and then Finschhafen, where he boarded the *Nashville*. Again Kinkaid thought that neither he nor Krueger should be present, but he was probably not consulted. Following his own rule, he remained close to his communications at Port Moresby throughout the operation. A few weeks later he explained, in a memorandum for the general, why he believed Krueger (and MacArthur by inference) should not take a destroyer to the next operation, an assault on Wakde Island: "I can see no earthly reason why the Commander, Attack Force, should be saddled with this additional hazard [the presence of Krueger]. It is a definite hazard for, in addition to taking a badly needed destroyer from the scene, the presence of General Krueger is a mental hazard both to the Commander, Attack Force, and the Commander, Landing Force; he does interfere despite his protests to the contrary and the best of intentions; and some day there will be a flare-up which is distinctly not desirable and might actually be detrimental to operations."[35] From Kinkaid's perspective, the complicated Hollandia operation went exceptionally well. Mitscher's raids on the Palau Islands had not only eliminated a large number of Japanese aircraft that might have replaced those destroyed by Kenney's airmen but had also driven Japanese surface forces so far to the west that they could not possibly have interfered with the landings. Control over the Hollandia area, with its three airfields, was established more quickly than had been expected. Even if the landings at Aitape led to a prolonged battle with the Japanese caught between SWPA armies to the east and those that had just landed, U.S. naval control of the sea off New Guinea meant that fresh troops and supplies could be fed to the army ashore while the Japanese depleted their munitions and food resources. Very obviously, time would be on the side of the SWPA troopers.[36]

Hollandia had been seized to provide a major base of operations for the final six months' drive toward the Philippines. From its field headquarters at Port Moresby, MacArthur's staff finished planning its next moves against Wakde Island, Biak Island, Noemfoor Island, and Sansapor, all a part of the New Guinea campaign. Actually, planning went on constantly in GHQ, in Kinkaid's headquarters, in Barbey's command ship, and in Krueger's headquarters at Finschhafen. With the pace accelerating, plans for future operations were drafted before a current campaign had been concluded. Because new divisions reached New Guinea from the Solomons and Stateside, MacArthur's troops could have some rest, and not every regiment had to take part in every landing. On the other hand, though staffs grew in size, those in the planning and logistics divisions worked particularly hard. So did the fighting ships, for the same cruisers, destroyers, and landing craft were called on week after week. As a result the crews could not be properly rested; maintenance on the vessels had to be kept to a minimum. Seventh Fleet Service Force floating drydocks and repair ships took care of drydocking for repairs and exterior hull cleaning, but it was hard to spare the time for the various vessels to get to Brisbane or Sydney for the traditional rest and recreation.[37]

Following the Hollandia operation, as plans were being completed to seize Wakde and Biak, Kinkaid and MacArthur remained in Port Moresby. This put them just an hour and a half by air from Krueger's headquarters at Finschhafen. Communications to the field, or to Brisbane, were excellent, and there were regular flights to Brisbane for mail purposes. When time was available, Kinkaid usually visited the general's porch for an exchange of ideas or simply to smoke. On April 30 he was somewhat startled when MacArthur bared his political soul. On the previous day he had issued a public statement that he had never been a candidate for the presidency, and were the nomination offered to him, he would refuse it. As he smoked with Kinkaid he elaborated on his views. The latter reported the conversation to his wife. "He said that it was obvious that a general at the front in time of war could not be a candidate for such a position, that he had no qualifications for the job unless it was that of honesty and he would be like putty in the hands of the politicians who do not go in strong for honesty, that he thought a 42 year old ex-District Attorney did not have much chance against Roosevelt, that because of the war situation he thought the President should be reelected although he did not approve of him or believe that any man should have a fourth term in the White House."[38]

With the Wakde plans being distributed and the Biak planning well advanced, Kinkaid returned to Brisbane early in May. The Wakde operation (STRAIGHT LINE) was scheduled for May 17, with Biak ten days later. Wakde and its airfield, plus two nearby fields on New Guinea, were needed as bases for aircraft to support the Biak invasion and as a means of keeping the Japanese from using them against the Hollandia area. The seizure of Wakde, about 115 miles west of Humboldt Bay and lying 2 miles off the coast, would be completed quickly. Because Barbey was on leave, Rear Admiral William Fechteler oversaw STRAIGHT LINE, and Captain A.G. Noble commanded the attack force which put troops ashore opposite Wakde on May 17. The next day small craft carried the invaders to the island. The defenders were quickly wiped out, and the Wakde airdrome was ready to handle its first fighter squadrons on May 21.[39]

The landings at Biak, on May 27, provided a change of pace for the Seventh Fleet. For a year SWPA amphibious operations had taken place without significant enemy naval opposition. Occasional Japanese submarines would enter an area where an assault was occurring, or land-based naval aircraft would make sporadic appearances, but on the whole the Japanese navy had remained clear of the New Guinea coast from Milne Bay to Wakde. With evidence pointing toward an assault against Biak, however, the Imperial Navy felt that it had to take action. SWPA's purpose in seizing Biak was to use its three airfields for operating heavy bombers against the Palau Islands and Halmahera, on the road to Mindanao. Japanese interest in Biak was as an air base to protect the Palau Islands and to block any American approach into the Celebes Sea. Used effectively, Biak could help block farther westward movement by MacArthur's forces.

At the time of the original landings on Biak, the Seventh Fleet provided two covering forces: Force A (TF 74), commanded by Rear Admiral V.A.C. Crutchley, R.N. consisted of the Australian heavy cruisers *Australia* and *Shropshire* and four destroyers, two of which were Australian. Force B (TF 75), commanded by Rear Admiral Russell S. Berkey, included light cruisers *Phoenix*, *Nashville*, and *Boise* (CL-47), plus six destroyers. These covering groups alternated in providing night coverage of the Biak area and withdrew toward Hollandia at daylight.

On June 3 intelligence estimates convinced Kinkaid that the Japanese would be trying again to reinforce Biak, perhaps as early as June 4. He ordered Task Forces 74 and 75 combined into one force under Crutchley. With *Shropshire* now en route to Sydney for refit, the combined force consisted of four cruisers and fourteen destroyers. During the first day's operation (June 4), Japanese aircraft attacked Crutchley's force, and *Nashville* suffered waterline damage from a near miss. The vessel stayed on station for the first night's operation but then withdrew to Humboldt Bay for repairs. On June 7 Kinkaid informed Crutchley that another reinforcement convoy was headed for Biak. Rear Admiral Naomasa Sakonju was en route with two cruisers and six destroyers with twenty-five hundred soldiers on board or being towed in barges. At midday, B-25s from Hollandia sank one Japanese destroyer and badly damaged another. But the Japanese continued toward Biak. Just before midnight Sakonju learned about the size of the American force awaiting him and decided again that retreat was the better part of valor. There ensued the "Battle of Biak," a three-hour stern chase in which Crutchley would fight but Sakonju would not.[40]

For Kinkaid's Seventh Fleet, particularly its Seventh Amphibious Force, the conclusion of fighting on Biak meant freedom for the next

movement westward of MacArthur's SWPA forces. GHQ decided to move
swiftly against Noemfoor, an island with three airfields lying about sixty
miles west of Biak. Besides denying its airdromes to the Japanese, occupation of Noemfoor would make it possible to bring forward more medium
bomber and fighter groups to use against enemy bases on the Vogelkop
Peninsula and in the Halmahera Islands. The invasion date for Noemfoor
was set for June 30 and was then changed to July 2.

Kinkaid moved quickly and issued his operation order on June 17.
Barbey's staff finished its planning within a week. The invasion force,
some seventy-one hundred troops built around the 158th Regimental
Combat Team, was covered by three cruisers and ten destroyers led by
Admiral Berkey in *Phoenix* and Commodore John A. Collins, R.A.N., in
Australia. Another fourteen destroyers, constituting fire support and escort groups, could also intervene should some form of enemy naval resistance occur. None did. The landing was unopposed. By July 6 the first
airdrome was ready for use.[41]

The final New Guinea campaign, against the Japanese in the Vogelkop, was anticlimatic by comparison with the operations since Kinkaid's
takeover of the Seventh Fleet the previous November. The Japanese
navy, badly bloodied in the great Philippine Sea battle of June 19-21, had
withdrawn to anchorages in Singapore (Lingga Roads), the Philippines,
and home waters. The Japanese army and navy air flotillas had been deci-
mated in the Palaus, in defending western New Guinea, and in combat
with Mitscher's carriers off Saipan. With Japanese air bases on the Vogelkop Peninsula almost empty of aircraft, defense of the area would be in the
hands of the Japanese troops left behind. Unopposed landings were made
on the western side of the Vogelkop at Sansapor and Mar on July 30. Engineering troops immediately set about constructing two air bases in the
area; both were operational by September 3, in time for the planned assault on Morotai in the Halmahera Islands.[42]

On a much smaller scale, the Morotai operation was a rehearsal for the
anticipated landing on Mindanao at Sarangani Bay. For the first time since
Hollandia, Pacific Fleet escort carriers would be present to provide air
cover over the beachhead and the invasion force. Also available if needed
were the fast carriers of Rear Admiral J.S. McCain (TG 38.1) and their
deadly air groups. The Seventh Fleet, as usual, supported the operation
with Admiral Berkey's two task units. The landings were unopposed, and
the almost twenty thousand troops in the assault had little trouble mopping up the four hundred Japanese present.

The purpose in seizing Morotai was to provide airfields for operations
against the southern Philippines and Japanese bases to the west and south
of the island. It was planned to have a fighter strip available on D + 2 of
the operation. Though that deadline could not be met, a major airdrome

was constructed on the south side of Morotai and was operational in time to provide assistance to the Leyte assault in the third week of October.[43]

Early in September, Kinkaid and his staff happily moved from Brisbane to Hollandia. Now he was not only "at the front" but could also take a more direct part in the planning.[44] When he and his staff set up shop on a hillside overlooking Lake Sentani, the Morotai operation was ahead of them, and they expected next to seize the Talaud Islands, midway between Morotai and southern Mindanao. But all of that was to change. Instead of invading the Talauds on October 15 and Sarangani Bay (southern Mindanao) on November 15, MacArthur's forces would land on Leyte, in the central Philippines, on October 20. And therein lay a tale of opportunity seized.

Between the issuance of his two plans for the invasion of Mindanao (MUSKETEER I) and Luzon (MUSKETEER II), MacArthur fought a successful engagement against the navy. Rather than invade Luzon, Admiral King wanted to move against Formosa. From there he would invade the China coast, set up air bases protected by the Chinese armies, and turn B-29s loose against Japan. Nimitz and his staff sought to avoid a difficult campaign and heavy casualties in assaulting Formosa by moving to China only after Leyte was in hand. MacArthur dissented vigorously. This three-cornered argument was settled at Pearl Harbor by President Roosevelt. After hearing Nimitz and MacArthur in person on July 26-27, the president sided with the general.[45]

The change in schedule, including the abandonment of the Sarangani Bay operation, came with the Morotai and Palau invasions. In order to reduce the possibility of Japanese air or naval interference with the two amphibious assaults, Halsey's Third Fleet, spearheaded by TF 38's fast carriers, bombed and strafed enemy air bases on Morotai, the Palau Islands, Yap, Mindanao, and the Visayan Islands (including Leyte) in the central Philippines. The Japanese response seemed unexpectedly weak. Following discussions with his staff, Halsey radioed Nimitz on September 13 that the invasions of Yap, Morotai, the Palau Islands, and Sarangani Bay should be scrapped, that Leyte could be invaded immediately with the troops en route to the planned invasions, and that the Third Fleet should cover the operation. Nimitz agreed with most of Halsey's ideas, though he did feel that the Palau Islands expedition was still necessary. He forwarded Halsey's views, plus his own, and tossed in the Third Amphibious Force and the Twenty-fourth Army Corps, which could be diverted to Leyte from its planned invasion of Yap.

CINCPAC's radio message went to the Joint Chiefs, who were then meeting with their British counterparts in Quebec. Also present were Prime Minister Churchill and President Roosevelt. After discussions among themselves, the Joint Chiefs sought MacArthur's views. As luck would have it, the general was riding *Nashville* to the Morotai landing and was observing radio silence. His chief of staff, Sutherland, answered the query enthusiastically. SWPA forces would be ready to hit the beaches at Leyte on October 20. The Joint Chiefs then approved the modification.[46]

Kinkaid's activities now moved into high gear, since the two-month advance in the target date for the Leyte landing meant that there would be less time for planning. But the environment for such work was almost ideal. Krueger and Barbey were fairly close together in Hollandia, and MacArthur and his staff were but a half mile away. On September 17 Vice Admiral Theodore S. ("Ping") Wilkinson, commander of amphibious forces, Third Fleet, arrived to participate in the planning. Originally scheduled to bring the army's Twenty-fourth Corps from Oahu to Yap, he would instead deliver it to Leyte. Kinkaid invited Wilkinson, an old friend, to share his quonset apartment with him. Wilkinson stayed for seventeen days.[47]

For Dan Barbey and his staff, this period of planning was exceptionally frantic. The Seventh Amphibs were still engaged in resupply activities associated with Morotai, some of the troops they would carry to Leyte were in the Admiralty Islands, far to the rear of Humboldt Bay, and some of their craft were yet to arrive from the Pacific Fleet. As "Uncle Dan" later noted, some of the troops would be carried in slow-moving LSTs and would have to leave Manus by October 4. This was about the date that the plans for KING II (the Leyte landings) were completed.[48]

By mid-August the question of command of the Leyte attack force had been settled. In late July Kinkaid had told Nimitz that he expected Barbey to command the Philippines attack force and that three junior Pacific Fleet amphibious commanders should join him. Nimitz forwarded Kinkaid's ideas to Admiral King with the observation: "This would place the largest amphibious operation in the Pacific to date under Barbey, assisted by Fechteler, Cecil, Conolly, Royal and Reifsnider." More serious would be the fact that Turner, Wilkinson, Hill, Fort, and Blandy with their experienced staffs would be unemployed between STALEMATE (the Palau operation) and CAUSEWAY (the Formosa operation). He recommended that, if large ships and forces from the Pacific Fleet were to be lent to Kinkaid, then some of the experienced commanders should go with them.[49]

King quickly saw what was bothering Nimitz and on August 17 proposed a solution to Kinkaid. "I assume that you will command, under MacArthur, all the Naval Forces involved directly in the operation, and that you will coordinate their activities with Admiral Halsey as Commander of the Third Fleet Covering Force." He then suggested that Barbey and Wilkinson each command one part of the attack force. He further assumed that Barbey and Wilkinson would each command a number of rear admirals. As overall attack force commander, Kinkaid would have

Barbey and Wilkinson reporting to him. As matters were thus arranged, Barbey, a rear admiral, would not be under Wilkinson's command, nor would Kinkaid have to request that Wilkinson, a vice admiral, serve under Barbey.[50]

Taking into consideration the estimated 21,000 Japanese troops on Leyte, plus the reinforcements that could be expected during the first week of operations ashore, GHQ believed that the invasion should be a two-corps assault by four divisions with a two-division reserve.[51] Along with these major units, totaling about 133,000 troops, there would be almost 70,000 troops in special units such as tank battalions, artillery, engineer, amphibian truck and tractor battalions, signal companies, hospitals, and so forth. There would be, in other words, a staggering accumulation of people to organize, lift to the beaches, supply, and protect.[52]

The immediate task was to seize the Leyte Gulf-Surigao Strait area, then establish air, naval, and logistic bases to support further operations into the Philippines.[53] The initial target area was the east coast of Leyte between the cities of Tacloban and Dulag, where some half-dozen airfields and airstrips would be captured.[54] From these fields, or from newly constructed ones, Kenney's squadrons could take over the air defense of the area, permitting the navy's aircraft carriers to return to the Pacific Fleet.

Kinkaid created three task forces under him as commander, central Philippines attack force (CTF 77). He would directly command four task groups. TG 77.1, the creation of his new chief of staff, Commodore V.H. Schaeffer, consisted of the fleet flagship, *Wasatch* (AGC-9), and light cruiser *Nashville*, which would embark General MacArthur, and four destroyers. It was assumed that once in Leyte Gulf the flagship group could maneuver as a unit and would have sufficient firepower to defend itself under air attack. TG 77. 2, the bombardment and fire support group under Rear Admiral Jesse B. Oldendorf, had been lent by the Pacific Fleet and consisted of six old battleships, all reconditioned survivors of the Pearl Harbor attack, three heavy cruisers, four light cruisers, including *Nashville*, and twenty-one destroyers. TG 77.3, the close covering group under Rear Admiral Berkey, consisted of cruisers *Phoenix, Boise, Australia, Shropshire*, and seven destroyers. TG 77. 4, commanded by Rear Admiral Thomas L. Sprague, consisted of sixteen CVEs (escort carriers) on loan from the Pacific Fleet, plus an accompanying nine destroyers and twelve destroyer escorts. The CVEs, in turn, were organized into three task units: TU 77.4. 1 (Rear Admiral T.L. Sprague) with four carriers; TU 77.4.2 (Rear Admiral, F.B. Stump) with six carriers; TU 77.4.3 (Rear Admiral C.A.F. Sprague) with six carriers. TG 77.5 was the minesweeping and hydrographic group, TG 77.6 the seven beach demolition groups; TG 77.7 consisted of Service Force Seventh Fleet vessels such as oilers, ammu-

Kinkaid and Barbey planning an operation; *below*, U.S.S. *Wasatch*. Courtesy U.S. Naval Institute.

nition ships, provision ships, water tankers, net tenders, salvage vessels, and so forth. It can be seen that task groups 77.1, 77.2, 77.3, and 77.4 made up a "scratch" battle force for the Seventh Fleet were it necessary to confront a portion of the Imperial Navy.[55]

Task Force 78, Barbey's Seventh Amphibious Force, had been designated the northern attack force. Barbey's job was to land the Tenth Corps (Major General Franklin C. Sibert) on the Leyte beaches, roughly in the area three miles south of the Tacloban airport. He divided his force into two attack groups, each landing a division of the Tenth Corps. Fire support for Barbey's assault would be provided by Rear Admiral G. L. Weyler with the battleships *Mississippi* (BB-41), *Maryland* (BB-46), and *West Virginia* (BB-48) and a handful of destroyers, plus Admiral Berkey's cruisers if needed.

Task Force 79, the southern attack force, came to the Leyte operation from the Pacific Fleet, and with it came Wilkinson as its commander. Unlike Dan Barbey, "Ping" Wilkinson preferred to leave the management of his two assault groups to experienced amphibious commanders he brought with him. Wilkinson's groups had the task of landing the Twenty-fourth Corps (Major General John R. Hodge) on the beaches between the small cities of San Jose and Dulag. As with the northern force, the two attack groups each would be responsible for landing a division. Prelanding bombardment and fire support during the assault would come from Rear Admiral Oldendorf's battleships and cruisers.[56]

Before the two attack forces ever entered Leyte Gulf, Kinkaid's plan of operations required seizure of certain islands in the Surigao Strait-Leyte Gulf area to prevent enemy interference with the landings. Also, during the three days before the actual landings on Leyte were to begin, Oldendorf would oversee the sweeping of mines from Leyte Gulf, clearance of any underwater obstacles in the approaches to the landing beaches, and elimination by bombardment of enemy gun emplacements, fortified points of resistance, and any other military targets worthy of a four-inch destroyer shell or fourteen-inch battleship high-capacity shell.[57]

While Kinkaid's reinforced Seventh Fleet was designed to escort, protect en route, and defend in Leyte Gulf the more than seven hundred vessels that constituted the central Philippines attack force, Kinkaid did anticipate assistance from Halsey. The mission of the Third Fleet was to cover and support the Leyte operation by:

1. Containing or destroying the Japanese fleet

2. Destruction of hostile air and shipping in the Formosa, Luzon, Visayas, and Mindanao areas

3. Destruction of ground defenses and installations and shipping in the objective and adjacent enemy supporting areas

4. Providing direct support of the landing and subsequent operations by fast carrier aircraft as required.[58]

These general tasks were made more specific in Nimitz's plan and in Halsey's own orders to his force. Nimitz broadened the scope of operations for the Third Fleet when he added: "In case opportunity for destruction of major portion of the enemy fleet is offered or can be created, such destruction becomes the primary task." As we shall see, this sentence became central in controlling Halsey's activities once the Japanese had decided to attempt the destruction of the Leyte expeditionary force.[59] It should be remembered that MacArthur controlled the Seventh Fleet through Kinkaid, but Nimitz was Halsey's immediate superior. At the scene of action in the Leyte Gulf area, there were two independent fleet commanders, working cooperatively, with no one directly in a position to command the two of them.

Before putting to sea and heading for Leyte, Kinkaid in early October reviewed the KING II plan with all of his senior commanders and their staffs. Kinkaid and Krueger started the briefings, followed by Wilkinson and Barbey. Then each of the task group commanders reviewed his responsibilities and tasks. It was a way to inform everyone about the total operation and the role of each subordinate commander. Oldendorf later commented that in the case of KING II for the first time he was able to discuss a major operation before implementing it. Rear Admiral F.B. Stump, one of the CVE task unit commanders (TU 77.4.2) was surprised to be there, particularly since he was the only representative from TG 77.4. Captain R. W. ("Rafe") Bates, who was Oldendorf's chief of staff and a specialist in battle analysis, later mentioned to Kinkaid that he admired Kinkaid's calm, straightforward approach when briefing his flag officers. Bates felt that it inspired great confidence in his commanders.[60]

Wasatch, with Kinkaid and Krueger aboard, departed Humboldt Bay at 0622 on October 15. The last leg on the return to the Philippines had begun, and Kinkaid was pleased to be at sea again. He started his daily letter to Helen, "It is good to feel the throb of the engines again and to be away from the dust and insects."[61]

In the early morning of October 20, A-Day, the command ships, transports, cargo carriers, and escorting combatant vessels passed boldly into Leyte Gulf. With daylight the bombardments began on all beaches to be assaulted, and the landing craft were lifted out and filled. Following aerial bombardments and a final pulverizing of the beach areas by rocket-firing LCIs, the troops at 1000 hit the beaches and scrambled inland. The casualties were few, as the prelanding cannonading had driven most of the enemy away from the beach areas. As at Biak and Peleliu, and later at Okinawa, the Japanese had decided to mount their principal resistance inland.

With planes overhead from the CVEs and two of TF 38's task groups, MacArthur decided it was time officially "to return." In the early afternoon the general took a motor whaler from *Nashville* and stopped at the transport *John Land* to pick up the Philippine president, Sergio Osmeña, the Philippine secretary of national defense, General Basilio Valdez, and the president's aide, Brigadier General Carlos Romulo. The boat then put its distinguished passengers ashore on Red Beach, near the city of Palo. After wading ashore and visiting for a time, MacArthur, Osmeña, and Romulo delivered radio messages to the Filipino people. The general's began: "People of the Philippines, I have returned. By the grace of Almighty God our forces stand again on Philippine soil."[62]

The general paid visits to other beaches on October 21 and 22 and then led a procession of senior officers and Philippine officials to the steps of the provincial capitol on Monday, October 23. Kinkaid, Wilkinson, and Barbey represented the navy; about a dozen army officers were part of MacArthur's entourage. The ceremony was brief but meaningful. Civil self-government was restored to the Filipinos, and President Osmeña was there to take charge, although his authority was complete in only a few areas.[63]

Kinkaid regretted the two and a half hours taken up by the Tacloban ceremonies because recent dispatches had indicated that the Japanese were on the move. At 0700 that morning, messages had come from several of Christie's submarines that two groups of enemy ships, traveling north to the west of Palawan, had been attacked and four cruisers had been sunk or badly damaged. Most important, it was now clear to Kinkaid and Halsey that a major force was probably headed for the Sibuyan Sea and the San Bernardino Strait between Luzon and Samar.[64] This large force, commanded by Vice Admiral Takeo Kurita, consisted of five battleships, ten heavy cruisers, two light cruisers, and sixteen destroyers. Japanese plans called for the First Striking Force, led by the eighteen-inch gun battleships *Yamato* and *Musashi*, to cross San Bernardino Strait during the night of October 24-25, steam south down the coast of Samar, and enter Leyte Gulf. Here, of course, the Japanese expected to destroy the American invasion forces. By daylight on October 24, Kurita's striking force had lost to submarine attacks the cruisers *Atago*, *Maya*, and *Takao*, the latter badly damaged and returning to Brunei. And now, in the Sibuyan Sea, Halsey's TF 38 fell on them.

Another Japanese force, led by Vice Admiral Shoji Nishimura, had departed Brunei Bay after Kurita on October 22 and on October 23 had crossed the Sulu Sea and entered the Mindanao Sea, destination Surigao Strait. This so-called southern force had battleships *Yamashiro* (flagship) and *Fuso*, heavy cruiser *Mogami*, and four destroyers. It was to be joined during the night of October 24-25 by a cruiser force led by Vice Admiral Kiyohide Shima. Not under Nishimura's command but operating cooperatively, Shima's group included heavy cruisers *Nachi* (flag) and *Ashigara*, light cruiser *Abukuma*, and seven destroyers. The Nishimura-Shima force had the mission of entering Leyte Gulf by way of the Surigao Strait and, simultaneously with Kurita's First Striking Force, annihilating Kinkaid's central Philippines attack force. As was the case with Kurita, Halsey's flyers located Nishimura's ships at about 0900 on the October 24 and commenced attacking them. Because of the route he took, from the north, Shima's cruisers escaped detection and attack en route to the Surigao Strait.

To the Seventh Fleet staff, it was fairly obvious what their tasks would be to meet the oncoming Japanese forces. The CVEs had to continue to attack enemy airfields in the central Philippines and provide combat air patrol over the gulf and beaches. Since there were only two passages into Leyte Gulf, by Surigao Strait from the south and from the open ocean to the east, the battleships, cruisers, and CVEs under Kinkaid would provide a last-gasp defense were the Third Fleet to prove unable to stop the Japanese. With the submarine sighting reports, it was reasonably clear on the twenty-third that Kurita's force would approach by way of the San Bernardino Strait. But still a mystery was the location of the Japanese carriers: were they at sea, and how would they attack? At this point there was no evidence that a southern force existed.

On the twenty-third, Halsey's carrier groups (TG 38.2, 38.3, and 38.4) had been concentrated to the northeast of Samar, providing the "strategic cover" called for in KING II. During the night of October 23-24, the groups moved to a position about 125 miles east of central Luzon. Here, during the forenoon watch (0800-1200), three waves of enemy land-based aircraft, consisting of more than fifty planes in each group, attacked Rear Admiral Frederick C. Sherman's TG 38.3. While they experienced enormous losses, the Japanese did manage to damage irreparably light carrier *Princeton* (CVL-23). In trying to save the ship, which was ordered sunk in the late afternoon, light cruiser *Birmingham* (CL-62) and destroyers *Morrison* (DD-560) and *Irwin* (DD-794) were damaged by explosions in the carrier. *Birmingham* suffered 236 dead and 400 wounded, more than twice the losses in *Princeton*.[65]

As Sherman's task group was undergoing its trial by fire, Rear Admiral R.E. Davison's TG 38.4 and Rear Admiral G.F. Bogan's TG 38.2, cruising off Samar, sent out morning search missions to the west to locate the enemy forces known to be at sea and found them. At 0905, Davison's searching Helldivers spotted Nishimura's southern force and called for assistance from 38.4's flat-tops. At about the same time, Bogan's search planes located Kurita's First Striking Force a few miles east of Mindoro in the Sibuyan Sea. Given the size of this fleet, Halsey ordered all three of the task groups, including Sherman's beleaguered TG 38.3, to attack Kurita's force. He also ordered Vice Admiral J.S. McCain's TG 38. 1, currently en route to Ulithi for rest and recreation with five carriers, to return to the fray.[66]

The air attacks on the twenty-fourth were disastrous for the Japanese, but they were not the knockout blows that were reported by Halsey's pilots. Before their orders to concentrate on the ships in the Sibuyan Sea, Davison's squadrons in three forenoon attacks had dealt remarkably light damage to Nishimura's ships. Practically speaking, they were unimpeded in their progress toward Surigao Strait. Shima's force, while spotted several times during the twenty-fourth, was never attacked.[67] Kurita's force, as might be expected, received almost the full attention of all three task groups. When he was ordered to join the attacks against Kurita's ships, Sherman was also directed to have his carriers search to the north and northeast for the missing enemy carriers. Bedeviled by his own problems, Sherman's searches did not get off until the afternoon. At 1540 a small force consisting of the two hermaphrodite battleship carriers, *Ise* and *Hyuga*, plus light forces, was spotted and an hour later the carrier force was located, approximately 190 miles north of Sherman's task group. This latter body consisted of the fleet carrier *Zuikaku* and light carriers *Zuiho*, *Chitose*, and *Chiyoda*, plus two light cruisers and assorted destroyers. Not immediately evident was the fact that only twenty-nine aircraft remained on the carriers.[68]

Kinkaid met with his group commanders at noon on October 24. He designated Oldendorf, CTG 77. 2, as commander of the battle group which would meet the Japanese in Surigao Strait. He would have his six old battleships, three heavy and two light cruisers that had come with him from the Third Fleet, and a mixture of twenty-six Third and Seventh Fleet destroyers. Kinkaid had also ordered Berkey, with his two light and one heavy cruiser, to serve under Oldendorf's command. Some thirty-nine Seventh Fleet motor torpedo (PT) boats were likewise added. Rear Admiral T.L. Sprague's sixteen CVEs (TG 77.4), with their destroyer escorts, were disposed about fifty miles east of the gulf entrance in three groups within supporting distance of one another. The CVEs were expected to keep the area clear of Japanese aircraft and submarines and to be ready to attack the enemy ships if they were called upon to do so. All transport and cargo vessels that were unloaded were gathered into a convoy, allocated a couple of escorts, and sent out in the gulf toward Manus. Finally, the three amphibious command ships present, *Wasatch*, *Blue Ridge* (Barbey's), and *Mount Olympics* (Wilkinson's), *Nashville*, and twenty-eight Liberty ships at the north end of Leyte Gulf, were all pulled together and allocated a screen of destroyers and patrol craft. At the close of the conference, with dispositions made, Kinkaid then let Halsey know by dispatch that the Seventh Fleet could handle the southern force and that he expected the Third Fleet to take care of the central force, the term used for what was later identified as Kurita's First Striking Force.[69]

By 1600 on the twenty-fourth, Admiral Halsey was fairly confident that he had already defeated Kurita's fleet, the central force. From 1030 to 1600 his carrier groups had launched 259 sorties against the Japanese. The super battleship *Musashi* had been sunk and the heavy cruiser *Myoko* severely enough damaged to force it to return to Brunei. Hits had been made on three other battleships, but all were able to continue. However, TF 38 airmen gave such glowing reports of their accomplishments that Mitscher and Halsey were convinced that a major naval victory had been won in the Sibuyan Sea. The clincher, from Halsey's perspective, came at 1600, when a flyer from *Intrepid* observed the enemy fleet turn to a westward heading, apparently leaving the field of battle. No one saw that at 1715 the central force again countermarched and shaped course for San Bernardino Strait. Kurita was bloodied but unbeaten. Halsey, convinced that the Japanese were no longer a threat to Kinkaid's fleet, by 1700 had turned his attention to the carriers north of him.[70]

While TF 38 was mauling Kurita's central force, the Seventh Fleet was preparing a trap for Nishimura's southern force. Once he had finished with Kinkaid, Oley had Bates draft the operations order. Then he had his subordinate flag officers report to his flagship, *Louisville*, for conference. The battle plan was basically simple. The battleship line would steam across the end of the Surigao Strait on an east-west line. To the south of the line would be two cruiser groups, a left and right flank unit, also steaming on an east-west line. South of the cruisers, close to the shores on each side of the straits, would be the destroyer squadrons. Finally, strung out down the strait to the south would be thirteen groups of three motor torpedo boats each. The MTBs would give the first warning of the enemy's presence and then attack; next the destroyers would attack with torpedoes; and finally the cruisers and battleships would open fire when reasonably sure of scoring a high percentage of hits. The battleships were short on armor piercing fourteen-and sixteen-inch shells and did not want to waste any by firing too early. Kinkaid later reported: "Fire was to be held until the destroyers had launched torpedoes and the enemy had closed to within 17,000 to 20,000 yards of our battleline."[71]

As Halsey's strikes against Kurita's central force were reaching a climax, the admiral had to make plans for the next phase. Were Kurita to be turned back, then TF 38 aircraft would continue attacks the next day until the survivors were beyond the reach of the carrier planes. If Kurita continued eastward through San Bernardino Strait, then it was clear that a surface engagement was likely. To prepare for this contingency, at 1512 Halsey flashed a "preparatory dispatch" to all task group commanders in TF 38, designating four battleships and their supporting cruisers and destroyers which were to become a surface battle group. Vice Admiral Willis A. Lee would command this TF 34 if it was formed. To make sure TF 38 understood that this was a preparatory dispatch, Halsey informed his commanders by TBS: "If the enemy sorties, Task Force 34 will be formed when directed by me." An hour and a half after his 1512 dispatch, Halsey finally had reliable information that an enemy carrier force was at sea to his north. This was Ozawa's two-part northern force. Following a couple of hours of indecision on Halsey's part, he sent a dispatch to Kinkaid: "Central Force heavily damaged according to strike reports. Am proceeding north with three groups to attack carrier force at dawn." From "Bull" Halsey's flag bridge, it appeared that Kurita's force was no longer a genuine threat, so he was now turning north toward a force worthy of a carrier task force's attention.[72]

Halsey's decision to attack an enemy carrier force to the north did not particularly worry Kinkaid. His radio crew had intercepted Halsey's 1512 radio concerning TF 34. He and his staff now assumed that Halsey had turned north with three carrier groups (TG 38.2, TG 38.3, and TG 38.4) and had left Admiral Lee's TF 34 to guard San Bernardino Strait. As Kinkaid's chief of staff remembered it: "We notified Halsey of our expected night engagement with the enemy Southern Force and that we would be able to take care of them without any assistance from him if he would handle the Jap Center Force."[73]

From the perspective of the Seventh Fleet, the night battle in Surigao Strait was a smashing success. Nishimura's force was almost totally destroyed. Shima's force, steaming in Nishimura's wake, had the good sense to reverse course to prevent total destruction. The big guns and torpedoes of Oldendorf's forces had sunk two battleships and two destroyers in the main engagement. During the pursuit by the cruisers, another destroyer was sunk and heavy cruiser *Mogami*, too badly damaged to keep up with Shima's fleeing cruiser-destroyer force, was sunk by the Japanese. Though Shima's smaller force escaped major damage in the gun battle, fuel shortage limited its speed and range of movement, and two of his cruisers were destroyed by air attack during the next ten days. Of the Nishimura-Shima forces, only heavy cruiser *Ashigara* and four destroyers escaped the Battle of Surigao Strait.[74]

During both the preparatory period and the battle itself, Kinkaid and his staff remained in *Wasatch*, close to their communications. There was not a whole lot they could do; the battle dispositions had been made. During the afternoon and evening, they received a stream of reports, some delayed, from Halsey about the carrier attacks against Kurita's central force. But there was nothing in them to make Kinkaid or his staff anxious, unless it was information that the damaged central force had moved to the area between Burias and Masbate islands, a position twenty-five miles east of its 1935 position. As his staff kept watch through the night, monitoring reports from the Surigao Strait area, Kinkaid did decide to reinforce a previously ordered search of the San Bernardino Strait entrance. At 1225 Kinkaid had ordered three of his patrol planes to search at night the sector 341 to 017 degrees to a distance of 600 miles from Tacloban but starting through the entrance to the gulf. No reports had come in from the planes during the evening. At 0156 (on October 25) the admiral ordered a dawn search of sectors 340 to 030 degrees to a distance of 135 miles from Suluan Island, at the entrance to Leyte Gulf.[75] This search would also take in the entrance to San Bernardino Strait.

Finally, after having spent most of the night together, Kinkaid asked his staff if there was anything they had overlooked. Captain R.H. Cruzen, staff operations officer, observed, "We've never asked Halsey directly if Task Force 34 is guarding the San Bernardino Strait." Kinkaid said to send a dispatch, and at 0412 the question was asked. However, despite its urgent priority, it was not answered for several hours.[76]

During the two hours between the message asking Halsey whether TF 34 was guarding the San Bernardino Strait and sunrise at 0614, Oldendorf and T.L. Sprague began operations to pursue the defeated Nishimura-Shima forces. Given the slowness of the old battleships, surface pursuit was a cruiser-destroyer action. At the same time, T.L. Sprague's Task Unit 77.4.1 (Taffy 1) loaded torpedoes or armor-piercing five-hundred-pound bombs into its planes in preparation for early strikes. On board *Wasatch*, Kinkaid read a detective story and the staff relaxed as it awaited further developments. More than two hundred miles to the north, Halsey's TF 38 was about to hold reveille for Admiral Ozawa's carrier force.

At 0647 a plane on antisubmarine patrol from the CVE *Kadashan Bay*, a part of Rear Admiral Stump's TU 77.4.2 (Taffy 2), reported being fired upon by an unidentified group of ships. It included battleships and cruisers and bore about 340 degrees, distance twenty miles, from Rear Admiral C.A.F. ("Ziggy") Sprague's TU 77.4.3 (Taffy 3). The three Taffies of TG 77.4 lay about sixty miles offshore and were strung out in three groups, from north (Taffy 3), to south (Taffy 2, then Taffy 1), with about thirty miles between each group, Ziggy Sprague's Taffy 3 lying sixty miles north-northeast of Suluan Island. Taffy 3 was the only group of ships that directly engaged the Japanese force, Kurita's center force, in surface combat. At 0658 the enemy commenced firing on Taffy 3, and three minutes later Sprague called for support. Six escort carriers were no match for four battleships, six cruisers, and eleven destroyers. Kinkaid received the contact report in *Wasatch* at 0704. It was now quite obvious that TF 34 was not guarding San Bernardino Strait.

Kinkaid promptly took three actions. At 0707 he informed Halsey of the situation and requested assistance at all possible speed; he directed the air support commander on board *Wasatch* to have the aircraft from all of the Taffies concentrate against the attacking center force; and at 0725 he ordered Oldendorf to concentrate his battle line at the eastern entrance to Leyte Gulf. As Oley was gathering his heavy ships, Kinkaid also provided him with the light cruiser *Nashville* and nine destroyers from inside Leyte Gulf and even recalled several destroyers escorting a convoy of empty transports and cargo ships toward Manus.[77]

Before Oldendorf had time to concentrate his forces, Admiral Kurita decided to retreat back through San Bernardino Strait. It has never been absolutely clear why the center force commander reversed course and left the field of battle, thus terminating the "Battle off Samar." Whatever the reasons for the Japanese retreat, Ziggy Sprague looked upon it as a Heaven-sent dispensation. *Gambier Bay* and *St. Lo* had been sunk, and it had looked as if nothing could save Taffy 3. Probably few of Oldendorf's warriors shed tears at missing a second gun battle in one day. Oley's battleships and cruisers were low in the number of armor-piercing projectiles on board after their previous fight, and so they might have been in trouble had a gun fight with the center force been protracted.

Halsey's attack on Ozawa's northern force was as successful as Oldendorf's shootout in the Surigao Strait. His flyers quickly sank a destroyer and three of the four carriers which had been the lure for TF 38. Battleship-carriers *Ise* and *Hyuga*, lightly damaged, were chased back to Formosan waters. The fourth carrier and another destroyer were attacked and sunk by cruiser fire. Because of Kinkaid's insistent calls for assistance for the Taffies, Halsey finally at 1115 turned his battleships south, but none of the big ships reached the San Bernardino Strait area in time to attack Kurita's retiring force. Halsey's TF 38, in fighting the "Battle off Cape Engaño," had won another smashing victory over the Japanese at no cost in ships of his fleet.[78]

Although there was glory enough for all involved—and perhaps a special place in the pantheon of naval heroes for the officers and men of *Johnston* (DD-821), *Hoel* (DD-768), and *Samuel B. Roberts* (DE-413), which so ably defended Taffy 3 off Samar—the Battle for Leyte Gulf sparked more than forty years of controversy about the actions of Halsey and Kinkaid. As might be expected, Kinkaid and almost all naval commanders present in Leyte Gulf or in the Taffies believed that Halsey should not have taken Task Force 38 north against the decoy northern force of Ozawa. Had he remained on guard at San Bernardino Strait, they argued, he could have smashed Kurita's central force, and the Taffies would merely have joined the attack. Halsey, of course, disagreed. He cited the paragraph in his instructions from Nimitz which stated that, "in case opportunity for destruction of major portion of the enemy fleet offers or can be created, such destruction becomes the primary task." He did have a "major portion of the enemy fleet" at hand, but once he heard of Ozawa's northern force, with its aircraft carriers, then it became the "major portion" to be attacked. After that decision had been made, then the decision to let Kinkaid worry about Kurita's central force became a matter of assumptions and rationalizations. Halsey and his staff assumed that Kurita's force had been heavily damaged and significantly weakened by TF 38's airmen in the Battle of the Sibuyan Sea. He further assumed that Oldendorf's battleships would be finished with the Surigao Strait action in time, and in shape, to meet and defeat Kurita. He further assumed that the sixteen CVEs in TG 77.4 could provide the necessary striking power to assist significantly in stopping the central force and to defend against shore-based enemy aircraft. The rationalizations came later. None of the troubles that beset the CVEs would have occurred had Kinkaid not mistakenly assumed that TF 34 had been formed and had he ordered proper surveillance of San Bernardino Strait by Seventh Fleet aircraft. Furthermore, even had Kurita broken into Leyte Gulf, his force could not have significantly damaged the American beachhead. And finally, had there been a single person in overall command, instead of the two fleet commanders present, without a coordinating authority, then communication between Halsey and Kinkaid would have been clear. The latter would have known that TF 34 had never been formed and left behind when Halsey took TF 38 north to attack Ozawa.[79]

Not until December 11 did Admiral King ask Kinkaid about the arrangements he had made to assure himself that during the night of October 24-25 the Japanese center force had not passed through the San Bernardino Strait and was heading toward Leyte Gulf. In his reply, Kinkaid explained that he had ordered a night search by aircraft from TG 77.4. He told of intercepting Halsey's message concerning the formation of TF 34 off San Bernardino Strait and assumed it had been left at the Strait when Halsey took his three carrier task groups north. He noted that the PBY search had led to nothing, and that the CVE search had not gotten off in a timely manner. To his credit, Kinkaid placed no blame on Admiral T.L. Sprague for not seeing that the CVE morning search was pressed or on Rear Admiral Felix Stump, commander of Taffy 2, among whose CVEs the dawn search should have originated. Kinkaid had been urged by Admiral Wilkinson and his chief of staff, Commodore P.P. Powell, to order Admiral C.A.F. Sprague specifically to be prepared for morning air attacks against the Japanese battleships and to do some dawn searches. In describing this incident on board *Wasatch*, Powell noted: "I suggested that such an order was good enough for Felix and Tommy Sprague, but not enough for 'Dopey.' Tom got very annoyed with me because I insisted that he had to tell 'Dopey' to do some night scouting and be ready to launch everything he had at dawn."[80]

Despite the controversy that has surrounded the actions taken by Kinkaid and Halsey (or the lack thereof), the Battle for Leyte Gulf remains one of the U.S. Navy's greatest sea fights. The area that was encompassed, the fighting of four engagements (Sibuyan Sea, Surigao Strait, off Samar, off Cape Engaño), the "crossing of the T" in the Surigao Strait, the drama of the Taffies' predicament, the heroics of the destroyermen, and the immense damage to the Japanese navy all help to raise this battle above all others in the Pacific war. Samuel Eliot Morison, the great historian of U.S. naval operations in World War II, concluded regarding this epochal battle: "However you look at it, the Battle for Leyte Gulf should be an imperishable part of our national heritage."[81]

Four days after the great sea battle, Kinkaid in *Wasatch* joined a convoy returning ships to Ulithi, Manus, and Hollandia. Once in Hollandia, Kinkaid and his staff began final planning for the amphibious assault on the southwest coast of Mindoro (Operation LOVE-3, or L-3) scheduled for December 5, and for the great invasion of Luzon at Lingayen Gulf (Operation MIKE-1, or M-1), targeted for December 20, 1944. The two operations were intimately related. The purpose of invading Mindoro was to construct air bases from which Fifth Air Force fighter and bomber squadrons could attack Japanese air bases and their squadrons in Luzon and neighboring islands. Those aircraft suppression attacks would make it possible for the Lingayen attack force to reach the gulf without hindrance from shore-based Japanese aviation.

On November 15, Kinkaid flew into Tacloban, where he learned from MacArthur that the situation was still not well in hand. Japanese air power had not been silenced. The navy people in Leyte, which included Nimitz's plans officer, were pretty well agreed that the Mindoro and Lingayen operations, still scheduled for December 5 and December 20, should be delayed until the Fifth Air Force could gain control of the air over Leyte and the Sulu Sea and thus assure safe passage to the landing sites. MacArthur strongly disagreed, since agreement would require postponement.

On November 16, with Kinkaid at hand, the general sent a long dispatch to Nimitz which indicated that he intended to stick to his plans. He radioed: "The obvious intention of the enemy to make a strong fight for the Philippines can best be frustrated by immediate attack in strength to prevent his preparations for the defense of Luzon which he is pushing at top speed at the present time. For that reason I intend to adhere to the present target dates for the L-3 [Mindoro] and M-1 [Luzon] Operations." MacArthur went on to admit that Kenney's air bases were not far enough along to "saturate enemy airfields and beat down enemy air strength in Luzon and the Visayan area." He therefore requested further Third Fleet attacks throughout Luzon and the Visayas preliminary to the two operations ahead.[82]

Nimitz's reply created a genuine dilemma for the general. The admiral said that he understood the need to assist Kenney's airmen in seizing control of the air prior to the Mindoro landing, and to continue assistance until the shore-based squadrons in Leyte and Mindoro could handle the situation, but Halsey's carriers and their squadrons had to have at least two weeks of rest and replenishment before the Mindoro operation in December.[83] The dilemma for MacArthur, of course, was to shift Kenney's Fifth Air Force into Leyte in such strength that Halsey's carriers could leave the Philippine area by November 26. Unfortunately, neither the weather nor the Japanese were under the command of the general.

Kinkaid returned to Hollandia on November 17 with a copy of Nimitz's radio in his briefcase, and three days later boarded *Wasatch* for the five-day passage back to Leyte Gulf. During that time, Kenney's planners on November 21 informed Krueger about Fifth Air Force's capabilities to cover him. If the navy's carriers could handle the air defense of Leyte and protect the convoys on the first day to Mindoro, then Kenney's pilots could cover the rest of the operation. But here was a major proviso. Operations would depend on being able to base ashore ten day-fighter squadrons, one night-fighter squadron, and one navy medium bomber squadron.[84] Unfortunately, airfield space for twelve squadrons could not be developed in time to cover the Mindoro convoys, which would depart on December 2. Kinkaid received a copy of this memorandum when he got to Tacloban on November 25.

Once ashore Kinkaid received more disquieting information, this time from Rear Admiral Arthur D. Struble, who would command the amphibious landing at Mindoro. He had drafted an "estimate of the situation" for Kinkaid, and it was filled with foreboding predictions and conclusions. He stated that the Japanese could launch strong air attacks against the Mindoro expedition, and that the number of aircraft available for attacks was growing as planes were staged into Luzon from Formosa. Given the weakness in army air coverage for the expedition, Struble recommended "That Naval Air provide air cover for the convoys and over the beach area if the Army is unable to provide such cover."[85]

As if to underscore the correctness of Struble's "estimate," Third Fleet carriers off Luzon suffered serious damage during the afternoon of November 25—Kinkaid's first day back in Leyte Gulf. Kamikazes struck Task Groups 38.2 and 38.3 and damaged four of the nine fast carriers. The next day Halsey had had enough. He canceled further strikes in the Visayas and Luzon and sent three of his four task groups back to Ulithi to repair damage and rest the crews.[86]

On the same day that Halsey sent his fast carriers back to Ulithi, November 26, MacArthur called a meeting to lay out the final details for assaulting Mindoro on December 5. In his opening remarks, the general made it clear that he planned to stay on schedule. Kenney estimated that his Fifth Air Force could handle its mission. Krueger simply stated that his troops were ready to go. Kinkaid and his chief of staff, Commodore Schaeffer, became the wet blankets. After a few generalizations, Kinkaid asked Schaeffer to give his estimate. The chief of staff was honest, painting a grim picture of the air menace to the Mindoro attack force. Pressed for an estimate of damage to transports and landing ships, Schaeffer (who was a naval aviator) guessed 25 percent. Krueger let everyone know that he could not accept such casualties, particularly if he was going to have to meet General Yamashita's armies in Luzon after another amphibious expedition. MacArthur then tossed the ball back to Kinkaid and asked if the navy could send some escort carriers to provide its own air cover for the Mindoro force. The answer was yes. Kinkaid would put together a small task force of six escort carriers and would provide them and the convoys with antiaircraft and heavy gunfire support from three battleships, three light cruisers, and eighteen destroyers.[87]

Back on board *Wasatch*, Kinkaid and his staff began having second thoughts about the wisdom of their decision to hit Mindoro on schedule. On November 29, three days before the Mindoro expedition was scheduled to depart, Rear Admirals Struble and Theodore D. Ruddock, commanders of the invasion force and heavy support group, proposed that the whole Mindoro-Lingayen plan be reconsidered. Both had been shocked by successful attacks on the big ships in Leyte Gulf. Struble commented, "The two recent attacks on the battleship force are not indicative to me of a waning Jap air power in the Philippine Area." He concluded, "I do not consider the L-3 operation sound at this time, and recommend L-3 be converted to a much shorter thrust into Jap territory." Ruddock's paper was similar.[88]

Kinkaid faced the same dilemma that had beset his predecessor. Carpender had elicited the wrath of MacArthur and his staff during 1942 and 1943 because he did not want to risk naval vessels in dangerous waters along the New Guinea coast.[89] Now Kinkaid was being ordered into an expedition that his subordinate officers considered too dangerous under the existing timetable. To those officers, and Kinkaid too, MacArthur appeared to be letting vanity stand in the way of sound judgment. He wanted to stick to the timetable set by the Joint Chiefs. He would not permit a delay in the Mindoro operation until Japanese air power had been more thoroughly smashed.

The controversy reached a climax on November 30, when the Seventh Fleet commander twice confronted MacArthur. The admiral's career now hung in the balance. In the morning, Kinkaid went to the general's headquarters in Tacloban and had a two-hour discussion with him and Sutherland. He had prepared a long memorandum arguing his case and proposing cancellation of the Mindoro and Lingayen operations and substituting short moves to nearby islands. He presented these ideas orally but did not leave the paper. The admiral made absolutely no progress. As he later noted: "The General insisted upon not delaying the operation and that Jap air was weak and would cause very little trouble. He said he could not change the plans at that late date."[90]

Frustrated and determined to take the only action he could under such circumstances, Kinkaid returned to his command ship and drafted a dispatch to King. In this message Kinkaid explained his concerns and MacArthur's refusal to give them credence. He stated candidly:

General MacArthur declines to accept my evaluation of present conditions and my strong recommendation that the Mindoro operation be not, repeat not, conducted now. General MacArthur believes that we must push forward now. I believe that it is not possible from the naval and air standpoint at the present time and that it would be disastrous to do so. I am under orders to carry out the operation. To meet the scheduled date of 5 December the convoy and its covering force, including CVE's, must pass through Surigao Strait the night of 2-3 December. I regret the necessity for sending this despatch but as COM 7th Fleet it is my duty to do so. I can find no alternative. I request immediate action on this despatch. [91]

Marked for information to MacArthur and Nimitz, this dispatch could hardly have failed to ignite explosions at GHQ in Tacloban, on Makalapa Hill in Pearl Harbor, and at Main Navy in Washington. Fortunately for Kinkaid, the message was not sent, and the "alternative" which he could not find was brought to him by his communications officer.

Nimitz knew of Kinkaid's predicament. He had heard about it from Halsey and probably, in person, from his plans officer, Rear Admiral Forrest Sherman, who had returned to Pearl from Tacloban. To meet Halsey's need to give his carriers time for repairs and rest, Nimitz sent a dispatch to MacArthur which arrived, fortuitously, after Kinkaid had left on the morning of November 30. In this message he called attention to the dangers for naval vessels operating in restricted waters where the Japanese could still strike through the air. He noted that Halsey's carriers had spent a long period on the line and needed time to recover. He said that TF 38's carriers could go again immediately, but their striking power was greatly diminished. Given a longer period in Ulithi, the fast carriers could come back and thoroughly smash the Japanese air bases and make the landings at Mindoro and Lingayen a sure success. He said that Halsey had given him some suggestions and he was forwarding the message separately to the general. [92]

As might be expected, Kinkaid, whose communications staff had received Nimitz's radio message for the general, sent a copy ashore with his intelligence officer. At 1700 hours the admiral again went ashore to GHQ. He took with him his long and carefully drafted estimate and delivered it personally to the general. "I fully expected that my detachment would be requested but I could find no other justifiable course of action," Kinkaid later wrote to his deputy. Another two-hour argument ensued, then they went to dinner. [93]

Halsey's dispatch, which Nimitz had forwarded, arrived for dessert. In his message he said his carriers would be much more effective if there were at least a ten-day delay. [94] After the meal, MacArthur and Sutherland

withdrew for a short conference, then returned to announce that the Min-
doro expedition would be delayed ten days, until December 15, and the
Lingayen assault for twenty days, until January 9, 1945.[95] Much relieved,
Kinkaid returned to *Wasatch* and buried in the files his unsent dispatch to
King.

The ten-day respite was a godsend to the navy and equally important
to Krueger. Unable to finish off the Japanese in the monsoon-soaked terrain of northwest Leyte, Krueger was able to plan and stage two landings
on the west coast of the island during the extra time allowed. Struble
found that, with a strong escorting force present, his passage to Mindoro
was almost trouble free. On December 14, as the assault force began its final approach to the island, Halsey's fast carriers returned for three days of
attacks on everything that flew or moved in Mindoro and central and
southern Luzon. When Struble passed the word to "land the landing
force," the sky overhead was not free of Japanese planes by any means,
but the Americans clearly commanded the air.

Struble's December 15 landing on Mindoro was a complete success.
The army, more than twenty-seven thousand combat and engineering
troops, quickly eliminated the one thousand Japanese and took control of
the island. Airfields were promptly constructed, and by December 20 the
first squadrons had begun operations. The reason for seizing Mindoro had
been to provide air coverage over the last half of the eight-hundred-mile
route between Leyte and Lingayen gulfs and, above all, to make it possible to protect the Lingayen area during the assault phase. Fortunately for
all, the soil and rainfall were such that field construction did not suffer the
delays experienced by the engineers in Leyte. However, because the island faced onto the South China Sea, American bases and airfields were
exposed to surface and air raids by the enemy, as were the convoys sent to
resupply the bases.[96]

While the army worked to bring Mindoro under American control,
the largest amphibious operation in the Pacific to date was taking shape.
SWPA's invasion of Leyte had been simply the overture in the program;
the main event was to be the invasion of Luzon. From Kinkaid's view-
point, the general outline of the navy's role in the coming campaign was
not significantly different from what had been done for Leyte. Even the
planning took on some aspects of déjà vu. Upon his return to Hollandia on
November 3, Kinkaid found "Ping" Wilkinson and Oldendorf ready to finish up the plans for the Luzon operation. As had been the case with the
Seventh Fleet staff, the Third Fleet people had been at work on their own
plans. Now with Kinkaid at hand some of the final questions could be answered. One decision, concerning leadership, had been made, but the
subject was reopened anyway. Wilkinson suggested that he should command the attack force, as Kinkaid had done at Leyte, and that the latter
should exercise broad command all of the Seventh Fleet naval forces, in-

cluding the attack force. Perhaps as a measure of their close friendship, Kinkaid was not offended by Wilkinson's suggestion, but he had no intention of accepting it. He understood, as perhaps Wilkinson did not, that the general still did not wish to place his amphibious commander, Barbey, under a Third Fleet commander. Possibly, too, MacArthur wanted to ensure that everyone knew this was an SWPA show, and not Nimitz's or Halsey's. Amazingly, given the problems at Leyte, the issue of a single commander for all naval forces did not emerge. Halsey and Kinkaid would still have to work cooperatively, with no single person in command at the scene of action.[97]

As commander, Luzon Attack Force (CTF 77), Kinkaid would command all army troops and naval vessels in the expeditionary force until Krueger took command ashore. Two army corps (the First and the Fourteenth) consisting of four divisions and a plethora of supporting units, would be immediately landed on January 9 (S-Day) and then followed by service troops, in all some 203,000 troops in the first two days. Later landings by Eichelberger's Eighth Army would swell the total to almost 400,000 soldiers. In December GHQ had estimated that there were 152,000 Japanese troops of all categories on Luzon. Unless massive enemy reinforcements were brought in from outside the Philippines, MacArthur had more than enough troops to subdue the Japanese.[98]

Sixth Army plans called for landing two corps (four divisions) abreast on the beaches of Lingayen Gulf. To accomplish this goal, Kinkaid created two attack forces. The San Fabian attack force (TF 78), led by Barbey, was to land the First Corps (Major General Innes P. Swift) near the village of San Fabian in the southeast corner of the Gulf. Wilkinson's Lingayen attack force (TF 79), charged with landing the Fourteenth Corps (Major General Oscar W. Griswold), was also to consist of two assault groups. Wilkinson's groups would go ashore on the beaches between the small cities of Dagupan and Lingayen in the southwest corner of the Gulf. While Barbey's First Corps came largely from the New Guinea area, Wilkinson had to collect the the Fourteenth Corps divisions at Bougainville (the Thirty-seventh) in the Solomons and Cape Gloucester (the Fortieth) on New Britain.[99]

Further paralleling the Leyte experience, Kinkaid established a variety of task groups from his naval forces to handle the many missions that were vital to the success of the assault. Oldendorf was given TG 77. 2, the bombardment and fire support group, made of six Pacific Fleet old battleships, six cruisers, and eighteen destroyers. Again following previous experience, the beach demolition group was put in charge of Oldendorf. Now a Seventh Fleet fixture, Berkey commanded TG 77. 3, the close covering group. His command consisted of three light cruisers and six destroyers. For TG 77.4, the escort carrier group (Rear Admiral C.T. Durgin), Nimitz again lent eighteen CVEs plus twenty-seven destroyers and destroyer escorts. Not only did Durgin's carriers provide air cover for the huge convoys from New Guinea to Lingayen Gulf, but the CVEs were expected to provide antisubmarine coverage. Also, their air groups would attack targets ashore when called upon. For his own purposes, Kinkaid set up a fleet flagship group (TG 77.1), which consisted of *Wasatch* (AGC-9), *Boise* (CL-47), and four destroyers.[100]

Oldendorf's TG 77. 2 sortied for Lingayen on January 3 in company with some of the CVEs; it soon became a lightning rod for Japanese special attack squadrons. On January 4, while forty miles west of Panay, *Ommaney Bay* (CVE-79) was struck by a twin-engine kamikaze and mortally damaged. Unable to save the burning carrier, Oley ordered the vessel sunk by a screen destroyer's torpedo. The next day saw no sinkings in the convoy, but kamikazes damaged two cruisers, including Oldendorf's flagship, *Louisville* (CA-28), escort carrier *Manila Bay* (CVE-61), and three lighter vessels. On January 6 TG 77. 2 entered Lingayen Gulf and was met by the full fury of the "Divine Wind," as the special attack squadrons were called. Battleships *New Mexico* (BB-40) and *California* (BB-44) were struck, with Rear Admiral T. E. Chandler being fatally wounded on board *New Mexico*. The Australian heavy cruiser, *Australia*, which had been struck on the fifth now took two more kamikaze hits, as did cruisers *Louisville* and *Columbia* (CL-56). Nine lighter vessels were also struck, and among them a destroyer minesweeper, *Long* (DMS-12), was sunk. It is little wonder that Oldendorf, after surviving the attacks on his flagships, sent a pessimistic dispatch to Kinkaid: "Additional damage may seriously and adversely affect this as well as important subsequent operations. More damage may invite action by the Japanese fleet for which this command is becoming progressively less prepared. Should suicide bombers attack transports, results might be disastrous. Recommend Fifth Air Force be informed seriousness of situation and need for more air support. Recommend Third Fleet be ordered this area immediately[to] provide additional air and surface cover urgently needed. Consider this matter of such serious import as to warrant serious consideration of present plans."[101]

Oldendorf's dispatch must have given Kinkaid and his staff a dash of cold water, especially since *Wasatch* had left Leyte's secure anchorage just a few hours earlier. Forgetting the niceties of command relationships, Kinkaid radioed Halsey directly and requested assistance from the "Big Blue Fleet," a favorite term around Pearl Harbor for the Third/Fifth Fleet. Kinkaid not only asked that enemy airfields in northern Luzon be smothered but "further request that you give consideration to moving Third Fleet to westward of Luzon to give direct air support objective area [Lingayen Gulf] which will be specially required during period loaded transports in that area."[102]

The reply to Kinkaid's dispatch came in a radio from Nimitz to Mac-

Arthur. Nimitz reminded the general that the Third Fleet would soon have other commitments and could not be tied to Lingayen affairs too long. He expressed the belief that Third Fleet attacks on Formosa, Okinawa, and perhaps the China coast would be as effective in protecting the Gulf as parking TF 38 in the area. From this dispatch, and other exchanges between Halsey and Nimitz, it appears that CINCPAC's staff might have thought that Kinkaid was exhibiting a slight case of operational jitters.[103]

Despite the grimness of the sixth, Japanese air attacks were diminishing. Oley's minesweepers went about their dangerous business and had the vital areas of the gulf cleared by S-Day. The bombardment vessels found that real targets were relatively scarce. As at Peleliu and Leyte, the Japanese had evacuated the beach areas in order to prepare defenses to the rear. The same lack of serious work to do was evident when the underwater demolition teams looked for beach obstacles. There were not many.[104] On January 7 only two ships were struck by kamikazes, both minesweepers, and both were sunk. On S − 1 (January 8), however, the Japanese returned in force and hit six ships. *Australia* was again struck twice by kamikazes, and two CVEs, *Kadashan Bay* (CVE 76) and *Kitkun Bay* (CVE 71), suffered extensive damage but remained on station. Unknown to the Luzon attack force, the Japanese had shot their bolt. Halsey's attrition operations, and the destruction of enemy aircraft over the convoys and in Lingayen Gulf by the CVE squadrons and Fifth Air Force fighters, had reduced Japanese aviation to near impotence. They had shaken Kinkaid and his commanders badly, but General MacArthur's return to Luzon was not to be stopped.[105]

Despite assurances from Filipinos ashore, air reconnaissance, and what could be seen from Oley's ship, that the Japanese were not emplaced at the Lingayen Gulf beaches, TG 77. 2 did its usual thorough job of bombarding the shore before the troops landed. The first soldiers were on the beach at 0927; by sunset some sixty-five thousand troops had come ashore. At about 1400, General-of-the-Army MacArthur and a handful of his senior staff left *Boise*, the cruiser they had ridden to the gulf, and paid a visit to the troops near San Fabian. Given the opportunity to step ashore onto a makeshift pier, the general opted for his traditional wade. As his best biographer has noted, "the Barrymore side of MacArthur's personality could not resist another big splash of publicity and surf."[106]

As was the case at Leyte, Kinkaid's operations in Lingayen Gulf involved constant personal danger. From the day he left the anchorage off Tacloban until S + 5 (January 14) in Lingayen Gulf, his flagship's war diary reported air attacks on his ship and those around him, but his luck continued. *Wasatch* was never struck by bombs, torpedoes, or kamikazes. Earlier in the war, when *Enterprise* (CV 6) had been his flagship, Kinkaid had felt the jolt of bombs hitting his flight deck, but the island structure had ben spared. Of the four navy Distinguished Service Medals that he had been awarded, three recognized that he had earned them in the crucible of combat. Only in the Aleutians had he not been actually under fire.

Toward the end of the month, Kinkaid took *Wasatch* down the Luzon coast to observe Struble's management of a January 29 assault near the city of San Antonio on the Zambales coast. His task force landed almost forty thousand Eleventh Corps troops of Eichelberger's Eighth Army from Leyte. From their landing sites, the troops were expected to strike due east and cut off any possible movement into the Bataan Peninsula by Japanese forces retreating before Krueger's Sixth Army. Two days after Struble's operation, Kinkaid looked in on a smaller assault being managed by Fechteler, Barbey's subordinate who was landing several Eighth Army units on the south Luzon coast at Nasugbu in eastern Batangas Province. Coming ashore only fifty-five miles south of Manila, these forces would drive toward the city and compel the Japanese to hold troops in place that might have moved north to oppose the main American force coming down from Lingayen Gulf.[107]

Upon his return to *Wasatch's* anchorage off Tolosa in Leyte Gulf, Kinkaid moved into his fairly new Seventh Fleet headquarters. Because Tolosa was to be his headquarters until he could move into Manila, Kinkaid had his staff brought forward from Hollandia, including the few members who had remained in Brisbane. Though it was four hundred miles from Manila, Tolosa was an appropriate location for Kinkaid's headquarters because Seventh Fleet operations now turned to eliminating the Japanese from areas in the Philippines and Borneo that had been bypassed as SWPA forces took control of Leyte, Samar, and Luzon.

During most of 1945, Barbey's Seventh Amphibious Force operated with three attack groups, each commanded by a rear admiral. Admirals Fechteler, Struble, and A.G. Noble were regular members of the Seventh Amphibs command, while Rear Admiral F.B. Royal was a "loaner" from the Pacific Fleet's Third Amphibious Force. Among themselves, these four group commanders carried out more than twenty major and minor amphibious assaults, starting with the difficult Corregidor and Mariveles Point landing of February 15 and ending with the capture of Balut Island, off the southernmost tip of Mindanao, on July 20. Barbey's command was, of course, a part of the Seventh Fleet, but he operated on a very loose rein from Kinkaid. All of Barbey's operations came at the order of MacArthur, through Kinkaid, but they were definitely not at the order of the Joint Chiefs. It had been the intention of the Joint Chiefs to leave the central and southern Philippines in a "bypassed" status after Luzon had been taken, but the general would not have it. He considered it a sacred obligation to free all of the Filipinos from Japanese control as quickly as possible and not wait for liberation to come with a final surrender at some distant day. As for Kinkaid and Barbey, they simply carried out the general's commands.[108]

The weeks and months passed slowly for Kinkaid in Tolosa. The general remained in Manila, close to the operations of the Sixth and Eighth armies as they liquidated General Yamashita's last troops. Kenney was there also, and so was most of MacArthur's staff. Kinkaid thus became the senior officer in the Leyte area. He knew that plans were being considered in Pearl Harbor and Washington for the invasion of Japan, or possibly Formosa or the China coast, but the Seventh Fleet had received no orders to start planning. So the admiral kept up with the reports, swam daily until the Gulf became too polluted, pitched horseshoes, attended dances held by the army nurses and Women's Army Corps officers, read detective stories each night, and wrote daily letters to Helen. On April 6 there was a break in routine. Kinkaid and Rear Admiral J.L. ("Reggie") Kauffman, who had been Naval Academy roommates for four years, had the unique pleasure of pinning new collar devices on each other. Kinkaid now wore the four stars of an admiral and Reggie the three of a vice admiral, both to date from April 3. Had the promotion dispatch arrived on April 3, the promotion party could have done double duty, since that was the admiral's fifty-seventh birthday.[109]

On May 5 Kinkaid finally received a dispatch ordering him to Washington for consultations with King and his staff. Following the meetings, he was authorized six weeks' delay before returning to his command. He had last seen Helen in November 1943. The eighteen months of separation had seemed like an eternity, but she would be in Washington to meet him when his command transport set down at Naval Air Station Anacostia on May 12.[110]

Upon returning from leave, Kinkaid spent two weeks catching up on his reading of dispatches and preparing for the move to Manila. Since the time of his promotion, there had been a change in the command responsibilities in the Pacific. With the invasion of Okinawa, the war had been brought to Japan's doorstep. The division of the Pacific into a Southwest Pacific area, North Pacific area, and central Pacific area no longer had much justification. The Joint Chiefs in April finally decided that there should be one commander for all naval forces in the Pacific (Nimitz) and one commander for all army forces in the Pacific (MacArthur). They had wanted to appoint a single commander for the final invasion of Japan but could not reach agreement. The Chiefs did decide that Nimitz, or a commander under him, would plan and carry out the amphibious assault in cooperation with MacArthur's designated commander. Once ashore, land forces and aviation in support of the land forces would be under MacArthur. All of this information Kinkaid learned from visits to Nimitz's headquarters on Guam and while in Washington. He also understood that the Seventh Fleet was now under CINCPAC's direct command, rather than COMINCH's, but he and his fleet would continue to serve Mac-Arthur.[111]

The war ended before Kinkaid's role in the planned invasion of Japan (OLYMPIC) had been clearly decided upon. He knew that he was to command all naval forces in Japan once the invasion had been accomplished. He also quickly discovered, once the occupation of Japan began after the cease fire, that his Seventh Fleet would be used to assist with the occupation of Korea and China. This assignment precluded Kinkaid's participation in the surrender ceremonies on board *Missouri* (BB-63) on September 2.[112]

Kinkaid and the Seventh Fleet remained in China waters for the remainder of his tour as commander. Relieved by Admiral Barbey on November 19, Kinkaid boarded his command seaplane for the air trip to Alameda. Four and a half years later, on April 28, 1950, a final retirement ceremony was held for the admiral on board *Enterprise* (CV-6), one of his best remembered flagships. He had completed almost forty-six years of naval service from his entry at the Naval Academy as a callow "plebe" of sixteen to his retirement at sixty-two, a four-star admiral, laden with honors from a naval career well spent in the service of his country.

There is little doubt that Admiral Kinkaid's service under General MacArthur's command was the most important of his naval career. He had been successful in Alaska, and the third star on his collar was tangible recognition of that service. He was assigned to SWPA because of his reputation for working smoothly and effectively with the army, air corps, and Canadians. But service under MacArthur, from the naval point of view, opened the door to potential professional disaster and future assignment to a backwater command. On the other hand, upon his arrival in Brisbane, Kinkaid found the general ready to launch a long series of amphibious operations, designed to isolate the Japanese stronghold at Rabaul, and badly needing a senior naval commander who would exert positive leadership in carrying out SWPA plans.

Besides his battle-tested savvy, Kinkaid brought good judgment, a fund of common sense, and a fundamental understanding of how to deal with people, both superiors and subordinates. To many of his contemporaries, he was colorless, almost dull to be around. But most, when asked, agreed that he was a good listener and respectful of the opinions of those he consulted. He had obviously learned early in his career that not much could be learned by monopolizing a conversation. It is also clear from a study of his career that he believed in the delegation of authority. Kinkaid trusted subordinates with as much authority and responsibility as he thought they could manage until they proved otherwise. He recognized quickly that Admiral Barbey was a "charger" who could produce handsomely. He might have been annoyed by Barbey's pushiness and occasionally self-serving behavior, but Dan Barbey handled amphibious operations with consummate skill, and that ability counted with Kinkaid. He found "Count" Berkey to be a dynamic leader, at times impulsive but intelligently courageous. Like Barbey, he enjoyed command under a loose rein. Admiral Oldendorf was another individual in whom Kinkaid placed great trust. Less flashy than Barbey or Berkey, Oley was the solid, goal-oriented-type commander. He enjoyed responsibility, took early initiatives when he understood the whole picture, and saw projects through to completion. When he expressed reservations about a plan, as he did in preparing for Lingayen, Kinkaid knew how to keep him moving ahead. Ironically, Kinkaid's staff was the source of the greatest criticism concerning him. He accepted its members as he found them, molded them to his approaches to problem solving, and kept most of them with him during 1944 and 1945. He clearly won their loyalty and at all times remained supportive of them as individuals. Yet many outsiders considered his staff "dumb" or "second-rate." The perspective of history clearly shows that Kinkaid's staff served him well and deserved the loyalty he gave it.

In an army environment, Kinkaid won the approbation of his fellow commanders for performance under fire. At both Leyte and Lingayen he was present physically as the Japanese suicide pilots attacked his ships. While Oldendorf and the Spragues met the enemy at close quarters, Kinkaid was close enough to each engagement to command effectively and act in the interest of his subordinates. His type of leadership and personal courage were readily identifiable by MacArthur and his GHQ as the hallmarks of a true master of naval warfare.

Finally, it is clear that Kinkaid's loyalty to MacArthur's leadership and plans was repaid in kind. Kinkaid was no sycophant. He knew that he was working for the army, but when planned operations conflicted with his professional naval judgment, he was willing to confront the general. In case of the Mindoro operation, Kinkaid was almost forced to risk MacArthur's anger to the point of possible recall. Fortunately, Nimitz and King recognized his dilemma and provided the necessary leverage to force a change upon the general. The ultimate success of the operations at Mindoro and Lingayen Gulf was enough to eliminate any lingering doubts in MacArthur's mind about the value of his naval commander. A few days after pinning on his fourth star, Kinkaid visited MacArthur in Manila, and before leaving his office, he thanked the general for his assistance in arranging the promotion. MacArthur answered him simply, "the four stars are due entirely to Tom Kinkaid."[113]

Robert L. Eichelberger

MacArthur's Fireman

JAY LUVAAS and
JOHN F. SHORTAL

Robert Lawrence Eichelberger was born on March 9, 1886, in Urbana, Ohio, the youngest of five children. His father was a prominent lawyer who had served with the Union army in the Civil War; his mother, who came originally from Port Gibson, Mississippi, had witnessed the ravages of the Vicksburg campaign as a young girl. His own boyhood was spent on a farm near Urbana that his father had purchased "more as a place in which to raise his family than to provide a livelihood." Here he led an active life with his three brothers, sharing the farm chores, riding horses, and often listening to the war stories of old veterans. One of the veterans had a large Civil War library, and Eichelberger in later life claimed that he had read "every book in it." After his freshman year at Ohio State University, his father's law partner, a local judge, offered him an appointment to the U.S. Military Academy. He accepted.[1]

From the first Eichelberger had been fascinated with things military. Besides a compelling interest in the Civil War, he had eagerly followed events of the Spanish-American War, had worn his own "Rough Rider" suit to the state capital to see Colonel Theodore Roosevelt campaign for vice president, had visited a National Guard camp near Lake Erie, and had watched the Corps of Cadets drill at the Pan-American Exposition in Buffalo in 1901. By the time he reached West Point in the summer of 1905, he looked forward to a military career. He graduated in 1909, sixty-eighth in a class of 103, then reported for duty with the Tenth Infantry at Fort Benjamin Harrison, Indiana. The following spring this regiment formed part of an experimental "maneuver division" that was assembled in San Antonio to keep a watchful eye on Mexico. "There were maneuvers, long practice marches and many of the dull things that made up camp life in those days," he recalled. So many officers were relieved that Eichelberger, although only a second lieutenant, was given command of a company. While at San Antonio, Eichelberger saw for the first time two officers who would later shape his destiny—Captain Douglas MacArthur, a "very handsome," "aloof," and reserved person who did not seem to mingle much with the others, and Lieutenant George Catlett Marshall, a "high brow" recently graduated from the Staff College at Leavenworth.

In September 1911 Eichelberger accompanied his regiment to Panama, where he met and married Emma Gudger, daughter of Judge H.A. Gudger, chief justice of the Canal Zone. "Miss Em," as she was affectionately called, became his lifelong companion, confidante, and ardent champion—a model army wife. They had no children, and Miss Em so lavished her affections upon "Bobby"—which he fully reciprocated—that at times her anxiety for his safety and success contributed, without her knowledge, to the pressures he would feel in the performance of duty. In Panama, too, Eichelberger first encountered tropical jungles, an experience that "helped a bit" many years later when he found himself fighting in New Guinea.

In 1915 he was transferred to the Twenty-second Infantry, then in Arizona helping to guard the border against incursions by Mexican revolutionaries under Pancho Villa. Eichelberger witnessed combat for the first time when Villa attacked government forces at Agua Prieta, one thousand yards from his observation post in an old slaughterhouse. "We were neutral, but stray bullets know no international law."[2] A few days later Eichelberger was astonished to learn that some of his fellow officers had remained in the officers' club playing cards instead of grasping the opportunity to watch the battle—a lesson that he would remember when he assumed command during his first battle in New Guinea.

In 1916 Eichelberger went to Kemper Military School in Boonville, Missouri, to spend a year as professor of military science and tactics. He then joined the Twentieth Infantry at Fort Douglas, Utah, and with the expansion of the army on the eve of American entry into World War I he was soon promoted to captain and given command of a battalion of the Forty-third. After a brief stint as instructor at the Third Officers' Training Camp in Camp Pike, Arkansas, he was assigned to the General Staff in Washington, where he served under Major General William S. Graves, the executive assistant to the chief of staff. When Graves left the War Department to command the Eighth Division at Camp Fremont, California, in July 1918, he took Eichelberger with him as his G-3 (Operations). Although the division had been scheduled to leave shortly for France, it was sent instead to Siberia as the American contingent to a joint Allied military action aimed ostensibly at saving some seventy thousand Czech soldiers, former Russian prisoners of war, and deserters from the Austrian army then reportedly making their way across Siberia with the hope of finding transportation to France to continue the fight.

Here Major Eichelberger, as assistant chief of staff and later as chief intelligence officer, made extended trips into the field to observe military operations, investigate atrocities, and assess the motives of America's allies. He frequently came under fire and was once captured by the White Russians, when for several long hours his life was in jeopardy. In March 1920 Miss Em joined him in Vladivostok, and accompanied him later on assignments to Japan, China, and the Philippines. He returned to Washington in 1921 to serve with the Military Intelligence Division in the War Department. He was then assigned as liaison officer with the Chinese delegation to the Washington conference on the limitations of naval armaments and Far Eastern questions. In 1924 Eichelberger, by this time a colonel, transferred to the adjutant general's department, where chances for promotion seemed brighter.

The following year Eichelberger attended the Command and General Staff School, emerging at the end of a strenuous year at the top of a list of "distinguished graduates." (Dwight D. Eisenhower stood number one in the class.) He remained at Leavenworth for three more years as adjutant general and instructor, after which he attended the Army War College. In August 1931 he returned to West Point as adjutant and secretary of the Academic Board. Four years later he became secretary to the War Department General Staff. The chief of staff at that time was Major General Douglas MacArthur.

Eichelberger had positive memories of his first tour with MacArthur. The "Chief" worked unconventional hours, making it difficult to maintain a regular schedule, but he was friendly, courteous, often scintillating, and willing to face uncomfortable facts. "He told me many of his troubles . . . so that I could carry over this information to the new regime." For his part MacArthur seemed to be impressed with Eichelberger's "comprehensive grasp of the Army's major problems, and of the War Department functioning," and paid tribute to his "tact, loyalty, intelligence and initiative."[3]

When MacArthur left to become military adviser of the Commonwealth government in the Philippines, he was replaced by General Malin Craig, whom Eichelberger always regarded as "a wise and understanding mentor." He enjoyed the same kind of association with Craig that he had experienced with Graves. Craig kept reminding him that he deserved to be with troops in case of war, and long after their ways had parted, General Craig's wise and sane letters helped to sustain his spirit during dark days in the Pacific.[5]

As war clouds began to darken over Europe, Eichelberger requested transfer to the infantry. He attended the Infantry School at Fort Benning in 1938 and then assumed command of the Thirtieth Infantry at the Presidio. For the next two years he made up for the time spent behind a desk as he improved the morale and efficiency of his regiment, in the process serving "as just about everything" from division commander to chief of staff at maneuvers that at times involved three divisions and gave him some experience in amphibious exercises. He was happy to be back in close contact with troops, and his performance soon caught the attention of superiors. In 1940 Eichelberger was promoted to brigadier general and was subsequently named superintendent of the Military Academy.

To hear him talk about these years at the Military Academy, one could easily form the impression that his most important accomplishment had been to recruit Earl "Red" Blaik to rebuild army's sagging football fortunes. Eichelberger worked hard, however, to bring both the training and the education of cadets in line with the demands of the times. He introduced fatigue uniforms, expanded the time devoted to military training and instruction, arranged for cadets to maneuver with nearby National Guard units, and cut back on horseback riding so that cadets could devote more time to developing skills relevant to the "gasoline age." He even tightened the ties between the academy and the air corps by increasing the emphasis upon flying and arranging for cadets who so elected to obtain their wings before graduation. In July 1941 Eichelberger received his second star.[5]

When Japan attacked Pearl Harbor, Eichelberger requested a command in the field and was given the Seventy-seventh Division, then being organized at Fort Jackson, South Carolina. In June 1942 he was ordered to form the Eleventh Corps in Chicago and two weeks later was given command of the First Corps, which had originally been intended for use as an amphibious corps in the forthcoming landings in North Africa. In August, however, Eichelberger and his staff were suddenly summoned to Australia—presumably because he knew MacArthur and had some experience in amphibious training—where MacArthur was organizing his forces for a counteroffensive in New Guinea. "When there is a war," Miss Em remarked, "you always seem to go to the queerest places."[6]

To those familiar with current career patterns in today's army, it must seem incredible that a man with such limited experience with troops over twenty years should be considered fit for such a command. But these were not normal times, and Eichelberger had prepared himself well. During his tour on border patrol and in Panama he had observed that pomposity, lack of interest, and discipline by rank rather than personality on the part of an officer inevitably lowered morale and efficiency in a unit.[7] He had trained troops before being sent to Siberia and again with the Thirtieth Infantry and during amphibious maneuvers in 1939. His experience in Siberia and at the Washington Disarmament Conference had given him an advanced education in geography, politics, and the capricious behavior of his fellow men.[8] He had worked closely with Graves, MacArthur, and particularly Craig, his mentor in every sense of the term. Eichelberger's lively sense of curiosity coupled with a lifelong habit of reading—which enabled him to view events in historical perspective—would compensate for much that he had not yet experienced, and he had given some thought to problems of amphibious warfare. But as Eichelberger himself would soon discover, conditions that he was about to encounter in New Guinea lay completely beyond the experience of most of his fellow officers, whether or not they had served in France or had spent the interwar years with troops.

Eichelberger arrived in late August 1942 to learn that the only two U.S. combat divisions in Australia, the Thirty-second and the Forty-first, had been sent initially to reinforce Australia against possible invasion and had accordingly been deployed half a continent apart. Both were National Guard divisions that had been activated in 1940 and had been forced to absorb a large number of draftees to achieve assigned strenth—a condition further complicated by the fact that each had come under a different Australian command responsible for defensive training. This situation had improved somewhat by the time Eichelberger reached the scene, but there was still a marked difference in the readiness of the two divisions. The Thirty-second had left its original camps near Adelaide—where the terrain and winter climate offered no opportunity to train for jungle warfare—and was constructing a camp near Brisbane, while the Forty-first had recently moved to a far better location at Rockhampton, some three hundred miles to the north, where the semitropical climate made possible more realistic battle training.

In the midst of these preparations, the Japanese offensive in New Guinea, aimed at the capture of the strategic Australian base of Port Moresby, was approaching its culmination. Australian forces were in the process of defeating the flanking column that had landed at Milne Bay and containing the main attack along the Kokoda Trail over the Owen Stanley Mountains. Before the Japanese commander could reorganize his forces, replenish stores, and restore the health of his troops for his final push, he was ordered back to the Buna-Gona area by Imperial General Headquarters because of the deteriorating situation on Guadalcanal. On September 18 the Japanese began to withdraw across the hostile Owen Stanleys.

Now it was MacArthur's turn. With sufficient Australian troops to defend Port Moresby, he hoped to insert an American regimental combat team to outflank the main Japanese column strung out along the Kokoda Trail, but his main objective was to use an entire division to capture the Buna-Gona area in Papua, which the Japanese had seized in July. On October 1 GHQ issued its plan. The Australians would "engage the enemy in a frontal action along the Kokoda Trail," the second axis of advance "would involve a wide flanking movement over the Owen Stanleys east of Port Moresby against the enemy lines of communications and supply, and the third . . . would consist of large-scale infiltration from Milne Bay along the northeastern coast of Papua." All three approaches would eventually converge on the fortified beachheads at Buna, Gona, and Sanananda, where a final assault would be made against the Japanese stronghold.[9]

Eichelberger hoped to be involved in these operations, for on September 14 MacArthur outlined for him his plan and clearly intimated that Eichelberger would be the task force commander. But when Eichelberger inquired whether General Richard K. Sutherland, MacArthur's chief of staff, had been told of this plan, MacArthur responded: "No, but I'll tell him tomorrow morning."[10] The next day Sutherland informed him that the plan was off. The marine regiment originally slated to leapfrog up the north shore from Milne Bay in small landing craft was not available, and a growing lack of confidence in Australian troops, together with deep anxiety on the part of the Australian war cabinet about the deteriorating military situation, had prompted MacArthur instead to send Field Marshal Sir Thomas Blamey, commanding Allied land forces, to New Guinea personally to take charge and "energize the situation." Blamey in turn soon became convinced that the unresponsive commander of New Guinea force, which comprised all Allied units in Australian New Guinea, was a part of the problem and sent for Lieutenant General Edmund F. Herring to take command. While Eichelberger would select one of his divisions for the coming campaign, in other words, he would not be directly involved in the planning or fit into the chain of command. Furthermore, MacArthur had already instructed him to have as little as possible to do with the Australians.[11]

Beyond selecting the Thirty-second Division—which was scheduled to move its camps once again in order to be near the Forty-first at Rockhampton—to go to New Guinea, Eichelberger was not directly involved during the first weeks of the Papuan campaign. Indeed, before mid-November he was not even permitted to accompany the Thirty-second in order to learn at first hand the nature of the problems encountered so that he and his staff might plan a realistic training program to enhance the fitness of the Forty-first for combat. When he finally did receive permission to visit New Guinea, MacArthur told him when he arrived that he could not cross the mountains to visit his troops. Sutherland then ordered him back to Australia the next morning, explaining that his role was to be primarily a training one. "A fly," Eichelberger later reflected, "may not know when its wings are being pulled off, but I did." The difficulty lay not so much with MacArthur as with his chief of staff, who apparently had reasons of his own for not wanting Eichelberger on hand and hence treated him "more like a lieutenant than a lieutenant general." After the campaign, Eichelberger decided that the trouble lay in the timing: he arrived at GHQ at a "most unfortunate" moment, when Allied troops were supposed to be making their triumphant entry into Buna and Gona and were instead hopelessly mired down in jungle mud.[12]

Troops from the 32nd Division cross a branch of the Eroro Creek, New Guinea, 1942. Courtesy National Archives.

MacArthur's initial plan to take Buna-Gona had gone awry. By mid-November the Australian Seventh Division and two U.S. regimental combat teams had negotiated treacherous mountain trails, landed at primitive airfields, or moved by coastal shipping in the dark to be safe from enemy air attacks and were within striking distance of the Buna-Gona beachhead. Most American soldiers considered the campaign almost over once the logistical problems had been solved. The Japanese were falling back, patrols made little contact with the enemy, and pilots reported no signs of enemy troops from the air. Consequently, Major General Edwin F. Harding, commanding the Thirty-second Division, accepted the estimate of his G-2 (intelligence) that the "Buna area was garrisoned by not more than a battalion with purely defensive intentions," while word spread through the ranks that "there is nothing around Buna but a few sick Japs." In reality, the recent arrival of fresh and experienced troops had increased Japanese strength in the area to about sixty-five hundred men. They were deployed behind formidable works that had been under construction for nearly two months.[13]

On November 16 the Allies resumed their advance. It was like walking into a hornets' nest. "Our troops were pinned down everywhere," wrote one American officer. "It was dangerous to show even a finger . . . , and it would immediately draw a burst of fire." Stunned by this unexpected resistance, the Americans were soon halted in their tracks. They renewed the assault the next day, again without success. The terrain channeled the attacks through jungle swamps, while circumstances beyond Harding's control—transportation difficulties, enemy action, and orders from New Guinea force—had scrambled his units, causing confusion, additional administrative burdens, and problems in supply and evacuation. On November 23 and again on the thirtieth in response to MacArthur's orders to make an all-out effort "regardless of cost," Harding renewed his attacks but in vain. The Japanese defenses stood intact; American forces made "not so much as a single penetration of the enemy line."[14]

Meanwhile MacArthur was growing impatient. Losses did not seem heavy—about five hundred battle casualties for the two regiments engaged over a period of two weeks—and from his headquarters in Port Moresby he could not have appreciated how many riflemen were too sick and worn out to fight aggressively or even the extent to which terrain and shortages of ammunition and supplies had limited the tactical possibilities. Australian generals visiting the American front reported signs of poor morale and discipline, and MacArthur's own G-3 and chief of staff confirmed his conviction that leadership in the Thirty-second Division was unaggressive. On November 29, the day before Harding's final attack was scheduled to take place, MacArthur summoned Eichelberger to Port Moresby. As Eichelberger later recalled the conversation: "Bob, I'm putting you in command at Buna. Relieve Harding . . . [and] all officers who won't fight. . . . If necessary put sergeants in charge of battalions and corporals in charge of companies—anyone who will fight. Time is of the essence. . . . *I want you to take Buna, or not come back alive.*"[15]

Eichelberger took over command on November 30. The next day he visited the front. He never forgot what he saw there: no frontline discipline, no thought of going forward, men loitering about in rear areas. To Eichelberger and his staff there appeared but one solution: Harding and his principal subordinates must be replaced. In later years, Eichelberger regretted the need to relieve a West Point classmate, but he had been ordered to assumed command, the responsibility was now his, and he had faith only in those of his First Corps staff whom he now placed in command. Eichelberger's arrival struck his immediate superior, General Herring, as "a very pure breath of fresh air" that "blew away a great deal of the impurities that were stopping us getting on with the job."[16]

His first task was to reorganize and regroup the badly intermixed forces. He halted all offensive action for two days until he could unscramble his units, tightened the chain of command, attacked the supply problem, which had already begun to improve with completion of the airstrip at Dobodura on November 21, and provided the dynamic leadership that would infuse new life into his units at every level. He visited the front to see and be seen. To his staff he "set an example . . . by being cheerful." He gave pep talks to troops trudging up the line and direct orders to cautious or indecisive subordinates. Occasionally he resorted to "strange words of profanity" if there was no other way to motivate. In his daily letters to Miss Em, he declared that he almost felt "destined to become an inspirational speaker of the Billy Sunday type," while at the front "his three stars were in evidence to the tired, dirty doughboys that the high command was taking a very personal interest in the fight."[17]

On December 5 Eichelberger set about trying to solve his tactical dilemma. The Japanese held a heavily fortified area about three and one-half miles long and three-quarters of a mile deep, with both flanks secure and open to frontal assault only along two narrow corridors through jungle swamps. This situation had forced Harding to establish two separate fronts, known as Warren front (on his left) and Urbana front, after the Ohio hometowns of two of the American generals involved. Although only two or three miles apart by air, the fronts were separated by impassable swamps and thick jungle, so that, whereas the Japanese could reinforce either flank in a matter of minutes, it took American patrols six or seven hours to follow the tortuous native trails from one flank to the other and a two-day roundabout march over Jeep trails for any extensive movement.

Brigadier General Albert W. Waldrom, the division's artillery commander to whom Eichelberger had given the Thirty-second when Harding was relieved, had planned a frontal attack on both fronts, preceded by an air strike and artillery bombardment. On Warren front the main thrust, supported by five Australian-manned Bren-gun carriers that had just arrived, was to be along the coast. On Urbana front the objective was to seize designated points in the Japanese perimeter around Buna Village. Neither the small air strike nor the artillery bombardment did much damage to Japanese defenses on Warren front, and the Bren-gun carriers failed in their role as tanks; left to its own resources, the infantry managed to gain only forty yards. Things went better on Urbana front, where a platoon managed to reach the sea and dig in, completing the encirclement of Buna Village. When Waldron was wounded at the front while leading his men by personal example, Eichelberger's chief of staff, Brigadier General Clovis B. Byers, assumed command of the Thirty-second.

The events of the day convinced Eichelberger that the Japanese position was too strong to be breached by frontal attack: he would await the arrival of Australian reinforcements and tanks, which had been promised two days earlier, before making another major effort. Meanwhile, he ordered "continued pressure and advance by infiltration," tried to devise new methods of reducing pillboxes, insisted upon more aggressive patrolling, particularly at night, and built up supply and ammunition reserves. Obviously there was no school solution to what had become known as a "Leavenworth Nightmare." The long line of communications was absorbing precious manpower in engineers, supply, and hospital troops, while the rifle companies were down to an average strength of about sixty-five men. Eichelberger's greatest difficulty, however, was not lack of numbers but lack of maneuver space along both narrow fronts. He could not afford to continue his "pallid siege" while the Japanese had the capacity to reinforce the Buna garrison. Eventually, fever was certain to reduce the American forces "to nothing."

Eichelberger's solution was to hold at Warren front, using more aggressive patrols and infiltration rather than frontal infantry attacks, and to make his main effort with Urbana force. After three days of savage combat that reminded one correspondent of "trench fighting . . . , of stomach-twisting bayonet charges behind lifting artillery barrages, [and] of nerve-wracking night patrols" characteristic of the World War I, the Japanese, on the night of December 13, evacuated Buna Village. "We shall reorganize and push on," Eichelberger assured Sutherland. The next objective, a nearby coconut grove, was taken by assault by elements of a battalion that "has found its soul." "As a matter of fact," Eichelberger wrote Sutherland, "the boys are coming to life all along the line."[18]

On December 18 he renewed attacks along both fronts. Warren force, reinforced by two Australian infantry battalions and two troops of tanks, seized the Duropa plantation, "a mass of fortifications which the infantry alone could probably never have stormed," while Urbana force, now containing a fresh regiment that had recently arrived, resumed the attack against Buna Mission. There would be no further lulls in the fighting, even on Christmas Day. On the thirtieth, Eichelberger confided to Sutherland: "If I don't get Buna Mission today I am surer than hell to reorganize tomorrow, for my men have been battered day after day since before Christmas." Not until January 2, however, were his frustrations and "bitter disappointments" over so that he could finally announce victory.[19] But the campaign was not quite terminated: there remained two weeks of what GHQ called "mopping up operations" at Sanananda, where "some of the hardest fighting" was about to take place. When MacArthur and Blamey returned to Australia, Herring took over New Guinea force at Port Moresby, leaving Eichelberger in command of all Allied forces in the forward area. Not until January 22 was all organized resistance of the Japanese in Papua finally ended, leaving Eichelberger free to return to Australia to absorb and incorporate the valuable lessons learned from recent experience in new and improved training programs.

The lessons that Eichelberger himself learned from his recent experience, however, had more to do with human nature than battle tactics. Once GHQ had revealed that he was the mystery general in charge at

Eichelberger and Blamey at Buna, January 1943. Courtesy Australian War Memorial.

Buna, Eichelberger attracted headlines, and his picture was plastered on the cover of *Life* magazine. "When these articles began to come back from the States," Eichelberger recalled after the war, "General MacArthur sent for me" and said, " 'Do you realize I could reduce you to the grade of colonel tomorrow and send you home? . . . Well, I won't do it.' " Eichelberger was forewarned. Although he enjoyed praise, the incident taught him to fear a certain kind of publicity more than anything else. "I would rather have you slip a rattlesnake in my pocket," he later confided to a friend in the Bureau of Public Relations, "than to have you give me any publicity."[20] "Sarah," which was short for Sarah Bernhardt, the great French actress whose name he used whenever referring to General MacArthur in letters to Miss Em, obviously did not take kindly to it.

Nor was Eichelberger "exactly covered with honors" for his part in the victory. MacArthur recommended him for the Distinguished Service Cross, along with some other officers who had not even been in combat, but he did not approve a recommendation that Eichelberger be awarded the Medal of Honor. The situation was further complicated with the arrival in February 1943 of the U.S. Sixth Army under Lieutenant General Walter Krueger. Krueger's appearance on the scene was in no way intended as an affront to Eichelberger, although it obviously dimmed his prospects for future employment in combat, since forthcoming operations were not of sufficient dimension to involve an entire army corps and Krue-

ger outranked even the Australians. "One must develop a hide like a rhi-
noceros," Eichelberger confided to his wife, "or rather one must develop
the habit of happiness."[21] In this way Eichelberger hoped to keep his own
spirits high, although the war seemed to be moving away from him. It
would be a long eight months before his military and personal disappointments were over.

The strength of Eichelberger's character and his unselfish commitment to the nation were best exemplified throughout 1943, in Australia.
His relationship with MacArthur was severely strained, and his career
seemed in eclipse. His opportunities for future combat command, promotion, and public recognition appeared negligible. Furthermore, Mac-
Arthur had assigned him the tedious and unglamorous job of training the
Twenty-fourth, Thirty-second, and Forty-first divisions for combat. However, in performing this mission, Eichelberger set an example of profes-
sionalism for all his subordinates in the theater to emulate. Placing his
personal feelings behind him, he threw himself into this task with dedica-
tion and commitment.

Eichelberger was profoundly affected by his experiences at Buna.
During the tough fighting there, he promised himself that he would never
again lead untrained American soldiers in battle. The next time, he
wanted the Japanese to worry about facing veteran American soldiers. He
wanted the enemy to know fear. In order to accomplish this goal, he had
to develop a realistic training program. Many American soldiers had died
at Buna because they had not been prepared for battle. During the fighting at Buna, Eichelberger had described to MacArthur the impact of inadequate training on the battle: "The regiments of the 32nd Division
needed training in the simple things such as scouting and patrolling. We
saw these things the first time we went to Tambourine and reported their
battle efficiency as low. In scouting and patrolling, for example, lieutenants have been found to take out patrols, stay for a while in the grass, and
come back with a full report of certain areas that they have never been
near."[22]

Eichelberger's answer was small unit combat training that emphasized scouting, patrolling, fire control, and security measures. He was
sure that this combination, together with an effective chain of command,
would produce a highly effective combat unit. At Buna, he told the men of
the Twenty-fourth Division, "time and again the simple everyday principles that you have learned in training was the difference between success
and failure in battle." He stressed his point:

On one occasion I told the commander of a force on the left flank to go into a certain place and find out what was there. He said he couldn't get the men to go into
that place. I asked him if he realized that what I was asking him to do was nothing

more than simple scouting and patrolling. He said "oh!" as though he was greatly surprised and went out and got the information. . . .

Security seems to be a simple thing. Yet it is of the utmost importance in fighting an enemy as cunning and aggressive as the Japanese. There were cases when guards would fail to fire on small groups of Japanese because they were afraid the Japanese would return their fire. . . .

The fact that your training will bear fruit in battle could be illustrated by many true stories. For example, let me tell you about "G" Company, 127th Infantry. . . . This company was the spearhead of the drive to the sea. It demonstrated such teamwork, such skill that nothing could stop them. I found out that this company had been the outstanding company in small unit combat training before the unit had left Australia. Small unit training was here paying dividends.[23]

Eichelberger's divisional commanders understood the value of small unit training and until their deployment for combat devoted half their training time to "small unit tactical problems."[24]

Eichelberger also stressed the importance of developing initiative within the chain of command. His training philosophy reflected the maxim that "the amount of initiative officers (and men) display in war will probably be in direct proportion to the effort made to inculcate it in peacetime training."[25] Eichelberger's views on the chain of command were expressed in letters written to Major General Horace Fuller during the Battle of Buna. "You will find that you must follow the chain of command. Develop sergeants and corporals that will really take charge of their men."[26] "One of the greatest difficulties we find up here is a shortage of junior officers and noncommissioned officers with guts and ability to lead small units."[27] The First Corps deputy chief of staff explained Eichelberger's technique for stressing chain of command: "The next item is what Eichelberger calls the 'chain of command' and the responsibility of every officer and noncommissioned officer in the chain. Hold the sergeant responsible for his section and all its equipment, to include the gun truck. Hold the lieutenant responsible for his platoon, and so on. When you see something wrong don't correct the individual soldier. Give the sergeant hell for failing to see trouble before you did and make him correct it."[28]

Eichelberger's emphasis on the chain of command during the training of First Corps in 1943 was not a new idea. Rather, it was a commonsense response to a serious deficiency noted at Buna, where the chain of command's inefficiency in inspecting, supervising, and enforcing discipline was "one of the most glaring causes of failure." This experience had led him to believe that "Nothing of importance can be left to the individual inclination of the soldier. The taking of quinine, the care of insect bites, the maintenance of weapons, shaving and bathing, avoidance of sleeping on the ground are all subjects about which specific instructions must be issued and diligently enforced." Eichelberger observed that the units in which the chain of command enforced standards of discipline, cleanliness, and maintenance of equipment were the units with the highest morale, efficiency, and fighting spirit.[29]

In addition to stressing small unit training and development of the chain of command, Eichelberger insisted upon conditioning his troops for the environmental and situational factors they would encounter in battle. Eichelberger realized that all future operations would have to be conducted in the jungle and that the American soldier was not naturally prepared for this environment. Anticipating numerous streams, swamps, and rivers, he insisted that the soldiers learn how to swim and that all units conduct extensive training in stream-crossing operations. Furthermore, since the jungle would be an extremely physically demanding environment, Eichelberger instituted a physical hardening program which included forced marches, hand-to-hand combat, bayonet training, and obstacle courses.[30]

Eichelberger's training program also prepared the soldier to fight in the jungle at night. This was a major weakness of the Thirty-second Division at Buna, where Eichelberger had discovered that, in the twenty months before deploying to combat, this unit had had only one night training exercise.[31] Therefore, Eichelberger had his troops conduct extensive small unit night training in such operations as night raids, night attacks, night defenses, night withdrawals, and night infiltrations. To add realism to these operations and to prepare his soldiers for the noise and confusion of the battlefield, he had the artillery fire live ammunition overhead.

Eichelberger also conducted extensive day and night training in amphibious operations. He realized that all future operations would commence with an amphibious landing; therefore, he devoted a great deal of time to rehearsing this type of operation under conditions that were as realistic as possible.

Throughout 1943, as Eichelberger prepared the First Corps for battle, MacArthur conducted a series of brilliant operations which cut the Japanese line of communication to Rabaul. This enabled him to neutralize completely the Japanese forces at this location without conducting a bloody frontal assault. By January 1944, however, MacArthur had moved only 240 miles north of Buna and still had 2,240 miles to go before reaching Manila. At that pace it would take another ten years to reach the Philippines. In order to speed up the advance, MacArthur decided in April 1944 to move six hundred miles up the coast of New Guinea in a single amphibious operation. His objective was to seize the airfields and natural harbor at Hollandia. To ensure the success of this operation, MacArthur selected Eichelberger, his best field commander, to command the operation.[32]

The Hollandia task force consisted of the Twenty-fourth and Forty-first divisions (less 163rd RCT) plus supplementary support units. Each division had been vigorously trained by Eichelberger to ensure that the problems encountered at Buna were not repeated. The total command strength for this operation was 37,527 combat troops and 18,184 service troops. Eichelberger assigned Major General Frederick Irving and the Twenty-fourth Division responsibility for the Tanahmerah Bay landing, while Major General Horace Fuller was to lead the Forty-first Division ashore at Humboldt Bay. D-Day was set for 22 April. Once ashore, Eichelberger envisioned both divisions, acting like pincers, rapidly driving inland and linking up on the airfields.[33]

The key to success would be speed. Eichelberger did not want to get bogged down in a siege like that which had occurred at Buna. That type of battle always resulted in attrition and high casualties. Instead, Eichelberger expected his troops to take full advantage of surprise and move so fast that the enemy would be kept off balance and would be unable to construct a coherent defense. The Japanese should not be allowed to recover from their shock. He wanted to break through their defenses and seize the airfields before they could react.[34]

On April 22, 1944, at 0700 hours, the navy simultaneously landed two regiments of the Twenty-fourth Division at Tanahmerah Bay and two regiments of the Forty-first Division at Humboldt Bay. The loading and unloading of the landing craft and the seizure of the beachhead were conducted flawlessly.[35] As Eichelberger, with a great deal of satisfaction, later described the landings: "Our long training in amphibious assault was rewarded. The landings were classical in their precision. Down to the most minute detail of planning, everything went off as scheduled."[36]

At Humboldt Bay, the two regiments of the Forty-first Division (162nd and 186th RCTs) landed at four separate beaches. Tactical surprise was complete, and General Fuller, who came ashore at 1005 hours, rapidly pushed his forces inland.[37] Eichelberger described the tactical situation in Humboldt Bay on the morning of April 22, 1944: "The surprise of the Japanese was so great that most of them fled at once from the beach area. Breakfast bowls of rice were only half consumed, and teapots were found still boiling when our first wave landed."[38]

The situation at Tanahmerah Bay was not as good. Although the Twenty-fourth Division also achieved tactical surprise, an impenetrable swamp prevented the division from moving inland from its main landing site. However, this intelligence error did not become a major catastrophe, thanks to the drive and determination of the battalion commander at the secondary landing site.[39]

Lieutenant Colonel Thomas E. Clifford (First Battalion, Twenty-first Infantry) displayed great initiative by quickly moving his unit, without waiting for reinforcements, up a steep cliff to a trail that led toward the airfields where the division's objectives lay. The long hours of grueling

physical training paid handsome dividends as the soldiers were able to ne-
gotiate the 60-degree slope and push rapidly inland. Despite harsh jungle
terrain and constant fear of enemy contact, the physically fit unit, which
had trained in the jungle, covered six miles before sunset. That night the
battalion halted and prepared a defensive position. So highly trained was
the unit in night operations that the Japanese night attack on its positions
failed to dent the perimeter. In fact, after this unsuccessful night attack,
the Japanese made no further attempt to cut the trail behind the
battalion.[40]

The flawless execution of the landing phase completely surprised the
Japanese at both Humboldt and Tanahmerah bays. The initiative displayed by Colonel Clifford and the flexibility of the Twenty-fourth Division's staff allowed the momentum of the Tanahmerah pincer to be
sustained. The Japanese were never able to gain the initiative or recon-
struct a defense. Eichelberger later wrote that, "for the soldiers making
the pincer movement on the dromes [airfields], there was nothing for it
except slog, slog, slog. Fuller's troops [Forty-first Division] had twenty-
one miles to go; Irving's troops [Twenty-fourth Division] had only fourteen miles to go, but their going was harder. They had fourteen streams to
cross."[41] Neither terrain nor the enemy slowed the advance. The Americans relentlessly and aggressively pushed to their objectives. It took only
five days for Eichelberger's troops to seize the Japanese airfields and end
the tactical phase of the operation. General George C. Marshall described
this operation as a "model of strategical and tactical maneuver."[42]

Eichelberger did not have much of an opportunity to relax after the
Hollandia operation. Six short weeks later MacArthur sent for him to salvage a desperate tactical situation on the island of Biak.

On May 27, 1944, MacArthur landed a division on Biak with the mission of seizing three airstrips that the Japanese had constructed there.
MacArthur hoped to use these airfields to conduct bombing missions
against Japanese bases in the Philippines, only eight hundred miles away.
Since he had expected the task force to have seized and built up at least
one airfield by June 10, he had promised the Joint Chiefs of Staff that he
would support Admiral Chester W. Nimitz's invasion of Saipan, scheduled for June 15, 1944, with planes from these airfields. Unfortunately,
the Japanese were in much greater strength on the island than Mac-
Arthur's intelligence had indicated; by June 15 the invading force had
failed to secure any of the airfields. Therefore, on that date, Eichelberger
was sent in to give the invasion new life.[43]

Eichelberger solved the tactical dilemma for MacArthur in less than
one week. He had also proved conclusively that he was the nonpareil of
tacticians in the theater. As soon as he arrived on Biak, he immediately
went to the front personally to assess the situation. Drawing on his experi-

ence at Buna, Eichelberger decided not to try to seize the airfields by a frontal assault. Instead, he planned to go around the Japanese positions and occupy the high ground to their rear. When it had been executed, this plan resulted in complete victory at a minimum cost in American lives. Eichelberger later credited the Japanese with having given him the solution for cracking their defenses. He had carefully examined all their operations in World War II and believed that the Japanese tactics in Malaya would provide the method of ending the stalemate on Biak. In Malaya, each time the British forces prepared a defensive line, the Japanese enveloped it. Once the British discovered that the Japanese were in their rear, the whole defensive line collapsed, and the British withdrew to establish another, a process that was repeated down the entire peninsula. Eichelberger believed that the Japanese perimeter at Biak would break down when the Japanese found Americans in their rear. He was proved correct. [44]

Eichelberger returned to Hollandia on June 28, 1944, with his reputation as the theater's most capable field commander secure. It had taken him only five days to seize the three Japanese airfields and break the enemy's main line of defense. At a cost of four hundred American lives, forty-seven hundred Japanese had been killed. With Biak secured, MacArthur could move on to his cherished operations in the Philippines. [45]

General MacArthur, obviously impressed by Eichelberger's innovative tactics and dynamic leadership at Biak, rewarded him with command of the new Eighth Army. Because an experienced army headquarters staff that had been trained in the United States and had already functioned as a unit for several years was then en route for Hollandia, all that remained was for Eichelberger to pry his chief of staff and G-3 away from First Corps to fill comparable positions at army headquarters. On September 9 he officially took over Eighth Army—too late to be involved in the forthcoming invasion of Leyte. Not until December 26, when MacArthur declared that organized resistance had ended, did the Eighth Army assume control of all combat units on Leyte, leaving Krueger's Sixth Army free to concentrate on the forthcoming invasion of Luzon.

For Eichelberger—and especially for the men who had to endure the "bitter, exhausting, rugged fighting" in what MacArthur inadequately described as "mopping up" operations—it was Sanananda all over again. Once Sixth Army had commenced landing operations in Lingayen Gulf on January 9, 1945, public attention quickly shifted to events on Luzon despite the fact that Eighth Army between Christmas day and the end of the campaign killed more than twenty-seven thousand Japanese—over one-third of all Japanese casualties on Leyte. This was done by troops who received no public recognition, for the existence of the Eighth Army had not yet been officially announced. [46] "I do not know why," Eichelberger confided to Miss Em the day after he took over command on Leyte; "the best explanation I can think of is that *two armies* would indicate more tools than it is desired to admit."[47]

After a month of "mopping up" operations, during which it was also the responsibility of Eighth Army to prepare the units in Leyte for future operations elsewhere, Eichelberger was at last given the opportunity to show what his new command could do. From the first, MacArthur had intended to use the Eighth Army in subsidiary landings on Luzon. By the last week in January, after Sixth Army had secured its communications and had begun its final push toward Manila, he ordered Eichelberger to land one regimental combat team from the Eleventh Airborne Division at Nasugbu Bay, fifty-five miles south of Manila, to make a "reconnaissance in force." Eichelberger was to ascertain enemy strength, deployment, and intentions in the Nasugbu-Tagaytay region; if circumstances seemed promising, he could then land the entire division and contain Japanese forces in southwestern Luzon.[48] Since some of MacArthur's directives were verbal, it is difficult to know precisely what he had in mind, but he was impatient with the slow and deliberate advance of Sixth Army from the north, and it is altogether possible that he was using the rivalry between his two army commanders to produce quick military results, an established command technique that goes back at least as far as Napoleon. At any rate, nobody at Eighth Army headquarters was about to let this opportunity slip through their fingers. They had waited long enough for public recognition and for the chance to put Eighth Army on the map—particularly when the map was Luzon.

Initially Eichelberger had hoped to land in Luzon on January 29, when Eleventh Corps (commanded by Lieutenant General Charles P. Hall) hit the beaches north of Subic Bay, but when he learned that this force would soon afterward come under Krueger's control, he backed out. Hall's mission was to open Subic Bay to American shipping, cut off Japanese forces on the Bataan peninsula, and then move swiftly to join Sixth Army in advancing down the central valley to Manila. Although the operation was planned and staged by Eighth Army, Eichelberger remained on hand only until the landings had been made and Japanese strength could be determined. His plans, he wrote Miss Em the previous evening, "are a bit uncertain and are governed to an unusually large extent by the enemy. . . . I am prepared to draw back or stay depending on conditions. . . . If the resistance is very light or non-existent, I think I shall stay ashore until I have discovered whether or not the Japs have pulled out of the section where we land. . . . *I might try a fast drive to Manila.*"[49] The landings were unopposed, Hall assumed command ashore the next morning, and simultaneously control of Eleventh Corps was passed to the Sixth Army.

Eichelberger's presence was needed elsewhere. On January 31 two regiments of Major General Joseph M. Swing's Eleventh Airborne Division were scheduled to land at Nasugbu, forty-five miles southwest of Manila. Eichelberger had to be on hand to make two critical decisions: "whether or not to change the 'reconnaissance in force' into a real landing, and . . . to drop the 511th Parachute Regiment on Tagaytay Ridge."[50]

The landing caught the Japanese by surprise and was accomplished without loss. That evening Eichelberger's staff learned with delight that the latest release from GHQ had identified the Eighth Army in connection with the landings. During the next twenty-eight hours, Swing's troops advanced some nineteen miles inland, encountering growing resistance as they assaulted Japanese defenses in the mountains west of Tagaytay Ridge, which was vital terrain more than two thousand feet high. From here a concrete road led downhill to Manila. Eichelberger gave the order for Swing's third regiment to be dropped by parachute on the ridge itself, and during the night of February 3, his patrols, with help from armed guerrillas, pushed forward another eighteen miles. The next day Eichelberger reached Los Piñas, where he could observe Manila through field glasses. When "things seemed to be going a bit slow," he drove thirty miles back to Tagaytay Ridge to speed up the forward movement, and later he returned to the outskirts of Manila. "The fires in Manila were bright enough so that we did not need a flashlight. After I went to bed we started pounding the Japanese with artillery and they began to reply. It sounded as though these shells were coming in one window and out the other."

Press releases that day stated that the Eighth Army was knocking at the southern approaches. "Our gamble," he wrote, "had been successful. Four days after landing at Nasugbu we had a beachhead . . . sixty-nine miles long and five hundred yards wide." It was several days, however, before Eichelberger had specific information on the progress of Sixth Army from the north. Although General MacArthur announced on February 6 that the Japanese garrison was surrounded by converging columns and "their complete destruction is imminent," desperate resistance would continue for another four weeks, and the victory parade would have to be postponed. "It is high time for me to be getting out," Eichelberger confided to Miss Em two days later. He had had enough of so-called mopping-up operations, and it would never do for him to enter the city before the "Big Chief" had made his official entrance. Besides, the hidden objective had already been accomplished: the Eighth Army was indeed "on the map."[51]

While Eichelberger was driving on Manila he had his staff work day and night to prepare for the Eighth Army's next mission, the liberation of the central and southern Philippines. The VICTOR operations, as the campaign was known, finally provided Eichelberger with the opportunity to display his full talents as a combat commander. This time he would not be expected to correct someone else's mistake on the battlefields; instead, he would be solely responsible for every aspect of the operation's planning and execution.

MacArthur's decision to conduct the campaigns in the southern and central Philippines has been severely criticized by a number of historians. Most recently, Ronald Spector has stated that the campaign had "no strategic value whatsoever." During the course of VICTOR operations, MacArthur transferred five divisions, the Twenty-fourth, Thirty-first, Fortieth, Forty-first, and Americal, from the Sixth Army to the Eighth Army. This transfer seriously curtailed the operations of the Sixth Army on Luzon. General Krueger felt that he needed every available division in the theater to reduce General Yamashita's formidable mountain strongholds in northern Luzon, and he deeply resented the removal of every man, weapon, and division that MacArthur took from him and gave to Eichelberger.[52]

Despite the historical controversy over the strategic necessity of this campaign, there has never been any disagreement over Eichelberger's performance—it was brilliant.

As Krueger plodded forward on Luzon, the Eighth Army conducted a clinic in amphibious warfare. In a series of lightning campaigns, Eichelberger opened the San Bernardino Straits and recaptured Palawan, Panay, Zamboanga, Bohol, the Sulu Archipelago, and twenty-two other Visayan islands in the central and southern Philippines. Although the term "amphibious operations" has become synonymous with the Marine Corps, Eichelberger and his Eighth Army conducted thirty-five amphibious assaults between February 28 and April 3, 1945. Eichelberger used his meager forces (he had five divisions to Krueger's fifteen) with great skill and daring. These amphibious landings ranged in size from company- to division-level task forces, and all were successful. The coordination of these landings were complicated by the immense size of the Philippines, which measured one thousand miles from north to south. Yet Eichelberger and his efficient staff never missed a beat in the successful liberation of thirty islands in the central and southern Philippines.[53]

Eichelberger's success enhanced MacArthur's reputation as a military genius. While the bulk of his forces were tied up in the methodical advance of the Sixth Army on Luzon, Eichelberger's bold and audacious campaigns filled the headlines for MacArthur. Good publicity always brought out the best in MacArthur. On March 30, 1945, he told General Clovis Byers that Eichelberger's "progress in these Eighth Army operations was brilliant and that nothing in the history of this war would suppress what Bob [had] done with the meager forces available to him in such lightning-like strokes." On April 10, 1945, Eichelberger was summoned to a meeting with MacArthur, who stated that the operations in Palawan, Zamboanga, the Sulu Archipelago, and the Visayans had been executed "just the way he would have wanted to have done it had he been an Army commander—speed, dash, brilliance, etc." MacArthur's operations officer told Eichelberger that the "Visayan campaign would some day be considered a classic."[54]

Eichelberger relished this high praise from MacArthur. His treatment after this campaign was markedly different from what he had received after Buna. His lightninglike operations appeared even brighter when compared to the Sixth Army's operations in Luzon. A comparison was inevitable, and on April 10, 1945, MacArthur described Krueger as an "old-fashioned Army general who wants to do everything by the rules." MacArthur also confided to Eichelberger that, every time he assigned a mission to Sixth Army, its commanders protested that they needed "twice the number" of troops allocated. However, Eichelberger's Eighth Army was always innovative enough to accomplish its assigned mission with the number of troops allocated for the operation.[55]

By April 20, 1945, the only Japanese resistance left in the entire archipelago was centered in northern Luzon and in Mindanao. MacArthur strongly wanted the 95,000 Filipinos on Mindanao to be liberated from the Japanese occupation. In order to accomplish this demanding assignment, he again sent in his best—Eichelberger.

MacArthur realized that Mindanao was a difficult undertaking for two reasons: first, the size of the island, which was 36,546 square miles and the second largest in the archipelago, made it difficult to secure. Even more important, however, was the strength and disposition of the enemy garrison on Mindanao. Expecting MacArthur to commence his invasion of the Philippines with Mindanao, the 50,000 Japanese on the island had been preparing their defenses for three years.

The bulk of these forces was concentrated in Davao City, the island's largest and most important city. Envisioning an American frontal attack through Davao Gulf, the Japanese had erected strong coastal defenses along the shoreline, including a large concentration of artillery and anti-aircraft batteries. Furthermore, the entire gulf was heavily mined to prevent an amphibious landing. The Japanese had also prepared their defenses in depth, in order to prolong the campaign as much as possible. They anticipated withdrawing into the jungle, falling back from Davao into prepared defensive bunkers.[56]

General MacArthur was well aware of the strength of the Japanese fortifications on Mindanao through his intelligence system. The fighting on Luzon had also prepared him for the tenacity with which the Japanese would fight to hold onto the island. In April 1945 the campaign on Luzon had already lasted for three months, and by war's end it would still not be over. However, MacArthur was confident that Davao City could be captured in four months and the huge harbor in Davao Gulf opened soon after.

Mindanao was Eichelberger's finest hour and most brilliant campaign. He was forced to conduct this campaign with one corps, the Tenth, which was composed of only two divisions—the Twenty-fourth and the Thirty-First. However, Eichelberger devised a daring plan for overcoming the superb defenses and numerical superiority of the Japanese on Mindanao. Instead of making the frontal assault into the heavily mined Davao Gulf that the Japanese expected, he would land his troops at Illana Bay and then have the infantry march 110 miles through the jungle to take Davao City from the rear. He believed that if his troops moved quickly enough, the city could be seized before the Japanese had time to react. Success would depend on the speed and beachhead performance of the first units to land at the Illana Bay.[57]

Eichelberger's plan worked perfectly. On May 3, 1945, only fifteen days after the landing on Mindanao, Davao City was captured. Delighted by Eichelberger's success, MacArthur paid him his greatest compliment: "You run an Army in combat just like I would have done it."[58]

Eichelberger's contributions to victory in the Southwest Pacific are distinctive. At Buna he inherited a desperate situation yet quickly managed to instill a new fighting spirit and confidence in his sick and tired troops and provide dynamic and determined leadership throughout the chain of command. As one Australian historian has put it, "Eichelberger was surely one of [Field Marshal] Wavell's 'robust generals.' He accepted the order to take Buna or not come back alive. He put up with Sutherland looking over his shoulder as he prepared his attacks. But he was distressed that neither MacArthur nor Kenney visited him and that the congratulations from MacArthur were belated and begrudgingly given."[59]

Normally, for the tide of battle to be changed, some new element must be inserted—more troops, better equipment, or a change in command. There were no reinforcements to speak of even after Eichelberger had assumed command, and he never had what was needed in the way of artillery or air support. The difference therefore was Eichelberger. By his victories at Buna and Sanananda he gave MacArthur the necessary sites for airstrips vital to any further advance along the coast. Buna was the first victory won over Japanese forces fighting to hold a fortified position since the Allies first began their offensive at Guadalcanal, and Eichelberger quickly converted his unique experience into improved training methods that greatly enhanced the ability of American troops in future battles with the Japanese.

At Hollandia Eichelberger performed "a logistical miracle" by maintaining a rigorous schedule in the face of unforeseen difficulties. Equally miraculous was the quick and efficient way that Eichelberger established his forces ashore and constructed the bases and airfields necessary to support forthcoming operations at Wakde-Sarmi and Biak.

Again at Biak, Eichelberger was introduced at the eleventh hour to accelerate operations that seemed stalled. And as at Buna, he reorganized the forces, devised new tactical plans, and pumped life into a sagging offensive, so that within a week after his arrival he had captured the main objectives and the critical phase of the battle had ended. Biak then became a vital site for the construction of heavy bomber fields.

And finally, although this kind of accomplishment does not gain headlines, Eichelberger prepared Eighth Army staff for the complex and demanding operations that lay ahead. Throughout the Philippine campaign this staff demonstrated great versatility in the tempo of the operations it planned and staged, in one span of forty-four days conducting fourteen major landings and twenty-four small operations. Eichelberger freely gave the credit to his "pick and shovel boys" for the accomplishment of such marvels, but it was "the old man" himself who provided the leadership, the example, and above all the atmosphere of mutual confidence which inspired loyalty in his subordinates.

His crowning achievement was the role played by the Eighth Army in the liberation of the Philippines. In spirit he belonged among the successful exponents of blitzkrieg in his insistence upon rapid exploitation and the unexpected thrust and sustained tempo of his operations. Speed and constant pressure upon the enemy in the long run would save lives, he insisted, and his operations followed a consistent pattern—strategic and tactical surprise in the amphibious assault, quick exploitation to seize key objectives and to keep the enemy off balance, and the final mopping up. It was a new kind of war that he conducted in the Philippines, and in his skillful execution—if in no other characteristic—Eichelberger successfully articulated the concepts of the "Big Chief," whom he resembled in his particular genius more than he would probably have cared to acknowledge.[60]

Ennis C. Whitehead

Aerial Tactician

DONALD M. GOLDSTEIN

In any large war such as World War II, there are always a few brilliant and dedicated commanders who through dislike of publicity or oversight—deliberate or unintended—on the part of superiors fail to receive the plaudits of the public or the recognition merited by their performance. The Southwest Pacific theater seemed to have more than its share of such individuals, and foremost among them was Lieutenant General Ennis Clement Whitehead, U.S. Air Force serial number nine. Few air commanders accomplished as much with as little as did Whitehead. Yet his successes remain obscure and his name largely forgotten. He deserves a better fate.

Whitehead was born September 3, 1895, on a farm in Glenwood Community, a small hamlet eighteen miles northeast of Burlington and thirty-two miles southeast of Emporia, Kansas. He was the oldest of three children born to J.E. and Celia Whitehead, who had moved to Kansas from Indiana in 1850. His father was a farmer and his mother a schoolteacher.[1]

He entered grade school at the Glenwood District School, a county school near Westphalia, in 1902, where he went through the eighth grade, graduating in 1910. In 1911 he entered Burlington High School. In 1914 he matriculated at the University of Kansas, intending eventually to seek a law degree.[2]

Upon America's declaration of war against Germany on April 6, 1917, Whitehead joined the army and was sent to the officers training camp at Fort Riley, Kansas, where he volunteered for the air service. Following completion of ground school at the University of Illinois at Champagne-Urbana, Illinois, he was sent to Chanute Field, Rantoul, Illinois, to begin pilot training. On October 19 he passed the test for reserve military aviator. After a short leave, he sailed for France on November 14, 1917. When he arrived in Europe, he was ordered to the Third Aviation Instruction

Center at Issoudun to complete pursuit training. He was then sent to the gunnery school near Bordeaux. In the summer of 1918, he became a test pilot and remained one until the war ended.[3]

After the war, Whitehead was briefly assigned to Rockwell Field at San Diego before he received his discharge. He returned to Kansas University and majored in journalism. He completed his undergraduate degree in February 1920, then took a job with the *Wichita Eagle* as a reporter in order to make enough money to attend law school.[4]

But Whitehead had been bitten by the flying bug, even though he did not at first care for army life. When the time came for the decision between law school and flying, his love for flying won out. He applied for a regular commission as a first lieutenant in the air service of the U.S. Army, which was granted on September 11, 1920. Before reporting back to the military, he went to Newton, Kansas, and, on September 25, 1920, married Mary Nicholson, his college sweetheart. Thus Whitehead began a career in the military service which was to last thirty-one years.[5]

Whitehead's first assignment was March Field, California, where he was a flying instructor in dual instruction. In February 1921 he joined the First Pursuit Group at Kelly Field near San Antonio and was given command of the Ninety-fourth Pursuit Squadron. With this squadron he also returned to flying the Speed Scout, the fastest pursuit airplane developed during World War I. He now had an opportunity to lead men and at the same time to acquire administrative experience available only at the squadron level which would be of great value to him later in his career. Major Carl Spaatz, a future chief of staff of the air force, wrote Whitehead's efficiency report, rating him "superior," with high marks for leadership and administrative abilities.[6]

In the meantime, Billy Mitchell had persisted in his claim that the bomber spelled the end of sea power. Mitchell's vision of air power, rather than naval power, touched off a feud that culminated with bombing tests in Hampton Roads, Virginia, early in 1921. These involved pitting American aircraft against the captured German battleship *Ostfriesland*, which had been classified by many experts as unsinkable. Whitehead and a number of his associates were ordered to Langley Field to take part in these bombing tests. This was the first time in the history of aviation that an air group had flown to sea on a military mission. Individual planes had been sent on such military missions, but no nation had ever sent a full squadron out one hundred miles from home base and seventy miles from the nearest land for an aerial attack.

In a letter to his family Whitehead described the test: "Pursuit made the first attack. We left our base with eleven planes at 8:15 A.M. It took us one hour and fifteen minutes to reach the target. We formed our circle, and made our attack. Of course we were carrying 25 pound bombs, but we took off the smoke stacks, and the ship settled two feet after we finished.

As soon as we were through, the Martins came over with 300 pound bombs. After seventeen minutes from the time of our attack, the G1O2 [*Ostfriesland*] sunk. One 300 pound bomb hit the center and blew the ship four ways."[7]

In June 1922 the First Pursuit Group moved to Selfridge Field, Mount Clemens, Michigan, where Whitehead remained for three years. During this time he flew air missions all over the Midwest, testing and evaluating the landing facilities throughout the region.[8] While performing these functions he continued to meet other young pioneers who were to become his close associates when his career was at its zenith.

In September 1926 Whitehead and nine other pilots assembled at Kelly Field to prepare for a goodwill flight around South America. After three months of intensive training, they began the twenty-four-thousand-mile journey on December 21. The five ships flew from San Antonio down the east coast of Mexico to Puerto, then over to Salina Cruz before proceeding down the west coast of Central America to Panama. From Panama the flight continued southward, crossing the Andes through a pass about five hundred miles south of Santiago, Chile, before circling back up the east coast of South America, branching off at the Windward and Leeward Islands to Trinidad in the British West Indies. From the West Indies the planes passed over Puerto Rico, Haiti, and Cuba, then followed the East Coast of the United States to Washington, D.C.[9]

The first half of the trip was accomplished smoothly. In Buenos Aires, however, the planes took off for a fifteen-mile flight to obtain servicing at the local Argentine army airfield. Just as the five airplanes were about to descend, the airplane *New York*, flown by Whitehead and flight commander Major Herbert A. Dargue, collided with *Detroit*, flown by Lieutenants Clinton F. Woolsey and Lieutenant John W. Benton. In a spectacular collision, the two planes began to fall with their wings intertwined. At about 800 feet, the two fell apart. Whitehead and Dargue, wearing parachutes, jumped to safety, but Woolsey and Benton were not wearing theirs (parachutes were optional) and were killed. Whitehead suffered a slightly sprained ankle; Dargue was not injured. Whitehead vividly described the accident in a letter to his wife:

I was falling head down and spinning a bit in the air. I had my hand on the ripcord, but the New York had made a turn of her spin and it seemed to me that if I pulled the ripcord that my descent and forward speed would be checked and the New York might hit me. I waited until the New York turned away from me in her spin and jerked the ripcord, which by the way I lost much to my disgust. The parachute functioned perfectly and I was snapped from a head down to a horizontal position rather sharply. . . . As soon as I landed I got free of my chute and went to the planes. I knew that Woolsey and Benton were dead for I had watched the air carefully during my descent and knew that no other parachutes were out.[10]

The tragic accident did not stop the flight. Whitehead took a boat to Panama, picked up a spare plane, and met the other three planes at Maracay airfield in Venezuela. The flight then continued without mishap, and the four planes arrived at Bolling Field on May 2, 1927, completing the twenty-four-thousand-mile flight. [11]

The early years of Whitehead's air service career were filled with such memorable events. Another took place on February 20, 1930, when Whitehead, Major Jacob E. Fickel, First Lieutenant Albert F. Hegenberger (hero of a recent flight from San Francisco to Hawaii), and radio operator Staff Sergeant Kenneth D. Wilson took off from Miami for a nonstop flight to Panama, a distance of 1,140 miles. The flight began at 6:10 A.M. EST and ended at 5:30 P.M. EST. The men flew in a Ford C-9 airplane equipped with three Wright J-6 motors. Four extra gas tanks, each with a capacity of 110 gallons, were installed in the fuselage, making the plane able to hold as much as 740 gallons of gas. Special radio equipment was furnished by the Pan American Airways and the American Fruit Company, so that the pilots could contact these agencies' radio stations during the trip. The trip went off so smoothly that the plane arrived in Panama unexpectedly and undetected by the U.S. coastal defense, thereby graphically illustrating the weakness of American detection devices. [12]

In July 1930 Whitehead was assigned to the Air Corps Tactical School at Langley Field. He was promoted to captain during this tour and graduated in June 1931. Rejoining the First Pursuit Group at Selfridge Field, he received his second command, the Thirty-sixth Pursuit Squadron. [13]

Whitehead and his family (now consisting of his wife, his daughter Margaret, and his young son Ennis, Junior, who was born in 1926) left Selfridge Field for Albrook Field, Panama Canal Zone, in November 1932. Assigned to the Sixteenth Pursuit Group, Whitehead had ample opportunity to apply his extensive background in aircraft testing and in materiel, maintenance, and logistics. He also served as post intelligence officer, an experience that was to prove valuable later in his career. [14]

In 1934 Whitehead returned to the United States. Following three months with the Twentieth Pursuit Group at Barksdale Field near Shreveport, Louisiana, he was transferred to the newly formed General Headquarters Air Force at Langley Field. Here Whitehead spent less than one year in the post operations division. While at Langley he was promoted to major and was sent to the Command and General Staff School of the Army at Fort Leavenworth, Kansas. Upon graduation in June 1938, Whitehead was assigned in Washington, D.C., to the War Department General Staff in the G-2 (Intelligence) Division. Specifically, he was placed in charge of the European division of G-2, where he closely followed the rise of Hitler. [15]

After his promotion to lieutenant colonel in December 1940, Whitehead renewed his attempts to leave his desk position and return to the air. His wish was granted in February 1941, when he was transferred to Luke Field near Phoenix, Arizona, to train pilots. They would soon be needed: on December 7, 1941, the Japanese attacked Pearl Harbor and ushered the United States into war. [16]

During the first eight months of the war, the triumphant Japanese swept down through China and across Thailand. They marched through Malaya and Burma and captured what had once been called the impregnable port of Singapore. They took the Philippines and lost no time in adding Sumatra, Java, Borneo, and Celebes to the imperial realm of Hirohito. They occupied New Britain, New Ireland, and the small group of islands opposite the Dutch West Indies, and when they took the Solomons, only New Guinea stood between them and the projected conquest of Australia.

Their tactics were relatively simple. As they pushed south against token opposition, they built airfields so that the bomb line could be extended and targets in the next projected area of attack could be saturated by their air arm. In the early days, when the Japanese were not making mistakes, no land or sea force moved anywhere until it was assured of effective air cover. Maximum harmony existed between the army, navy, and air force. Thus using their air power to the maximum extent possible against token resistance from the Allies, the Japanese took their objectives with a high degree of precision and little expenditure of human life. There were no massive attacks with men marching shoulder to shoulder. There was no front line of the World War I pattern. Instead, the Japanese fought as an invisible enemy. They hid behind retiring British columns, blocked roads, and staged ambushes. When the battle grew too hot, they disappeared into the jungle. The simplicity of the Japanese tactics, more than anything else, made them a formidable foe. [17]

The Allies were unprepared for war, as witness the devastating attack on Pearl Harbor and the subsequent Allied defeats throughout Asia. Against the type of tactics employed by the Japanese they were doubly unprepared. Their errors were initially to underestimate the capabilities of the Japanese armed forces and then, following the early Japanese victories, to overestimate them. Thus the myth of the invincible Japanese superman was born and played an important role in Japan's early victories. This myth was nurtured by Japanese propaganda and by credulous war correspondents who wrote about the enemy's invincibility.

As the supposedly invincible Japanese drew closer and closer to Australia, there was a change in the Allied high command. On April 18, 1942, General Douglas MacArthur formally became supreme Allied commander in the Southwest Pacific area, which included Australia, the Philippines, and New Guinea. Admiral Chester Nimitz was given responsibility for the rest of the Pacific. He was made commander in chief of the Pacific area, with headquarters at Pearl Harbor. To keep the division of control simple, Admiral Nimitz broke his vast command into three sectors—the North, the central, and the South Pacific areas.[18] By agreement between MacArthur and Nimitz, the operational dividing line between SWPA and South Pacific air units was set on the east at the 159th meridian and south from the equator.[19]

As the Japanese pushed further south toward New Guinea and Australia, MacArthur in Australia began to consolidate the few forces he had. The Japanese, after securing their flank with a victory in Tulagi, in the south Solomons, paused in northern New Guinea to regroup. Their several options included an attack on Hawaii or the Aleutians or consolidation of their defenses and waiting for the Allies to move against them. But after some deliberation they realized that their flank was exposed to the Allied forces in Australia and New Zealand. They reasoned that, in order to protect what they had won, they would have to capture both Australia and New Zealand. With this in mind, early in May 1942 a Japanese fleet sailed for New Guinea with a force of two aircraft carriers, seven cruisers, seventeen destroyers, two submarines, one submarine tender, and twenty-one troop transports. Their objective appeared to be Port Moresby, the gateway to Australia. American naval and air forces engaged the huge Japanese convoy from May 7 through May 9, 1942, in the famous Battle of the Coral Sea. In this engagement the Japanese lost 1 carrier, 4 cruisers, 2 destroyers, 4 gunboats, 4 transports, and 100 planes. American losses were the carrier *Lexington*, 1 destroyer, 1 tanker, and 17 aircraft. When the battle concluded, it became obvious that the Japanese had been soundly defeated.[20]

The Coral Sea debacle did not cause the Japanese to relinquish their plans for capturing more territory in the Pacific. They next sought to extend their bases further eastward by trying to seize Midway Island. A feint at the Aleutian Island chain, near the coast of Alaska, did not deceive the U.S. naval command, and American naval forces and carrier planes were in a position to deal the Japanese the most lethal blow that they had received in the Pacific to that date. Japanese losses included four carriers, two cruisers, three destroyers and one transport. The United States lost the carrier *Yorktown*, one cruiser, and one destroyer.[21]

The Coral Sea and Midway battles in May and June 1942 were significant for four reasons. First, they were the first major defeats for the Japanese in World War II and discredited the thesis of Japanese invincibility. Second, they proved the value and effect of air power, even though it was naval air power, against ships out at sea. Third, the two victories slowed the Japanese offense, which had been irresistible for almost six months, to a temporary standstill. Finally, the immediate threat to Australia was effectively stymied.

Whitehead left San Francisco for Australia early in July 1942. He arrived in Australia on the eleventh and reported to General MacArthur's

SWPA headquarters at Melbourne the next day. The two men hit it off immediately, and a deep and lasting friendship quickly developed.[22]

Shortly thereafter, Whitehead was sent to Port Moresby. General MacArthur had shaken up his command in an effort to stem the tide of the Japanese advance, assigning Major General George C. Kenney to lead the Allied air forces in the SWPA. Kenney had inherited a command of broken and incomplete elements that had been formed under great pressure during the first eight months of the war. Its mission had never been defined, and the responsibilities of each component were not clear. Kenney had reorganized the American fighter and bomber units into the Fifth Air Force and broke up the Australian and other Allied components into separate but equal units. Under the new reorganization, the Royal Australian Air Force was assigned the mission of the defense of Australia, while the U.S. Fifth Air Force was given the offensive mission of regaining New Guinea. Kenney therefore wore two hats: he was both commander of Allied Air Forces SWPA and commander of the Fifth Air Force.[23]

Whitehead had been at Port Moresby for only two days when he was designated commander of Allied Air Forces in New Guinea. Two months later, after General Kenney created the Fifth Air Force, Whitehead became deputy commander of the Fifth Air Force and commanding general of the advanced echelon of the Fifth Air Force.[24]

Whitehead surmised that, if his forces were to be effective in the implementation of Allied strategy, he would need more airfields so that there would be more room for the concentration of all the available Allied air strength in SWPA. Forward airfields on New Guinea were necessary because pilots from Australia, staging through Port Moresby for targets in Japanese-held territory, flew missions which took them from thirty-six to forty-eight hours away from their home base, so that crews had to fly as much as eighteen hours to drop a load of bombs. Adding to the problem, the Japanese usually met them over the target with swarms of fighters. Under the above-described adverse conditions, the efficiency of both planes and crew suffered. Such circumstances pointed to the necessity of obtaining air bases, not merely staging areas, on the north coast of Papau. Many of the same unfavorable conditions impelled the Japanese to seek an air base on the northeast coast of Papua. Thus when the Japanese landed at Buna on July 21, 1942, they proceeded immediately to build airstrips there.[25]

Whitehead devoted much of his time during his first months in New Guinea to obtaining a substantial increase in engineer troops and equipment for construction of the additional airdromes, operating facilities, and housing. He pushed engineering construction efforts with unlimited energy, and he personally selected sites and visited work camps on almost a daily basis.[26]

For the conquest of Papua and New Guinea, the strength of American air forces in New Guinea and Australia was meager, consisting of three bombardment groups, three fighter groups, and two partly equipped troop carrier squadrons. While military tables of equipment and organization called for a fighter group to consist of four squadrons, each with fifteen aircraft, and a bomber group of four squadrons, each with twelve aircraft, Whitehead's fighter squadrons were lucky to have eight operational aircraft and his bomber squadrons, six. Thus SWPA air forces were constantly understrength.[27]

The Royal Australian Air Force had thirty squadrons of assorted aircraft, but twenty-seven of them were outmoded. The Australians had to turn primarily to the United States for new aircraft. The Dutch Air Forces consisted of one B-25 squadron. Two American medium bombardment squadrons had been detached to help the South Pacific forces' invasion of Guadalcanal and the rest of the Solomon Islands operation. Also supporting the Guadalcanal and Solomon Islands campaign, which was top priority in the Pacific under the ELKTON plan, which envisioned the reconquest of New Britain, was one bombardment group which belonged to SWPA. The bombers in this group were a great help to the South Pacific forces but were badly needed by General MacArthur. The forces under Whitehead were just a fraction of those under the command of the Fifth Air Force. Besides the above-mentioned American aircraft there were two squadrons of the Thirty-fifth U.S. Fighter Group at Port Moresby. In addition, at Port Moresby there was one squadron of the Twenty-second Medium Bombardment Group equipped with Martin B-26s and two depleted squadrons of the Third Attack Group equipped with A-20s. The third squadron of the attack group had lost its last dive-bomber a few days before Whitehead reported to Australia. Whitehead thus had about seventy bombers to work with.[28]

A shortage of aircraft and equipment was not the only problem that Whitehead faced. Upon taking command of the Allied air effort in New Guinea, he found that the organization, operation, and morale of his units left much to be desired. A lack of confidence, pride, leadership, and direction by the group and squadron commanders had permeated to the lower echelons of the command. Whitehead acted quickly to remedy these problems.[29]

Whitehead had little time to forge an effective air weapon, as the situation was grave. Despite constant harassment from the air, the Japanese continued to push south. Within two months they were through the gap of the Owen Stanley Range and only thirty miles from Port Moresby. Whitehead's bombers attacked their supply lines, but they kept advancing. It soon became a case of survival. The Japanese, fighting for every mile, edged closer and closer to Port Moresby, but finally heavy bombing

of the enemy supply lines and stiff ground resistance by Allied forces began to pay off, and the enemy was halted approximately eighteen miles
from its goal.[30]

By November 2, 1942, Allied forces were able to push the Japanese
back across the Owen Stanley Mountains, shattering forever the myth of
Japanese invincibility. Later that month, Japanese forces at Buna, Gona,
and Sanananda were enveloped.

Although the enemy, with their backs to the wall, fought valiantly,
the constant bombing and strafing by Whitehead's airplanes and the pressure of Allied ground troops were too much for the starving adversary to
overcome. Gona fell on December 9, and Buna and Sanananda on January
3, 1943.[31]

But the Japanese did not give up. They realized that if they were to retain even a foothold in eastern New Guinea and Papua, it was imperative
that they strengthen their bases at Lae and Salamaua. Because these bases
lay on MacArthur's left flank and were the key to New Guinea, they also
perceived that their capture was essential to the Allied long-range strategy, and as long as they held them they could keep the Allies from advancing against their positions in the rest of the SWPA. Therefore, on
January 6, 7, and 8 in 1943, they sent several small convoys to reinforce
Lae. Although they lost a few transports, the Japanese managed to land
troops and supplies.[32] This encouraged them to send a bigger convoy in
March. Kenney directed Whitehead to intercept, and Whitehead moved
swiftly. He determined that he would strike the convoy as soon as his air
arm could reach it. When the convoy came within the range of his low-level
B-25 bombers and their fighter escorts, he planned to hit it with all the
heavy and medium bombers in his command. From the middle of February, he kept the Kavieng Harbor and its vicinity under surveillance to gain
advance knowledge of the gathering of the convoy and subsequently to
discover whether the route to Lae and Salamaua was to be south or north
of New Britain. In addition, he had the Fifth Bomber Command practice
coordinated attacks and maneuvers again and again.

An American freighter, stranded near Port Moresby, was used as a
practice target. Whitehead's rehearsals employed almost every type of
bombardment aircraft in the Allied inventory. B-25s approached the practice target at high speeds, changing their altitude rapidly and practicing
violent evasive action at full throttle until they had descended to an altitude of approximately five hundred feet. About fifteen hundred yards
from the target they approached in pairs, one plane attacking the vessel
from its head to its stern and the other plane strafing the vessel at a 90-
degree angle. Australian flyers also participated in these complicated
dress rehearsals, using the Beaufighter, a twin-engine, two-man crew aircraft with tremendous firing power. It carried four cannons in the nose
and six machine guns on the wings.[33]

On March 1 a reconnaissance report was flashed to Whitehead's head-quarters that a radar-equipped B-24 had sighted a large convoy heading west from Kavieng. With this information, Whitehead could predict the route of the convoy. It appeared to be heading on a course which would carry it along the north coast of New Britain to the Vitiaz Straits and then south to Lae. Whitehead alerted his heavy bombers for the strike. He ordered the Fifth Bomber Command to keep the convoy under constant surveillance. On March 2, the convoy was sighted through broken clouds. Twice during the day bombers of the Fifth Bomber Command attacked and hit several ships, but the convoy continued. The question in White-head's mind was: would the convoy, after the initial Allied air attacks, attempt to fulfill its original mission of reinforcing Lae and Salamaua, or would it give up this mission and disperse?[34]

At daybreak on March 3, the answer came from the trailing aircraft: "Convoy heading south through the Vitiaz Straits [toward Lae]—weather over target clear and unlimited." This information was what Whitehead had been waiting and hoping for. Now the many hours of planning and training could pay off—and pay off they did! The entire Fifth Air Force, accompanied by a squadron of Australian Beaufighters, headed for the enemy. B-17s and B-24s struck, just preceding a low-level attack by B-25s. While Beaufighters and A-20s strafed the Japanese vessels, the fighter escort engaged a swarm of Zeros that arose in defense. The attack annihilated the convoy, and not one man in the Japanese division being transported by the convoy reached Lae or Salamaua.[35]

The Japanese defeat in the Bismarck Sea, which MacArthur later called the decisive aerial engagement in his theater of war, so discouraged the enemy that they made no further attempt to run supplies into the Lae area. In three days Whitehead's flyers had cut off the enemy's supply line to the New Guinea area, making their collapse in this sector only a matter of time.

Of perhaps equal importance with the destruction of the enemy supply line was the successful employment of new Allied aerial tactics. The Bismarck Sea victory was made possible by careful preparation and an accurate evaluation of intelligence. MacArthur emphasized these two points in a cable to the men of the Fifth Air Force on March 11, 1943, declaring that success was due to "the complete anticipatory diagnosis of enemy plans and intentions and careful preparation for and exact execution of coordinated medium and low-altitude bombing."[36]

The carefully rehearsed tactics would probably not have been possible without the remarkable technological developments accomplished within the theater—the A-20 with its skip bombing, the B-25L with its stepped-up firepower, and a new fuse, the M-106, which had been modified for naval attack in New Guinea only twenty-four hours before the battle.

Statistics emphasized the magnitude of the victory. There were four hundred sorties connected with the Bismarck Sea. A total of 5,711 bombs were dropped on the ships of the convoy. Figures on the number of Japanese aircraft shot down and the number of ships in the convoy varied. First reports indicated that twenty-two ships were sunk. This was the number which the press and news media used, but after the war, interrogation reports, diaries, and confiscated Japanese documents indicated that there had been only sixteen ships in the convoy and that all had been sunk. The Joint Army-Navy Assessment Committee, appointed by the War Department, concluded that there had been a total of sixteen vessels in the convoy and that only twelve had been sunk.[37]

The number of ships actually destroyed will probably never be known. The Japanese kept their records on four-by-five sheets of tissue paper. Many of these records, not being very durable, were destroyed or ruined. Regardless of which figures are accepted, it was a great triumph for the Allied forces, won by concentrating virtually all available air power against a single enemy objective. It would have been difficult to carry out the attack if the Japanese had sent out other convoys at the same time or if they had immediately renewed their attempt to resupply their forces in New Guinea. Having access to the intelligence information on the movement of the convoy and knowing approximately where and when the ships were going was definitely a great advantage.[38]

It certainly could not be assumed that the Allied positions in New Guinea were secure. In fact, there was a need to guard against the overconfidence engendered by the tremendous upsurge in Allied morale following the Bismarck Sea victory. According to Marlin Spencer, Associated Press news correspondent, both MacArthur and Kenney were aware of the danger of overoptimism. Spencer paraphrased MacArthur's views given out at a press conference as follows: "We are waging a holding war in this area. Nothing more. We have hardly enough even to do that. The Japs at Lae are punch drunk but we don't have sufficient troops or equipment to deal the knock out blow."[39]

Nevertheless, the Allies had much to be thankful for. The bleak days of early 1942 were a thing of the past. The Allies in Australia were hardly safe, but the threat to Port Moresby and Australia itself was far more remote than it had been in February.

In summary, the reasons for the Allied success during the first six months of Ennis Whitehead's command included the reorganization of the SWPA command; excellent leadership by MacArthur, Kenney, and Whitehead; over-extension by the Japanese of their lines of communications, supply, and operations. All of these elements made important contributions to Allied success. However, in the final analysis, the ingenuity and unorthodox methods used by the Fifth Air Force enabled it to get the job done in spite of the shortage of men and aircraft.

One such example of the ingenuity used by Whitehead and his men was the introduction of skip bombing. In skip bombing the plane dived close to the water and released the bomb so that it would bounce off the water and into the side of the enemy ship, creating damage with as great an effect as a torpedo. Skip bombing involved the same principle as the skipping of a stone across the surface of a small lake or pond. Major William Benn, former aide to General Kenney, introduced the tactic of skip bombing in the SWPA. Whitehead quickly saw its value. By the middle of 1943 most B-17s and B-25s specialized in the skip bombing method, and torpedo training was discontinued in the Fifth Air Force. Skip bombing played an important part in the Battle of the Bismarck Sea.[40]

Another example of ingenuity which helped the Fifth Air Force accomplish its mission was the parafrag bomb, a twenty-pound bomb with a parachute attachment. The pilot dropped it from low altitudes, and in the few seconds that it took for the bomb to reach the target, the aircraft was flown out of the range of the bomb fragments. Because the bomb was usually released at low altitudes, it was fairly accurate. Among all the various types of bombs used by the Allies, the Japanese feared the parafrag the most because they had no defense against it. They could not shoot up at the parachute because that would bring the bomb down faster on their heads, and if they exposed themselves by running away, skilled Allied snipers who were using aircraft deploying parafrag bombs for close air support would pick them off.[41]

A third innovation involved the placing of additional firepower on each bomber aircraft. This became necessary because the Japanese in New Guinea concentrated their air defense weapons in constricted zones. The heavy firepower of these defenses made them tough to penetrate. If Allied bombers were ever going to be successful in cracking them, they would need additional firepower. In order to rectify this deficiency, the men of the Fifth Air Force's advanced echelon, with the consent of Whitehead and under the direction of Lieutenant Colonel Paul I. Gunn, experimented with the installation of additional guns in each bomber's nose. Since only local Australian materials were available, it was necessary to fabricate each installation by hand. After several experiments and extensive combat tests, eight fixed, forward-firing, fifty-caliber machine guns were established as standard equipment. They proved so efficient and effective that by the first part of 1943 two groups of B-25s had been fully equipped and were operating against Japanese targets at minimum- instead of medium-altitude missions. By the middle of 1943 production models with this equipment were arriving directly from the United States—made in accordance with the specifications developed in the SWPA.[42]

A fourth major innovation by the airmen of the SWPA was an increase in the range of all aircraft assigned the Fifth Air Force. Although the increase of firepower on strafer-type airplanes had given the Allies a strong weapon against Japanese airstrips, ground installations, and shipping, their range was still limited. Beginning with their retreat in New Guinea, the Japanese, as the Allied strikes became more effective, pulled their forward bases back beyond what they considered the range of Allied aircraft. This countermeasure in turn required that the Fifth Air Force either establish new forward bases or extend the range of its weapons. The former solution obviously was not easy to achieve; the second solution, with a little resourcefulness, was.

Additional gasoline tanks were installed on all aircraft. This installation on the B-25s eventually gave them a combat radius of from 720 to 750 nautical miles. Fighter ranges from points of takeoff were increased to more than 700 nautical miles; heavy bomber formations flew missions of from 860 to 1,020 nautical miles; and night bombers and reconnaissance planes continually flew fourteen- to sixteen-hour missions. Thus, with the added fuel capacity, it became possible to provide fighter-escorted strikes to places where the enemy had felt secure.[43]

Other new methods employed by Whitehead's men included the use of heavy bombers for low-level attacks on pinpoint targets, the placing of high air-burst phosphorus bombs over airfields to burn enemy aircraft and personnel on the airstrip, and finally the addition of eighty millimeter cannons on heavy bomber aircraft, making them almost like deadly flying buzz saws.[44]

Whitehead had created an effective air weapon, and the results were obvious. By the close of the Papau campaign, General MacArthur had become loud in his praise of air power: "The continuous, calculated application of air power with its adaptability, range and capacity of its transport in an effective combination with ground forces represents a change in my concept of warfare. Air power has proved its value and the slow costly island by island advance may no longer be necessary."[45]

In January 1943 Allied strategy for the next stage in the Pacific came up for consideration. General George C. Marshall, U.S. Army chief of staff, urged implementation of tasks 2 and 3 of the ELKTON plan. Task 2 called for the capture of all of New Guinea and task 3 the seizure of Rabaul. This set off a debate among the planners of the Joint Chiefs of Staff which raged for four months. The major issue revolved about who should command the forces involved in the task 2 and task 3 operations. Under ELKTON the command of forces for these two tasks was assigned to MacArthur, in whose area the operation in both New Guinea and Rabaul lay. But to Admiral Ernest King, chief of naval operations, control of the Pacific Fleet and command were indivisible. He believed that, if MacArthur controlled operations, the strategic flexibility of movement afforded by the fleet would be jeopardized. MacArthur's planners countered with the arguments that their air and ground forces were as flexible as the navy and that all military forces in the area should be under one commander.[46]

Despite the argument, the Allied Combined Chiefs of Staff gave MacArthur a green light to continue his planned capture of Rabaul as outlined in the original ELKTON plan. The Joint Chiefs of Staff, meeting at Casablanca with other Allied leaders in July 1943, confidently predicted that Rabaul would fall to MacArthur's forces by late 1943. But in March 1943, upon receipt of MacArthur's plan for such an operation, it became apparent to the Joint Chiefs that, without sizable reinforcements, he could not possibly take Rabaul in 1943.

Because the war in Europe took priority, reinforcements for the Pacific were not available. As a result, a less ambitious plan was substituted. Given the code name CARTWHEEL it called for an advance in 1943 to Bougainville by Admiral Halsey and to western New Britain by MacArthur. Strategic direction of both advances was assigned to MacArthur; however, Nimitz, as commander of South Pacific forces, was given control of all naval forces participating in the plan. The capture of Rabaul was assigned as the ultimate objective of both commands.

Specifically, the plan ordered MacArthur to move his forces up the coast of New Guinea through New Georgia and the Huon Peninsula, so that the Fifth Air Force would be in better position for neutralizing Japanese airfields at Rabaul, Kavieng, Baka, and Buin. CARTWHEEL next called for the occupation of Bougainville by South Pacific forces, with SWPA forces simultaneously landing on Cape Gloucester and Arawe in New Britain. After the capture of Gloucester and Arawe, a landing at Gasmata and another at Talaud would complete the preparation for a joint offensive by both South Pacific and SWPA forces against Rabaul. The timetable foresaw the completion of these operations by October 31, 1943.[47]

For future planning, MacArthur desired the consolidation of both SWPA and South Pacific forces for a series of moves along the coast of New Guinea to the Philippines and then ultimately to Japan. However, the navy had other ideas. It wanted a direct advance across the central Pacific through the Marshall and Gilbert islands toward Guam and into Japan.[48]

While the navy and army were arguing over whether to take the central route from the Marshalls to the Carolines to Guam and Japan or the route from New Guinea through the Philippines to Japan, MacArthur went on the offensive in New Guinea. Meanwhile, the South Pacific forces, after winning the Solomons in late 1943, began their advance toward the Carolines and Marshalls. After several months of bickering, both sides agreed that the argument would wait until the bomb line had been extended and both forces were closer to Japan.[49]

Although the strategic planning for the New Guinea campaign was to be performed by Allied general headquarters in Australia, the man who developed the tactical air aspects of the plan was Ennis C. Whitehead. "Ennis the Menace," as he was affectionately called, would be the guiding force behind the success of the Allied air forces in the New Guinea campaign. He brought great imagination and energy to the task, planning major operations at Rabaul, Wewak, and Gloucester. Without exception the men who served with Whitehead in the Pacific and whom I interviewed claim that Whitehead was the dynamic and driving force that inspired his officers and men to great efforts.[50]

Whitehead's tactics to extend the bomb line were simple. Using his air reconnaissance and concentrating his air power on individual targets rather than spreading his forces thin over many targets, he would first gain air superiority in a given area, then isolate the enemy in this area on both land and sea by bombing and cutting him off from supplies and reinforcements, and finally blast his ground position with heavy and medium bombers. He was to use these tactics repeatedly at such places as Rabaul, Wewak, Gloucester, and Saidor.[51]

The Fifth Air Force began its extension of the bomb line by reassigning its First Task Force to Dobodura, a small hamlet just over the Owen Stanley Range from Port Moresby. It was this task force's primary job to construct seven all-weather airfields so that operations against Rabaul and other Japanese air bases could begin as soon as possible. To protect his new major base at Dobodura from an offshore attack and to obtain fighter bases near Rabaul, surprise landings were made by Allied forces on Woodlark and Kiriwana on June 22 and 23, 1943. After their capture, Whitehead immediately directed that airfields be established on these islands.[52]

Development of the bases at Dobodura gave Whitehead's air units the capability of operating against the sea and air bases at Rabaul without the prohibitive restrictions of weather and the formidable Owen Stanley Mountains. Strategically, it was one of the most important supporting actions of the war because of the assistance which it rendered the Solomon Islands and central Pacific campaigns in support of the ELKTON plan. Rabaul now had to contend with SWPA and South Pacific air raids as well as continuing navy attacks. An all-out effort against Rabaul was planned and executed from Dobodura. The devastating effects of this effort were best demonstrated by a Fifth Bomber Command raid which took place on October 12, 1943. On this date, 87 B-24s, 114 B-25s and 135 P-38s expended 350 tons of bombs and 250,000 rounds of ammunition to destroy 34,000 tons of Japanese shipping and 126 enemy aircraft. This was strategic bombing at its best. Additional sorties were flown on November 19, 23, and 25. The attacks from Dobodura made the Japanese sea and air bases at Rabaul so untenable that the enemy was never again able to use Rabaul as a major threat against the Allied advance up the New Guinea coast. From the results of these air and naval attacks, the Allied Supreme Command decided not to attempt to capture Rabaul, which was almost impregnable, but to isolate the base by the use of aerial bombardment. This decision was to prove fruitful, and at the end of the war 100,000 Japanese from Rabaul surrendered to the Allies almost without firing a shot.[53]

In the meantime, because of the great distance to Wewak from Allied bases in New Guinea, Allied fighters could not escort their bombers to this island. Consequently, when the bombers did attack this Japanese stronghold, they experienced heavy losses. The enemy, grasping the Allied predicament, began to use this base as a sanctuary.

In early July, desiring to destroy Wewak, to increase pressure on other enemy bases further to the west, and to help furnish air support for operations designed to capture Lae, Salamaua, and Finschhafen, Whitehead established the second of his task forces, the 309th Bomber Wing, at Nadzab. Australian and American airborne infantry had been flown into this area in a well conducted air drop by Whitehead's troop carrier forces and had taken this town a week before. From Nadzab this same airborne force captured by air envelopment Marilinan in the Markham Valley.[54]

With the capture of Marilinan, which was forty miles southwest of Lae and Salamaua, Allied aircraft were able to refuel there when returning to Dobodura from flights over Wewak. Bombers flying to Wewak now had the protection of fighter escorts, and Wewak was no longer a Japanese sanctuary.

When Whitehead's bomber force had fighter protection at Marilinan, he planned an all-out attack against the Japanese sanctuary at Wewak. Using his reconnaissance aircraft, he discovered that the Japanese were massing the greatest force of planes that they had ever assembled anywhere in the Wewak area.

After careful and comprehensive planning, on August 17, 1943, two and one-half groups of Allied B-25s, covered by fighter-bombers and fighter escort, bombed and strafed the Japanese airfields at Wewak. The attack was complete and devastating. The enemy was caught by surprise, with many of its planes lined up wing tip to wing tip on the runways. As a result of this attack and a repeat attack the next day, more than 200 Japanese aircraft were destroyed, 184 on the ground and 31 in combat. The cost to the Allies was six bombers. Wewak was never a serious threat to the Allies again.

With Wewak neutralized, the Allies decided, as they had done for Rabaul, to bypass this enemy stronghold and keep it isolated by air interdiction rather than to attempt to occupy it. However, two more air bases were needed to secure the right flank of eastern New Guinea. They were Cape Gloucester on New Guinea and Saidor on New Britain.[55]

The planning by General MacArthur's staff for the Cape Gloucester operation began in September. Whitehead was ordered by Kenney on

Whitehead's B-25s on a mission (note bombs under wing); *below*, MacArthur confers with Whitehead, New Guinea, 1943. U.S. Air Force photos.

September 7 to coordinate his air plan with naval forces of the South Pacific area under the command of Admiral Barbey. Despite some friction between Barbey and Brigadier General Frederic H. Smith, Whitehead's task force commander, a plan was worked out for a joint attack by both commands on Cape Gloucester.

As the war progressed, Whitehead was to apply the concept of preparation used in the Gloucester invasion for other amphibious operations. For this reason, an analysis of this operation in more depth is in order. The Cape Gloucester operation, above all, demonstrated Whitehead's understanding of tactical fundamentals.

Whitehead began the operation by intensifying his attacks on the target with night and day missions one week before the invasion. In addition, when the weather permitted, he had photoreconnaissance carried out daily to assess bomb damage and to pinpoint new targets. Through careful planning with the navy and the use of coordinated sea patrols, the Cape Gloucester area was sealed off from Japanese reinforcement and resupply. Naval gunfire and air-supported attacks during the assault itself were coordinated and conducted subsequent to the landing. Air response to ground requests for support was timely and even included low-level bombing by B-17s against enemy redoubts and dugouts. By the time the Allied troops landed, the Japanese garrison was worn out and starving. Its artillery, both field and antiaircraft, had been almost completely destroyed. Many of the prisoners taken were in a state of shock and exhaustion.[56]

After the capture of Gloucester, only one more area was needed on the Allied left flank to complete the disposition of the Allied forces in New Guinea. On January 2, 1944, after a short but thorough air preparation and well-coordinated prelanding strafing and bombing of every possible enemy position, Allied troops by amphibious assault invaded Saidor. They encountered little opposition, and after obtaining control, the Allied forces quickly restored the airfield to operative condition. With the capture of Saidor, Allied positions in eastern New Guinea were secure. It was nevertheless a long way to the Philippines, and Whitehead had to obtain other bases if he hoped to extend his bombing so that the Philippines could be recovered.[57]

Since their main bases at Wewak and Rabaul had been virtually destroyed by Allied aircraft, in February 1944 the Japanese began to concentrate their air forces at Hollandia in Dutch New Guinea. In a carefully planned operation between March 30 and April 3, 1944, Whitehead personally directed an attack by the Fifth Bomber Command on the three Japanese airstrips at Hollandia. When the smoke cleared, Whitehead's airmen had destroyed 288 Japanese aircraft on the ground and 25 in air combat. Whitehead employed the same tactics at Hollandia that he had used to neutralize Wewak, Rabaul, and Gloucester. Excellent reconnaissance and the coordination of heavy, medium, and light bombers with the aid of long-range fighters dealt the Japanese another great setback. From the standpoint of the bombs and ammunition expended, the raid on Hollandia was one of the heaviest raids of the war in the Pacific. The destruction of Hollandia cleared the way for Allied naval supremacy up through the waters off Dutch New Guinea.[58]

On April 22 Allied amphibious forces made a five-hundred-mile leap from eastern New Guinea to Hollandia and Aitape, bypassing Wewak. Because of the heavy bombing by the Fifth Air Force and the dispersion of the Japanese defending forces, they encountered little resistance.

With the fall of Hollandia in April 1944, most of New Guinea was now in Allied hands, but the battle to extend the bomb line continued. Much to Whitehead's dismay, he found out that Hollandia itself was a mud hole and a poor prospect as a station for Allied heavy bombers. He needed another facility to allow the Fifth Bomber Command to continue "leapfrogging" without being congested in one area. Whitehead and his staff selected Biak, an island 230 miles west of Wakde and 350 miles from Hollandia. On May 27, after another tremendous bombing assault by the Fifth Air Force, Biak was invaded; it was captured one month later. This allowed Whitehead's B-24 low-altitude bombers to stage out of Nadzab through Wakde and Biak to hit shipping in Davao, on the southern tip of the Philippine Islands, making the strategic reach of Allied fighters almost 2,000 miles. Now both fighters and bombers from Biak and Wakde could bomb the southern approaches to the Philippines with regularity. The Japanese, realizing the value of Biak and Wakde, sent a convoy to attempt to retake these two island bases; but Whitehead's reconnaissance aircraft spotted the ships. On May 29 the convoy was intercepted by his aircraft and forced to turn back. Another attempt in June by a Japanese task force was hit by ten B-25s off Waigero Island; when this air attack was over, four Japanese destroyers and five troop transports were on the bottom of the Pacific.[59]

Airstrips were never built fast enough for Whitehead's forces. In some instances it was ironic that, almost as fast as the strips were built, they became obsolete as the bomb line was extended. Thus, a lot of hard work was done in vain. In August 1944 Whitehead selected Biak and Owi as the major bases for Allied heavy and medium bombers, and the Fifth Bomber Command moved into these areas in late 1944. To add depth and dispersion to fighter aircraft operations, the island of Noemfoor, west of Biak, was systematically bombed and captured on July 2 for future fighter air bases. On June 25, 1944, the naval air power in the area was transferred to the central Pacific command and the Thirteenth Air Force was reassigned to the SWPA. To command both the Fifth and Thirteenth air forces, a new air command was created; it was called Far East air forces. General Kenney became commander of FEAF, and Whitehead took command of the Fifth Air Force. By now, the Fifth Air Force, with almost thirteen hundred assorted aircraft, was second to none in size and striking power among all the numbered air forces in the U.S. inventory.[60]

The never-ending drive to extend the bomb line continued. Allied intelligence selected Morotai as the next objective. However, before this island could be attacked, Japanese bases at Palau, in the Halmaheras, and in the eastern Celebes had to be destroyed. This task was assigned to the Fifth Air Force. In a series of raids from September 9 to September 15 Whitehead's forces attacked and destroyed these bases. On September 15 Allied troops made an unopposed landing at Morotai. Airfield construction was vigorously prosecuted by Whitehead, and within thirty days fighters were based there.[61]

In spite of Whitehead's tremendous successes in the Papuan and New Guinea campaigns, there was a noticeable lack of publicity about him in the national press. MacArthur and Kenney received most of the plaudits for the Allied victories in the Pacific. However, the enemy were quick to identify Ennis C. Whitehead as the man behind the scenes who was responsible for the Allied air successes in New Guinea, and they began to call him the "Murderer of Moresby."[62] A few reporters also began to notice his activities. In a feature story by Pat Robinson of the International News Service, written early in 1943, Whitehead at long last received some overdue recognition. Robinson wrote: "If there is one American the Japs fear the most and hate more than any other it is Brigadier General Ennis C. Whitehead of Kansas City." In March 1943 he was promoted to major general.[63]

As Allied forces moved closer to the Philippines, their lines of communication became longer, while Japanese lines of communication became shorter. Allied planners could readily see that the projected invasion of the Philippines would be unlike any of the previous assaults on the tiny atolls and islands to the east and different from the jungle beachheads in New Guinea. In these operations it had been possible to neutralize the few scattered and isolated enemy airfields, but in the Philippines there were too many airfields (from sixty to seventy) available to the enemy, and they were too far apart for all of them to be completely neutralized. Furthermore, Japanese airfields in the Philippines were too close to Formosa and other areas to be cut off from reinforcements. The Allies, five hundred miles from their nearest airfields and entirely dependent upon carrier-based planes for protection, were at a grave strategic and tactical disadvantage. To add to the Allied dilemma, the winding passages through the various Philippine Islands, presumably mined and covered by Japanese land-based planes, were denied to the attacking Allied forces but remained open to their Japanese adversary.

So impressed and worried was the Allied high command that, as late as mid-September 1944, their plans called for three amphibious operations, in addition to the invasion of Morotai and Palau, before the invasion of Leyte was to be attempted. [64]

The plan for these three amphibious operations and the reconquest of the Philippines (RENO I) was drafted by the high command in Washington in July 1944. It called for a landing on Yap Island as a continuation of the western Carolines campaign by the POA forces. The date for this operation was set for September 26, 1944. In the meantime, MacArthur's SWPA forces were to advance from Morotai toward the Philippines via Talaud Island. This invasion of Talaud was to commence on October 15, 1944. From Talaud Island the POA and SWPA forces were to seize Sangihe Island on November 14, proceed to the large Philippine Island of Mindanao, then invade Leyte, Mindora, Visayas, and finally Luzon. The invasion of Leyte was to take place December 20, 1944, with the landing on Luzon scheduled for sometime in April or May of 1945. Thus the Philippine campaign assumed somewhat the shape of the long struggle for the Solomons and New Guinea. [65]

Then came a sudden and dramatic change in the whole concept of strategy for the campaign. On September 7 Admiral Halsey, who had a large carrier task force in the central Pacific operating east of the Philippines, reported that, in probing and striking Japanese airfields on Luzon, Leyte, and the Visayas, his pilots had reached the conclusion that the enemy air power to Leyte was a "hollow shell" and that Leyte lay before the Allies almost undefended. [66]

The Octagon Conference was then in progress at Quebec. Admiral Halsey radioed the Joint Chiefs of Staff, who were attending the conference, of his pilot's findings. He also wired General MacArthur in Hollandia and Admiral Nimitz in Hawaii. [67]

In his report Halsey recommended that all preliminary operations be dropped in favor of an immediate start on KING II, the code name for the invasion of Leyte. He believed that the Yap, Talaud, and Mindanao operations were no longer necessary because the Third Fleet was faced with a weak enemy air force and could provide the air support that was supposed to come from land-based aircraft stationed on these islands. [68]

Despite Whitehead's and Kenney's doubts about the validity of moving up the invasion time, General MacArthur and the Allied Supreme Command decided to advance the proposed Leyte invasion date to October 20, 1944. This plan allowed only one month to prepare for the operation.

The secret of Whitehead's success in Leyte was to be the organization and strategy employed by his forces. In the last stages of the New Guinea campaign and at Leyte, by trial and error he "worked the rough spots" out of the Fifth Air Force organization and reached what he believed was the best solution for fitting the weapon to the task. His new organization, with which he experimented in 1943, was relatively simple. He created two commands, the Fifth Bomber Command and the Fifth Fighter Command. Under them various task forces were fashioned, as the situation dictated, to perform assigned missions.[69]

The unique composite task forces of bombers and fighters, consisting of aircraft and men from his two major commands, gave Whitehead maximum flexibility in his operation. His bomb wings or air task forces did not perform any administrative functions. Their sole task was to control combat operations. When one of his moving air task forces participated in an amphibious assault, separately from the rest of the Fifth Air Force, Whitehead delegated to the task force commander complete authority for carrying out the aerial function of the mission.[70]

The aircraft available to Whitehead in October 1944 for his three task forces and the Leyte campaign was a great deal more than he had had in January 1944. For Leyte, Whitehead's air arm consisted of more than twelve hundred assorted types of aircraft, while for the campaign to extend the bomb line and capture all of New Guinea he had had fewer than six hundred aircraft.[71]

The air strategy for the New Guinea and Leyte campaigns, as formulated by Whitehead and his staff with the concurrence of MacArthur and Kenney, was to leapfrog the three task forces (or bomb wings) so that two established wings would cover the advance and assault upon a new military target, while the third wing was physically moving forward by either naval cargo vessels or air transports. Using this system, the echelons of Whitehead's air force were seldom out of action. Light-maintenance air echelons of the combat units, which traveled with each task force, kept the airplanes flying during the approximately two-week period required to move heavy maintenance echelons (by naval cargo ship) from their old location to the new one. This system made it possible for the air units to be flown forward and miss only one or two days of fighting.[72]

In this way three-fourths of the Fifth Air Force's air power was brought to bear continuously against the Japanese, and each combat unit of the Fifth Air Force performed major strategic movements of approximately three hundred miles every time they leapfrogged to a new base. Little combat effort was sacrificed during these moves, and Whitehead's forces were able to remain in all-out combat against the Japanese almost every day of the Philippine campaign. As one of Whitehead's subordinate commanders said: "It worked the hell out of everybody and everything, but it sure won wars."[73]

Once the Leyte beachhead was secure, Whitehead found that his major objective was to cut down the numbers of aircraft which gave the Japanese their air superiority. This he set out to do in a slow and methodical way. His first area of concentration was Celebes and Negros islands. Japanese aircraft based at these two islands had been a thorn in the Allies' side since the beginning of the invasion of Leyte. Starting on November 15,

1944, and lasting almost one month, Whitehead's bombers based at Leyte and Morotai began to blast the two islands in repeated raids around the clock. Not only were airfields hit but also fuel lines, ammunition dumps, and communications and supply depots.

As the Allied air forces began to grow in numbers, isolation of the battlefield of Leyte became another primary mission of the Fifth Air Force. The record shows that Whitehead's men performed this task in a most efficient way. From October 20 to December 13, Fifth Air Force planes attacked and harassed eleven large enemy convoys that were heading for Leyte's western beaches, sinking fifty-four ships and destroying an unknown number of barges and small landing craft. Based on the known loading figures of Japanese vessels, it was estimated that 80,000 Japanese soldiers, together with artillery supplies and equipment for more than 100,000 troops, were lost to Whitehead's aircraft in these attacks, at a cost of only 53 Allied aircraft.[74]

As the balance of air power over Leyte passed to the Allied side, Whitehead intensified attacks on Japanese airfields. Fighters and bombers strafed planes in hidden and dispersed locations; by the first week in December, 643 enemy airplanes had been destroyed to 47 Allied losses. In an air battle on December 6, 1944, 65 Japanese planes were shot down over Leyte. The Allies lost 2. The last large air battle took place in late December, when more than 60 Japanese fighters from Clark Field, near Manila, rose to meet Whitehead's bombers. This was the last time the enemy seriously challenged the Allied air force at Leyte and in the Philippines; by January 2, 1945, the air battle had been won.[75]

While the Allies were preparing for the invasion of Luzon, they prepared to seize Mindoro, on December 15, 1944. The attack on Mindoro illustrated the strategy employed in the Philippine operation by the SWPA force—invade Leyte, secure a foothold, slash across Mindoro, cut the Philippines in two, invade Luzon and win the big battle there, then at will divide, cut, and absorb the southern Philippines.[76]

Whitehead's mission in complementing this strategy was to coordinate the role of his forces with the carrier-based aircraft in protecting the U.S. invasion convoy to Mindoro. The convoy was to take a route which six weeks before had been traveled by the mightiest ships of the Japanese navy. Several Japanese suicide planes annoyed the convoy, but except for the sinking of an ammunition ship and damage to the naval command ship, the convoy got through without significant loss.

Resistance to the invasion of Mindoro was negligible. Because the island was much higher above sea level than Leyte, it was possible for Allied aircraft to move in as suitable fields were captured, and Whitehead's air arm, flying out of Mindoro, immediately began to intensify its strikes on Luzon.[77]

As soon as the date for the invasion of Luzon was confirmed, units of the Thirteenth Air Force moved into bases vacated by the Fifth Air Force in New Guinea and Morotai. While the Fifth moved to Leyte, which was closer to Luzon and would allow them to concentrate on supporting its invasion, the Thirteenth was given the mission of interdicting the Japanese forces in the Netherlands East Indies. [78]

Thus realigned, Whitehead began at once to concentrate his air force on the captured airfields of Leyte and Mindoro. By January 1, 1945, he was able to place five bombardment groups, or approximately 148 bombers, in the Philippines. The Japanese were estimated to have 3,657 aircraft in the area, the Allies 1,099. Although the airfields in the Philippines were in a deplorable and crowded condition, he could take a chance and crowd his forces on these fields because the Japanese air force failed to challenge him. Short of trained pilots, fuel, and spare parts, the Japanese by the end of December had lost all their air capability and potential in Leyte and Mindoro except for limited reconnaissance at night and an occasional raid by one or two airplanes. [79]

On January 1 a final conference for air coordination was held. After careful deliberation, the conferees concluded that the Japanese would cause them more trouble during the Luzon invasion than they did during the Leyte invasion because of the many airfields which they had located on Formosa and Okinawa. Accordingly, it was agreed that, to counteract the expected Japanese air attacks, Allied air forces would be assigned special missions against the various segments of the enemy air force. The Third Fleet's fast carrier forces were assigned the strategic interdiction of Japanese air forces in the north. Whitehead's Fifth Air Force was ordered to neutralize Japanese airfields in the Philippines from central Luzon southward and to destroy certain ground targets throughout Luzon as part of the overall invasion plan. [80]

The air strikes in the implementation of this strategy began on January 2 and reached their peaks between January 5 and 9. At first Japanese air opposition was heavy, but by January 9, the day of the assault, Whitehead reported that only three enemy planes were seen over the objective area.

Through meticulous and careful planning, Whitehead provided land-based air cover for the great invasion force of more than six hundred assorted ships, from Leyte to Luzon. Sixty fighter aircraft were kept over the convoys for protection during the daylight hours. Fifth Air Force strikes against Formosa, the Philippines, and the Japanese airfields in the immediate vicinity were so effective that the greatest invasion task force of the Pacific war reached its objective unscathed. Not one ship was damaged or sunk. The continuous bombing assault by Whitehead's aircraft destroyed not only enemy military and industrial targets but also fuel depots and spare-part reservoirs and thus prevented many Japanese aircraft from taking the air. As one observer was to write later, the convoys' success can be measured directly by the decline of Japanese air strength.[81]

In a little over one month from the day of the first assault on Luzon, Manila was captured and the assault phases of the battle for Luzon were over. Whitehead's Fifth Air Force had turned out another excellent performance. They had virtually destroyed the Japanese air force in the area, had gained air superiority, and had isolated the battlefield.[82]

With the capture of Luzon, land was provided for the extension of the bomb line, and Whitehead immediately made plans for airfield development. By May 1, after several prodigious engineering feats, nineteen airstrips were in use on Luzon.

Whitehead was not involved in the making of strategy for the final assault on Japan, but he was involved with the tactics which would be used in implementing this strategy. Thus he was very interested as the Allied planners in Washington began to formulate the strategy for the invasion of Japan. As the weeks went by, the Fifth, which was committed to northern Philippine operations, played a lesser role in this area. When airfields were finally built on Luzon, the Fifth left the southern area completely to the Thirteenth and began to increase its attacks on southern Japan.

On Easter Sunday 1945, 548,000 men of the army, navy, and Marine Corps, transported and accompanied by 318 combatant and 1,139 auxiliary vessels, began the invasion of the Ryukus Islands without immediate opposition. Airfields at Kadena and Yontan were captured the first day and were immediately put into operation. For the first six days, American army forces had their own way, but the enemy, short on aircraft, pilots, and fuel, did not give up easily.[83]

From desperation, on April 6 the Japanese began kamikaze (suicide) attacks, sending five hundred aircraft from southern Japan in a twenty-four-hour air assault on Allied naval forces off Okinawa. About 116 planes fought through interception attempts by Allied carrier pilots. Combat air patrol over the beachhead, provided by Whitehead's fighters, sliced the number to sixty-one. Antiaircraft gunners shot down thirty-nine more, but twenty-two completed their mission and did considerable damage. Repeat attacks by kamikazes occurred on April 11, 12, 27, and 29 and May 3, 4, and 11. The Japanese used all types of aircraft in the kamikaze assault—new models, fresh from the factory; obsolete varieties; and specially designed "piloted bombs" which were small, winged craft without landing gear, released at some distance from the target with no hope for survival.[84]

Whitehead believed that his forces were not used properly in the Okinawa campaign, and in two letters written to Kenney after the war discussed how he believed his forces could have been used for masthead and strategic bombing and for tactical interdiction. Instead, he wrote, "we sat

Arnold meets with Kenney, Whitehead, and Major General Clements Mc-Mullen at Manila, June 1945. U.S. Air Force photo.

around with nothing to do twiddling our thumbs and waiting for assignments of targets which the navy was reluctant to give us."[85]

The Okinawa campaign lasted eighty-one days. The United States paid dearly for its victory. Thirty-three warships were sunk and 223 were damaged, most of them by the kamikaze planes. The total number of Americans killed was 11,260: 3,633 army and 7,627 navy and marines; 33,769 army, navy, and marines were wounded.[86]

By July 15 half of the Fifth Air Force—eleven bomber and fighter groups consisting of five hundred aircraft—was operating out of Okinawa. For almost a month they took part in the round-the-clock bombing of Japan. The bomb line was extended for the last time at Okinawa.[87]

Although Whitehead's air arm did not play an important role in the invasions of Iwo Jima and Okinawa, it did in the neutralization of Formosa. This neutralization began on January 22, 1945, and, according to many of the Japanese officials who were interrogated after the war, tremendously hindered the Japanese war effort.

The Japanese oil fields at Balikpapan in the Dutch East Indies also felt the destructive power of the Fifth Air Force's bombers. For more than two years, Whitehead's intelligence had reported that about two-thirds of all Japanese fuel was refined at Balikpapan. As soon as his bombers and fighters were within range of the big Japanese oil fields, Whitehead planned to knock them out. Morotai's capture in September 1944 placed fighter-bombers in range of Balikpapan; this airfield even offered Whitehead the luxury of fighter support. In a coordinated effort with the Thirteenth Air Force, two raids were planned to destroy the Japanese refineries. Balikpapan was attacked on October 10 and 14, 1944. Despite tremendous enemy antiaircraft fire, Allied aircraft neutralized the oil fields, contributing immensely to the Japanese shortage of fuel and the eventual defeat of the Japanese air force. As the Fifth Air Force moved north, the Thirteenth continued the attacks on the Japanese oil fields, and they were never again of any use to the Japanese war effort. [88]

While the Fifth Air Force was moving to Okinawa for the all-out assault on Japan, other targets were not forgotten. Shanghai was hit in a big raid on July 24. Formosa continued to be bombed, as were Hong Kong, Canton, and other Chinese areas. For a while, with the B-29s doing most of the bombing from Guam, it looked as if there would be no mission for the Fifth's bombers to perform. But once they became operational in Okinawa, they played a major role in the bombing and subsequent defeat of Japan.

With a desire to get into the final action, Whitehead submitted a plan to Kenney on April 8 that directed the movement of his forces into Okinawa to execute the following mission: one, neutralize the Japanese air arm in western Japan; two, cut the Japanese sea lanes to the mainland of Asia; three, destroy coastal enemy sea lanes to Kyushu and the enemy rail lines to this southern island from Osaka west; four, furnish air cover for an amphibious assault on Kyushu to seize an airfield area from which the first three missions could be pursued; and five, cut the Japanese lines of communication and transportation into Tokyo. Whitehead's "Air Plan OLYMPIC" also called for speed in action. [89]

Kenney took Whitehead's ideas into account, and the basic strategic air plan for the invasion of Japan included the five principles of the plan.

In the meantime, during April and May 1945, the Joint Chiefs of Staff forwarded their plan to the Pacific theater, outlining the strategic concept of the invasion of Japan. DOWNFALL was divided into two operations. The first part, given the code name OLYMPIC, called for the invasion of southern Kyushu on November 1, 1945. Following the establishment of thirteen airfields, the Kanto Plains around Tokyo were to be invaded by three armies in the spring of 1945 in an operation called CORONET. [90]

On April 6, 1945, in an attempt to create a more workable structure in the Pacific for the decisive operation against the Japanese empire, General MacArthur was chosen supreme commander of the Allied forces. Under him were placed all the army, navy, and air forces involved in the operation. The army forces were responsible for the basic invasion plans. The navy forces were to carry the army forces to the objectives and help establish the beachheads. B-29s were to perform heavy bombardment missions as required by the overall operation.[91]

For OLYMPIC, Japan was divided by a north-south line just west of Osaka. East of this line, strategic air forces from Guam were to continue their heavy raids throughout Japan. Whitehead's air force was responsible for all air activities west of the line, with special emphasis on targets which would ensure the success of OLYMPIC. The naval carrier forces were to work on both sides of the dividing line, hitting targets as the period and situation demanded.[92]

The Fifth Air Force and the Thirteenth Air Force were to coordinate the air operations involved in OLYMPIC and to move their forces to Okinawa as fast as possible. The Fifth Air Force was to carry the major load of the preinvasion strikes and be stationed at the Kanto Plains airfield. The Thirteenth Air Force was to establish bases in Kyushu and supervise the air strikes for CORONET.[93]

Working in conjunction with the Sixth Army, and using as a basis the elements in his letter of April 8 to Kenney, Whitehead completed the tactical plans for the invasion of Japan on July 28, 1945. These plans were comprehensive and detailed and called for preinvasion strikes, counter air operations, isolation of the portions of Kyushu below the thirty-second parallel, and finally the isolation of the individual battlefield in cooperation with the army. The general scheme of Whitehead's plan was the isolation, neutralization, and destruction of the enemy's air, ground, and naval forces. Within the plans themselves, the major objectives were further broken down into smaller specific objectives, which were carefully studied, analyzed, and assigned attack aircraft in proportion to the available aircraft, which now consisted of close to twelve hundred planes—six fighter groups with three hundred aircraft, nine bomber groups with four hundred aircraft, four groups with two hundred troop transports, fifty photoreconnaissance aircraft, and one hundred miscellaneous planes. Although only approximately one-half of his aircraft (six hundred assorted planes) were in place, in early July the Fifth began to bomb Japan from Okinawa.[94]

Air operations prior to the Japanese surrender went off smoothly, and it was necessary to make only minor changes to Whitehead's basic plan. Effective air attacks were carried out against Japanese shipping at sea and in harbors and docks. Military installations and lines of communication were destroyed or harassed. Whitehead's strafers and bombers repeatedly assaulted cities such as Kagoshima until they were leveled. Japanese airfields in western Japan and Korea were bombed around the clock.[95]

In July, shortly after the fighting in Okinawa had ended, Halsey boldly took his Third Fleet into Japanese waters and struck at targets throughout the length of the Japanese home islands. Launching raids with as many as one thousand carrier aircraft and shelling east coast installations as well, Halsey's forces contributed materially to the destruction of Japanese industry while they tightened the blockade of the home islands. Opposition to Halsey was light.

At the same time that Halsey's fleet was maneuvering in Japanese waters, Whitehead's Fifth Air Force and B-29s from the Twentieth Air Force stationed in Guam began laying aerial mines on a scale heretofore never equaled. Later interrogations revealed that this mining was quite successful in blockading the main Japanese islands. Meanwhile, American submarines continued their unheralded campaign against Japanese shipping and helped to draw the noose even tighter about a starving and industrially crippled Japan.[96]

By August 1, 1945, the outcome of the war was no longer in doubt. Whitehead's force had more than doubled its number of air strikes; seven hundred aircraft of the approximately twelve hundred aircraft assigned (60 percent of the Fifth Air Force) were in place in Okinawa.[97] The Japanese were not challenging the Fifth Air Force, preferring to save their aircraft for the final battles which they knew were to come. The isolation of Kyushu was completed on August 6. When Japanese civilians on Kyushu began to wave white flags at FEAF aircraft, Whitehead was convinced, as he wrote his brother, that "the Nips are done for."[98]

On the afternoon of August 6, the first atomic bomb was dropped on Hiroshima. On August 8, Russia declared war on Japan, and on August 9, the second atomic bomb fell on Nagasaki. Japan's leaders saw the futility of further resistance and on August 10 asked for peace.[99]

The Fifth Air Force had come to the end of a long road that had begun at Port Moresby and had ended in Tokyo Bay. The war was over. Ahead now lay the occupation of the Japanese islands and all the problems which encompassed such a task. As he stood at the surrender ceremony, Whitehead could look with pride upon his accomplishments and the magnificent performance of the airmen of the Fifth Air Force. He had forged a mighty air weapon, giving MacArthur the key to victory.

Whitehead remained in Japan after the surrender as commander of the Far East air forces and MacArthur's chief air officer, helping to administer the occupation and demobilize American air bases in the area. In 1949 he left to head the Continental Air Command. At Mitchel Field, Long Island, he was instrumental in the division of this organization into the Tactical Air Command and the Air Defense Command. He retired in 1951 and died in Newton, Kansas, of emphysema in 1964.[100]

Although Whitehead's subordinates have no doubt that their boss was the foremost air tactician of the war in the Southwest Pacific, he never received due credit for his accomplishments. George Kenney has usually been viewed as the man most responsible for Allied air success. Certainly Kenney believed that he was. At the annual birthday celebrations following MacArthur's retirement, Kenney often boasted about the great victories in the Pacific, while Whitehead sat back, listened intently, and from time to time smiled as Kenney tossed him a compliment or two. [101]

While Kenney's achievements were substantial, especially in educating MacArthur about the proper use of air power, Whitehead's contributions should not be overlooked. The uses to which he put troop carrier aircraft, skip bombing, napalm, aerial reconnaissance, the parafrag bomb, and fighter-bombers were milestones in American air warfare. True, he did not originate these ideas, but he implemented them as no one had ever done before. He was the driving force behind the Fifth Air Force. [102]

Whitehead was an accomplished aerial tactician. The tactical air plans for such operations as the Bismarck Sea, Rabaul, Wewak, Hollandia, Leyte, Mindora, and OLYMPIC were written by Whitehead and his staff. MacArthur and Kenney simply told Whitehead what they wanted, and he planned the tactics to achieve the objective. [103]

Kenney and Whitehead made a superb team. Their personalities and skills blended well to produce an impressive record of aerial victories in the Southwest Pacific. Although the senior Kenney received most of the credit, these great accomplishments would not have been possible without the tactical genius of Ennis C. Whitehead.

Daniel E. Barbey

Amphibious Warfare
Expert

PAOLO E. COLETTA

Amphibious operations played a central role in the defeat of Japan in the Southwest Pacific, and Daniel E. Barbey was the man who made them work. Born in Portland, Oregon, on December 23, 1889, he graduated from the U.S. Naval Academy in 1912, then rotated from sea to shore billets of ever-increasing responsibilities. Photographs of special landing craft, with hinged bow ramps, that the Japanese had used during an assault on Tientsin, China, in 1937, sparked Barbey's interest in amphibious warfare. In 1940 he updated the navy's almost useless landing manual of 1918 and produced the modern amphibious bible in Fleet Tactical Publication No. 167, *Landing Operations Doctrine, United States Navy.*[1]

Until this time, the navy had shown little interest in amphibious warfare. Although the Gallipoli campaign of World War I was perennially studied in American service schools during the 1920s and 1930s, with special attention given to the British use of the landing ship *River Clyde*, which had a ramp bow, battleships were considered to be the prime index of naval power, and few naval officers called for the development of special boats or doctrine for amphibious purposes. Charged after the Spanish-American War with such developments, the Marine Corps created an advanced based force in 1901 that became the fleet marine force in 1933. Also created was the Marine Corps Equipment Board, which sought to solve the problems of getting troops and their equipment from ships to enemy-held beaches. For doctrine the staff and students at the Marine Corps Schools, Quantico, Virginia, produced the *Tentative Manual for Landing Operations* in January 1934.[2]

During the 1920s the marines developed Troop Barge A, a fifty-foot, twin engine, armored boat with a bow ramp, and Walter Christie came up with an amphibious tank. Both proved unsatisfactory. The thirty-six-foot Andrew J. Higgins *Eureka* boat for disembarking personnel was tested in

1938 and 1939, yet in February 1940 the navy had only thirty-five thirty-foot landing boats, five tank lighters, and six artillery lighters. As late as the fall of 1941, when he participated in exercises in the Atlantic, Barbey saw marines and army troops leaping over the bows of ships' boats to the beach six to eight feet below. In 1940 and 1941 he assisted in training the First Marine Division and First Army Division for amphibious warfare. While the army thought it could use dock facilities such as those at Cherbourg and Le Havre to transfer troops to Europe, Barbey concentrated on developing techniques to land troops on Pacific beaches.[3]

In early 1940 Barbey began serving as chief of staff to the commander of the service force, Atlantic Fleet, Rear Admiral Randall Jacobs, who had amphibious warfare as additional duty. Although the navy accepted the Higgins boat in September 1940, not until June 1942 did an "amphibious ships and craft" subsection in the office of chief of the naval operations supersede the "auxiliary vessels" subsection.[4]

The navy considered APs (large transports able to carry small landing craft), AKs (cargo ships also able to carry such craft), and APDs (destroyer-hulled transports) useful only for providing logistic support, and of these only two AKs were in the Pacific.[5] As Barbey noted, "At the time of the Japanese attack on Pearl Harbor, the U.S. Navy did not have a single oceangoing ship that could run its bow onto the beach and deliver a cargo of big tanks and other heavy equipment directly to the shore without benefit of piers or cranes."[6] After the fall of France in June 1940 and the abortive expedition against Dakar, North Africa, however, Prime Minister Winston Churchill pressed the need for personnel and vehicle carriers and support craft for amphibious operations. Churchill made their desired characteristics, including a "Spirit Room" for larger ones, known to Americans and asked that substantial numbers of them be provided Britain under lend-lease. Later, Lord Louis Mountbatten came over to help formulate a common nomenclature for amphibious ships and craft.[7] Because higher priorities were given to larger warships, few British landing craft were built. Only after the attack on Pearl Harbor was part of America's industry diverted into the amphibious craft program.

With the British conceding the Pacific Ocean to the United States, the Joint Chiefs of Staff divided it into a Pacific area, with Admiral Chester W. Nimitz in command after December 31, 1941, and a Southwest Pacific area under command of General Douglas MacArthur. On June 4, 1942, Admiral Ernest J. King, both CNO and commander in chief, U.S. Fleet, established an amphibious warfare section under his COMINCH readiness section and chose Barbey to head it. From a tiny office in the ninth wing of Main Navy, Barbey provided liaison between the readiness section and the Bureau of Ships. He was greatly helped by a single aide, Lieutenant Commander William E. Howard, until the fall of 1942, when four more officers joined him. Howard, a 1928 graduate of the U.S. Naval Academy and a bright engineer, had formerly been with the Bureau of Ships. The bureau maintained liaison with the British delegation in Washington. In that bureau was a young naval engineer named Schuyler N. Pyne, who saw much of Barbey and thought that he was "a hell of a nice guy," but he never became as close to him as Howard, who called him, "Uncle Dan."[8]

By mid-1942 $1 billion had been granted the amphibious craft program. With most large American shipyards busy, the Bureau of Ships ordered "miracle ships" built by any bridge builder, small boat manufacturer, or new construction firm that could produce them along a waterway. Many of them were "cornfield" builders located along the Ohio and Mississippi rivers. During the summer of 1942 Barbey took a ride in an LVT down Fourteenth Street in Washington, crossed the Potomac, and slid into a lake—and was given a summons for invading a wildlife sanctuary![9]

All amphibious vessels over two hundred feet in length are called "landing ships"; those under that length, "landing craft." The ungainly LST, popularly known as "large, slow target," though rated at eleven knots usually made eight or nine. It was of about four thousand tons' displacement and 328 feet long, with a draft of fourteen feet, and had water ballast tanks forward which, when pumped out, permitted it to land in shallow water on a relatively flat beach. It could carry tanks on its tank deck and miscellaneous cargo on an upper deck. The tanks landed directly onto the beach through ramp doors. An elevator dropped the upper deck cargo below for discharge. Living accommodations aft were provided for 160 men; tank crews and assault troops used compartments in wing walls. The first LST was completed at Newport News Shipbuilding Company on October 28, 1942, less than a year after it had been designed.[10]

The ramp-bowed LCT was originally 105 feet long but was lengthened to 118 feet in order to give it a speed of nine to ten knots. Built in three sections, it could be transported on freighters and bolted together at its destination. It was to be used only for runs of about seventy-five miles' radius near shore bases and had no living accommodations. Much faster—of about fourteen knots—were the LCIs, which carried a crew of two officers and twenty-two men and could transport 205 troops and thirty-two tons of cargo. The troops reached the beach by means of gangways rigged along both sides of the bow. With watertight hulls and caterpillar tracks, LVTs and DUKWs could travel on land, through water, and over reefs.

Responding to a request from MacArthur for an amphibious commander, on December 15, 1942, Admiral King directed now rear admiral Barbey to report to Vice Admiral Arthur S. Carpender, commander, Allied naval forces, SWPA, as commander, amphibious forces, SWPA, and also as commander of the Seventh Fleet service force after the SWPA naval forces were redesignated the Seventh Fleet on March 13, 1943.

Flying to San Francisco and from there on December 26, 1942, to

Pearl Harbor, Barbey was an overnight guest of Admiral Nimitz, who showed little interest in what MacArthur was doing.[11] Similarly he was an overnight guest, in Noumea, New Caledonia, of Admiral William F. Halsey, the new commander of the South Pacific area and force. He then called on Rear Admiral Richmond Kelly ("Terrible") Turner, commander, amphibious forces, SOPAC, who told him of the problems he had faced during the amphibious landings at Guadalcanal-Tulagi caused in part by the early retirement of designated aircraft carrier forces. Barbey came away impressed with the need to reduce the unloading time of ships and craft and determined to demand continuous air cover and adequate naval surface cover of a landing area.[12]

On January 10, 1943, when Barbey assumed command of it, the amphibious force, SWPA—later Seventh Amphibious Force—was born. It consisted of himself, one aide, ships yet to arrive or even to be built, and men still to be assigned. His area of responsibility stretched from Australia to the Netherlands East Indies. His forces were seven thousand miles away from the nearest home base, and the Japanese forces, three thousand. Moreover, he saw that Australia's industrial and transportation facilities were woefully inadequate to meet the demands of a major military buildup. Last, only the troops, supplies, and ships that the United States could spare from Guadalcanal, North Africa, and the desperate antisubmarine campaign in the Atlantic could be expected in SWPA. No wonder he said, "If you have to fight a war, don't do it at the end of the line."[13]

Barbey learned from Carpender that, until he himself obtained additional naval forces, MacArthur could move only by air or land, that he had been unable to provide much naval support during the "Bloody Buna" campaign declared ended on January 24, 1943, and that MacArthur had had to depend for water transportation upon his as yet ineffective engineer special (small boat) brigade. These "webfoots" operated from shore to shore rather than from ship to shore and used only LCVPs and LCMs. A second ESB reached the Southwest Pacific area in October 1943 and a third one in May 1944.[14]

Barbey further learned from Carpender that, except for PT boats, ships could not operate in the waters of the western Solomon Sea until the Allies obtained control of the air and the area was better charted. Some available charts dated back to 1792, and while army charts had great details on topography, they turned blue at the water's edge. Nimitz could spare no ships, and Carpender's unwillingness to use his cruisers and destroyers in uncharted waters strained his relations with MacArthur.[15]

With MacArthur and his chief of staff, Lieutenant General Richard K. Sutherland, in New Guinea when he arrived in Brisbane, Barbey called upon the staff operations officer, Brigadier General Stephen J. Chamberlin, who outlined MacArthur's plans. After Buna, an attack would be made on Lae and then across Vitiaz Strait to the western end of New Britain in order to encircle the Japanese stronghold at Rabaul. Meanwhile Halsey would proceed northward through the Solomons. Naval support would be needed on the northern New Guinea coast so that MacArthur could obtain airfields from which he could move forward under his own air umbrella and keep the promise he had made to return to the Philippines. "The General [everyone knew who "The General" was] expects you and your amphibious force to do just that," Chamberlin told Barbey. The latter knew that Allied strategy called for getting Hitler first and that the U.S. Navy planned to defeat Japan by driving through the central Solomons. He wisely kept quiet but wondered whether MacArthur knew how the Joint Chiefs were thinking. Since MacArthur had fired one naval commander and his successor was already in trouble, Barbey asked himself, "How long will I last?"[16]

Although MacArthur commanded the forces of many nations, every senior officer on his staff was an American, and he used an army rather than a joint or combined staff. There was thus no planning under one roof. Later, after MacArthur had come to depend upon Barbey to move his troops, Barbey called for joint planning with American or Australian generals and the army air force, with the latter often failing to cooperate. Because MacArthur charged the navy's leadership with conspiring against his theater's interest, a United Press correspondent noted that "the war between the Yanks and the Japs is only exceeded by the war between the Army and the Navy."[17] Not only did MacArthur's staff vie with each other to get close to "The Great Man," but a small group, "the Bataan Club," tried to insulate him from the influence of anyone else.[18]

Soon after MacArthur's return to Brisbane, Barbey called upon him and found him to be "friendly but deadly serious. He never smiled. There was no light touch to his words nor the informality and comaraderie that was so evident around the Pacific Fleet Headquarters of Admiral Nimitz." Rather than asking about how Barbey's special knowledge of amphibious warfare could be used in his theater—and his success would depend upon Barbey—he spoke of current operations and future plans, adding that the reconquest of the Philippines must be given priority over all other objectives in the Pacific. "Your job," he said, "is to develop an amphibious force that can carry my troops in those campaigns." The only question he asked Barbey, was, "Are you a lucky officer?"[19]

In his book, *MacArthur's Amphibious Navy: Seventh Fleet Amphibious Force Operations, 1943-1945*, Barbey wrote that he was jarred when MacArthur said that whatever he reported about him to the Navy Department "will come back to me." Barbey nevertheless admitted that "General MacArthur proved to be the finest commander I have ever worked for. . . . He gave his subordinates a job and then left to them the details of how it was to be done. If the job was not being done to his satisfaction, he simply found another man to do it." On the other hand, "MacArthur was never able to develop a feeling of warmth and comradeship with those about him. . . . He could not inspire the electrifying leadership Halsey had. He was too aloof and too correct in manner, speech, and dress. He had no small talk, but when discussing military matters he was superb."[20]

Barbey had asked Captain M.T. Farrar to criticize the statement he would make to MacArthur, especially to counter the latter's idea of using the ESBs as amphibious forces. After the war, Farrar wrote Barbey:

Your presentation speech to MacArthur was very good. . . . So, it was made clear that the Navy was in full command and charge of all amphibious planning, loading, and operations from departure until the beachhead had been secured. And the Army would NOT establish its own duplicate amphibious (small boat) department. But the Great Man never gave you a chance to tell him off. . . . You returned so goddamn mad you were blubbering. . . . I can't quote you exactly, but you said something like "Here I come out to fight the Japanese and that goddamn so-and-so wants to make me a school-teacher." . . . It all worked out, but it took a longer time to establish the point that you intended to talk about.[21]

By the last remark Farrar meant that the ESBs would eventually be absorbed into Barbey's command. At least General Chamberlin was happy because, rather than using pack animals for future operations, with Barbey's landing craft "we could go around the mountains by water rather than go over them."[22] When asked later who the greatest military and naval leaders of World War II were, Barbey named MacArthur as the greatest ground commander and—without explanation—Admiral Raymond A. Spruance as the finest American naval commander.[23]

While he awaited a directive from MacArthur, Barbey met the latter's subordinates. From Lieutenant General Robert L. Eichelberger, First Corps commander, he learned about the horrible conditions on New Guinea. Because he was a warm person who did not shun publicity, but also because he was sometimes belligerent and outspokenly critical of the Big Chief, MacArthur kept Eichelberger in training roles in Australia for more than a year.[24]

Lieutenant General Walter Krueger, commander, Sixth Army, scorned red tape, followed orders, and shunned publicity—the last was a plus with MacArthur. Short, stocky, and dynamic, Lieutenant General George Kenney commanded the Allied air forces and the Fifth Air Force. His policy was to avoid long jumps because his planes would be useless and aircraft carriers might have to be called in from the "godamn-navy." He had no interest in anything except his aircraft, especially his bombers. It was also his policy not to fly his fighters at dawn, dusk, or in darkness or bad weather; bad weather apparently did not bother the Japanese. Nor did he provide constant combat air patrol over an objective area. While Barbey had to bring the engineers and equipment to build his airfields, thereafter Kenney had influence with MacArthur because his aircraft were the only means of transportation over the jungle. However, after Barbey mentioned to MacArthur his need of aerial photographs with which to chart waters and beaches, the general nudged Kenney and the latter obliged.[25]

Major General Sir Thomas Blamey, the top field commander of the Australian army since September 1939, did what he could to help Barbey. The liaison officers he sent Barbey included Brigadier General Ronald N. L. Hopkins, who eased Barbey's way in dealing with Australian service leaders. Via Hopkins, Barbey exchanged data on amphibious warfare matters with Lord Mountbatten, chief of British Combined Operations.

In his hurry to reach Australia, Barbey disregarded advice that he should choose a good staff to take with him, instead letting the Bureau of Naval Personnel select it for him. As his officers and men reached him he learned that 98 percent of the officers were reserves commissioned directly from civilian life and with an average service age of eight months. Included were some "retreads" from World War I, such as James Van Zandt, who had retired from Congress and joined Barbey early in 1943. Barbey, who was quick to praise a man for good work and equally quick to dismiss an incompetent, soon learned that Van Zandt was as capable at sea as in representing his Pennsylvania district.[26]

Even before Barbey's staff was fleshed out, on February 8, 1943, MacArthur directed him to command all amphibious training in SWPA and train all of his troops, then consisting of one Australian and two American divisions. Lacking sufficient staff, a training program, and ships, Barbey inspected available base and repair sites. He chose Toobul Point, near the mouth of the Brisbane River, and Port Stephens, Nelson's Bay, one hundred miles north of Sydney. With no Seabees or Australian naval personnel available at his bases, his men "scrounged" and built their own facilities. The original training officer, Captain Bern Anderson, an amphibious combat veteran of Guadalcanal, soon gave way to Commander John W. "Red" Jamison, who had attended the Marine Corps schools and served as a beachmaster for the Casabalanca operation.[27]

MacArthur's directing Barbey to use the procedures contained in U.S. Navy Fleet Publication No. 167 meant that troops had to be trained to land in small boats carried by APAs. Lacking an APA, Jamison trained troops to climb down cargo nets hung on a cliff to the sides of a mockup landing craft. On January 8, however, the first LSTs and LCTs arrived in Sydney, and on Easter Sunday thirteen LCIs reached Port Stephens. While Jamison shifted training to include their use, Barbey was so cautious that he decided to employ the new craft on reinforcement runs rather than as assault forces. Even so, boat crews had to learn to trim their craft properly by the stern so that their bottoms would conform to the slope of a beach. Improper trim would call for the use of sixty pontoons that were awkward to carry and handle. Training was a unique part of Barbey's policy, and as noted below he established several forward amphibious training centers.[28]

Meanwhile on Admiral King's order Admiral Turner transferred the APA *Henry T. Allen* to Barbey for use as his flagship, and the Australian government began converting three passenger ships so that they could each carry twelve hundred troops. In addition Barbey was provided with many of the 584 steel craft and 1,090 wooden powered craft built in Australia.[29]

The *Henry T. Allen* was in such disrepair that she could not be used in forward areas, and so Barbey used her for troop training exercises in rear areas. Although a landing exercise he carried out with two APAs proved to be disastrous, he decided to use his landing craft for both assault and reinforcement purposes. Because these as yet lacked ship support and air cover, they had to beach in undefended areas about two hours before high tide at dawn and leave about four hours later. He had to operate with crews that had never been to sea before, without hospital, repair, and supply ships, tankers, and water barges, and he was extremely short of spare parts. Barbey therefore sent an officer to Washington to see Rear Admiral Jacobs, now chief of the Bureau of Personnel. The officer recalled that "it was not long before things with which to fight began to come into our area."[30]

The Navy Department answered MacArthur's request for a naval adviser and planner by sending him Captain Raymond D. Tarbuck, who would head up the forty to fifty naval officers at his general headquarters. Tarbuck, a 1920 graduate of the U.S. Naval Academy, had served at army staff and aviation schools and had worked with Barbey in the Bureau of Navigation in the late 1930s. He found the naval officers at GHQ spread around. When he tried to put a navy section together so that it could answer any naval questions put to it, the Bataan Club prevented him from doing so. For eighteen months Tarbuck headed MacArthur's red team of planners, the other two being white and blue, with the three being able to plan ahead and leapfrog over each other on a map. "While wearing Navy blue," he later told Barbey, he "felt like a bastard at a family reunion."[31]

On April 26, 1943, Halsey and MacArthur conferred about Operation CARTWHEEL, in which thirteen amphibious operations would be undertaken in six months and would end in a combined assault on Rabaul. MacArthur would operate on New Guinea; Halsey, under his strategic direction, in the Central Solomons. CARTWHEEL called for landings on Kiriwina and Woodlark islands on June 30; New Georgia, June 30; the Salamaua-Madang area, September 1; southern Bougainville, October

15; and Cape Gloucester, New Britain, December 1. The JCS approved except that Rabaul was to be bypassed, and King and Nimitz began considering operations against the Gilbert Islands to secure the lines of communication to SWPA and divert Japanese air and ships from the Solomons. CARTWHEEL was postponed for six weeks until various new ships reached Barbey, who on June 20 flew into Milne Bay in a little aircraft he used when not aboard a ship.

There being no unity of command in SWPA below MacArthur's level, Barbey, Carpender, Kenney, and Krueger planned Operation CHRONI-CLE for June 30, 1943. The objectives were the undefended Kiriwina and Woodlark islands about two hundred miles northeast of the eastern end of New Guinea, where airfields would be built from which Kenney's planes could hit Rabaul. Halsey lent MacArthur some ships, troops, and Seabees for the operation and in addition provided Barbey with both distant and close support. Barbey decided to have his craft approach the islands during darkness, unload, and retreat before daylight. He was so anxious for none of his ships to be lost that he told his operations officer, Captain Anderson, "that if that LST he planned to put on the northern shore of Kiriwina was sunk by the Japanese we would both go to jail."[32]

Barbey's first landing occurred while he had to train the widely separated second ESB and the Ninth Australian Division, scheduled for the next operation. With many high-ranking American officers observing, it was fouled up from the beginning. The landing craft approached the beach at about 2000, had difficulty in clearing the bar at the entrance to the channel, and once inside the harbor were about half a mile from the shore and could not navigate a gradually sloping beach. Barbey reported that the "grave inexperience and the lack of training of the personnel in handling their ships in landing operations will be disastrous against opposition." In any case, for the next two months his LCTs brought in the cargo needed at the islands.[33]

From this operation, in which 50 percent of the troops were seasick, Barbey determined to consider forecasts of sea conditions in future operations. Yet he had moved sixteen thousand men and their supplies 185 miles beyond Milne Bay through poorly charted waters subject to enemy action without the loss of a single ship. As Samuel E. Morison put it, in a bloodless occupation his operation had been a "thumping success" and provided a "template for future ship to shore operations in the Southwest Pacific," words echoed by both Australian and other American historians.[34] And a first step had been taken in the encirclement of Rabaul. But now he had to consider how future operations would succeed against air attack and shore opposition. These would be conducted about thirty-five days apart for the next eighteen months, with a landing not counted as such unless it was separated by one day and a distance of one hundred miles from the last. He himself spurred his men to do their best because he was always present at the scene of action.

To be closer to the operating area, Barbey and Krueger moved to Milne Bay. Lacking a hospital ship, on June 12 Barbey had improvised by having an LST converted into one and sought Navy Department approval. Although the Department disapproved, LSI-464 continued operating as before. In addition he converted some LCTs into badly needed water barges and repair craft and used some small wooden-hulled APCs, called "apple carts," as flagships for LCT flotilla commanders and floating post offices; one APC served as a planning ship with an office in which one junior-grade lieutenant and a third-class yeoman cut stencils and cranked out copies of operation plans and orders.

While the army relied heavily upon reconnaissance parties and coast watchers, Barbey preferred to obtain intelligence from overlapping aerial photographs. Plantation owners, he found, were not accustomed to seeing their beaches from seaward, but architects thought to be useless in amphibious operations proved skillful in photographic interpretation.

Barbey also had some highly trained and eager scouts. However, Major General Charles A. Willoughby, at GHQ, was in charge of coast watchers and flatly refused to let Barbey's men scout on their own. Barbey occasionally had his men, in rubber boats, obtain tidal information from unoccupied islands until he found better use for them during the invasion of Leyte Gulf. [35]

Barbey's next task was to transport the Ninth Australian Division to beaches adjacent to the village of Lae, located about 370 miles northwest of Milne Bay on Huon Gulf. Lacking information about the beach approaches, he got Major General G.F. Wooten to agree to a night approach and early daylight landing and to the light loading of landing craft so that they could retract quickly, escape enemy action, and be used in resupply echelons. In this case he was lucky because army commanders usually insisted upon getting as much material as possible to accompany assault troops and not gamble upon receiving it later. [36]

Fortunately for Barbey, for the first time in eighteen months of fighting in SWPA, Admiral Carpender was able to spare four destroyers to sweep Huon Gulf and bombard the shore. Although no air cover was expected during the approach, Kenney sent planes at daylight. To aid these Barbey had the destroyer *Reid*, which carried a fighter director team, stationed fifty miles to the east of the landing beaches. [37]

At MacArthur's request the Navy Department ordered twenty-five new officers to join Barbey's staff, but thirteen were siphoned off en route. With only two weeks following the completion of the resupply missions to Kiriwina and Woodlark islands for his ships to reach their jumping-off place at Milne Bay and Buna, he sent a newcomer, Commander Charles

LST unloading cargo. Courtesy U.S. Naval Institute.

Adair, to reconnoiter sites for a forward base for operations against Lae and Salamaua while he himself distributed operation plans, held rehearsals, and loaded troops and supplies. He was extremely anxious that all go well in his first beach assault.

Lacking a suitable flagship, Barbey rode the *Conyngham* (DD-371). Her crew originally resented his coming on board with six other officers and men, but as one of her crew noted, "He quickly won the respect of all hands by trying in every way to cause a minimum of trouble. Having him and his staff on board soon came to be a pleasure."[38]

With General Wooten on board, on September 2, 1943, Barbey led his troop-laden convoy on a thirty-six-hour run. With him also were six destroyers, various APCs, LCTs, and SCs, a service group, and an ESB.

No ship was sighted by the Japanese. Troops in small rubber boats from APDs were within twelve hundred yards of the beaches just eighteen minutes after sunrise and moved inland against only a few Japanese lookouts. When the landing craft approached the beaches, however, Japanese bombers and fighters bombed and strafed four LCIs. Yet in less than four hours the ESB got ashore, and LSTs and LCIs landed eight thousand troops, tanks, steel matting for road building, and fifteen hundred tons of stores. They then retracted. On September 4, Japanese aircraft damaged several LSTs and the *Conyngham*. Despite air attacks, much work normally accomplished by the service force was undertaken by Barbey's crews. After twelve days of fighting, the Japanese abandoned Lae, thus removing the last serious threat to southeastern New Guinea.[39]

With Lae taken more rapidly than expected, MacArthur wished quickly to seize Finschhafen, a small port one hundred miles up the coast from Lae that guarded the western side of narrow Vitiaz Strait between New Guinea and New Britain. On September 17 he asked Generals Blamey and Ennis C. Whitehead, the latter Kenney's deputy, how soon their forces could be ready. Blamey said "soon" but did not know exactly when. Kenney tried to beg off, but Whitehead said he would be ready the next day. Having anticipated MacArthur's decision, Barbey said he would be ready in one or two days but wanted more air cover than in the past because his ships must operate in the narrow waters of Vitiaz Strait. Nudged by MacArthur, Kenney promised to provide two layers of air cover over the beaches and two over the convoys beginning at daylight.

With September 22 chosen as D-Day, Barbey had only three days to prepare plans and assemble ships and load cargo and only six days to pick up troops at Buna and Lae. As General Wooten opposed a night landing, Barbey planned to beach his craft one hour before daylight and land not only the troops but fifteen days' worth of supplies. In this way time would be provided to build airfields from which aircraft could provide cover. As Commander Adair put it, Finschhafen "was not that bad when you consider that we landed, in about four hours, the following: 5,300 troops, 180 vehicles, 32 guns, and 850 tons of bulk stores."[40] However, the troops met such ground and air resistance that Finschhafen was not declared secure until October 3. "Finschhafen was easy," said MacArthur's chief planner, Colonel Bonner Fellers, "but *time consuming*. Then and there I decided that if we were to liberate Manila, which was some 2,500 miles away, we had better start taking some longer hops."[41]

While Barbey sent resupply runs to Finschhafen, MacArthur planned for a landing at Gasmata, on the south coast of New Britain. With it secured, he could then move onto Cape Gloucester and so clear both sides of Vitiaz Strait of enemy forces. Concerned about the feasibility of the operation, however, he called a conference at GHQ. With Gasmata only 193 miles from Rabaul and the nearest Allied air base 300 miles distant, Kenney said he could not guarantee air cover. Barbey said that he had no ships forthcoming and that any great loss of ships at Gasmata might cause the postponement of the Cape Gloucester operation. Unwilling to expose priceless transports to attack, he proposed to use only craft that discharged troops directly to the beaches. The issue was debated on November 2 by Major General William H. Rupertus, U.S. Marine Corps, Barbey, and Krueger's operations officer. With Admiral Carpender saying that the operation was impossible from the naval point of view, Barbey consulted with his own intelligence officer, William Mailliard, who knew that Carpender would admit to having made an error. When Barbey asked Carpender if he had not made an overhasty decision, the latter banged a fist on his desk and exclaimed, "Very well, I reverse myself."[42]

Barbey and Carpender then spent a night pouring over charts of New Britain's south coast and decided upon the little coral-infested harbor of Arawe, eighty-six miles closer to Finschhafen than was Gasmata. When the conference with MacArthur resumed next morning, Carpender noted that amphibious tractors and tanks rather than landing craft must be used. Kenney said that he would provide air cover, the fast carriers of the Pacific Fleet would contribute aircraft, and Krueger was happy, so that agreement was reached.[43]

At Arawe on December 15, Barbey's men located and marked reefs and channels while troops landed from tractors and Higgins boats. Although half of the men in the first wave became lost, a number of "firsts" had been recorded, including the first use of tractors, rockets, an LSD, an Australian LSI, LCTs as medical centers, a specially trained naval beach party, landing craft control officers (Barbey's brainchild), and the employment of carrier aircraft in close support. In an earlier test landing Barbey had conducted, one LST took three hours to unload, another four and a half hours.[44] At Arawe, LSTs unloaded in less than one hour. Meanwhile, lacking bases on New Guinea at which to conduct amphibious training for large numbers of men, Barbey established his first advance mobile training unit, at Milne Bay.[45]

With Arawe taken, Barbey's ships returned to Milne Bay. There Barbey learned that on November 26, 1943, Vice Admiral Thomas C. Kinkaid had relieved Carpender, who did not get along with MacArthur. Although but eight months older than Barbey, Kinkaid, a 1908 graduate of the U.S. Naval Academy, had like Barbey commanded many ships and task forces and had learned much about army ways when he had helped General Simon Buckner recapture the Aleutians. As Kinkaid saw the problem, "Carpender didn't want to operate the Navy the way the Army wanted [him] to."[46] Barbey agreed. He believed that part of the interservice problem lay in the insistence of Sutherland and Kenney that naval aircraft operating in SWPA do so under Kenney's control, and part of it in Sutherland's deliberately antagonizing ranking naval officers who visited

GHQ. However, MacArthur objected to Carpender's communicating directly with King and Nimitz and was convinced that he was not supporting him fully with his surface units.[47]

Fortunately for Kinkaid, MacArthur quickly took a liking to him even though the latter disagreed with his demand for a fleet, saying that a fleet could not fight the Japanese from Australia.[48] When Krueger and Sutherland told MacArthur that Barbey was tired, Kinkaid went to Milne Bay and spent an evening with him. He reported that Barbey was tired but not too tired to make another landing. Moreover, upon his return to Brisbane Kinkaid told MacArthur of Barbey's sole preoccupation: fear that the air force would not give him proper coverage. MacArthur called a conference at which Kinkaid repeated Barbey's complaint. He added that, while the navy tried to keep a combat air patrol over an objective area, the army kept its planes on the ground until it learned of possible attack. In addition, bomb holes on an airfield could be filled in, but a bombed ship might be lost. Said MacArthur, "You can tell Barbey, you can assure him that he will have adequate air cover to go into Gloucester, and he'll have better cover than he has ever had"—which turned out to be true.[49]

Following the Roosevelt-Churchill Quadrant Conference at Quebec, the Combined Chiefs of Staff directed that Rabaul be neutralized rather than assaulted. At any rate, just eight days after reaching Milne Bay, Barbey was leading a convoy carrying the First Marine Division for the assault on Cape Gloucester. With most of his ships running supplies into Finschhafen and Arawe, he had very little time for joint training with the 12,500 Marines. Instead of landing from APAs, as they had at Guadalcanal, they would use Barbey's landing craft. Yet the landings have been characterized as "the most nearly perfect amphibious assault in World War II,"[50] and as "the only one of the four major 1st Marine Division landings that went according to plan."[51]

Barbey knew that the flat trajectory of naval gunfire and even aerial bombs were of little value against pillboxes or rain forests extending almost to the shoreline. But how to obtain a plunging, high-explosive fire barrage just ahead of the troops as they hit the beach? In October 1943 the answer had come from his assistant repair officer, who took two LCIs alongside the repair ship *Rigel* and had racks holding twelve rocket launchers installed. The original allowance of 288 rockets was soon increased to 312, with a full reload. Each launcher could fire twelve 4.5-inch rockets in a pattern three hundred yards wide at a range of about twelve hundred yards. The rockets were aimed by the heading of the ship. If a salvo was fired each hundred yards that the ship made good, the troops would land behind a rocket barrage.[52] "The LCI conversion," Barbey later said, "was the result of a typical SWPA 'make do' attitude."[53]

Landings were to be made to the east and west of Cape Gloucester. With Guadalcanal and the recent carnage of the Second Marine Division at Tarawa in mind, the marines wanted to land enough equipment, ammunition, and food to last them for twenty-six days. They provided their own shore party while army drivers took loaded trucks from LSTs in a series of round trips to overlapping dumps. Barbey agreed to the arrangement even though his ships would be on the beach most of D-Day, December 26, 1943.[54]

Barbey commanded the more than one hundred ships that at 0600 on Christmas Day proceeded from near Buna for the twenty-four-hour run to Cape Gloucester. At first light on December 26 his bombardment ships opened up on the two-strip airdrome and beaches while men in small craft buoyed a channel through the reef and minesweepers swept for mines. Troops from APDs and LCIs made for the beaches as Kenney's bombers dropped high-explosive and white phosphorous smoke bombs and two LCI(Rs) and two DUKWs laid a flaming fire curtain ahead of them. The landing came as a complete surprise to the Japanese, who offered no opposition as Barbey landed thirteen thousand troops and seventy-six hundred tons of supplies.[55]

Three factors contributed to this most successful operation. First, thinking that Arawe was to be reinforced, Japanese aircraft struck there rather than at Cape Gloucester. Second, Australian radar on H.M.A.S. *Shropshire* performed exceedingly well. Third, casualties were handled expeditiously by being transferred to hospital LSTs, which then sailed to base hospitals. So well did the LCI(Rs) work that Barbey had another sixteen of them modified for the purpose. Some of the craft could also lay down smoke screens, had equipment and teams to fight fires both in ships and ashore, and carried explosives for blasting channels through reefs so that LSTs could berth.[56]

During the next four months, while the marines cleared the Japanese from the western end of New Britain, Barbey's craft brought in supplies while others engaged in still more landings. On December 16, 1943, meanwhile, the commodious communications and command ship *Blue Ridge* (AGC-2) reported to him for duty. To her he transferred his staff and most of his force's administrative personnel.

Barbey's hope that some respite might be granted to his tired men and ships was blasted when, six days before the Cape Gloucester landings, MacArthur directed that on January 2, 1944, he land 7,500 men and 3,000 tons of equipment and supplies at Saidor, 115 miles west of Finschhafen. This may have been the occasion when, upon being told that plans could not be prepared in a week, he replied, "Then do it in four days"— and it was done.[57]

In Allied hands a Japanese landing strip near Saidor would enable Fifth Air Force planes to patrol Vitiaz Strait and support Cape Gloucester. At Sio, seventy-five miles to the west, were twelve thousand enemy troops. The Saidor landing, said Barbey, was an excellent example of

MacArthur's concept of "hit them where they ain't," and bypass strong-points—in other words, "big gains with little losses."[58]

Leading a fifty-five-ship convoy in the *Conyngham*, Barbey landed the troops fifteen minutes before sunrise. His surprise move more than offset the fact that Kenney's bombers did not reach the area until an hour later. After employing his customary shore bombardment with guns and rockets, he sent his LCIs and then LSTs to the beach. Perhaps because it contained no dramatic moments, the assault received little notice in the press. "The whole operation was just too perfect to be newsworthy," Barbey remarked.[59] He could have added that, except for the capture of Madang, little remained to be done to complete the neutralization of Rabaul and that with his operation against the Gilbert Islands on November 20, 1944, Nimitz had begun his central Pacific drive.

Although the next operation, against the Admiralty Islands, was not scheduled until April 1944, most of Barbey's ships and crews had been employed on extended duty well forward of all normal support for more than six months. Everyone was exhausted from lack of sleep caused by constant air raid alerts. Shore recreation was limited to walking, swimming, and an occasional softball game. There were the heat and the rain—as much as sixteen inches of rain a day at Cape Gloucester fell during the wet season—and fear of air attack meant that movies had to be shown in stifling heat below decks. While the food was good, ice, ice cream, and beer were rarities. The answer lay in more ships and more replacement personnel. Since these were not forthcoming, both ships and men must remain on duty.

Fortunately, Barbey's casualties were few, illnesses involved mostly malaria and skin irritations, he knew of no racial problems, psychiatric cases (combat fatigue) were few, and the overwhelming number of men did their jobs well and uncomplainingly and often gave more thought to the welfare of their shipmates than to themselves.[60] And Barbey agreed with many others that those who lived in ships did not have to face the problems created when female nurses, WACs, and Red Cross workers began arriving in the quieter sections of the combat zones. As he put it, "Women were not fitted for the crude conditions of outdoor living. A few among thousands of men often led to trouble. They would have served their country better by remaining in the rear areas."[61] As for sex, one of his physicians told him, "it did not exist because there wasn't any."[62]

To complete the neutralization of Rabaul and let 100,000 Japanese troops there wither on the vine, the JCS had directed MacArthur to capture the Admiralty Islands and Hansa Bay on the north coast of New Guinea and Admiral Halsey to move his forces up the Solomons and capture Kavieng. But MacArthur's and Nimitz's concept of "advance" differed greatly. To Nimitz, and to King as well, moving westward meant reaching Formosa and China and bypassing the Philippines. Although

MacArthur opposed the central Pacific drive and was determined to return to the Philippines, General H. H. Arnold, chief, army air forces, supported the navy because he wanted bases in the Marianas from which B-29s could raid Japan. In meetings held in Washington on March 11 and 12, Nimitz and MacArthur's chief of staff, General Sutherland, had their say. On the twelfth the JCS ordered MacArthur to occupy Hollandia, New Guinea, on June 15 and Nimitz to seize the Marianas beginning the same day. The JCS also ordered Nimitz to provide cover for MacArthur at Hollandia and during subsequent operations in his theater. To coordinate the campaigns, Nimitz spent March 25-27 conferring with MacArthur in Brisbane. [63]

About 200 miles north of Cape Gloucester and 345 miles northwest of Rabaul, the main Admiralty Islands, Manus and Los Negros, contained Seeadler harbor, fifteen miles wide and four long. Separated by only a narrow strait, both islands had airfields and contained perhaps four thousand Japanese troops. These would be assaulted by Major General Innis P. Swift's First Cavalry Division. To facilitate joint planning, Barbey proceeded to meet Swift in Oro Bay. By February 23, four possible landing areas had been studied, and it had been agreed to land the troops on four beaches inside Seeadler Harbor. On the next day, as a result of Kenney's statement that Los Negros was ripe for the picking, MacArthur directed Swift to land a "reconnaissance in force" of 882 men on Los Negros within five days. It was the old "hurry up" again. Lacking sufficient APDs, Barbey had to use destroyers as transports. At any rate, he and Swift then visited General Krueger, who would coordinate the planning, at Finschhafen. [64]

Meanwhile carrier aircraft strikes of February 16 and 17 had revealed that Japanese defenses on Truk and presumably on other islands were weak and that elements of the Japanese fleet at Truk had been withdrawn farther westward. One of MacArthur's planners, Bonner Fellers, feeling that progress was being made too slowly, began planning for a long leap to Hollandia.

As D. Clayton James has noted, "There was better Army-Navy cooperation during these hectic days than the Southwest Pacific command had experienced in its nearly two years of existence." [65] However, plans for assaulting the Admiralties were not sent out until the night of February 26, and H-Hour was set for 0815 on the twenty-ninth. As Barbey's last ships loaded at Oro Bay on the twenty-seventh, MacArthur and Kinkaid flew staff officers to confer with him. When the *Phoenix* arrived at Oro Bay, Barbey told MacArthur and Kinkaid that he would remain there to complete plans for reinforcement echelons and that a new man, Rear Admiral William M. Fechteler, would command the attack force. Fechteler, a 1916 graduate of the U.S. Naval Academy, had reported as Barbey's deputy on January 27, 1944.

The reconnaissance force reached Hayane Harbor on February 29 and surprised its defenders. However, Japanese resistance then became so furious that Krueger visited Barbey on March 3 to learn what he could do. The nine troop-laden destroyers and three APDs sent by Barbey turned the tide, and Krueger informed MacArthur on the fifth that the Admiralties were secure.[66] The navy waited until April 3 to do so. Admiral King characterized the operation as "a brilliant maneuver."[67] However, it had taken a year for the Allies to advance 240 miles northward from Buna—and Manila was still 2,240 miles ahead.

The next assault was scheduled for Hansa Bay. Seeing the need for a longer hop, one he thought would shorten the war by three months, Bonner Fellers spoke with Captain Tarbuck and an air force planner. According to Tarbuck, when Kenney asked him how many aircraft carriers would be needed at Hansa Bay, he said three, but Kenney told MacArthur that Tarbuck had said that "the Navy could not support the landing."[68] When Fellers disclosed his Hollandia scheme to him, General Chamberlin "hit the ceiling and ordered me to drop the wild scheme," Fellers later told Barbey, adding, "We continued to work on our plan anyway." Being on terrible terms with Sutherland, Fellers then spoke with MacArthur's aide-de-camp, who passed the word to MacArthur, who approved. Livid, Chamberlin fired Fellers for having bypassed Sutherland.[69] As a result MacArthur decided to ask the JCS to cancel the Hansa Bay, Wewak, and Kavieng operations and substitute a three-pronged attack on Humboldt Bay, Aitape, and Tanahmerah Bay—more simply Hollandia—and sent Sutherland to Washington to press for its adoption. If the JCS approved the greatest amphibious operation yet to be attempted in SWPA, some of the Nimitz's combatant ships must be transferred to it and in addition auxiliaries to support the nearly eighty thousand men who would be involved.

Barbey felt that, while amphibious operations were the navy's business, they were being directed by the Army, "and this was not working too well." To improve the situation, on March 28, 1944, he suggested to Kinkaid that GHQ prepare an operational directive and, after conferring with the Seventh Fleet, army, and AAF leaders, in general terms spell out the mission, method of accomplishment, and approximate forces to be employed. The service leaders would then select their attack force commanders, provide operating directives, and submit them to their superiors for approval. Evidently the suggestion came to nothing, and Barbey often bickered with Krueger over differences in their attack plans. He resented Krueger's giving him orders to send his ships here and there and asked Kinkaid to see MacArthur and solve the problem. Kinkaid replied, "I gave Barbey orders that he was not to fight with the Army, and if he had any fights send them up to me and I'd do the fighting."[70]

To help plan the Hollandia landings, Barbey joined Krueger, Eichel-

berger, and others in Finschhafen. These men proceeded to GHQ to con-
fer with Nimitz and his chief of staff, Rear Admiral Forrest Sherman.
Nimitz promised support but submitted arguments in favor of the central
Pacific drive to the JCS.[71]

JCS approval for the Hollandia operation set the future course of the
Pacific war. Nimitz would occupy the Marianas beginning June 15 and the
Palaus September 15. MacArthur, supported by the Pacific Fleet, would
begin occupying Mindanao on November 15. Thereafter Formosa would
be occupied either directly or via Luzon. With the phasing out of the
SOPAC thereafter slated for August 1, a reorganization of forces was
planned. Halsey would transfer six army divisions to MacArthur and
many naval units to Kinkaid. The latter thereupon assigned command of
the two amphibious forces that he now had to Barbey, who on December
9, 1944, was promoted to vice admiral. As Barbey told Kinkaid, he would
use two of his forces for assault purposes, each capable of transporting a
reinforced division, and the third for training, maintenance, repair of battle damage, and support operations in rear areas.[72]

Plans for the Hollandia operation had to be prepared in just two weeks
and delivered to 217 ships, some of them as far away as Goodenough Island, one thousand miles distant. Barbey warned the army leaders that his
photographic intelligence people had from the foliage of mangroves determined that there was a huge swamp behind the beach at Tanahmerah
Bay. Although Krueger supported him, Eichelberger instead depended
upon information furnished him by a native, with results noted below.[73]

Barbey then disagreed when Krueger recommended using four AKs
for the operation, saying that they carried few boats and would be vulnerable to air attack if they remained in the forward area until they were unloaded. The incident was typical of cases in which army men saw their
equipment as expendable but failed to realize that the loss of a ship meant
the loss of a complete unit that could not be replaced in the near term.
Barbey therefore assumed a calculated risk in agreeing to have two lightly
loaded AKs move to Hollandia with the D-Day convoys but leave on
D + 2 whether they were unloaded nor not. Kinkaid sweetened the pill
for the army by providing six LSTs and also by having all large assault ships
carry extra landing craft.[74]

D-Day was set for April 22. Noting increases in Allied ship movements and loading operation, the Japanese anticipated an attack on Hansa
Bay or Wewak rather than on Hollandia, which they thought was too far to
the westward for the Allies to reach. Meanwhile Barbey for the first time
enjoyed good liaison with the AAF by exchanging some of his planning officers with some of Kenney's. Moreover, Kenney's planes, navy land- and
tender-based aircraft, and the aircraft of Vice Admiral Marc A. "Pete"
Mitscher's fast carrier task force, ensured that Japanese aircraft at Hansa
Bay, Wewak, and Aitape would offer little resistance at Hollandia. While

Mitscher would depart the day after the landings, Thomas L. Sprague's escort carriers would remain in the area for ten days and so would give Kenney time to move up his aircraft. MacArthur had 750,000 men in SWPA in all services. Although he had good intelligence on the numbers and types of Japanese forces at Hollandia, it remains unknown whether he passed this information on to Barbey.[75]

Plans for Operation RECKLESS called for a triple play—simultaneous daylight landings on April 24 at Humboldt Bay (Hollandia), Tanahmerah Bay, thirty miles to the westward, and Aitape, 120 miles to the eastward. Though the last had no harbor, the airfield there, when taken, could be used to cover Hollandia. Short of staff, Barbey sent members of his own staff to Fechteler, who would command at Humboldt Bay, and others to his own chief of staff, Captain Albert G. Noble, who would command at Aitape with "Red" Jamison as his deputy. Barbey himself, at Tanahmerah, would supervise all three task forces. With his flag lieutenant as his only aide, he was in overall command of the entire operation except for the fast carriers.[76]

To Barbey's dismay, on April 10 MacArthur told him that it might be necessary to assault Wakde Island immediately after the Hollandia landings. Aircraft from a small Japanese field on Wakde, with some from fields on the mainland, he said, might harass efforts to develop a naval and air base at Hollandia. Krueger was to submit naval, air force, and army requirements by April 22. While dispersing his staff for the Hollandia operation, Barbey had to submit his requirements for the Wakde operation.

To deceive the Japanese, Barbey's first convoy sailed from Finschhafen to the Admiralty Islands, then westward toward Hollandia. Two convoys followed at twenty-four-hour intervals. In his flagship, now the *Swanson* (DD-443), was Eichelberger, who commanded the troops of the western and central attack forces in his first amphibious operation. Krueger, the overall army commander, rode the destroyer *Wilkes*, and MacArthur the cruiser *Nashville*.

On D − 1 Noble's force split off for Aitape, where for the first time in the Pacific war pontoon barges were used. Soon thereafter Fechteler's force headed for Humboldt Bay while Barbey continued toward Tanahmerah Bay. At the last moment, following the usual shore bombardment, a preliminary air strike was canceled because of little opposition, and Barbey hastened his landing craft forward. When the landing force was halfway to the beach Mitscher's planes strafed and bombed the shoreline. Then Barbey's rocket ships opened up. By the time the firing stopped the troops had reached the beach—unopposed—as was the case also at Hollandia and Aitape. But because the Tanahmerah beaches were unsuitable, only one division was landed there and the other sent to Humboldt Bay. Blocked by a sago swamp behind the beach, that division spent three weeks there and had eaten up its reserve rations before it was taken off.[77]

At his call, Krueger, Eichelberger, and Barbey joined MacArthur on a visit to the beach. There, according to correspondent Frazier Hunt, MacArthur said of Barbey, "There goes just about the Number One amphibious commander in the world." After returning with his commanders to the *Nashville* and reviewing the day's events, MacArthur startled his guests by suggesting that they strike Wakde Island while the Japanese were still off balance. Could Barbey carry out his part in such an operation? Although the new operation meant carrying out three landings in eighteen days, Barbey replied that he was "all for it"; his preliminary planning was finished and any changes in plans could be made by radio. While Krueger was noncommittal, Eichelberger was vehemently opposed on the ground that initial success did not obviate heavy fighting later. Why start a new operation until the one at hand was further along? MacArthur agreed with Eichelberger and postponed the Wakde operation.[78]

To Hollandia, Barbey's "brood of chickens" had carried 79,800 army personnel, 50,000 tons of bulk stores, and more than 3,000 vehicles. But as Walter Karig has written, "they weren't just moving people. They were moving gas stations, bulldozers and construction equipment, lumber and saw mills, bridges, telephone companies, hospitals, tool shops, gasoline and dry goods stores, and explosives. They were even bringing along a post office for good measure. It was like picking up a city the size of Galveston, Texas, and planting it in three different locations along the coast of Florida.[79]

A problem that plagued every operation was that of beach control. At Eichelberger's insistence, Barbey loaded so many supplies for Hollandia that they and many ships piled up on the beaches. During the second night of the operation at Tanahmerah Bay a Japanese plane bombed the middle of the beach and destroyed twelve precious LST cargo loads. Although no ships were lost, twenty men were killed and one hundred were seriously wounded, and explosions and fires among the gasoline and ammunition dumps continued for four days. In addition the AK *Etamin* was hit by an aerial torpedo while off Aitape. Her damage supported Barbey's contention that such large ships should not be used in early convoys, and in subsequent operations he thinned out both ships and supplies.

Edwin Hoyt has alleged that "one thing Nimitz had not liked about Barbey's amphibious technique was the piling or storage of ammunition and other supplies on the beachhead" and that Kinkaid would later worry that he would do the same thing at Leyte Gulf. Hoyt added that Kinkaid implicitly trusted Theodore S. Wilkinson, a senior amphibious commander in the Pacific fleet, but "thought Barbey a little too ambitious, but he gave the latter credit for being a very fine amphibious commander."[80] The statement stems from Kinkaid's comment in his oral reminiscences: "Well, Barbey, to me, was difficult personally. Barbey was a good amphibious commander, but became a little too ambitious. I think he spent a good part of his time wondering how long I was going to stay there." But when Nimitz commented negatively about Barbey as an amphibious commander, Kinkaid defended him, even saying that the SWPA people did a better job of clearing a beach of landed stores than did Wilkinson's or Turner's people. In sum, Kinkaid disliked people who sought press attention, and in this matter he thought Barbey "too pushy." However, he did not mention this fact in the fitness reports he wrote on Barbey. In a report dated November 28, 1943, he called Barbey "an outstanding officer of excellent personal and military character" and give him a 4.0 for both his executive and his administrative work. A report dated April 1, 1944, was marked 4.0 and contained the comment that "Vice Admiral Barbey has displayed a high order of leadership and initiative in amphibious operations against the enemy." With respect to later mopping-up operations in the Philippines and Borneo operations, he rated Barbey between 3. 6 and 4.0 and commented that "all operations were well and efficiently conducted."[81]

MacArthur privately praised his subordinates for good work but usually referred only to his "forces" in public releases. For this reason Barbey had an officer trained in journalism serve part time "to improve the PR of the Seventh Amphibious Force." Moreover, after he obtained the *Blue Ridge* he carried up to ten war correspondents with him, who popularized him. In *Newsweek* for October 23, 1944, for example, Robert Shaplen wrote about him in an article headed "The Duck-billed Admiral: Amphibious Daniel E. Barbey Sets MacArthur's Troops Ashore." In *Life* for November 20, 1944, John Walker's headline read "Uncle Dan Barbey: An Amphibious Admiral Moved MacArthur's Army." These and other reporters gave Barbey the unofficial titles of "Founder of Modern Amphibious Warfare" and "Grandfather of U. S. Amphibious Warfare."

Shaplen saw Barbey as a "stocky, gray-haired man with a constant smile . . . able to improvise brilliantly and to get along on a shoestring." He found his training program to be "the most unique feature of the Seventh Amphibious Force."[82] And John Walker told the American people that Barbey "possesses one of the most common physical badges of the top-notch fighting man, a big, jutting nose. The rest of his features—chin, ears, cheekbones, brow—are big in proportion and the whole Barbey countenance, with dark brown eyebrows and iron-gray hair, silver-plated at the temples, adds up to something like a Roman senator."[83]

On D + 3 Barbey relinquished command and prepared to leave Hollandia. While still there, however, he was told by Mitscher's new chief of staff, Arleigh Burke, that Mitscher's fast carriers must return to the central Pacific. Barbey disagreed when Eichelberger recommended that Mitscher not leave. When Eichelberger appealed to MacArthur, the latter refused to refer the appeal to Nimitz.[84] In any event, in his action report on the Tanahmerah Bay landing, Barbey wrote, "This operation was the forerunner, in many ways the prototype, of the operations to be conducted in the future when battleships, fast carriers, cruisers, and CVEs were all to be employed in [a] tactical unit to produce uniformly successful amphibious landings."[85]

While Barbey shipped additional troops and supplies to Hollandia, he also had to prepare for the Wakde Island invasion set for May 15 and the Biak operation set for the twenty-seventh. In addition he established his second advance ATC at Hollandia and his third at Cape Torokina, Bougainville.

While Fechteler planned the Biak operation, Barbey made a quick trip to Washington to present his case for more ships and personnel. His visit was badly timed. Interest there centered upon the impending invasion of Normandy. The Joint Chiefs less Admiral William D. Leahy had left for England to witness the great event, and priority for the building of large landing craft had been given to the European campaign for the first five months of 1944. Barbey wanted to go over as an observer and learn what he could for the projected Mindano invasion. When lack of time and transportation precluded his doing so, he consoled himself with the thought that the conditions at Normandy were so different from those in SWPA that he could not have learned anything useful.[86]

King returned to Washington on June 19 and, in Barbey's words, "the war, as fought in the Pentagon, went on as before."[87] The Joint Chiefs had approved plans in which Nimitz would assault the Palaus and MacArthur the island of Morotai, the northernmost island of the Moluccas which guarded the eastern approaches to the Philippines. King impressed upon Barbey that Mindanao would be the western terminus of MacArthur's campaign and that emphasis would center upon Nimitz's central Pacific drive, which would bypass the northern Philippines and assault Formosa and thus isolate Japan. However, MacArthur—to whom he revealed persistent hostility—could contribute to the operation by establishing some air bases on Mindanao useful in neutralizing Japanese airfields on Luzon until Nimitz established himself on Formosa. King ended the talk with the sarcastic remark that MacArthur seemed to be more interested in making good his promise to return to the Philippines than in winning the war.[88]

Upon his return to Brisbane on July 2 Barbey excluded King's comments about him when he reported the results of his trip to MacArthur. All that could be expected in SWPA were two amphibious headquarters ships and, when the pressure of operations in the Atlantic eased, some increase in ships and personnel. But King had stressed that the augmentation would be limited to what was needed for an invasion of Mindanao and that, if his wishes were met, there would be no invasion of the islands of Leyte and Luzon. Disregarding his report, MacArthur directed Barbey to

begin planning not only for the invasion of Morotai and of southern Mindanao but also for that of Leyte and Luzon and then for mopping-up operations for the other Philippine islands.[89]

The Wakde Island operation was set for May 15 and the Biak operation for the twenty-fifth. Because spongy soil prevented the building of
airfields capable of handling heavy bombers at Hollandia and at most of
New Guinea to the westward, and because MacArthur wanted to keep the
Japanese off balance, he wanted Wakde taken as soon as possible and Biak
quickly thereafter. Bridling at the early date for Wakde, at a conference
held on the *Nashville* Eichelberger told MacArthur that the ships combat
loaded for Hollandia could not be prepared in time to reach Wakde. According to him, Krueger and Barbey remained silent. He erred, for Barbey was greatly disturbed. How could he plan for Wakde unless he knew
what landing craft and naval and air support would be available? He therefore recommended postponing D-Day to May 21, when there would also
be a higher tide than on the fifteenth and the congestion at Hollandia
would be relieved. Krueger and Kenney supported him, with the result
that MacArthur had the entire operation recast: the Sarmi portion of it
was canceled and the move to Biak was delayed by ten days.[90]

Captain Noble, now Barbey's chief of staff, was the assault commander for the Wakde Island operation, which included enough ships to
carry twenty thousand troops and air force personnel, yet Barbey wondered whether air support would be available and merchant ships could
maintain the flow of supplies. According to labor union regulations, merchant ship crews worked only from 0800 to 1630 during weekdays. Barbey
therefore had to fight the unions as well as the war. In any case, on May 17
his landing craft lifted troops to the small village of Toem, on the mainland
opposite Wakde Island. Against no resistance, artillery was sited with
which to bombard Wakde while ships fired at it, aircraft bombed it, and
LCI(Rs) employed their rockets. The defenders lost 759 men, the U.S.
Army 110, and the U.S. Navy 10.[91]

Wakde Island is one and a half miles long; Biak, forty-five miles long
and also wide. As soon as his ships were released from Wakde, Barbey assigned them to Fechteler as the assault commander for Biak. Using Barbey's now well-seasoned landing plan, Fechteler put the thirty thousand
troops ashore. Barbey correctly expected the Japanese to send aircraft
against the LSTs, which because of a reef had to transship cargo to
DUKWs, LVTs, and LCTs. Fortunately, American submarines attacked a
Japanese convoy embarked in Shanghai and destined for Biak and caused
it to retire, leaving the Japanese in the immediate area only those aircraft
that Mitscher had not destroyed during the Hollandia operation. However, the Japanese were able to get 184 planes to the Vogelkop Peninsula
by June 1, and at Mindanao on May 31 they embarked twenty-five thousand troops escorted by a battleship force. The latter might have over-

whelmed the four Allied cruisers and fourteen destroyers in the SWPA force, but after the troops were landed the naval commander retired to Mindanao.

Beginning on June 2 Japanese pilots attacked the Americans on Biak. On that day they damaged an LST but lost twelve planes. On June 3 forty-one planes attacked. Eleven of them were destroyed and inflicted no damage. In subsequent raids the Japanese suffered more losses than they inflicted, while Allied bombers from Hollandia partly destroyed a resupply convoy that attempted a "Tokyo Express" run. [92]

Because of the importance of Biak in their planning, on June 10 the Japanese high command sent two eighteen-inch-gun battleships and some cruisers and destroyers to eliminate the Allied naval forces in the Biak area and land sufficient troops to retake the island. When the Japanese learned that Nimitz's carrier planes had attacked Guam and Saipan on June 11 and 12, however, they canceled the Biak operation and ordered all fleet units to concentrate in the Philippine Sea and the aircraft at Vogelkop to fly to bases farther north. Had the attack on the Marianas been delayed by a mere week, the recalled Japanese naval squadron could easily have destroyed the Allied ships at Biak, gained command of the sea, and possibly so delayed MacArthur's advance as to reorient the direction of the war, for example by bypassing Luzon and moving directly onto Formosa. While the great American victory in the Battle of the Philippine Sea freed MacArthur to move toward the Philippines, the Japanese could still throw powerful naval and air forces in his path. [93]

After being detained in Brisbane by Kinkaid to help plan operations for the Philippines, Barbey returned to Hollandia. On July 1, 1944, the commander of the Seventh Fleet service force relieved him of the service tasks he had hitherto performed. Meanwhile his own ships poured reinforcements into Biak, which became a key air base and staging area for the invasions of Noemfoor, Sansapor, Morotai, and Leyte Gulf.

In July, finally, Barbey had enough ships to divide them into two groups. Using Barbey's staff, Fechteler would serve as his deputy until ships were provided for him as commander, Amphibious Group 8 (formerly Amphibious Group 1) and Rear Admiral Arthur D. Struble assumed command of Amphibious Group 9 (formerly Amphibious Group 2). With their staffs augmented, by the time of the Leyte Gulf operation in October both could plan directly with appropriate army generals. And by early 1945 Amphibious Group 6 would be formed under command of Rear Admiral Forrest Royal, transferred from the Pacific. [94]

On June 15, 1944, MacArthur directed his senior commanders in the forward area to prepare to assault Noemfoor on July 2. With Japanese aircraft in the area called away to the Marianas, Barbey said that the assault was "more like a training exercise than an attack on a supposedly well defended island." [95]

While Barbey's ships brought reinforcements and supplies to Noemfoor, on July 3 MacArthur ordered plans drafted for an assault on Cape Sansapor on the Vogelkop Peninsula on July 30. Now that the cape had been taken, except for some mopping up, his New Guinea campaign would end and he could seize island stepping-stones on his way to the Philippines. And Kinkaid's Seventh Fleet had now grown to respectable strength.

The Japanese had few planes at their thirty-one airfields within striking range of the Vogelkop Peninsula. Rather than assault defended airfields at Sorong and Manokwari, MacArthur would land at a point midway between them and have airfields built. With these and the bomber bases at Biak, Noemfoor, and Sansapor, he could provide air support for the troops that would seize Morotai, his last step on his way to the Philippines.

Planning for the Vogelkop operation was simplified because most of the senior commanders were in Hollandia. Expecting no opposition and with good beaches available, Barbey had only to run a ferry service. The beach chosen was twelve miles northeast of Sansapor. There on July 30 Barbey's forty-eight amphibious craft landed 13,500 combat troops, 7,000 service personnel, and 7,000 air force people with only one casualty, but the dreaded tick and scrub typhus infected more than 800 troops by the end of August, before remedial steps, including the spraying of DDT, ended the scourge. There was no serious fighting on the Vogelkop, and with the Sansapor operation over, Barbey needed only to provide resupply. At Sansapor his force ended a year-long trek of fifteen hundred miles from one end of New Guinea to the other, with eleven hundred miles covered in the last two months. And with the north coast of New Guinea now in hand, MacArthur had airfields and bases to support operations against Morotai.[96]

Barbey now proceeded to GHQ and sent representatives to Krueger's headquarters to work on plans to assault the Morotai and Talaud islands. Morotai would be invaded on September 15, the Talauds soon thereafter, and Sarangani Bay, on the southeastern end of Mindanao, on November 15. Meanwhile Nimitz would assault the islands of Peleliu, Ulithi, and Yap and would cover both series of operations. While the SOPAC theater was designated a rear area, Halsey would continue to command the Third Fleet but not be tied to any area. As already noted, the JCS had said nothing about MacArthur's movements beyond Mindanao, but the latter had ordered plans drafted for an invasion of Leyte Gulf. Sutherland and Tarbuck took these plans to the JCS for approval.[97]

While Sutherland and Tarbuck were in Washington, MacArthur was summoned to Honolulu by July 26. There President Roosevelt and Admirals Leahy and Nimitz had already discussed the conflicting views of Nimitz and MacArthur on Pacific strategy. The president left the matter hanging, but MacArthur believed that Leahy supported him. In any event, the JCS soon directed MacArthur to land on Leyte but advised that they would decide later whether Luzon would be occupied before Formosa.

With these decisions made, Barbey began planning for the invasion of Morotai, which he would command. While Kenney's planes and those from Admiral Thomas L. Sprague's CVEs eliminated Japanese air from the surrounding area, he had PT boats engage in search-and-destroy operations. With American planes controlling the skies he could fully load his LSTs and land them on the west side of the Gila Peninsula.

Although the staging plan was the most complicated one since the Hollandia operation, the preinvasion tactics and makeup of the Morotai invasion convoy—100 ships carrying 16,842 troops—differed little from earlier ones. Because reefs and coral heads fouled the approaches to the beaches, pontoons were used until engineers had built a pier able to accommodate Liberty ships. Soon after the initial landing MacArthur startled Barbey by saying that Halsey had noted great Japanese weakness in the central Philippines and recommended to Nimitz the canceling of all intermediate landings and landing in Leyte Gulf on October 20 rather than December 20. Nimitz concurred, the JCS plan to land on Mindanao was scrapped, and MacArthur applauded. With Morotai in hand he had taken his last step on his return to the Philippines, and for operations there Nimitz offered him the use of his Third Amphibious Force, commanded by Vice Admiral Wilkinson. But only thirty-five days were left for the completion of plans for invading Leyte Gulf.[98]

Barbey did not know that Nimitz, King, and Kinkaid had corresponded about command relations for the Leyte Gulf operation. Nimitz knew that Kinkaid expected Barbey to command the Joint Expeditionary Forces, indeed had requested that Nimitz furnish him with three junior amphibious commanders. "This would place the largest amphibious operation in the Pacific to date under Barbey, assisted by Fechteler, [Charles P.] Cecil, [Richard L.] Conolly, Royal, and [Lawrence F.] Reifsnider," wrote Nimitz to King, who added that he would have five experienced amphibious commanders unemployed between the Palau and Formosa operations. Moreover, if large ships and amphibious forces from the Pacific Fleet went to Kinkaid, "then there should go with them some of the experienced officers who know how to handle large forces." King told Kinkaid, "My approach to the problem is that the First and Second Amphibious Groups in the 7th Amphibious Force (under Barbey) be built up by appropriate additions from the Amphibious Forces, Pacific Fleet. . . . Further, that the Third Amphibious Force, preferably under Wilkinson . . . be assigned amphibious tasks under you." With Barbey and Wilkinson in parallel, Barbey could proceed to make his plans with the army and army air forces in SWPA before Wilkinson arrived.[99]

Wilkinson thought that he should command at Leyte and wished to have Conolly lead one amphibious force and Barbey another. He had not counted on MacArthur's sturdy support for Barbey. "The reason for Kinkaid's decision," Conolly later said, "was that MacArthur did not want Barbey superseded, even though Wilkinson was very senior to him. He did not want anyone put over Barbey. (I don't think Kinkaid was too keen on Barbey.) We had come into the Southwest Pacific from the Central Pacific and we were considered outsiders."[100]

On MacArthur's order, the Leyte operation plan was prepared by Tarbuck's red planning team. While representatives of all the services conferred at GHQ from July 20 to August 6, army and navy commanders from the central Pacific flocked to Hollandia, where 589 ships had gathered by October 13. As Tarbuck planned, Barbey would land the two divisions of Major General Franklin C. Sibert's Tenth Corps, while Wilkinson landed the Twenty-fourth Corps troops of Major General John R. Hodge. Barbey divided his northern attack force so that each part would land one division. He gave Fechteler command of the northern half but retained control of the rest. He directed Struble, recently arrived from Normandy, to land the Sixth Ranger Battalion and his own scouts and seize two small islands guarding the eastern entrance to Leyte Gulf and a small island at the southern end of the gulf bordering on Surigao Strait. With these captured and navigation lights installed, minesweepers could go to work at the entrance to the gulf and in the vicinity of the landing beaches.[101]

While Kinkaid and British naval commanders discounted the possibility that Japanese naval forces would attack their ships in Leyte Gulf, Tarbuck submitted a paper on October 4 to General Chamberlin, copies to Kinkaid and Willoughby, the last MacArthur's chief intelligence officer. The paper showed that a Japanese southern fleet would make a night attack through Surigao Strait on the amphibious forces in the gulf and that another fleet would cross San Bernardino Strait and attack the gulf from the north. However, the generals disagreed with him, and Barbey felt confident that Halsey and his Third Fleet, off to the east, could handle the situation.[102]

Barbey left Hollandia on October 13, his *Blue Ridge* carrying several army commanders and their staffs and six reporters. Although his 119 ships proceeded at only six knots, "that was enough," he said, "to take us to a great moment in history."[103] As he entered the gulf he worried about mines and whether his ships would be in position on time and be able to beat off air attacks. He also wondered how MacArthur felt on the eve of his return to the Philippines. At 0400 on October 20 he led his ships, which arrived ninety seconds ahead of schedule, toward their beaches and anchored his flagship. She would remain stationary for the next five days. With his ships both on time and in the right position, Tarbuck stated, "No trained officer witnessing the perfect functioning of such a complex form

Meeting aboard a destroyer during the Hollandia operation, April 1944: Barbey, Major General Horace Fuller, Rear Admiral William N. Fechteler, and Eichelberger; *below*, Barbey welcomes Krueger and Kinkaid aboard his flagship off Leyte, October 1944. Courtesy U.S. Naval Institute.

of warfare could fail to admire the skill and professional judgment of Admiral Barbey and his staff."[104] That afternoon MacArthur landed in Barbey's area and announced his return to the Philippines. By 1950 the Tacloban and Dulag airstrips had been captured, and Barbey's ships had unloaded, loaded casualties, and stood out in the gulf. At 1600, meanwhile, General Sibert relieved Barbey of command of the northern operation.

On October 23 Barbey attended MacArthur at Tacloban, where the latter turned over the civil government of the Philippines to President Sergio Osmeña. With his combatant ships in the gulf under aerial attack, Barbey felt that the ceremonies were unreal. He was anxious to return to his job. Meanwhile his smoke-laying LCIs proved of immeasurable value in the Gulf, where kamikazes were the major threat to shipping. In addition his LST-464 provided medical services until hospital ships arrived three days later, and his firefighting LCIs did good work along the shore. He sweated out the news of the approach, as Tarbuck had predicted, of three Japanese naval surface forces until he heard that Oldendorf had destroyed two of them in Surigao Strait. He left out of his book what his PR man recalled: "When it got the hottest and we were not sure we were going to get out of the harbor you called me up and ordered me to get guns and ammunition for three (you, Mailliard, and me) with some food and a map of the Philippines. You were not sure if we might have to beach and blow up the [*Blue Ridge*] and go ashore with the Army to fight."[105]

Halsey, meanwhile, independent from MacArthur, acted under Nimitz's order to "cover and support" the landings. But Nimitz had offered him an option: to destroy "a major portion of the enemy fleet." Halsey interpreted his paramount mission as the destruction of a Japanese carrier force reported to the northward of the Philippines. By going north on October 25, however, he left San Bernardino Strait unguarded and let Admiral Takeo Kurita's battleship force slip through. Hoping to save some of his own ships, Barbey concentrated them in shallow San Juliano Strait, which separates Leyte from Samar. Kurita then sank one escort carrier and several destroyers and destroyer escorts in the northernmost of the three CVE groups to the eastward of Leyte Gulf. For reasons of his own, at about noon he retired. After sending Tarbuck at 1600 to obtain Kinkaid's permission to do so, Barbey sent five LCIs and two PCs to rescue survivors, the only part his forces played in the Battle of Leyte Gulf itself.[106]

With the arrival of a resupply convoy on October 26, Barbey sailed for Hollandia, where he would plan for an assault on Lingayen Gulf, Luzon. In reporting to Kinkaid he stressed the need to combat kamikaze attacks on landing ships and asked that in the future APAs not be used in assault landings, that assault waves be landed in a given sequence (namely APDs, LCIs, LSMs, and LSTs), and that group landing craft commanders use Coast Guard cutters or destroyers as headquarters ships. Moreover, by providing six LCIs and four LSMs for a battalion landing team, he could provide almost as much lift as an APA.[107] As for the six British LSIs recently arrived from England, they were so different from their American APA counterparts and in such poor condition that they were barely useful for training.[108]

On December 7, Tarbuck became Barbey's chief of staff, with promotion to commodore impending.[109] At about the same time Captain John D. Hayes joined up. Barbey used the latter to help plan future operations and, judging him the best writer on his staff, gave him the additional duty of writing his command history.

Lacking enough amphibious ships to resupply Leyte and also to make other landings before moving on to Lingayen Gulf, Barbey used Liberty ships to make most of the resupply runs. In reply to Kinkaid's request that he describe the lessons learned at Leyte and make recommendations for improvement, he said that he had learned little that was not evident from previous operations: on D-Day the smallest number of ships needed should be used and for the shortest possible time; follow-on echelons, including salvage parties, should unload on the day they arrived; emergency airstrips should be built at the earliest moment; hospital-rigged LSTs should be employed; and there should be unity of command for both the assault and service forces.[110]

The assault of Lingayen Gulf would be another joint operation under MacArthur's direction. Given that there were more Japanese on Luzon than on Leyte, more troops were called for and more ships to carry them. However, the slow progress of Eichelberger's men on Leyte and delays in the completion of army airfields from which convoys heading for Lingayen could be protected made it necessary to postpone the latter landing to January 9, 1945, and required the construction of airfields on some other adequate island. MacArthur chose Mindoro ("Land of Gold"), three hundred miles northwest of Leyte. It was a bold choice because while enemy airfields ringed Mindoro it was beyond the range of friendly aircraft from Leyte. However, none of his subordinates could persuade him to change his mind.

An important immediate task was to stop Japanese supply runs into ports on the west coast of Leyte, especially to Ormoc. In landing the Seventy-seventh U.S. Infantry Division there, Struble lost a destroyer and an APD and had another destroyer seriously damaged by kamikazes. MacArthur thereupon postponed the Mindoro landing from December 5 to December 15.[111]

The 169 ships in Struble's central Visayan task force carried 17,800 troops, 9,500 air force personnel, and 5,900 service troops. Although he was escorted by three battleships, six escort carriers, and three heavy cruisers with eighteen destroyers as a screen, he could not stop all kamikazes, which hit first the convoy and then the beached ships as they unloaded. Yet the twenty-seven LSTs unloaded on D-Day set a new record.[112] The first and second resupply echelons to Mindoro were also attacked, with heavy losses especially of LSTs. Whenever possible, Barbey did not immediately assign ships that had operated in forward areas for more than a year to new operations.

Barbey's plans called for the employment of more than nine hundred ships in Lingayen Gulf, a large, sheltered body of water about one hundred miles north of Manila that contained good beaches on which LSTs could unload directly over dry ramps. As ships in more distant ports departed early, Barbey on December 23, his birthday, attended a party given by those who would remain behind for those who would leave on a 2,150-mile journey. He shoved his small craft off on the twenty-fourth and followed in his faster *Blue Ridge* on the twenty-sixth.[113]

Ships of all types from many ports made up convoys in the greatest overseas expedition in history. Barbey's convoy would land 100,000 troops at San Fabian. Another convoy with another 100,000 troops followed. At no time would the convoys be more than twenty minutes flight time from more than seventy enemy airfields, ten torpedo boat bases, and two submarine bases.

Crossing Surigao Strait from Leyte Gulf, Oldendorf's bombardment force delivered harassing fire in Lingayen Gulf for three days while minesweepers and hydrographic groups operated inshore. On the morning of January 9, 1945, Barbey took his San Fabian group to Beach White, Fechteler took his ships to Beach Blue to the east, and Wilkinson landed to the south. Barbey's troops began disembarking at 0715. The first wave landed at 0930, the last at 0940. The troops landed unopposed because the enemy had retreated to defensive positions in nearby hills. Combatant ships and amphibious ships not yet unloaded anchored under cover of a dense smog laid by LCIs.[114]

On February 4 Barbey told Kinkaid that many of his officers and men were ill or exhausted and should be given leave in Australia or the United States. He asked Kinkaid to reverse his order that such leave not be granted and let his force commanders decide who should go. As for himself, both Admirals King and Jacobs had suggested that he and Fechteler be returned to the States "for a blow." Instead he requested two weeks' leave in Australia during February but asked that Fechteler be returned home for six weeks. In addition, his escort ships and landing craft badly needed overhauling.[115]

As the troops landed in Lingayen Gulf proceeded southward along the central Luzon plain, at MacArthur's direction Barbey landed the forty-four thousand men of the Eleventh Corps at an undefended beach at San Antonio, on Luzon's west coast about fifty miles northwest of the entrance to Manila Bay. Other troops landed a few miles south of the entrance were to join the San Antonio group and those coming from the north to invest Manila and so seal Bataan off from the Japanese. Meanwhile landings were made to capture the group of small islands guarding the entrance to the bay. Troops carried in Barbey's ships assaulted Mariveles on February 15, 1945, while army landing craft brought troops to help paratroopers secure Corregidor. On Barbey's order, Tarbuck destroyed the booths in Malinta Tunnel that controlled the mines in the channel north of Corregidor so that his ships could enter it. On March 1 Barbey in a PT boat took MacArthur on his return to "The Rock," which he had left on March 11, 1942. On March 27 a small amphibious force landed on Caballo and another on El Fraile (Fort Drum). Then, while troops cleared Manila, Barbey went to Leyte Gulf to be near MacArthur and to supervise the fourteen major and twenty-four minor landings in forty-four days, all that were needed to mop up other islands.[116]

Although he had returned for use in the Iwo Jima and Okinawa campaigns the ships lent him by the Pacific Fleet, Barbey now had more ships and men than ever before. Two years earlier he had had about forty ships; now he had more than one thousand. Two years earlier he had waited for staff members to arrive; he now luxuriated with three capable group commanders: Fechteler (later Noble), Struble, and Royal, the last on loan from the central Pacific. Each had his own staff and flagship and enough auxiliary ships to be able to operate independently and simultaneously. Barbey now also had advantages he had not enjoyed during the early days, for Allied air forces controlled the skies and Allied ships the seas. In any event, on February 28 he had Fechteler land troops at Puerto Princessa and Palawan, on March 18 at Panay, and then at Cebu, Negros, Bohol, and Mindanao while plans were drafted for a new series of operations to capture the rich oil ports of Borneo.[117] When Kinkaid returned temporarily to the United States for a month beginning on May 8, Barbey added command of the Seventh Fleet to his other duties.

The Borneo landings presented Barbey with new challenges. There were many more mines than he had ever seen, man-made beach obstacles made of iron rails set upright and connected with heavy wire had to be cleared, there was an extreme tidal range, there was mud instead of sand at the shoreline, and the attackers were from many nations. Australia provided the ground troops, and the naval forces included American, Australian, and Dutch ships. Berkey commanded the naval covering group, Royal the Amphibious Group 6.

The first objective was the small, oil-rich Tarakan Island off the east coast of Dutch Borneo. No surprise was attempted. Under cover of ship and aerial bombardment minesweepers swept mines for four days before Royal on May 1 landed eighteen thousand troops. Although the landing was unopposed, it took six weeks of fighting ashore before the island could be turned over to civil Dutch officials. And Barbey touched off a furor in Australia by saying that in making amphibious landings the Australians "were behind the times . . . , unskilled, and knew little about their equipment."[118]

For Brunei Bay, in North Borneo, with Berkey again providing naval cover, Royal had twice as many troops as those at Tarakan and an underwater demolition team to clear beach obstacles. One week sufficed to gain the objective, whereupon Royal retired to Leyte Gulf to prepare for his next assignment. But the stress of commanding one amphibious operation after another proved too much. He died of a heart attack on June 17.[119]

The third and last amphibious operation in the Borneo series was scheduled for Balikpapan, the oil center on Borneo's southeast coast. There were both Allied and enemy mines, shallow water prevented fire support ships from coming closer than five miles to the beach line, and the nearest Allied air base was more than four hundred miles away. Manmade obstacles lay in water a few hundred yards offshore. On the beach, in addition to mines and pillboxes, the defenders had dug wide trenches connected to oil tanks. If they were fired, blazing oil would greatly impede the attackers. Fortunately, Barbey was able to borrow a division of CVEs from the Pacific.

Barbey would be the overall naval commander, while Noble would command the amphibious task force and Rear Admiral Ralph S. Riggs the cruiser covering group. Again Australia would furnish the troops, and the naval forces would include American, Australian, and Dutch ships. Because Balikpapan was easy to defend, Allied planes bombarded it for sixteen days in one of the longest aerial bombardments of the Pacific war. For two weeks cruisers and destroyers covered minesweepers and the frogmen who cleared and buoyed a boat passage through obstacles.

On July 1, with the largest attack force in the SWPA since that used at Lingayen Gulf, Noble's two hundred ships with thirty-three thousand troops embarked anchored off Balikpapan. Against little opposition the Aussies scrambled ashore to find most of the defenses destroyed. As they went after Japanese holed up in the hills, MacArthur invited Barbey and others to accompany him on an inspection ashore. When MacArthur led his guests to within two hundred yards of the front lines, the rat-tat-tat of machine gun fire caused them to hit the dirt. MacArthur, however, unperturbably stood upright while studying a map. Upon rising Barbey blurted out something about fights ashore being no place for a navy man, but MacArthur said simply, "No, you did exactly right." In any event, with the Balikpapan operation Barbey's Seventh Amphibious Force completed a two-year record of fifty-six amphibious assault landings involving the overwater movement of more than a million men.[120] As Admiral King reported to the secretary of the navy, "These numerous amphibious landings were conducted on short notice and in many instances were so closely spaced that for all practical purposes they were concurrent operations.

Their successful completion on schedule reflects great credit on the commanders for their planning and execution."[121]

On August 14 the Japanese surrendered, thereby rendering superfluous plans that called for MacArthur to invade their home islands. However, a roll-up of rear bases to the Philippines by September 15 began with the more than 150 LSTs, LCTs, and LSMs in the Southwest Pacific area. For the first time Barbey's forces engaged in noncombat operations. Barbey then obtained leave in the United States prior to relieving Kinkaid as commander, Seventh Fleet. On August 15 he turned his amphibious forces over to Turner.

"The man who returned MacArthur to the Philippines" was one of the few American naval officers between World War I and World War II to be concerned with the development of amphibious materials and doctrine. As commander, Seventh Amphibious Force, he insisted upon training, simple language in operations orders, landing where the Japanese were not, and quick unloading of only those essentials needed on a beach. He was quite capable of holding his own in arguments with MacArthur's generals and with MacArthur himself. At his suggestion the latter several times postponed operations or changed objective beaches. Although Barbey was devoted to his men's welfare, no man was ever granted leave or sent to rest camp unless he was wounded. Nor did Barbey ever write a retirement plan. To his credit were the training of twenty-eight American and Australian army and U.S. Marine Corps divisions, and he made a great distinction between his shore-to-shore landings and the ship-to-shore landings that were made in the Pacific.

MacArthur's best biographer, D. Clayton James, evaluated Barbey as "a tough, energetic amphibious specialist who would prove indispensable in the future in planning and directing the landings during the amphibious operations in MacArthur's theater."[122] To Samuel E. Morison, "Barbey was King's gift to MacArthur."[123] Frazier "Spike" Hunt, a war correspondent in SWPA and also a biographer of MacArthur, noted that Barbey had "the MacArthur touch," that is, the ability to operate with few losses, and "knew the art of perfect timing."[124] To Major General Courtney Whitney, MacArthur's intelligence officer, Barbey was "an ingenious, daring leader who, like Halsey, was MacArthur's kind of admiral."[125]

Such admirals as Mark L. Bristol, Thomas C. Hart, Jonas A. Ingram, Adolphus Andrews, James O. Richardson, Nimitz, and Jacobs, all of whom he served, called Barbey as "an excellent officer," "thorough and capable," "active and forceful," "painstaking," "superlatively industrious and hard working," "a man who displayed a fine quality of leadership," and "displayed exceptional initiative."[126] The only comments critical of Barbey were Kinkaid's remark that he was "too ambitious" and a postwar comment by Fechteler, who also thought him "too ambitious," in this case for aspiring to be named ambassador to the Philippines. Mrs. Barbey has offered three comments regarding Barbey's "ambition." First, she averred that she knew of no naval officer who did not wish to be promoted. Second, Barbey enjoyed the company of the reporters who rode his ships; their relaxed life-style was an antidote to the pressures to which he was subjected. He liked them, and they wrote about him. Third, the ambassadorship to the Philippines was her idea, not his. She had many friends in the Department of State who "lived the life of Riley." Although he was too blunt and straightforward for such a post, according to Mrs. Barbey, he went along with her just to please her. When the word leaked out, it was all over.[127]

Barbey served in several important billets before he transferred to the retired list on June 30, 1951. For many years thereafter he served as civil defense director for the state of Washington and sought information from his shipmates for use in writing his book, which was published in 1969 and particularly praises the reserve officers who served him. Had he not written the book, there would be no history of the amphibious operations of the SWPA. He died on April 11, 1969, at the U.S. Naval Hospital, Bremerton, Washington. His name survives in the U.S.S. *Barbey* (DE-1088).

NOTES

ABBREVIATIONS

AMF	Australian Military Forces
AWM	Australian War Memorial
CAB	Cabinet Office (Great Britain)
CCS	Combined Chiefs of Staff
CG	Commanding General
CIGS	Chief of the Imperial General Staff
COS	Chiefs of Staff
LCMD	Library of Congress, Manuscript Division
Msg	Message
NOA	Navy Operational Archives
ONH	Office of Naval History
OPD	War Department Operations Division
OpOrder	operation order
OpPlan	operation plan
Phib For	amphibious force
PREM	Prime Minister's Office (Great Britain)
RG	record group
USAF	U.S. Air Force
USNI	U.S. Naval Institute
WO	War Office (Great Britain)

PREFACE

1. Douglas MacArthur, *Reminiscences* (New York, 1964), pp. 275-76.

2. Ibid., p. 145.

3. Daniel E. Barbey, *MacArthur's Amphibious Navy* (Annapolis, 1969), pp. 24-25.

4. Jay Luvaas, ed., *Dear Miss Em: General Eichelberger's War in the Pacific, 1942-1945* (Westport, Conn., 1972), p. 20.

5. Gordon Walker, "General Walter Krueger: Mystery Man of the Pacific," *Christian Science Weekly Magazine*, June 9, 1945, p. 3.

6. See Roger Olaf Egeberg, *The General* (New York, 1983), pp. 40-41, and Weldon E. Rhodes, *Flying MacArthur to Victory* (College Station, Tex., 1987).

7. D. Clayton James, *The Years of MacArthur*, 3 vols. (Boston, 1972-85), 2:538.

8. Leary, Interview with C.D. Eddleman, August 24, 1985.

DOUGLAS MacARTHUR AND THE WAR AGAINST JAPAN

1. The definitive biography of Douglas MacArthur is D. Clayton James, *The Years of MacArthur*, 3 vols. (Boston, 1970-85), of which vol. 2 covers World War II. Carol Petillo, *Douglas MacArthur: The Philippine Years* (Bloomington, 1981), explores the general's obsession with the islands and offers psychological insights into his personality. The volumes of the official series, *The United States Army in World War II: The War in the Pacific*, provide basic material on strategy, operations, and logistics. Louis Morton, *Strategy and Command: The First Two Years* (Washington, D.C., 1962), in the official series, and Ronald H. Spector, *Eagle against the Sun: The American War with Japan* (New York, 1984), are basic overall accounts.

2. Louis Morton, *The Fall of the Philippines* (Washington, D.C., 1953), pp. 79-90; Walter D. Edmonds, *They Fought with What They Had* (Boston, 1951), pp. 73-109; Robert F. Futrell, "Air Hostilities in the Philippines, 8 December 1941," *Air University Review* 16 (January-February 1965):33-45.

3. Carol M. Petillo, "Douglas MacArthur and Manuel Quezon: A Note on an Imperial Bond," *Pacific Historical Review* 48 (1979):107-17. See also Petillo, *MacArthur*, pp. 203-13. Petillo suggests that Washington approved the gift from fear that MacArthur was losing his nerve and needed this encouragement in order to continue a maximum effort against the Japanese.

4. Douglas MacArthur, *Reminiscences* (New York, 1965), p. 158.

5. Lida Mayo, *Bloody Buna* (Garden City, 1974), pp. 171-77.

6. Australia's military role is described in the multivolume official Australian and British histories, *Australia in the War of 1939-1945* and *History of the Second World War: The War against Japan*. Blamey is quoted from John Robertson, *Australia at War, 1939-1945* (Melbourne, 1981), p. 179, a separate one-volume account. See also David M. Horner, *Crisis in Command: Australian Generalship and the Japanese Threat, 1941-1943* (Canberra, 1978).

7. MacArthur to Army Chief of Staff General George C. Marshall, January 10, 1943, quoted in Morton, *Strategy and Command*, p. 375.

8. The statement was made by his chief of staff, apparently quoting MacArthur; ibid., p. 542, n. 60.

9. James, *MacArthur*, 2:864, n. 43; MacArthur, *Reminiscences*, pp. 181-82.

10. Quoted in James, *MacArthur*, 2:349.

11. Maurice Matloff, *Strategic Planning for Coalition Warfare, 1943-1944* (Washington, D.C., 1959), chap. 17; Robert W. Coakley and Richard M. Leighton, *Global Logistics and Strategy, 1943-1945* (Washington, D.C., 1968), chaps. 16-20.

12. Forrest Pogue, "The Military in a Democracy: A Review of *American Caesar*," *International Security* 3 (1979):60-62, 66-68.

13. E.B. Potter, *Nimitz* (Annapolis, 1976), p. 280.

14. James, *MacArthur*, 2:189.

15. MacArthur, *Reminiscences*, pp. 178-79.

16. Ronald Lewin, *The American Magic: Codes, Ciphers, and the Defeat of Japan* (New York, 1982), chaps. 8 and 12; Alexander S. Cochran, "MacArthur, ULTRA, et La Guerre du Pacifique," *Revue d'histoire de la deuxième guerre mondiale et des conflits contemporains* 34 (January 1984):17-27; Edward J. Drea, "ULTRA Intelligence and General Douglas MacArthur's Leap to Hollandia, January-April 1944," in Michael Handel, ed., *Intelligence and Military Operations* (forthcoming). I am indebted to Dr. Drea for a prepublication copy of his manuscript.

17. MacArthur to the Chief of Military History, March 5, 1943, quoted in John Miller, jr. [*sic*], *CARTWHEEL: The Reduction of Rabaul* (Washington, D.C., 1959), p. 173.

18. The most reliable accounts of the Luzon/Formosa controversy and the Pearl

Harbor conference are Robert Ross Smith, *Triumph in the Philippines* (Washington, D.C., 1963), pp. 3-17; James, *MacArthur*, 2:521-37. MacArthur himself seems to have been the intial source of the claim that Roosevelt accepted his recommendation in favor of Luzon while the president was in Hawaii. Major General Charles A. Willoughby and John Chamberlain, *MacArthur, 1941-1945* (New York, 1954), pp. 233-34; MacArthur, *Reminiscences*, pp. 214-16. In 1946 MacArthur told Herbert Hoover that Roosevelt had agreed to his plan in return for the general's guarantee of great military progress before the November presidential election. Michael Schaller, *The American Occupation of Japan: The Origins of the Cold War in Asia* (New York, 1985), p. 342. But MacArthur's return to the Philippines was not originally scheduled to take place until after the election, and there were surely enough other operations projected from July to November in both Europe and the Pacific to provide whatever military victories the president might have needed.

19. Quoted in Potter, *Nimitz*, p. 280.

20. MacArthur, *Reminiscences*, p. 216.

21. Matloff, *Strategic Planning*, p. 483. Indeed, sizable Japanese forces were still holding out in northern Luzon at the end of the war.

22. MacArthur, *Reminiscences*, p. 216.

23. William Manchester, *American Caesar: Douglas MacArthur, 1880-1964* (Boston, 1978), p. 328. Manchester's biography contains many statments of this sort, but see my critique of his statistics and interpretations. Stanley L. Falk, "Individualism and Military Leadership," *Air University Review* 31 (July-August 1980):98-100.

24. Quoted in James, *MacArthur*, 2:729; also see pp. 766-67; Matloff, *Strategic Planning*, pp. 482-83; General Headquarters, Far East Command, *Reports of General MacArthur* (Washington, D.C., 1966), 1:388-89.

25. Direct and indirect quotations of MacArthur's views appear in Department of Defense, *The Entry of the Soviet Union into the War against Japan: Military Plans, 1941-1945* (Washington, D.C., 1955), pp. 50-51, 80. MacArthur, *Reminiscences*, pp. 301-2; James, *MacArthur*, 2:763-65.

BLAMEY AND MACARTHUR

1. John Monash, *The Australian Victories in France in 1918* (Melbourne, 1923), pp. 319-20; Birdwood to Governor-General of Australia, October 28, 1918, Novar Papers, AWM, Canberra.

2. Shedden Manuscript, Book 4, Box 4, chap. 15, p. 2, Australian Archives, Canberra.

3. The Australian expeditionary force in World War I was known as the Australian Imperial Force. The Australian expeditionary force in World War II became the Second Australian Imperial Force.

4. John Hetherington, *Blamey: Controversial Soldier* (Canberra, 1973), p. 80; L.E. Beavis, review of Gavin Long, *The Final Campaigns*, in *Stand To* 91, (January-February 1964); Long, *The Six Years War* (Canberra, 1973), p. 22.

5. Hetherington, *Blamey*, p. 155. For a discussion of Blamey's performance, see D.M. Horner, *High Command, Australia, and Allied Strategy, 1939-1945* (Sydney, 1982), pp. 85-95.

6. Signal 3, MacArthur to Marshall, March 21, 1942, OPD Exec. 10, item 7D, RG 165, National Archives, Washington, D.C.; Blamey to Shedden, February 19, 1945, Blamey Papers, 23.11, AWM.

7. Assessment by Lieutenant General George Brett in Kenney Diaries, vol. 1, made available by Herman S. Wolk, Chief, General Histories Branch, Office of Air Force History, Bolling Air Force Base, D.C.

8. Memorandum of Chief of Staff from Richardson, July 28, 1942, Minutes of Conference, July 26, 1942, and Radio Message to MacArthur, August 3, 1942, RG 165, OPD 333, item 17, National Archives; Eichelberger Dictations, Book 4, p. VIII-37, copy courtesy of Jay Luvaas.

9. MacArthur's statement of March 18, 1943, is reproduced in "Notes of Discussions [by Shedden] with Commander-in-Chief, Southwest Pacific Area, Brisbane 25-31 May 1943," A 5954 (Shedden Papers), Box 2, Australian Archives. See also Douglas MacArthur, *Reminiscences* (New York, 1965), p. 162.

10. Blamey's Memoirs, chap. 3, p. 10, courtesy of Mr. T.R. Blamey; D. McCarthy, *South-West Pacific Area, First Year* (Canberra, 1959), p. 82.

11. J. Field to Gavin Long, February 14, 1945, Gavin Long Notes, AWM 577/7/32.

12. F.G. Shedden, "The Defence of Port Moresby," September 3, 1942, and memorandum by Shedden, October 3, 1942, A 5954, Box 587; Notes of Discussions with Commander in Chief, SWPA, 20-26 October 1942, A 5954, Box 2.

13. Sturdee to General Smart, July 20, 1942, AWM 425/11/12; Commander in Chief's Diary, Blamey Papers, item 144, AWM. He spent twenty-eight of the fifty-three days (August 1 to September 22) in Brisbane.

14. Blamey to Rowell, morning and afternoon, August 28, 1942, Rowell Papers, AWM.

15. Quoted in Christopher Thorne, *Allies of a Kind* (London, 1978), p. 263; MacArthur to Marshall, August 30, 1942, RG 165, OPD Exec. 10, item 23a, National Archives; Rowell to Vasey, August 30, 1942, AWM 225/2/5.

16. General Kenney in his book *General Kenney Reports* (New York, 1949) and in his diary claims that he met and spoke to Rowell. Rowell in his book and in speaking to me has denied that he did so. In his letters to Vasey he mentions having met Sutherland but not Kenney. Rowell's aide-de-camp, Captain Gordon Darling, wrote that he has no record of a meeting between Rowell and Kenney until September 24. His diary for September 12 reads: "We visited General Whitehead's Headquarters 1110 hours" (L.G. Darling to author, August 7, 1974). Lieutenant Colonel Vial, Rowell's chief intelligence officer confirms this point, as did his late brother, who was an air force liaison officer in Moresby at the time (R.R. Vial to author, August 25, 1974). This evidence makes it difficult to believe Kenney's account of the pessimism at Port Moresby.

17. MacArthur to Marshall, September 6, 1942, OPD Exec. 10, item 239, RG 165, National Archives.

18. Hetherington, *Blamey*, pp. 210-14; Minutes of Prime Minister's War Conference, Canberra, July 17, 1942, MP 1217, Box 1; F.T. Smith Reports, No. 13, July 23, 1942, National Library of Australia; Kenney, *Reports*, p. 29; Blamey's Memoirs.

19. Radio, MacArthur to Marshall, September 22, 1942, OPD Exec. 10, item 236, RG 165, National Archives; William Frye, *Marshall: Citizen Soldier* (Indianapolis, 1947), p. 328; entry for September 22 in Wilkinson Diary, quoted in C. Thorne, "MacArthur, Australia, and the British, 1942-1943: The Secret Journal of MacArthur's British Liaison Officer (Part II)," *Australian Outlook* 29 (August 1975).

20. Hetherington, *Blamey*, p. 240; notes of secraphone conversation between the prime minister and the commander in chief, Southwest Pacific area, September 17, 1942, MP 1217, Box 532, Australian Archives; R.A. Paull, *Retreat from Kokoda* (Melbourne, 1958), p. 247.

21. "Commander-in-Chief's Press Conference," Perth, July 9, 1945, Blamey Papers, 138.3; Dunstan to Rowell, September 29, 1942, Rowell Papers.

22. The controversial nature of Rowell's relief revolves around the widely held belief that Rowell had not failed as commander in New Guinea. Rather, it was believed by Blamey's critics that he had relieved Rowell to get rid of a possible rival. Blamey's supporters thought that Rowell had not given his superior the respect he de-

served. For a discussion of this episode, see Hetherington, *Blamey*; McCarthy, *Southwest Pacific Area*; S.F. Rowell, *Full Circle* (Melbourne, 1974); and D.M. Horner, *Crisis of Command: Australian Generalship and the Japanese Threat* (Canberra, 1978).

23. Wilkinson Diary, October 19, 1942, Churchill College, Cambridge; notes of discussions [by Shedden] with Commander in Chief, Southwest Pacific Area, October 20-26, 1942, MP 1217, Box 2; Lida Mayo, *Bloody Buna* (Garden City, 1974), p. 73.

24. Kenney Diaries, vol. 2, marked as October 16, 1942, but probably early November 1942.

25. Harding to Sutherland, October 14, 1942, AWM 581/3/5; Mayo, *Bloody Buna*, p. 120; Vasey to Blamey, November 25, 1942, Blamey Papers 171.2.

26. Eichelberger Dictations, Book 2, pp. VII-122, VII-123; Kenney, *Reports*, p. 151.

27. R.L. Eichelberger, *Our Jungle Road to Tokyo* (London, 1951), p. 42; Jay Luvaas, ed., *Dear Miss Em: General Eichelberger's War in the Pacific, 1942-1945* (Westport, Conn., 1972), p. 33.

28. For a sympathetic treatment of the relief of Harding, see Leslie Anders, *Gentle Knight: The Life and Times of Major General Edwin Forrest Harding* (Kent, Ohio, 1985), chap. 13.

29. Interview with Sir Edmund Herring, June 25, 1974; Blamey to MacArthur, December 27, 1942, Blamey Papers 43.631.

30. MacArthur to Blamey, December 28, 1942, Blamey Papers 43.631; Blamey to Herring, December 28, 1942, Blamey Papers 170.2.

31. Luvaas, *Miss Em*, p. 54; Hetherington, *Blamey*, p. 284.

32. Notes on Discussions [by Shedden] with Commander in Chief, Southwest Pacific Area, Brisbane, January 16-20, 1943, A 5954, Box 2.

33. Signal, MacArthur to Marshall, January 11, 1943, RG 4, MacArthur Memorial, Norfolk, Virginia; Walter Krueger, *From Down Under to Nippon* (Washington, D.C., 1953), p. 10; Interview Tapes, Papers of General George H. Decker, U.S. Military History Institute, Carlisle, Pennsylvania.

34. Long, *The Final Campaigns* (Canberra, 1963), p. 599; Diller to MacArthur, May 17, 1943, RG 4, MacArthur Memorial; Transcript of Interview with F.M. Forde, March 4, 1971, TRC 121/8, National Library of Australia.

35. Blamey to MacArthur, February 15, 1943, and "Alternative Proposal for Offensive Operations," February 22, 1943, AWM 515/5/5; GHQ Warning Instruction No. 2, May 6, 1943, AWM 589/3/1.

36. Commander, Allied Land Forces, Report on New Guinea Operations, 23 January 1943-13 September 1943, March 16, 1944, AWM 519/6/58; Report on Operations, New Guinea, 22 January-8 October 1943, by Lieutenant General E.F. Herring, January 17, 1944, AWM 589/7/1.

37. Notes of Conference, GHQ, 1700 hrs., July 15, 1943, Blamey Papers, 43/632; Berryman Diary, July 28, 1943, Berryman Papers, AWM; Kenney, *Reports*, p. 256; C.A. Willoughby et al., comp., *Reports of General MacArthur*, vol. 1: *The Campaigns of MacArthur in the Pacific* (Washington, D.C., 1966), p. 121; Berryman Diary, September 4, 1943; Blamey to Sturdee, September 16, 1943, Blamey Papers 6.1.

38. Memorandum for File, by General Chamberlin, n.d., and Notes of Conference on "Dayton" at Adv. GHQ, 2000 hrs., September 3, 1943, AWM 594/3/3.

39. Memorandum by General Berryman, November 6, 1944, Blamey Papers 54.1; Interview with Brigadier Sir Kenneth Wills, August 9, 1974; Blamey to Mackay, October 18, 1943, Blamey Papers 170.3; Memorandum, Herring to Mackay, September 26, 1943, AWM 591/7/21; Ivan Chapman, *Iven G. Mackay, Citizen and Soldier* (Melbourne, 1975), p. 279.

40. Daniel E. Barbey, *MacArthur's Amphibious Navy* (Annapolis, 1969), p. 27;

GHQ G-3 Journal, October 7, 1943, Notes of Discussions between MacArthur and Halsey, AWM 519/1/4; Louis Morton, *Strategy and Command: The First Two Years* (Washington, D.C., 1962), p. 520 and appendix 8.

41. War Cabinet Minute 2065, October 1, 1943, CRS A 2671, item 389/1943, Australian Archives.

42. Curtin to MacArthur, November 22, 1943, Blamey Papers 5.1; Notes of Discussions with the Commander in Chief, Southwest Pacific Area, Brisbane, November 29 to December 1, 1943, A 5954, Box 2; Notes of Discussion between Commander in Chief, Southwest Pacific Area and Secretary, Department of Defence, Brisbane, December 2, 1943, A 5954, Box 3.

43. Notes of Discussion between Commander in Chief, Southwest Pacific Area, and Secretary, Department of Defence, Brisbane, December 2, 1943, A 5954, Box 3.

44. MacArthur to Curtin, November 6, 1943, Cp 390/16, item bundle 1, Australian Archives; Blamey to Curtin, January 28, 1944, Blamey Papers 12; Hetherington, *Blamey*, p. 304.

45. AMF Policy Directive 1943-1944, December 23, 1943, Blamey Papers 23.11; extracts from a report on a visit to Australia, March 6-28, 1944, by Captain A. Hillgarth, R.N., PREM 3 159/9, Public Record Office.

46. Notes of Discussions with Commander in Chief, Southwest Pacific Area, Canberra, March 17, 1944, A 5954, Box 3.

47. Blamey's Memoirs; Interview with Sam Landau, December 13, 1978; Shedden Diary, A 5954, Box 16.

48. Cable, Northcott to Blamey, May 1, 1944, Blamey Papers 43.66; J. Ehrman, *Grand Strategy*, vol. 5, August 1943-September 1944 (London, 1956), pp. 459-61; Memorandum, Curtin to Churchill, May 17, 1944, Blamey Papers 1.2.

49. COS (44) 449 (0), May 22, 1944, Blamey Papers 1.2; Notes of Discussions with Commander in Chief, Southwest Pacific area, June 27, 1944, MP 1217, Box 3; Interview with Landau, December 13, 1978.

50. Notes of Discussions with Commander in Chief, Southwest Pacific Area, June 27, 1944, A 5954, Box 3.

51. Ibid.; Notes of Discussions with General MacArthur, Tokyo, May 1946, MP 1217, Box 3; Lumsden to Ismay, July 15, 1944, PREM 3 159/4, Public Record Office.

52. MacArthur to Blamey, Blamey Papers, 23.11; Draft of Report by General Blamey, c. August 11, 1945, Blamey Papers; Memorandum, Blamey to GHQ, July 21, 1944, MP 1217, Box 570; Memorandum of Interview [by Lumsden] with General MacArthur, August 1, 1944, CAB 127/33, Public Record Office.

53. Notes from an Interview with General MacArthur, August 1, 1944, CAB 127/33; Sutherland to Blamey, August 2, 1945, A 5954, Box 570; Long, *The Final Campaigns*, p. 23.

54. Planning File, Berryman Papers; *The Reports of General MacArthur*, 1:171.

55. Hamlin M. Cannon, *Leyte: The Return to the Philippines*, (Washington, D.C., 1954), p. 26; Blamey to Sturdee, September 27, 1944, Blamey Papers 30.2; Planning File, Berryman Papers; Commander in Chief's Press Conference, July 9, 1945, Blamey Papers 139.3.

56. Lumsden to CIGS, December 28, 1944, WO 106/3429; Signal, Blamey to Berryman, February 17, 1945, Blamey Papers, 43.68; Curtin to MacArthur, February 15, 1945, Blamey Papers 23.11; Signal, CA 50688, MacArthur to Marshall, February 26, 1945, RG 218, CCS 381, Pacific Ocean Area (6-10-430), sec. 11, National Archives.

57. Signals B 239 and B 240, Berryman to Blamey, February 20 and 21, 1945, Berryman Papers.

58. Signals and letters between Berryman and Blamey, February 15-17, 1945, Berryman papers; Blamey to Shedden, February 19, 1945, Blamey Papers, 23.11.

59. Curtin to MacArthur, February 27, 1945, Sutherland Papers, Correspon-

dence with Australian Government, National Archives; MacArthur to Curtin, March 5, 1945, RG 4, MacArthur Memorial; Gairdner to Ismay, May 30, 1945, WO 216/137, Public Record Office.

60. Curtin to MacArthur, March 23, 1945, Blamey Papers 23.11.

61. Long, *The Final Campaigns*, p. 47; Blamey to Curtin, April 5, 1945, Blamey Papers 2311.

62. For a discussion of these issues, see Horner, *High Command*, pp. 395-97.

63. Blamey to Fraser (Acting Minister for the Army), May 16, 1945, Blamey Papers 23.11; Signal to MacArthur, May 20, 1945, A 5954, Box 570; Teleprinter Message 1238, Shedden to Fraser and Blamey, Blamey Papers 23.11; Shedden to MacArthur, July 21, 1945, Sutherland Papers, Correspondence with Australian Government.

64. Notes of Discussions with Commander in Chief, Southwest Pacific Area, Canberra, September 30, 1944, A 5954, Box 3; Gairdner to Ismay, May 30, 1945, WO 216/137, Public Record Office.

65. This point has been discussed at length in Peter Charlton, *The Unnecessary War* (Melbourne, 1983). I state my own views in *High Command*, pp. 399-404, 407-10.

66. Curtin to MacArthur, March 23, 1945, Sutherland Papers, Correspondence with Australian Government; Signal, MacArthur to Curtin, April 18, 1945, RG 4, MacArthur Memorial; Blamey to Curtin, April 19, 1945, Blamey Papers 23.11; Signal, MacArthur to Chifley, May 20, 1945, Sutherland Papers; Notes on War Cabinet Agendum No. 209/1945, A 5954, box 570, File 3.

67. Chifley to MacArthur, July 21, 1945, Sutherland Papers, Correspondence with Australian Government; Beasley (Minister for Defence) to Blamey, July 21, 1945, Blamey Papers, 23.11. No reply to Chifley's letter has been found in the Shedden, MacArthur, or Sutherland Papers or in the GHQ Historical Record Card Index.

68. Hetherington, *Blamey*, p. 375.

69. Appreciation in Wills Papers, Folder 1, AWM.

70. A.J. Sweeting, "The War In Papua," *Stand To* 6, 6 (November 1958-January 1959).

71. Hetherington, *Blamey*, p. 223.

72. Ibid., p. 393.

73. MacArthur, *Reminiscences*, p. 163.

WALTER KRUEGER

Research for this essay was facilitated by an Advanced Research Grant from the U.S. Army Military History Institute at Carlisle Barracks, Pennsylvania.

1. "General Walter Krueger," n.d. [1945], Papers of Walter Krueger, U.S. Military Academy Library, West Point, N.Y.; Walter Krueger, Jr., to the author, May 20, 1985, author's collection.

2. Ibid. The biographical information is from material in the Krueger Papers.

3. Krueger to Fay W. Brabson, December 7, 1927, and September 2, 1928, Papers of Fay W. Brabson, U.S. Army Military History Institute, Carlisle Barracks, Pa.

4. Krueger to Brabson, September 2, 1928, and August 25, 1932, Brabson Papers.

5. Edwin T. Wheatley to Walter Krueger, Jr., August 21, 1967; copy provided to the author by Walter Krueger, Jr.

6. Marshall to Krueger, April 14, 1941, in Larry I. Bland, ed., *The Papers of George Catlett Marshall*, vol. 2 (Baltimore, 1986), pp. 473-74.

7. Krueger to Marshall, April 20, 1941, *Ibid.*, p. 474.

8. Notes on inspection of Fort Screvens, July 30, 1941, Krueger Papers.

9. William Henry Mauldin, *The Brass Ring* (New York, 1971), pp. 98-99.

10. *Time*, September 29, 1941; p. 30 J. Lawton Collins, *Lightning Joe: An autobiography* (Baton Rouge, 1979), pp. 111-15.

11. Chester F. Allen to C.D. Eddleman, August 24, 1985; copy provided to the author by C.D. Eddleman.

12. Ibid.; Krueger to Frank Kowalski, Jr., March 27, 1957, Krueger Papers.

13. Dan H. Ralls, Interview with General George H. Decker, November-December 1972, Military History Institute.

14. D. Clayton James, *The Years of MacArthur*, 3 vols. (Boston, 1970-85), 2:157-286; Samuel Milner, *Victory in Papua* (Washington, D.C., 1957).

15. MacArthur to George C. Marshall, January 11, 1943, Krueger Papers.

16. Krueger, "MacArthur," n.d., Krueger Papers.

17. Krueger to Brabson, April 30, 1943, Brabson Papers.

18. Krueger, Travel/Appointment Diary, Krueger Papers: Krueger, *From Down Under to Nippon* (Washington, D.C., 1953), pp. 3-4.

19. Krueger, *Down Under*, pp. 5-6, 8-15; James, *MacArthur*, 2:304-5.

20. Krueger, *Down Under*, pp. 12-14.

21. Krueger, Travel/Appointment Diary, Krueger Papers; Jay Luvaas, ed., *Dear Miss Em: General Eichelberger's War in the Pacific, 1942-1945* (Westport, Conn., 1972), p. 67. Krueger lay seriously ill in the hospital when he learned of Sutherland's death. "It was a good thing for humanity," he commented. L.G. Smith and M.G. Swindler, Interview with General Clyde D. Eddleman, January-April 1975, Military History Institute.

22. Allen to Eddleman, August 24, 1985.

23. Ibid.; Krueger, *Down Under*, p. 7.

24. James, *MacArthur*, 2:310.

25. Krueger, *Down Under*, pp. 19-21.

26. Ibid., pp. 24-25; John Miller, jr., CARTWHEEL: The Reduction of Rabaul (Washington, D.C., 1959), p. 50.

27. Krueger to Swift, October 20, 1943, Papers of George H. Decker, Military History Institute.

28. Krueger to Frank Kowalski, Jr., March 27, 1957, Krueger Papers. On the exploits of the Alamo Scouts, see Gilson Niles, "The Operations of the Alamo Scouts," Fort Benning, Ga, 1947; copy at the Military History Institute.

29. Krueger, *Down Under*, pp. 26-41; James, *MacArthur*, 2:344.

30. Robert Ross Smith, *The Approach to the Philippines* (Washington, D.C., 1953), details the New Guinea campaign.

31. Krueger, *Down Under*, p. 136; Krueger to J.L. Frank, August 20, 1944, Krueger Papers; James B. Bonham to the author, April 15, 1985, author's collection.

32. Palmer to the author, August 26, 1985, author's collection.

33. Remarks delivered on NBC Army Hour broadcast, September 18, 1944, Krueger Papers.

34. Ralls, Interview with Decker.

35. Smith and Swindler, Interview with Eddleman.

36. Krueger, *Down Under*, p. 137.

37. Ralls, Interview with Decker; Smith and Swindler, Interview with Eddleman.

38. M. Hamlin Cannon, *Leyte: The Return to the Philippines* (Washington, D.C., 1954), pp. 35-36; Ely to the author, May 21, 1986, author's collection.

39. James, *MacArthur*, 2:537-38; MacArthur, *Reminiscences* (New York, 1964), p. 212.

40. Krueger, *Down Under*, pp. 151-52; Ralls, Interview with Decker.

41. Krueger, *Down Under*, pp. 142-43; Krueger to MacArthur, July 2, 1944, Decker Papers.

42. Krueger, *Down Under*, p. 154.

43. Cannon, *Leyte*, pp. 60-62.

44. H.V. White to Krueger, Report on Interrogation of General Yamashita, October 3, 1945, Krueger Papers; Krueger, *Down Under*, p. 159.

45. James, *MacArthur*, 2:563.

46. Krueger, *Down Under*, p. 166

47. Stanley L. Falk, *Decision at Leyte* (New York, 1966), p. 220; Gregory M. Franzwa and William J. Ely, *Leif Sverdrup* (Gerald, Mo., 1980), pp. 193-94. For a detailed account of the engineering problems, see Hugh J. Casey, ed., *Engineers of the Southwest Pacific, 1941-1945*, 7 vols. (Washington, D.C., 1947-53), 1:207-23.

48. Krueger, *Down Under*, pp. 158-62.

49. Sixth Army to G-2, Tenth Corps, 1145 hours, November 3, 1944, and Tenth Corps G-2 Report, 1800 hours, November 3, 1944, Papers of Thomas F. Hickey [chief of staff of Tenth Corps], Military History Institute.

50. Krueger, *Down Under*, pp. 168-69; Telephone Conversation between Eddleman and Hickey, 1350 hours, November 4, 1944, Hickey Papers.

51. Falk, *Leyte*, p. 245.

52. Ronald H. Spector, *Eagle against the Sun* (New York, 1985), p. 514.

53. Yamashita Interrogation; Smith and Swindler, Interview with Eddleman; Krueger Biographical Sketch, n.d., Krueger Papers.

54. *Reports of General MacArthur*, 2 vols. in 4 (Washington, D.C., 1966), vol. 2: *Japanese Operations in the Southwest Pacific*, pt. 2, pp. 409-11; David W. Gray to the author, May 8, 1985, author's collection.

55. Krueger, *Down Under*, pp. 174-77; Falk, *Leyte*, pp. 258-59.

56. Krueger to Andrew D. Bruce, September 18, 1949, Papers of Andrew D. Bruce, Military History Institute. Bruce commanded the Seventy-seventh Division on Leyte.

57. Krueger, *Down Under*, p. 187.

58. Quoted in Cannon, *Leyte*, p. 367.

59. Ibid., p. 248.

60. Krueger, *Down Under*, pp. 214-15.

61. Ibid., pp. 218-19.

62. Ibid., p. 226.

63. Ibid., pp. 228-29.

64. Ibid.; Krueger, Travel/Appointment Diary, Krueger Papers; Roger Olaf Egeberg, *The General* (New York, 1983), pp. 115-16.

65. James, *MacArthur*, 2:623; Krueger, *Down Under*, pp. 233-34.

66. Krueger, *Down Under*, pp. 239-45.

67. Ibid., pp. 246-52.

68. James, *MacArthur*, 2:629; Robert Ross Smith, *Triumph in the Philippines* (Washington, D.C., 1963), p. 141; Yamashita Interrogation.

69. James, *MacArthur*, 2:670-71, 689-90.

70. *Time*, January 29, 1945 pp. 29-30; Frank L. Kluckhorn, "Master of Amphibious Warfare," *New York Times Magazine*, December 31, 1944, pp. 11, 32; Luvaas, *Dear Miss Em*, p. 214; Krueger to L.B. Massie, May 29, 1945, Krueger Papers.

71. H. Ben Decherd, Jr. [Krueger's long-time aide-de-camp], "Beans, Bullets, and—Mail," n.d. [1945], Krueger Papers; Ralls, Interview with Decker.

72. Gray to the author, July 28, 1985, author's collection.

73. Tolson to the author, May 10, 1985, author's collection.

74. Collins, "Walter Krueger," *Infantry* (January-February 1983):15-19.

75. Decherd, "Bean, Bullets, and—Mail."

76. Ibid.; Decherd to Joseph I. Greene, November 5, 1944, Krueger Papers.

77. Oscar W. Griswold to Krueger, January 11, 1945, Krueger Papers; James, *MacArthur*, 2:681.

78. Krueger, *Down Under*, pp. 298-99; Smith, *Philippines*, pp. 449-67, 491-95.

79. Krueger, *Down Under*, pp. 299-300.

80. Smith, *Philippines*, p. 497.

81. Ibid., pp. 503-4; Krueger, *Down Under*, p. 302.

82. Krueger, *Down Under*, p. 307.

83. Ibid., p. 318.

84. Luvaas, *Dear Miss Em*, p. 176; Falk, *Leyte*, p. 309. Decker later commented: "I sometimes feel that our situation in Korea would have been a bit different had General Krueger been the ground force commander" (Ralls, Interview with Decker).

85. Krueger, *Down Under*, pp. 333-40, 350, 369.

86. Ibid., pp. 369-71; Krueger, Travel/Appointment Diary, Krueger Papers.

87. *Christian Science Weekly Magazine*, June 9, 1945, p. 3.

88. Tolson to the author, May 10, 1985; Collins, "Walter Krueger."

89. Drea, *Defending the Driniumor* (Fort Leavenworth, Kans., 1984), p. 138; Spector, *Eagle against the Sun*; James, MacArthur, 2:629.

90. Martin Blumenson and James L. Stokesbury, *Masters of the Art of Command* (Boston, 1975), pp. 155-63.

91. *Richmond News Leader*, November 13, 1945. The comments of the unidentified soldier are quoted by Freeman in the same editorial.

GEORGE C. KENNEY

1. USAF Oral History Interview 806, James Hasdorff with General George C. Kenney, Bay Harbor Islands, Florida, August 10-21, 1974.

2. USAF Biographical Study No. 101, Office of Air Force History, Washington, D.C.

3. USAF Oral History Interview 806.

4. Ibid.

5. See Herman S. Wolk, *Strategic Bombing: The American Experience* (Manhattan, Kans., 1981), pp. 14-15.

6. USAF Oral History Interview 806.

7. Ibid.

8. Ibid.

9. Notebooks of General George C. Kenney, vol. 1, entry for July 12, 1942, hereafter cited by volume and date.

10. Ibid.

11. Msg 1610, DeWitt, Commanding General, Fourth Army, to General Mac-Arthur, July 17, 1942, vol. 1.

12. Msg 359, General MacArthur to Commander General, Fourth Army, July 19, 1942, vol. 1.

13. Vol. 1, entry for July 13, 1942.

14. Ibid., July 14, 1942.

15. Ibid., July 29, 1942.

16. George C. Kenney, *General Kenney Reports: A Personal History of the Pacific War* (New York, 1949), chaps. 2, 3.

17. Vol. 1, entry for August 3, 1942; Wesley F. Craven and James L. Cate, eds., *The Army Air Forces in World War II*, 7 vols. (Chicago, 1948-58), 4:98-99.

18. Vol. 1, August, 3, 1942.

19. Ibid.

20. "Fifth Air Force Aircraft by Type," as of August 1942, Kenney notebooks, vol. 1.

21. Vol. 1, August entries.

22. USAF Oral History Interview 806.

23. Ibid.

24. *Kenney Reports*, p. 76.

25. The lone B-17 lost in this attack was piloted by Captain Harl Pease, Jr., of Plymouth, New Hampshire. He was not scheduled to take part in this attack, one engine of his plane having failed the previous day in a bombing mission over New Guinea. With just three hours' rest, Pease took an unserviceable plane, and according to Kenney, "somehow he got it operating and followed the rest of the group into Port Moresby and although he had one missing engine he took off with the rest of the gang for Rabaul. Said he wouldn't miss this show for anything. Just before reaching the target the bad engine quit. . . . he stayed in position, took the brunt of the attack but when another engine was hit could not keep up and was shot down. I put him in for the Medal of Honor. General MacArthur OK'd it" (War Department General Order No. 59, November 4, 1942; Kenney notebooks vol. 1, entry for August 7, 1942).

26. Vol. 1, August 7, 1942.

27. *Kenney Reports*, p. 118.

28. Vol. 3, November 20, 1942.

29. Msg A 1192, Kenney to Arnold, November 27, 1942, vol. 3.

30. Vol. 3, November 27, 1942.

31. Vol. 3, December 10, 1942.

32. Arnold to Kenney, December 6, 1942, vol. 3.

33. Ibid.

34. Vol. 3, December 10, 1942.

35. Kenney to Arnold, December 14, 1942, vol. 3.

36. Vol. 3, December 10, 1942.

37. Kenney to Major General Muir S. Fairchild, Director of Military Requirements, December 8, 1942, vol. 3.

38. Vol. 3, December 16, 1942.

39. D. Clayton James, *The Years of MacArthur*, 3 vols. (Boston, 1970-85), 2:298.

40. Vol. 4, March 12, 1943.

41. Ibid.

42. Ibid.

43. Vol. 4, March 16, 1943.

44. Vol. 4, March 17, 1943.

45. Arnold to Kenney, March 30, 1943, vol. 4.

46. Kenney to Arnold, July 28, 1943, vol. 6.

47. Arnold to Kenney, August 31, 1943, vol. 6.

48. Kenney to Arnold, October 29, 1943, vol. 7.

49. Vol. 5, April 19, 1943.

50. *Kenney Reports*, pp. 251-79.

51. Whitehead to Kenney, August 20, 1943, vol. 6.

52. *Kenney Reports*, pp. 281-96.

53. Arnold to Kenney, September 23, 1943, vol. 7.

54. Notes to Conference, by Brigadier General S.J. Chamberlin, September 10, 1943, SOPAC and SWPA, vol. 7; *Kenney Reports*, p. 312.

55. Kenney to Arnold, October 10, 1943, vol. 7.

56. *Kenney Reports*, p. 321.

57. Kenney to Arnold, November 6, 1943, vol. 7.

58. Ibid.

59. Ibid.

60. Kenney to Whitehead, November 7, 1943, vol. 7; Kenney to Whitehead, November 9, 1943, vol. 7.

61. Ibid.

62. Diary of Kenney's appointments in Washington, D.C., January 3-11, 1944, vol. 8; *Kenney Reports*, pp. 339-49.

63. Vol. 8, January 23-27, 1944; *Kenney Reports*, pp. 369-71.

64. Charts, Fifth Air Force Advanced Echelon "Wewak Air Blockade," vol. 8; *Kenney Reports*, pp. 372-73; Craven and Cate, *Army Air Forces* 4:588-91.

65. Summary of Sorties, March 1944, Thirteenth Air Force, vol. 8; Craven and Cate, 4:646-51.

66. Fifth Air Force Summaries, vol. 8; Craven and Cate, 4:chap. 18.

67. *Kenney Reports*, p. 433.

68. Vol. 9, September-October 1944; "Summary of Results of Balikpapan Strikes," vol. 9, "Balikpapan Refineries and Bay-Damage Assessment," vol. 9.

69. Vol. 9, October 19, 1944; Kenney to Arnold, November 14, 1944, vol. 9.

70. Kenney to Arnold, November 14, 1944, vol. 9.

71. Craven and Cate, 5:368-89.

72. Kenney to Arnold, November 14, 1944, vol. 9.

73. Ibid.

74. Msg, GHQ, SWPA, to Commanding Generals, FEAF, et al., April 9, 1945, vol 10; Memorandum, GHQ, SWPA, to CINCs, Army (Pacific) and U.S. Pacific Fleet, April 15, 1945, vol. 10.

75. Vol. 10, June 17, 1945; Msg, War Dept, to Commanding Generals, All Theaters, et al., July 13, 1945, vol. 10.

76. Msg, 181936Z, Arnold to Kenney, August 19, 1945, vol. 11.

THOMAS C. KINKAID

1. *New York Times*, October 27, 1943.

2. Thomas B. Buell, *Master of Sea Power: A Biography of Fleet Admiral Ernest J. King* (Boston, 1980), pp. 319-20; Minutes of COMINCH (Admiral E.J. King)-CINCPAC (Admiral C.W. Nimitz) Conferences, 1942-45, September 25, 1943, ONH, Washington, D.C. (hereafter cited as COMINCH-CINCPAC Conferences, September 25, 1943).

3. Buckner to Kinkaid, November 3, 1943, Thomas C. Kinkaid Manuscripts, Office of Naval History (hereafter cited as Kinkaid MSS).

4. Kinkaid to Helen Sherbourne Kinkaid, November 17-27, 1943, Kinkaid MSS, ONH (hereafter cited as TCK to HSK).

5. *Courier Mail* (Brisbane), October 27, 1943; *Telegraph* (Brisbane), October 27, 1943.

6. CINCSWPA to Chief of Staff, U.S.A., Brisbane, October 27, 1943; Chief of Staff to CINCSWPA, October 27, 1943, George C. Marshall Manuscripts, Marshall Library, Lexington, Va. (hereafter cited as Marshall MSS).

7. Gerald E. Wheeler, "KINKAID, Thomas Cassin," in Roger J. Spiller et al., eds., *Dictionary of American Military Biography*, 3 vols. (Westport, Conn., 1984), 2:565-69.

8. R.W. Christie to the author, November 11, 1976; Clay Blair, Jr., *Silent Victory: The U.S. Submarine War against Japan*, 2 vols. (Philadelphia, 1974), 1:475.

9. TCK to HSK, November 27, 28, 1943.

10. TCK to HSK, January 15, 1944.

11. Dudley McCarthy, *South-West Pacific Area—First Year, Kokoda to Wau: Australia in the War of 1939-1945*, ser. 1: Army, 7 vols. (Canberra, 1959), 5:27-29; Charles A. Willoughby, comp., *Reports of General MacArthur: The Campaigns of MacArthur in the Pacific*, 2 vols. (Washington, D.C., 1966), 1:109; D. Clayton James, *The Years of MacArthur, 1941-1945*, 3 vols. (Boston, 1970-85), 2:313-15.

12. Barbey to Philip A. Crowl, November 9, 1953, Daniel E. Barbey Manuscripts, Office of Naval History (hereafter cited as Barbey MSS).

13. Raymond D. Tarbuck, Oral History, Annapolis, 1973, p. 92.

14. Memorandum: Comments and Recommendations Submitted . . . by Captain R.C. Hudson, Pt. Moresby, November 28, 1943, Commander, Seventh Fleet, Files, Navy Operations Archives.

15. Seventh Fleet Confidential Notice 3CN-44: U.S. Seventh Fleet Organization, February 1, 1944, Navy Operations Archives.

16. *Sunday Mail* (Brisbane), November 28, 1943; Kinkaid, Oral History, 1961, pp. 81-82, 253-54 (typescript of first draft, Kinkaid MSS, ONH).

17. E.B. Potter and Chester W. Nimitz, ed., *The Great Sea War: The Story of Naval Action in World War II* (New York, 1960), pp. 278-79; 310-13; Robert Ross Smith, *The Approach to the Philippines* (Washington, D.C., 1953), pp. 106; Grace Person Hayes, *The History of the Joint Chiefs of Staff in World War II: The War against Japan* (Annapolis, 1982), pp. 403-9, 415-27, 488-94; Samuel Eliot Morison, *History of United States Naval Operations in World War II*, vol. 6: *Breaking the Bismarcks Barrier, 22 July 1942-1 May 1944* (Boston, 1950), pp. 3-8; Samuel Eliot Morison, *History of United States Naval Operations in World War II*, vol. 8: *New Guinea and the Marianas, March 1944-August 1944* (Boston, 1953), pp. 3-10; Maurice Matloff, *Strategic Planning for Coalition Warfare, 1943-1944* (Washington, D.C., 1959), pp. 453-55.

18. Walter Krueger, *From Down Under to Nippon: The Story of Sixth Army in World War II* (Washington, D.C., 1953), pp. 26-36; John Miller, jr., *CARTWHEEL: The Reduction of Rabaul* (Washington, D.C., 1959), pp. 1-5; James, *MacArthur*, 2:341-42; *Reports of MacArthur*, 1:100-1, 128-31.

19. Kinkaid, Oral History, pp. 273-76; Daniel E. Barbey, *MacArthur's Amphibious Navy: Seventh Amphibious Force Operations, 1943-1945* (Annapolis, 1969), p. 122.

20. U.S. Navy, Office of Naval History, Administrative History: Commander, U.S. Naval Forces Southwest Pacific, pp. 67-69 [Written by Captain A.D. Turnbull], Office of Naval History; Kinkaid, Oral History, p. 85; Miller, *CARTWHEEL*, pp. 316-17.

21. Miller, *CARTWHEEL*, p. 299; Barbey to Bern Anderson, October 19, 1952, Barbey MSS.

22. Hudson Memorandum, November 18, 1943; TCK to HSK, December 2, 15, 20, 1943.

23. TCK to HSK, December 31, 1943, February 7, 1944, March 4, 26, 1944; Paul F. Foster to C.E. Van Hook, December 12, 1943, Clifford E. Van Hook Manuscripts, Hoover Institution (hereafter cited as Van Hook MSS).

24. Miller, *CARTWHEEL*, pp. 312-13.

25. Miller, *CARTWHEEL*, pp. 320-36; Barbey, *MacArthur's Navy*, pp. 144-48, 151-53; George C. Kenney, *General Kenney Reports: A Personal History of the Pacific War* (New York, 1949), pp. 358-62; TCK to HSK, March 1, 1944; James, *MacArthur*, 2:380-83; Walter Karig, Russell L. Harris, and Frank A. Manson, *Battle Report: The End of an Empire*, vol. 4 (New York, 1948), pp. 167, 172.

26. Krueger, *Sixth Army*, p. 49; James, *MacArthur*, 2:384-87.

27. Douglas MacArthur, *Reminiscences* (New York, 1964), pp. 187-89.

28. Miller, *CARTWHEEL*, pp. 325-32; *Reports of MacArthur*, 1:136-40.

29. E.B. Potter, *Bull Halsey* (Annapolis, 1985), pp. 265-66; James, *MacArthur*, 2:388-91; Miller, *CARTWHEEL*, pp. 349-50; Forrest C. Pogue, *George C. Marshall: Organizer of Victory*, vol. 3 (New York, 1973), pp. 441-42; William F. Halsey and J. Bryan III, *Admiral Halsey's Story* (New York, 1947), pp. 188-90.

30. TCK to HSK, April 27 and May 3, 1944.

31. *Reports of MacArthur*, 1:142-43; Smith, *Approach*, pp. 13-20; Morison, 8:61-64.

32. Kinkaid, Oral History, pp. 261-63; Dispatches, MacArthur to Nimitz, 3/150115Z, and Nimitz to MacArthur, March 15, 1944. Douglas A. MacArthur Manuscripts, MacArthur Museum, Norfolk, Va. (hereafter cited as MacArthur MSS).

33. James, *MacArthur*, 2:399-402; E.B. Potter, *Nimitz* (Annapolis, 1976), pp. 389-92; Clark G. Reynolds, *The Fast Carriers: The Forging of an Air Navy* (New York, 1968), p. 164; TCK to HSK, March 25, 26, 27, 28, 1944.

34. James, *MacArthur*, 2:400-1; Potter, *Nimitz*, pp. 389-92; Smith, *Approach*, pp. 16-26; Barbey, *MacArthur's Navy*, pp. 158-66; Kenney, *Reports*, p. 377.

35. Kinkaid, "Memorandum for General MacArthur," May 3, 1944, Kinkaid MSS; James, *MacArthur*, 2:450; TCK to HSK, April 20, 1944.

36. Smith, *Approach*, pp. 53-83, 103-205; Morison, 8:49-90; *Reports of MacArthur*, 1:146-49; James, *MacArthur*, 2:445-54; Krueger, *Sixth Army*, pp. 56-75.

37. TCK to HSK, May 2, 1944; Krueger, *Sixth Army*, pp. 77-78.

38. TCK to HSK, April 3, 1944; James, *MacArthur*, 2:422-40.

39. Smith, *Approach*, pp. 206-8; *Reports of MacArthur*, 1:150-52; Barbey, *MacArthur's Navy*, pp. 185-91.

40. G. Hermon Gill, *Royal Australian Navy, 1942-1945*, ser. 2, vol. 2 (Adelaide, 1968), pp. 416-17, 420-34; Morison, 8:117-30; Blair, *Silent Victory*, 2:607-12; U.S. Strategic Bombing Survey, *Interrogations of Japanese Officials*, 2 vols. (Washington, D.C., 1946), 2:450-54.

41. Smith, *Approach*, pp. 397-424; Gill, *Navy*, pp. 441-43; Barbey, *MacArthur's Navy*, pp. 205-11; Morison, 8:134-40.

42. Smith, *Approach*, 425-49; Morison, 8:140-44; Barbey, *MacArthur's Navy*, pp. 211-16.

43. Smith, *Approach*, pp. 450-56, 475-79, 490-93; Samuel Eliot Morison, *History of United States Naval Operations in World War II*, vol. 12: *Leyte, June 1944-January 1945* (Boston, 1958), pp. 19-29; Barbey, *MacArthur's Navy*, pp. 220-28; U.S. Seventh Fleet, Seventh Amphibious Force, *Command History, 10 January 1943-23 December 1945* (Shanghai, 1945); *Reports of MacArthur*, 1:174-78.

44. TCK to HSK, September 2 and 17, 1944.

45. COMINCH-CINCPAC Conferences, San Francisco, May 6, 1944; Pearl Harbor, July 13-22, 1944; ONH. Buell, *King*, pp. 466-68; Potter, *Nimitz*, pp. 310-14, 317-19; Morison, 12:9-11.

46. M. Hamlin Cannon, *Leyte: The Return to the Philippines* (Washington, D.C., 1954), pp. 8-9; Morison, 12:12-16; Reynolds, *Fast Carriers*, pp. 247-48; Potter, *Halsey*, pp. 276-78; James M. Merrill, *A Sailor's Admiral: A Biography of William F. Halsey* (New York, 1976), pp. 133-37.

47. Karig, *Battle Report*, 4:308-9; Krueger, *Sixth Army*, pp. 136-41.

48. Barbey, *MacArthur's Navy*, p. 233.

49. Nimitz to King, July 3, 1944, Chester W. Nimitz Manuscripts, ONH, Washington, D.C. (hereafter cited as Nimitz MSS).

50. King to Kinkaid, August 17, 1944; Kinkaid to Barbey, August 26, 1944; Kinkaid to King, August 27, 1944; Barbey to Kinkaid, August 31, 1944, Kinkaid MSS; Richard L. Conolly, Oral History (Annapolis, 1960), pp. 253-55.

51. Cannon, *Leyte*, p. 22.

52. Ibid., pp. 26-27.

53. Ibid., p. 23.

54. *Reports of MacArthur*, 1:184-89.

55. Morison, 12:415-23.

56. Ibid.; *Command History, Seventh Amphibious Force*, 1:8-9, sheet 16; Barbey, *MacArthur's Navy*, pp. 232-36; Cannon, *Leyte*, pp. 31-34; Morison, 12:415-23.

57. CINCSWPA to CINCAAF and CINCPOA, September 9, 1944, MacArthur MSS; Commander, Seventh Fleet, to COMINCH, "Report of Action for the Capture of Leyte Island," January 31, 1945, Navy Operations Archives.

58. *Reports of MacArthur*, 1:184.

59. Quoted in Morison, 12:57-58.

60. Felix B. Stump, Oral History, Columbia University, 1964, pp. 181-85; Kinkaid, Oral History, pp. 278-86, 292-93; R.W. Bates to Kinkaid, August 13, 1945, Richard W. Bates Manuscripts, Naval War College (hereafter cited in Bates MSS).

61. TCK to HSK, October 15, 1944.

62. Morison, 12:130-38; James, *MacArthur*, 2:550-57; Carlos P. Romulo, *I See the Philippines Rise* (Garden City, N.Y., 1946), pp. 90-95.

63. Vicente Albano Pacis, *Osmeña*, 2 vols. (Quezon City, 1971), 2:243-46; Wilkinson, Diary, October 10, 1944, Theodore S. Wilkinson Manuscripts, Library of Congress Manuscripts Division (hereafter cited as Wilkinson MSS); TCK to HSK, October 23, 1944; MacArthur, *Reminiscences*, pp. 234-35; Romulo, *I See the Rise*, pp. 127-30.

64. TCK to HSK, October 23, 1944; Blair, *Silent Victory*, 2:724-31.

65. Morison, 12:177-83; Edwin P. Hoyt, *The Battle of Leyte Gulf: The Death Knell of the Japanese Fleet* (New York, 1972), pp. 107-24; James A. Field, Jr., *The Japanese at Leyte Gulf: The Sho Operation* (Princeton, 1947), pp. 43-56; C. Vann Woodward, *The Battle for Leyte Gulf* (New York, 1947), pp. 12-17, 20-24, 33-35.

66. Reynolds, *Fast Carriers*, pp. 264-65.

67. Commander, Task Force 77, Action Report, January 31, 1945, p. 14; Morison, 12:190-91; Field, *Japanese at Leyte Gulf*, pp. 54-55.

68. Morison, 12:192, 319; Frederick C. Sherman, *Combat Command: The American Aircraft Carriers in the Pacific War* (New York, 1982), pp. 250-52, 263-66.

69. V.H. Schaeffer to the author, April 3, 1978, author's collection; Commander, Task Force 77, Action Report, January 31, 1945, pp. 14-17; Morison, 12: 198-99.

70. Morison, 12:183-89; Reynolds, *Fast Carriers*, pp. 265-66; Hoyt, *Leyte Gulf*, pp. 125-55.

71. Commander, Task Force 77, Action Report, January 31, 1945, pp. 14-15; Jesse B. Oldendorf, "The Battle of Surigao Strait," *Blue Book*, March 1948, pp. 38-40; Morison, 12:198-202; Oldendorf to A.A. Burke, December 4, 1947 (copy), Kinkaid MSS.

72. William F. Halsey, "The Battle for Leyte Gulf," *U.S. Naval Institute Proceedings*, May 1952, pp. 488-90; Morison, 12;193-94.

73. Schaeffer to the author, April 3, 1978.

74. Morison, 12:233-40; *Interrogations of Japanese Officials*, 1:235-44.

75. Commander, Seventh Fleet, to COMINCH ("King's Eyes Only"), 12/160202z, Ernest J. King Manuscripts, ONH (hereafter cited as King MSS).

76. Commander, Seventh Fleet, to COMINCH, 12/160202Z; Commander, Task Force 77, Action Report, January 31, 1945, p. 25; Thomas C. Kinkaid, "Communication Breakdown at the Battle for Leyte Gulf," in John T. Mason, Jr., ed., *The Pacific War Remembered: An Oral History Collection* (Annapolis, 1986), pp. 271-73.

77. Commander, Task Force 77, Action Report, January 31, 1945, pp. 26-27; Morison, 12:289-94.

78. Halsey, "Battle for Leyte Gulf," pp. 491-95; Potter, *Halsey*, pp. 293-304; Morison, 12:317-32.

79. Commander, Third Fleet, to CINCPAC, 10/251317Z, Command Summary; Potter, *Halsey*, pp. 305-7; Morison, 12:193-96. The views of Admirals Kinkaid and Halsey are given at length in Hanson W. Baldwin, *Sea Fights and Shipwrecks: True Tales of the Seven Seas* (Garden City, N.Y., 1955), pp. 165-82.

80. COMINCH to "Eyes Only Kinkaid," 12/111504Z, King MSS; Commander, Seventh Fleet, to COMINCH ("King's Eyes Only"), 12/190202Z, Kinkaid MSS; Paulus P. Powell to R.W. Bates, November 3, 1953, Bates MSS.

81. Morison 12:338.

82. CINCSWPA to CINCPAC, 11/160101Z, MacArthur MSS, file NAVY 573.

83. CINCPOA to CINCSWPA, 11/170200Z, Kinkaid MSS.

84. Memorandum, Chief of Staff, Fifth Air Force to Commander General, Sixth Army, November 21, 1944, Kinkaid MSS.

85. Memorandum for Kinkaid by Struble, "Estimate of the Situation—LOVE THREE Operation," November 24, 1944, Kinkaid MSS.

86. Reynolds, *Fast Carriers*, p. 288; Morison, 12:357-60.

87. Kinkaid to Van Hook, December 10, 1944, Van Hook MSS; Schaeffer to the author, November 16, 1977, author's collection.

88. Memorandum, Struble to Kinkaid, November 29, 1944, Kinkaid MSS.

89. James, MacArthur, 2:231-32, 242, 282.

90. Kinkaid to Van Hook, December 10, 1944, Van Hook MSS.

91. Commander, Seventh Fleet, to COMINCH, n.d., marked "not sent," Kinkaid MSS.

92. CINCPOA to CINCSWPA, 11/292349Z, MacArthur MSS, file NAVY 576.

93. Kinkaid to Van Hook, December 10, 1944, Van Hook MSS.

94. Commander, Third Fleet, to CINCPAC, 11/290400Z, MacArthur MSS, file NAVY 576.

95. Kinkaid to Van Hook, December 10, 1944, Van Hook MSS.

96. Robert Ross Smith, *Triumph in the Philippines* (Washington, D.C., 1963), pp. 43-49; Samuel Eliot Morison, *History of United States Naval Operations in World War II*, vol. 13: *The Liberation of the Philippines, Luzon, Mindanao, the Visayas, 1944-1945* (Boston, 1959), pp. 17-32.

97. Wilkinson to Kelly Turner, December 7, 1944, Wilkinson MSS.

98. Smith, *Triumph*, pp. 26-30.

99. Morison, 13:308-11; Smith, *Triumph*, pp. 54-57; *Reports of MacArthur*, 1:254.

100. Morison, 13:303-14.

101. Commander, Task Group 77.2, to Commander, Seventh Fleet, 1/061210Z, Command Summary.

102. Commander, Seventh fleet, to Commander, Third Fleet, 1/061824Z, Command Summary.

103. CINCPAC to CINCSWPA, 1/070322Z; Commander, Third Fleet, to CINCPAC, 1/071044Z, Command Summary.

104. Smith, *Triumph*, pp. 67-69.

105. Morison, 13:111-19, 325-26.

106. James, *MacArthur*, 2:620-21; Morison, 13:326; Smith, *Triumph*, pp. 73-76.

107. Smith, *Triumph*, pp. 310-14, 221-23; Morison, 13:185-90; Barbey, *MacArthur's Navy*, p. 302.

108. James, *MacArthur*, 2:737-79.

109. TCK to HSK, April 3 and 5, 1945.

110. COMINCH to Kinkaid, May 5, 1945, Kinkaid Personnel File, Kinkaid MSS; TCK to HSK, May 5, 1945.

111. Hayes, *History of the Joint Chiefs of Staff*, pp. 686-95, 701-7.

112. TCK to HSK, August 22, 23, 26, 1945; Samuel Eliot Morison, *History of*

United States Naval Operations in World War II, vol. 14: *Victory in the Pacific, 1945* (Boston, 1960), pp. 356-57.

113. TCK to HSK, April 14, 1945.

ROBERT L. EICHELBERGER

1. Unless otherwise indicated, all information pertaining to the early career of General Eichelberger is taken form his voluminous dictations, 1952-60, a complete copy of which is deposited with the Eichelberger Papers in the William R. Perkins Library, Duke University. This material is hereafter cited as "Eichelberger Dictations."

2. Robert L. Eichelberger, *Our Jungle Road to Tokyo* (New York, 1950), p. xi.

3. MacArthur to Eichelberger, September 20, 1935, Eichelberger Papers; Eichelberger Dictations, March 28, 1955; Douglas MacArthur, *Reminiscences* (New York, 1964), p. 157.

4. Eichelberger, *Jungle Road*, p. xvii.

5. Ibid., pp. xviii-xxii; Thomas J. Fleming, *West Point: The Men and Times of the United States Military Academy* (New York, 1969), pp. 320-21.

6. Eichelberger, *Jungle Road*, pp. 3-4.

7. Eichelberger Dictations.

8. Jay Luvaas, ed., *Dear Miss Em: General Eichelberger's War in the Pacific, 1942-1945* (Westport, Conn., 1972), pp. 7-11.

9. Supreme Commander for the Allied Powers, *Reports of General MacArthur: The Campaigns of MacArthur in the Pacific* (Washington, D.C., 1966), 1:75.

10. Luvaas, *Dear Miss Em*, pp. 26-32; Eichelberger Dictations, December 2, 1957.

11. Luvaas, *Dear Miss Em*, pp. 30-31.

12. Ibid., pp. 28-29; Eichelberger, *Jungle Road*, pp. 14-16.

13. Samuel Milner, *Victory in Papua* (Washington, D.C., 1957), pp. 137-39.

14. Ibid., p. 195.

15. Luvaas, *Dear Miss Em*, p. 32. Emphasis added.

16. Jay Luvaas, "Buna, 19 November 1942-January 1943: A 'Leavenworth Nightmare,'" in Charles E. Heller and William A. Stofft, eds., *America's First Battles, 1776-1965* (Lawrence, 1986), pp. 211-12. On Harding's relief, see also Leslie Anders, *Gentle Knight: The Life and Times of Major General Edwin Forrest Harding* (Kent, Ohio, 1985).

17. Luvaas, *Dear Miss Em*, pp. 41-47; General Clovis E. Byers, "Combat Leadership," *Marine Corps Gazette* 46 (November 1962):27-29.

18. Luvaas, "Buna," pp. 215-18.

19. Ibid., pp. 218-20; *Dear Miss Em*, p. 57; Eichelberger, *Jungle Road*, pp. 57-62.

20. Luvaas, *Dear Miss Em*, p. 65.

21. Ibid., pp. 66, 78.

22. Eichelberger to MacArthur, December 24, 1942, Eichelberger Papers.

23. Eichelberger, Address to the Twenty-fourth Division, October 1943, Eichelberger Papers.

24. Colonel Frank S. Bowen to Eichelberger, February 18, 1944, Eichelberger Papers.

25. Richard Tindall, "Initiative" (1937), in Joseph Greek, ed., *The Infantry Journal Reader* (Garden City, 1943), pp. 316-17.

26. Eichelberger to Fuller, December 14, 1942, Eichelberger Papers.

27. Eichelberger to Fuller, December 22, 1942, Eichelberger Papers.

28. Colonel Ray Chandler to O. Chandler, May 18, 1943, Rex Chandler Papers,

World War II Miscellaneous Collection, Archives, U.S. Army Military History Institute.

29. Report of the Commanding General, Buna Forces, on the Buna Campaign: 1 December 1942-25 January 1943, pp. 72-73, Eichelberger Papers (hereinafter cited as "History of Buna").

30. Colonel Frank Bowen to Eichelberger, February 5 and 18, 1944, Eichelberger Papers. Eichelberger's training philosophy can be seen in Eighth Army Training Memorandum No. 1, October 1, 1944, which was circulated after the Hollandia operation and is in the Eichelberger Papers.

31. Jay Luvaas, "Buna—A Leavenworth Nightmare."

32. Eichelberger, *Jungle Road*, p. 101; Allied Forces, "Twenty-fourth Division History of Hollandia," p. 37, Eichelberger Papers; Robert Ross Smith, *The Approach to the Philippines* (Washington, D.C., 1953), p. 9.

33. Allied Forces, "First Corps History of the Hollandia Operation," p. 1; Allied Forces, "Twenty-fourth Division at Hollandia," p. 39, Eichelberger Papers; RG 407, 210-0.1-B.3017, "History of First Corps," p. 18, National Research Center, Suitland, Md. (hereafter cited as "History of First Corps").

34. FM 100-5 (1986 Version), p. 97; Eichelberger to his wife, March 31, 1945, Eichelberger Papers.

35. Smith, *Approach*, pp. 42-43.

36. Eichelberger, *Jungle Road*, p. 106.

37. Eichelberger Diary, April 22, 1944; Allied Forces, "First Corps History of Hollandia," p. 10, Eichelberger Papers.

38. Eichelberger, *Jungle Road*, p. 106.

39. Allied Forces, "First Corps History of Hollandia," p. 5, Eichelberger Papers.

40. Ibid., p. 6; Eichelberger, *Jungle Road*, pp. 108-9, Smith, *Approach*, pp. 58-60.

41. Eichelberger, *Jungle Road*, p. 109.

42. D. Clayton James, *The Years of MacArthur*, vol. 2: *1941-1945*, (Boston, 1975), p. 453.

43. Ibid., p. 459; George C. Kenney, *General Kenney Reports* (New York, 1949), p. 289; Luvaas, *Miss Em*, p. 125.

44. Eichelberger, *Jungle Road*, p. 146.

45. James, *Years of MacArthur*, 2:460.

46. Eichelberger, *Jungle Road*, pp. 181, 182. See also M. Hamlin Cannon, *Leyte: The Return to the Philippines* (Washington, D.C., 1954), pp. 367-69.

47. Luvaas, *Dear Miss Em*, p. 186.

48. Robert Ross Smith, *Triumph in the Philippines* (Washington, D.C., 1963), pp. 222-23; Luvaas, *Dear Miss Em*, pp. 194-200.

49. Ibid., p. 204.

50. Ibid., p. 215.

51. Ibid., pp. 210, 212; Eichelberger, *Jungle Road*, p. 196; James, *MacArthur*, 2:637.

52. Ronald H. Spector, *Eagle against the Sun* (New York, 1985), p. 526; James, *MacArthur*, 2:671; Smith, *Triumph*, p. 364; Eichelberger, *Jungle Road*, p. 205.

53. "Robert Eichelberger, Biographical Summary, 28 January 1948." p. 4; Eichelberger to his wife, April 3, 1945, Eichelberger Papers; Eichelberger, *Jungle Road*, p. 202; Spector, *Eagle*, p. 527.

54. Clovis Byers, Memorandum: "Interview with General MacArthur, Saturday, 30 March 1945"; Eichelberger Diary, April 8-10, 1945; Eichelberger Papers.

55. Eichelberger Diary, April 10, 1945; Eichelberger Papers.

56. Report of the Commanding General, Eighth Army, on the Mindanao Oper-

ation, pp. 2-9 and 17, Eichelberger Papers. Roscoe Woodruff, "A Narrative Account of the Twenty-fourth Infantry Division on Mindanao" (n.p., n.d.) p. 2, RG 407, 324-03 Box 7670, National Research Center, Suitland, Md.

57. Eichelberger, *Jungle Road*, pp. 218-20.

58. Eichelberger Diary, April 28, 1945, Eichelberger Papers.

59. D.M. Horner, "Generals in Battle: Problems of Command in the South-West Pacific Area, 1942-1943" (M.A. Thesis, University of New South Wales, 1975), p. 260.

60. Luvaas, *Dear Miss Em*, pp. 16-17.

ENNIS C. WHITEHEAD

1. Interview with Loren Whitehead (Ennis C. Whitehead's brother), May 22, 1964; Loren Whitehead to General Frederick H. Smith, December 16, 1964, author's collection.

2. Interview with Mrs. Ennis C. Whitehead, March 8, 1969.

3. U.S. War Department, "Personnel Order 709," May 5, 1918; Interview with Frederick H. Smith, June 10, 1969.

4. Interview with Warren Wattle (Whitehead's best friend in college), April 4, 1969.

5. Interview with Mrs. Ennis C. Whitehead, March 8, 1969; Interview with Loren Whitehead, May 22, 1969.

6. Efficiency report for Whitehead by Major Carl Spaatz, November 18, 1921, author's collection.

7. Whitehead to Loren Whitehead, July 23, 1921, author's collection.

8. Interview with Mrs. Ennis C. Whitehead, March 19, 1969. See also Whitehead, "Chronology," in the Papers of Ennis C. Whitehead, U.S. Air Force Historical Research Center, Maxwell Air Force Base, Alabama.

9. *Aviation*, December 27, 1926, p. 1072; "Chronology of Pan American Flight," *Army Navy Journal*, February 25, 1927.

10. Whitehead to Mrs. Ennis C. Whitehead, March 5, 1927, author's collection.

11. *Washington Star*, May 2, 1927.

12. Whitehead, "Chronology," C. Whitehead to Loren Whitehead, February 25, 1930, author's collection; *Dayton Daily News*, March 23, 1930.

13. Whitehead, "Chronology."

14. Ibid.; interview with Mrs. Ennis C. Whitehead, March 28, 1969.

15. Whitehead, "Chronology."

16. Ibid.

17. Pat Robinson, *Fight for New Guinea* (New York, 1942), pp. 5-15; Hugh Buggy, *Pacific Victory: A Short History of Australia's Part in World War II* (Melbourne, 1943), pp. 85-100.

18. Jealousy between the army and navy as to who was to head the whole show caused the command to be divided in the Pacific. See Whitehead to Kenney, April 8, 1943, Whitehead Papers.

19. Buggy, *Pacific Victory*, p. 15; Robinson, *Fight for New Guinea*, p. 45.

20. For a comprehensive study of the Battle of the Coral Sea, see Samuel E. Morison, *History of United States Naval Operations in World War II*, 15 vols. (Boston, 1947-62), vol. 4; Wesley F. Craven and James L. Cate, eds., *The Army Air Forces in World War II*, 7 vols. (Chicago, 1948-58), 4:18-21, 46; Vern Haughland, *The AAF against Japan* (New York, 1948), pp. 79-89; "Let the Bombs Talk," an undated and un-

published narrative of the air war in the Pacific by the men of the Far East air forces, copy in the author's collection; Robinson, *Fight for New Guinea*, pp. 19-54; Buggy, *Pacific Victory*, pp. 145-160.

21. Gordon W. Prange, *Miracle at Midway* (New York, 1981); see also Samuel E. Morison, *U.S. Navy in World War II*, vol. 4; M. Fuchida and M. Okumiya, *Midway: The Battle That Doomed Japan* (Annapolis, 1945).

22. The Whitehead Papers contain numerous letters from members of MacArthur's staff telling Whitehead how much MacArthur thought of him. Almost all of the fifty-seven people whom I interviewed spoke of a "close personal friendship."

23. "Let the Bombs Talk," p. 28; Kenney, *Kenney Reports* (New York, 1949), p. 18.

24. Interview with Frederick H. Smith, June 10, 1969; Whitehead, "Chronology."

25. "Let the Bombs Talk," p. 31; Buggy, *Pacific Victory*, pp. 1-21; interview with Lowell Thomas, March 26, 1969. Thomas said that New Guinea had some of the worst weather and most rugged terrain he had ever seen.

26. Whitehead to Kenney, August 17, 1942; September 19, 1942; October 28, 1942; and November 15, 1942, Whitehead Papers. For an excellent summary of the engineers in New Guinea, see Hugh J. Casey, *Engineers of the Southwest Pacific, 1941-1945*, 7 vols. (Washington, D.C., 1947-53), vol. 2.

27. Interview with General Frederick H. Smith (commander, Fifth Fighter Command), June 10, 1969, and Major General J.V. Crabb (commander, Fifth Bomber Command), February 28, 1969.

28. Statistics for the Allied order of battle appear in *Fifth Air Force History* (Melbourne, 1942), p. 5; "Let the Bombs Talk," pp. 29-30.

29. Interview with Frederick H. Smith, June 10, 1969, J.V. Crabb, February 28, 1969, and Major General John Allison, February 15, 1970.

30. See Robinson, *Fight for New Guinea*, and Buggy, *Pacific Victory*.

31. "Let the Bombs Talk," p. 17.

32. "Let the Bombs Talk," p. 42; see also Craven and Cate, *Army Air Forces in World War II*, 4:129-36.

33. "Let the Bombs Talk," p. 44; Whitehead to Kenney, February 27, 1943, Whitehead Papers; Haughland, *The AAF*, p. 162.

34. "Battle of Bismarck Sea," undated and unpublished account at the Office of Air Force History, Washington, D.C., pp. 1-1; "Commentary on the Bismarck Sea Action," undated, Whitehead Papers.

35. Whitehead to Kenney, March 9, 1943, author's collection; Interview with F.H. Smith, June 10, 1969. There is some controversy as to how many Japanese vessels were actually sunk, but all reports agree that no Japanese landed on Lae or Salamaua.

36. Telegram, MacArthur to Whitehead, March 11, 1943. Whitehead Papers.

37. "Fifth Bomber Command," an undated and unpublished narrative (in 3 volumes) by the men of the Fifth Bomber Command, Fifth Air Force, available in the author's collection. A joint army-navy committee was appointed by the secretaries of war and navy to assess the results of the battle. As one might expect, the Japanese indicated that their losses were low, while the Americans claimed great victories. The numbers are still in dispute.

38. The argument over the exact number has never been resolved. As late as 1963 Whitehead still claimed that twenty-two had been sunk. One author claims that thirty were sunk; see Haugland, *The AAF*, p. 79. See also Whitehead to J.V. Crabb, May 15, 1963, Whitehead Papers.

39. *New York Times*, March 7, 1943.

40. Kenney, *Kenney Reports*, devotes considerable time to skip bombing; also "Fifth Bomber Command," p. 5; "Let the Bombs Talk," pp. 32-42; *Fight for New Guinea*, pp. 147-49.

41. "Let the Bombs Talk," pp. 33; Robinson, *Fight for New Guinea*, p. 149.

42. Kenney, *Kenney Reports*, pp. 76, 144, 154, 155, 161-65; see also H.H. Arnold to Kenney, August 17, 1943, author's collection. Arnold did not like the idea of SWPA's making the modification. He felt that the burden on its resources was too great and that the modification should be made in the United States.

43. In 1944 Charles Lindbergh helped extend the range of the P-38's by having the pilots cut back on the richness of the gas and the power needed to perform specific maneuvers. He doubled the range of the fighters, but of course more engines were ruined, and maintenance difficulties increased (Kenney, *Kenney Reports*, pp. 411-15, 421). One attack on Wewak caught the Japanese unaware because they thought that the Allied aircraft could not reach them.

44. "Let the Bombs Talk," p. 41; Craven and Cate, *Army Air Forces in World War II*, 4:129-36. Although Kenney takes much of the credit for these innovations, Whitehead developed them, supervised training, and was responsible for their employment.

45. *New York Times*, February 19, 1943.

46. Morison, *History of U.S. Naval Operations in the Pacific*, vol. 1, chap. 1, discusses strategy and problems of command in the Pacific.

47. Kenney to Whitehead, October 14, 1943, Whitehead Papers; Craven and Cate, *Army Air Forces in World War II*, 4:134.

48. "Let the Bombs Talk," p. 17; Kenney to Whitehead, October 15, 1942, Whitehead Papers.

49. Craven and Cate, *Army Air Forces in World War II*, 4:x-xiii.

50. Interview with Frederick H. Smith, June 10, 1969; J.V. Crabb, May 17, 1969; K.B. Wolf, March 19, 1969; Major General John Allison, March 21, 1969; and General Mark Bradley, April 19, 1969. All agree.

51. Interview with Frederick H. Smith, June 10, 1969, and J.V. Crabb, March 19, 1969.

52. Whitehead to Kenney, March 15, 1943; Whitehead to Don Wilson, March 20, 1943; and Whitehead to Kenney, June 19, 1943; all in Whitehead Papers.

53. "Let the Bombs Talk," p. 46; "Fifth Bomber Command," pp. 13-14.

54. Kenney, *Kenney Reports*, pp. 281-311.

55. Kenney, *Kenney Reports*, pp. 251-79, discusses in depth the Wewak operation. See also Whitehead to Kenney, August 18, 1943, author's collection.

56. See "Report of Bombing in Gloucester," unpublished, undated, Whitehead Papers; interview with General F.H. Smith, June 10, 1969, and J.V. Crabb, March 19, 1969.

57. This concept of extending the bomb line before the beginning of a major operation was reported frequently.

58. Whitehead to Kenney, April 13, 1944, Whitehead Papers; "Let the Bombs Talk," p. 61. The Japanese claimed that only 130 aircraft were lost.

59. "Let the Bomb Talk," pp. 59-60, 66; "Fifth Bomber Command," p. 27.

60. Whitehead to Kenney, June 26, 1944, Whitehead Papers; *New York Times*, June 28, 1944.

61. A sketch of the Morotai operation, dated June 14, 1944, is in the Whitehead papers; see also Kenney to Whitehead, May 31, June 7, July 28, and August 1, 1944, Whitehead Papers.

62. Robinson, *Fight for New Guinea*, p. 179.

63. *Kansas City Star*, February 19, 1943.

64. This point is discussed in depth in Craven and Cate, *Army Air Forces in*

World War II, 1:129-35, 442, 551; 2:194; 3:194-95, 549, 552-53, 570-71; 4:571, 616, 652, 662, 661; 5:passim.

65. C. Vann Woodward, *The Battle for Leyte Gulf* (New York, 1966), p. 3.

66. Stanley L. Falk, *Decision at Leyte* (New York 1956), pp. 30-31.

67. Halsey to MacArthur, September 13, 1944, Whitehead Papers.

68. Halsey also recommended that Palau not be invaded, but the operation was already under way and could not be stopped.

69. Interview with F. H. Smith, June 10, 1969, and J. V. Crabb, December 17, 1969.

70. Ibid.

71. "Let the Bombs Talk," pp. 32, 55. See also Richard L. Watson, *Fifth Air Force in the Huon Peninsula Campaigns, October 1943 to February 1944* (Washington, D.C., 1947), p. 224. Many of his planes were obsolete and out of commission for parts. He actually had only four hundred or five hundred airplanes at any one time.

72. Interview with Frederick C. Smith, June 10, 1969.

73. Interview with J. V. Crabb, February 27, 1969.

74. "Let the Bombs Talk," p. 71; "Fifth Bomber Command," p. 33; Whitehead to Kenney, December 1944, author's collection.

75. Ibid. The figures on Japanese losses appear exaggerated, although they come from official bomber and fighter command records.

76. Kenney to Whitehead, December 6, 1944, Whitehead Papers. Kenney, *Kenney Reports*, pp. 415-31.

77. Craven and Cate, *Army Air Forces in World War II*, 5:390-412.

78. "Let the Bombs Talk," p. 83; Kenney to Whitehead, January 19, 1945, Whitehead Papers.

79. Whitehead to Kenney, January 2, 1945, Whitehead Papers.

80. Whitehead to Kenney, January 9, 1945; Whitehead Papers; interview with J. V. Crabb, March 19, 1969.

81. Krueger to Whitehead, January 2, 1945, Whitehead Papers.

82. "Let the Bombs Talk," pp. 90-91; "Fifth Bomber Command," p. 45; Whitehead to Kenney, January 31, 1945, Whitehead Papers.

83. See Craven and Cate, *Army Air Forces in World War II*, 5:passim, and Morison, *History of Naval Operations* 14:79-169.

84. Whitehead to Kenney, April 8 and April 11, 1945, Whitehead Papers. See also "Fifth Bomber Command." More men were killed on initial assault and on naval ships struck by kamikaze than in any other battle of the Pacific War.

85. Whitehead to Kenney, May 27, 1948, author's collection.

86. Memorandum from Whitehead to Kenney, "Casualties of the Okinawan Campaign," July 2, 1945, Whitehead Papers.

87. "Let the Bombs Talk," pp. 102-3; "Fifth Bomber Command," p. 87.

88. Near the end of the war it was generally known that the Japanese were short on fuel. Whitehead and Kenney believed that the reason was primarily their assault on Balikpapan. They justified this belief with reference to the integration of Japanese prisoners of war. See Whitehead to Kenney, February 15, 1945, and Kenney to Whitehead, March 21, 1945, Whitehead Papers. The navy deserves a lot of credit for its submarine and carrier action, however. Interview with Frederick Smith, June 10, 1969.

89. "Air Plan OLYMPIC," April 8, 1945, author's collection.

90. Craven and Cate, *Army Air Forces in World War II*, 5:689.

91. Kenney to Whitehead, July 3, 1945, Whitehead Papers.

92. Ibid.

93. Memorandum, Whitehead to Kenney, "Plans for the OLYMPIC Operation," July 28, 1945, Whitehead Papers. The statistics came from "Let the Bombs Talk,"

p. 205, and "The Fifth Air Force in the War against Japan," in *The Strategic Bombing Survey* (Washington, D.C., 1946), p. 11.

94. "Fifth Bomber Command," p. 66; "Let the Bombs Talk," p. 141.

95. Morison, *History of Naval Operations*, 14:298-309; Whitehead to Kenney, July 17, 1945, Whitehead Papers.

96. "Mission Accomplished," unpublished, undated interrogations of Japanese industrial, military, and civil leaders of World War II, p. 29, Whitehead Papers.

97. Whitehead to Kenny, August 2, 1945, author's collection.

98. Whitehead to Loren Whitehead, August 3, 1945, author's collection.

99. Craven and Cate, *Army Air Forces in World War II*, 5:730-32.

100. Interviews with Loren Whitehead, March 20, 1970, and Mrs. Ennis C. Whitehead, May 19, 1969.

101. Interviews with General Frederic H. Smith, June 10, 1969; Major General J.V. Crabb, February 28, 1969; Lieutenant General K.B. Wolfe, August 13, 1969; and General Mark Bradley, August 15, 1969.

102. Almost all of Whitehead's close subordinates were appalled at Kenney's boast at these dinners that he won the Battles of Buna Bay and the Bismarck Sea. Interviews with General Frederick H. Smith, June 10, 1969; Major General Jarred V. Crabb, February 26, 1969; and Lieutenant General K. B. Wolfe, August 12, 1969. These men and a number of others made the point several times in speaking to me.

103. It must be emphasized that the planning done by Whitehead was tactical and operational. He had nothing to do with strategic planning and the selection of areas to invade. His job was to support the strategic plans presented to him by Mac-Arthur and Kenney with tactical fighter- and bomber-aircraft missions. Many of the drafts of these tactical plans are in his own handwriting.

DANIEL E. BARBEY

1. Rear Admiral Schuyler N. Pyne to the author, February 17, 1986; Major General Hugh J. Casey, *Engineers in the Southwest Pacific*, 8 vols. (Washington, D.C., 1947-59), vol. 4: *Amphibian Engineer Operations*, p. 11; *Portland Spectator* (Oregon), May 8, 1945; Brigadier General William F. Heavey, *Down Ramp! The Story of the Army Amphibious Engineers* (Washington, D.C., 1947).

2. Jeter A. Isely and Philip A. Crowl, *The U.S. Marines and Amphibious War* (Princeton, 1951), pp. 35-67, 231-38, 310; Captain W.D. Puleston, *The Dardanelles Campaign* (Annapolis, 1926); O. Hough, Verle E. Ludwig, and Henry I. Shaw, Jr., *Pearl Harbor to Guadalcanal: History of U.S. Marine Corps Operations in World War II* (Washington, D.C., 1958), pp. 8-9. *The Landing Force Manual, United States Navy*, 1920, devoted 7 of its 760 pages to landing operations and the 1927 edition 5 of its 703 pages to the subject.

3. Barbey to Rear Admiral William E. Howard, Jr., September 14, 1960, Vice Admiral Daniel E. Barbey, Papers, Naval Historical Center, Operational Archives Branch, Washington, D.C.

4. Barbey to Vice Admiral Alfred G. Ward, January 30, 1962, Lons Landenberger to Barbey, February 2, 1961, ibid.

5. Vice Admiral George C. Dyer, *The Amphibians Came to Conquer: The Story of Admiral Richmond Kelly Turner*, 2 vols. (Washington, D.C., 1971), 1:209-10, 213-15.

6. Vice Admiral Daniel E. Barbey, *MacArthur's Amphibious Navy: Seventh Amphibious Force Operations, 1942-1943* (Annapolis, 1969), p. 11.

7. Captain T.A. Hussey to Barbey, July 1, 1964, Barbey Papers; David Dexter, *Australia in the War of 1939-1945: The New Guinea Offensive* (Canberra, 1961), p.

272; Arthur J. Marder, *Operation "Menace": The Dakar Expedition and the Dudley North Affair* (New York, 1976); L.E.H. Maund, *Assault from the Sea* (London, 1947), pp. 19-21; Stephen W. Roskill, *The War at Sea, 1939-1945*, 3 vols. (London, 1954-61), vol. 3, pt. 1, pp. 12-13; "Fiasco at Dakar," *Time*, October 7, 1940, pp. 32ff.

8. Admiral Pyne to the author, February 17, 1986, "Discussion-Interview with Admiral Pyne," February 14, 1986; and "The Reminiscences of Rear Admiral Schuyler N. Pyne, USN (Ret.)," Transcript of Oral Interview by Dr. John T. Mason, U.S. Naval Institute, Annapolis, Md., 1972, pp. 158-91; *New York Times*, April 13, 1969, p. 88, cols. 1-2; Rear Admiral Julius A. Furer, *Administration of the Navy Department in World War II* (Washington, D.C., 1959), pp. 153, 155, 176, and "Naval Research and Development in World War II," *American Society of Naval Engineers Journal* 62 (February 1950):21-54.

9. *New York Times*, April 13, 1969, p. 88, cols. 1-2; Captain Sir James Hussey to Barbey, July 1, 1964, Commander W.N. Swann to Barbey, June 28, 1961, Barbey Papers. Sketches and photographs of amphibious craft are found in Barbey, *MacArthur's Navy*, and in R. Baker and others, *British Warship Design in World War II: Selected Papers from the Transactions of the Royal Institution of Naval Architects* (Annapolis, 1983).

10. W.N. Swann, *Spearheads of Invasion* (Sydney, 1953), pp. 22-23; Rear Admiral Edward L. Cochrane, "From Rendova to Normandy: Biography of the LST," *Shipmate*, July 1944, pp. 12, 65; Rear Admiral Schuyler N. Pyne, "The L.S.T. Mock-up at Fort Knox," courtesy Admiral Pyne.

11. Barbey, *MacArthur's Navy*, p. 4.

12. Ibid., pp. 5-6.

13. Ibid., pp. 6-7.

14. For the history of the ESBs, see Casey, *The Engineers of the Southwest Pacific*, vol. 4: *Amphibian Engineer Operations*.

15. Douglas MacArthur, *Reports of General MacArthur*, 4 vols. (Washington, D.C., 1966), 1:45-48; D. Clayton James, *The Years of MacArthur*, 3 vols. (Boston, 1970-85), 2:173-78; Samuel E. Morison, *Breaking the Bismarcks Barrier, 22 July 1942-1 May 1944* (Boston, 1950), p. 4; John Robertson, *Australia at War, 1939-1945* (Melbourne, 1981), p. 134; Major General Charles A. Willoughby and John Chamberlain, *MacArthur, 1941-1951* (New York, 1954), pp. 62, 206.

16. Barbey, *MacArthur's Navy*, p. 9; James, *MacArthur*, 2:ix, 185-91.

17. Raymond D. Tarbuck to Barbey, May 19, 1961, Barbey Papers.

18. "The Reminiscences of Rear Admiral Raymond D. Tarbuck," Transcript of Oral Interviews by Commander Etta Belle Kitchen, U.S. Naval Institute, Annapolis, Md., 1973, p. 92.

19. Barbey, *MacArthur's Navy*, pp. 21-23.

20. Ibid., pp. 24, 232.

21. Farrar to Barbey, August 8, 15, 24, 1962, Barbey Papers.

22. Chamberlain to Barbey, September 8, 1960, ibid.

23. Barbey to Robert M. Ancell, Jr., August 24, 1960, ibid.

24. Barbey, *MacArthur's Navy*, pp. 25-27, 170; Jay Luvaas, ed., *Dear Miss Em: General Eichelberger's War in the Pacific, 1942-1945* (Westport, Conn., 1972), pp. 28, 33-34; William R. Manchester, *American Caesar: Douglas MacArthur, 1880-1964* (Boston, 1978), pp. 321-22.

25. Seventh Amphibious Force, Chronology, pt. 3 (d), Rear Admiral B. C. Lovett to Barbey, July 26, 1946, Bonner Fellers to Barbey, August 19, 1960, October 27, 1965, Barbey Papers; Henri I. Shaw, Jr., "Notes on a Discussion-Interview with Vice Admiral Daniel E. Barbey, USN (Ret.), at the Army-Navy Club, Washington, D.C., on May 22, 1962," copy in Barbey Papers; Barbey, *MacArthur's Navy*, p. 32. For an extreme excoriation of the Fifth Air Force, see Rear Admiral Carroll B. Jones, "My

Experiences with the Army Air Corps in World War II," Naval Historical Foundation, Washington, D.C.

26. Barbey, *MacArthur's Navy,* pp. 28-33. A physician in an LST that landed on Manus Island recalled that "Van Zandt posted himself at our ramp at the bow doors and as the soldiers walked off to do battle in that crummy jungle, Van Zandt would pat each soldier he could reach and say, 'Don't forget to write the folks back home, and say your congressman from Pennsylvania was right here with you to see you off to battle. Remember, Van Zandt, from Pennsylvania' " (Lloyd E. Green to Dr. Emmett Norwood, enclosed in Norwood to Barbey, July 21, 1961, Barbey Papers).

27. Jamison to Barbey, December 7, 1960, Barbey Papers. For Jamison's story, see his "We'll Learn 'Em" (1952), copy in ibid.

28. Renwick G. Congdon to Barbey, May 1, 1962, Barbey Papers; Morison, *Breaking the Bismarcks Barrier,* pp. 131-32; Swann, *Spearheads of Invasion,* p. 43.

29. Robertson, *Australia at War,* p. 186; Swann, *Spearheads of Invasion,* pp. 10, 15, 20.

30. Rear Admiral William E. Howard, Jr., to Barbey, August 26, 1960, Barbey Papers; Barbey, *MacArthur's Navy,* pp. 34-42.

31. Tarbuck to Barbey, November 24, 1959, March 30, 1961, Barbey Papers.

32. John Mosher to Barbey, March 8, 1961, and "Woodlark and Kiriwina Operation," draft copy, 1943, Barbey Papers; Barbey, *MacArthur's Navy,* pp. 47-57; General Walter Krueger, *From Down Under to Nippon: The Story of Sixth Army in World War II* (Washington, D.C., 1953), pp. 19-24.

33. Walter F.G. Wemyss to Barbey, March 23, 1961, Seventh Amphibious Force Chronology, July 4, 1943, Seventh Amphibious Force, Report on Operation CHRONICLE, October 1, 1943, and Action Report, Woodlark and Kiriwina Islands, November 23, 1943, Barbey Papers; John Miller, jr., *CARTWHEEL: The Reduction of Rabaul* (Washington, D.C., 1959), pp. 49-66; Henry I. Shaw, Jr., and Major Douglas T. Kane, *Isolation of Rabaul* (Washington, D.C., 1963), pp. 59-63.

34. Morison, *Breaking the Bismarcks Barrier,* pp. 133, 134. See Dexter, *Australia in the War of 1939-1945: The New Guinea Offensive,* pp. 222-23, and Miller, *The Reduction of Rabaul,* p. 50.

35. Barbey to Robert W. MacDonald, April 2, 1962, February 7, 1964, John D. Mosher to Barbey, March 8 and November 4, 1961; Sidney S. Chapin to Barbey, July 22, 1961, Barbey Papers.

36. Barbey to Bern Anderson, October 10, 1952, ibid.

37. U.S.S. *Reid,* "Report of Action against Japanese Attacks during Landing East of Lae, N.G.," September 10, 1943, and "Lae and Finschhafen Operations: Reports, Notes, and Miscellaneous Items, 1943-1947," Barbey Papers; Morison, *Breaking the Bismarcks Barrier,* pp. 259-60.

38. Richard F. Hanley, "Destroyer 371," *Blue Book Magazine,* August 1949, p. 40.

39. Barbey, *MacArthur's Navy,* pp. 68-87; Robert L. Eichelberger, in collaboration with Milton Mackay, *Our Jungle Road to Tokyo* (New York, 1949), pp. 94-95; James, *MacArthur,* 2:324-28; Captain Walter Karig and Commander Eric Purdon, *Battle Report, Pacific War: Middle Phase* (New York, 1947), pp. 425-26; Miller, *CARTWHEEL: The Reduction of Rabaul,* pp. 189-214; Morison, *Breaking the Bismarcks Barrier,* pp. 261-62.

40. Adair to Barbey, August 5, 1960, Barbey Papers. See also Seventh Amphibious Force, Commander, Task Force 76, Report on Finschhafen, Lae, Salamaua Operation, December 8, 1943, and Action Report, Commanding Officer, *Conyngham* (DD-371) to Commander in Chief, U.S. Fleet, via Commander, Task Force 76, and Commander, Seventh Fleet, September 22, 1943, ibid.

41. Fellers to Barbey, September 26, 1965, ibid.

42. Barbey to Robert W. MacDonald, February 7, 1964, ibid.

43. Barbey to Captain Dudley W. Knox, December 17, 1944, Tarbuck to Barbey, April 12, 1961, Barbey Papers; Barbey, *MacArthur's Navy*, pp. 92-100; Lieutenant Colonel Frank O. Hough and Major John A. Crown, *The Campaign on New Britain* (Washington, D.C., 1952), pp. 18-19.

44. Commander, Task Force 76, "Operation Plan, Arawe," December 10, 1943, Report of Arawe Operation, n.d., Barbey Papers; Karig and Purdon, *Battle Report, Pacific War: Middle Phase,* pp. 50-53; Morison, *Breaking the Bismarcks Barrier,* p. 373 n. 2; Shaw and Kane, *Isolation of Rabaul,* pp. 310-11; Frank Kluckhohn, "Aero House on a South Sea Island," *New York Times Magazine,* January 2, 1944; Daniel Fredenthal, "Night Landing on New Britain," *Life,* August 21, 1944, pp. 48-56.

45. Commander Hunt Clement, Jr., to Barbey, February 28, 1961, Barbey Papers; Barbey, *MacArthur's Navy,* pp. 103-4; Miller, *CARTWHEEL: The Reduction of Rabaul,* pp. 272-305; Shaw and Kane, *Isolation of Rabaul,* pp. 310, 334-56.

46. "The Reminiscences of Admiral Thomas C. Kinkaid," Transcript of Oral Interview by John T. Mason, 1962, Columbia University Oral History Program.

47. James, *MacArthur,* 2:357-58.

48. Kinkaid, "Reminiscences," p. 275.

49. Ibid., pp. 275-76.

50. Frank Hough, *The Island War: The U.S. Marine Corps in the Pacific* (Philadelphia, 1947), p. 149.

51. George Macmillan, *The Old Breed: A History of the First Marine Division in World War II* (Washington, D.C., 1949), p. 182.

52. Commander D.H. Dayton to Barbey, June 28 and August 19, 1961; Barbey, *MacArthur's Navy,* pp. 112, 199.

53. Shaw, "Notes on a Discussion-Interview . . . with Barbey."

54. Barbey, *MacArthur's Navy,* p. 120.

55. "Rear Adm. Barbey OpPlan 3B-43," and Report on Cape Gloucester Operation, February 3, 1944, Barbey Papers; Morison, *Breaking the Bismarcks Barrier,* pp. 381-82; Captain Frank O. Hough, "The Cape Gloucester Campaign," *Marine Corps Gazette* (March 1944):7-16.

56. Barbey, *MacArthur's Navy,* pp. 123-24; Hough and Crown, *Campaign on New Britain,* pp. 28-35, 48-66.

57. *New York Times,* April 13, 1969, p. 88, col. 1.

58. Commander, Seventh Amphibious Force, Report of Operation, Saidor, February 3, 1944. Barbey's remark appears in *MacArthur's Navy,* p. 128.

59. Barbey, *MacArthur's Navy,* pp. 131-32.

60. Joseph A. O'Neill to Barbey, January 8, 1960, Barbey Papers; Barbey, *MacArthur's Navy,* pp. 126-30.

61. Ibid., p. 142.

62. Wayne P. Chesbro to Barbey, April 10, 1961, Barbey Papers. Said the commander of LST Flotilla 7, Captain R.S Scruggs, with respect to the islands of Kiriwina and Goodenough, "Both were 'tropical paradises' but the 'angels' were too dark, and chewed betel-nut" (Scruggs to Barbey, July 16, 1962, ibid.). With respect to the men engaged in a rehearsal at a forward ATC, their colonel reported to Captain Jamison, in part, that "most of the personnel were hunting souvenirs or staring at the exterior lungs of the female fuzzy-wuzzies" (Lieutenant Colonel Chester T. Barton to Jamison, May 7, 1944, copy in ibid.).

63. Grace Person Hayes, *The History of the Joint Chiefs of Staff in World War II: The War against Japan* (Annapolis, 1982), pp. 554-60; Fleet Admiral Ernest J. King and Walter Muir Whitehall, *Fleet Admiral King: A Naval Record* (New York, 1952), pp. 328-29; Robert W. Love, "Ernest J. King," in Robert W. Love, ed., *The Chiefs of Naval Operations* (Annapolis, 1980), pp. 170-71.

64. Charles Adair to Barbey, April 10, 1961, Barbey Papers; Barbey, *MacArthur's Navy*, pp. 144-45.

65. James, *MacArthur*, 2:382.

66. Commander, Task Force 76, "OpPlan No. 1-44, Admiralties," February 23, 1944, Barbey Papers; "The Reminiscences of Admiral William M. Fechteler," transcript of oral interview by John T. Mason, 1962, Columbia University Oral History Program, pp. 39-40; James, *MacArthur*, 2:379-82; Krueger, *From Down Under to Nippon*, pp. 45-55; Morison, *Breaking the Bismarck's Barrier*, pp. 432-48.

67. Fleet Admiral Ernest J. King, *U.S. Navy at War, 1941-1945: Official Reports to the Secretary of the Navy* (Washington, D.C., 1946), p. 70.

68. "The Reminiscences of Admiral Tarbuck," pp. 129-32.

69. Fellers to Barbey, September 26, 1965, Barbey Papers.

70. Barbey, "Memorandum to Commander, Seventh Fleet," March 28, 1944, Admiral Thomas C. Kinkaid Papers, Naval Historical Center, Operational Archives Branch, Washington, D.C.; "The Reminiscences of Admiral Kinkaid," pp. 358-59.

71. Barbey, *MacArthur's Navy*, pp. 151-59; James, *MacArthur*, 2:358.

72. Seventh Amphibious Force Chronology, n.d.[c. May 1, 1945].

73. John Mosher to Barbey, March 8, 1961, Barbey to Major General F.R. Zierath, October 5, 1961, Zierath to Barbey, November 30, 1961, Barbey Papers.

74. A.G. Noble to Barbey, October 26, 1950, Barbey to Major General Orlando Ward, December 18, 1950, Barbey Papers; Robert Ross Smith, *The Approach to the Philippines* (Washington, D.C., 1953), pp. 36-39; Krueger, *From Down Under to Nippon*, pp. 66-75; Gavin Merrick Long, *The Final Campaigns* (Canberra, 1963), pp. 261-71; Samuel E. Morison, *New Guinea and the Marianas, March 1944-August 1944* (Boston, 1953), pp. 34-44, 46, 66-67. Barbey was told that "planning with the staff of the 6th Army, Army divisions, and Marines presented no problems. . . . Planning with the Air Force presented a number of problems. . . . The situation finally became so impossible that it was necessary to request 5th AF to provide liaison officers to be attached to the 7th Phib For to improve communications and even more so to bring about a better understanding of joint operations" (Commander Russell J. Schmidt to Barbey, September 18, 1961, Barbey Papers).

75. Commander, Task Force 78, "Hollandia OpPlan, 4-14-44," Barbey Papers; Morison, *New Guinea and the Marianas*, pp. 64-65. For the Hollandia task force organization, see the latter, appendix 1.

76. Barbey, *MacArthur's Navy, p. 203*; James, *MacArthur*, 2:457-59.

77. Barbey, *MacArthur's Navy*, p. 207; King, *Official Reports*, 161; Krueger, *From Down Under to Nippon*, pp. 106-12; Morison, *New Guinea and the Marianas*, pp. 68-90; Smith, *Approach to the Philippines*, pp. 397-424.

78. Tarbuck to Barbey, November 3, 1965, Barbey Papers; Barbey, *MacArthur's Navy*, pp. 217-19; Eichelberger, *Our Jungle Road to Tokyo*, pp. 165-66; Frazier Hunt, *The Untold Story of Douglas MacArthur* (New York, 1954), pp. 333-37.

79. Karig and Purdon, *Batle Report, Pacific War: Middle Phase*, p. 190.

80. Edwin P. Hoyt, *The Battle of Leyte Gulf: The Death Knell of the Japanese Fleet* (New York, 1972), pp. 34-45.

81. "The Reminiscences of Admiral Kinkaid," pp. 357, 440; Gerald E. Wheeler to author, December 26, 1985, author's collection. Kinkaid's comments on Barbey's fitness reports are from the latter document, kindly furnished by Lieutenant Commander Robert A. Schultz, Naval Personnel Records Center, St. Louis, Mo. Barbey arrived in SWPA in January 1943, Kinkaid not until October. In any case, the *New York Times* carried three articles about Barbey and none about Kinkaid in SWPA in 1943; four articles about Barbey and one about Kinkaid in 1944, and seven articles about Barbey and four about Kinkaid in 1945, with three of the last dealing with their opera-

tions in Korea. In addition Barbey was featured in *Life, Newsweek, Reader's Digest,* and *Saturday Evening Post* and on the front cover of *U.S. News and World Report.*

82. Robert Shaplen, "The Duck-billed Admiral: Amphibious Daniel E. Barbey Sets MacArthur's Men Ashore," *Newsweek,* October 24, 1944, p. 31.

83. John Walker, "Uncle Dan Barbey: An Amphibious Admiral Moved MacArthur's Army," *Life,* November 20, 1944, pp. 16-18.

84. Bern Anderson to Barbey, August 8, 1952, Action Reports: Comments on the Tanahmera Bay, Hollandia, Landing, May 5, 1944, Seventh Amphibious Force, Report of Tanahmera Bay-Humboldt-Aitape Operation, with Enclosures, May 13, 1944, and Hollandia: History of the Hollandia (Reckless) Operation by the Hollandia Task Force, n.d., Barbey Papers; Barbey, *MacArthur's Navy,* pp. 178-79; Swann, *Spearheads of Invasion,* pp. 78-93.

85. Barbey, *MacArthur's Navy,* p. 183.

86. Ibid., pp. 176-80.

87. Ibid., p. 183.

88. Hayes, *History of the Joint Chiefs of Staff in World War II: The War against Japan,* p. 549; Henry L. Stimson and McGeorge Bundy, *On Active Service in Peace and War* (New York, 1948), pp. 200-5, 291; Love, "King," in Love, *The Chiefs of Naval Operations,* p. 164.

89. Barbey, *MacArthur's Navy,* pp. 181-83.

90. Bern Anderson to Barbey, August 8, 1952, Commander, Task Force 78, "WakdeToem OpPlan 44-44 Rev.," May 13, 1944, Barbey Papers; Smith, *Approach to the Philippines,* pp. 21-22.

91. Vice Admiral R.N. Smoot to Barbey, April 12, 1967, History of the Biak Operation, 15-27 June 1944, Barbey Papers; Krueger, *From Down Under to Nippon,* pp. 78-82; Smith, *Approach to the Philippines,* pp. 212-31.

92. Commander, Task Force 78, "Biak OpPlan No. 5-44," May 16, 1944; Amphibious Force, Task Force 77 Report of the Biak Operation, with Enclosures, n.d., Biak Operation: History, 15-27 June 1944, n.d., Barbey Papers; Barbey, *MacArthur's Navy,* pp. 184-202; Krueger, *From Down Under to Nippon,* pp. 83-91; Smith, *Approach to the Philippines,* pp. 280-303.

93. Barbey, *MacArthur's Navy,* p. 203; James, *MacArthur,* 2:457-59; Morison, *New Guinea and the Marianas,* pp. 95-114.

94. Commander, Seventh Amphibious Force, to Combined Amphibious Forces, Pacific Fleet, Subject: Information on Seventh Amphibious Force, May 22, 1945, Barbey Papers.

95. Barbey, *MacArthur's Navy,* p. 207; Morison, *New Guinea and the Marianas,* pp. 134-40. See also Commander, Task Force 78, "OpPlan No. 6044, Noemfoot," Barbey Papers.

96. Commander, Task Force 77, "OpPlan No. 8-44," August 20, 1944; Barbey Papers; Morison, *New Guinea and the Marianas,* pp. 140-44; Samuel E. Morison, *Leyte, June 1944-January 1945* (Boston, 1958), pp. 19-29: Smith, *Approach to the Philippines,* pp. 450-93.

97. Barbey, *MacArthur's Navy,* pp. 217-19; Morison, *Leyte,* pp. 3-6; E.B. Potter, *Nimitz* (Annapolis, 1976), pp. 281-82, 287; "Reminiscences of Admiral Tarbuck," p. 149.

98. Barbey, *MacArthur's Navy,* pp. 219-27; George Grand and Truman R. Strobridge, *Western Pacific Operations* (Washington, D.C., 1971), pp. 303-10; Fleet Admiral William F. Halsey and J. Bryan III, *Admiral Halsey's Story* (New York, 1947), pp. 198-201; James, *MacArthur,* 2:537-42; Morison, *Leyte,* pp. 19-25; Smith, *Approach to the Philippines,* pp. 275-93.

99. Nimitz to King, July 31, 1944, King to Kinkaid, August 17, 1944, with copy

to Nimitz, Admiral Chester W. Nimitz Papers, Naval Historical Center, Operational Archives Branch, Washington, D.C.

100. "The Reminiscences of Admiral Richard L. Conolly," Transcript of Oral Interview by Donald F. Shaughnessy, Columbia University Oral History Program, 1960, pp. 253-55.

101. Commander, Task Group 78.1, "OpOrder No. 1-44, San Pedro Bay, Leyte," October 7, 1944, Commander, Task Group 78.4, " OpOrder 1-44, Leyte," October 2, 1944, Captain R.S. Scruggs to Barbey, July 16, 1962, Barbey Papers; Barbey, *MacArthur's Navy*, p. 229; James, *MacArthur*, 2:545-46; Morison, *Leyte*, pp. 7, 56-58.

102. "The Reminiscences of Admiral Tarbuck," pp. 151-59, and enclosure B, copy in Barbey Papers; Barbey, *MacArthur's Navy*, pp. 229-37; Morison, *Leyte*, pp. 117-26. Barbey erred. Of historians who have written about the Battle of Leyte Gulf, six (Bernard Brodie, Samuel E. Morison, E.B. Potter, Clark G. Reynolds, Adrian Stewart, and C. Vann Woodward) are critical of Halsey; only one (Stanley L. Falk), believes he made the right decision in sailing north after a decoy Japanese carrier force.

103. Barbey, *MacArthur's Navy*, p. 237.

104. "The Reminiscences of Admiral Tarbuck," p. 10.

105. William Jibb to Barbey, September 28, 1960, Barbey Papers.

106. Commander James A. Baxter to Barbey, n.d., U.S.S. *Blue Ridge*, "Report of Action in Leyte Operation, Seventh Amphibious Force, Report Covering the Invasion and Occupation of Leyte, Philippine Islands, November 14, 1944, Barbey Papers; "Reminiscences of Admiral Tarbuck," pp. 166-67.

107. Barbey to Kinkaid, November 2, 1944, Barbey Papers.

108. Barbey to Major General F.H. Dewing, August 17, 1943; Barbey, *MacArthur's Navy*, pp. 257-58, 269-76.

109. To army personnel Tarbuck explained that "a commodore is a brigadier general who can swim" ("The Reminiscences of Admiral Tarbuck," p. 222).

110. Barbey to Kinkaid, November 9, 1944, Barbey Papers.

111. Rear Admiral Arthur D. Struble, Narrative Report, 18 August 1945, and Ormoc Attack Order, Attack Group, TG 78.3, December 1, 1944, Seventh Amphibious Force, Report of Resupply Echelon for the Ormoc Operations, January 31, 1945, ibid.

112. Commander, Task Group 78.3, "OpPlan 44, Mindoro," November 28, 1944; Barbey, *MacArthur's Navy*, p. 287; Morison, *Leyte*, pp. 34-36.

113. Barbey, *MacArthur's Navy*, pp. 285-91.

114. Report, Commander Luzon Attack Force, Commander, Seventh Fleet, Lingayen, January 9, 1945, Seventh Amphibious Force, Commander, Task Force 78, Report, Lingayen Gulf Operation, 9 January 1945, February 12, 1945, San Fabian Attack Force Report, Lingayen Operation, with Enclosures, February 12, 1945; Barbey, *MacArthur's Navy*, pp. 291-95; King, *Official Reports*, pp. 126-27; Morison, *Leyte*, pp. 95-115, 130-33, 137.

115. Barbey to Kinkaid, February 4, 1945, Barbey Papers.

116. Commander, Seventh Amphibious Force, Action Report on San Antonio-San Felipe Area, March 17, 1945, Commander, Task Group 78.3, "OpPlan No. 4-45, Bataan-Corregidor," February 10, 1945, Seventh Amphibious Force, Report on Mariveles-Corregidor Operations, December 18, 1945, Barbey Papers; Barbey, *MacArthur's Navy*, pp. 291-310; James H. Belote and William M. Belote, *Corregidor: The Saga of Fortress* (New York, 1967), pp. 194-251; James, *MacArthur*, 2:628-53; Samuel E. Morison, *The Liberation of the Philippines, 1944-45: Luzon, Mindanao, the Visayas* (Boston, 1959), pp. 185-210; "Reminiscences of Admiral Tarbuck," pp. 211-15, 220-27.

117. Seventh Amphibious Force, "Reports of . . . Zamboanga, Sulu Archi-

pelago, and Sarangani Bay Area," April 22, 1945, Barbey Papers; Barbey, *Mac-Arthur's Navy*, pp. 310-14; James, *MacArthur*, 2:738-51; King, *Official Reports*, pp. 183-86; Morison, *Liberation of the Philippines*, pp. 316-51.

118. Commander, Task Force 78, "Oboe ONE, OpPlan No. 1045, Tarakan," April 6, 1945; Barbey, *MacArthur's Navy*, pp. 314-15.

119. Commander, Task Force 78, "Oboe SIX, OpPlan No. 11-45, Brunei, Bay," May 17, 1945; James, *MacArthur*, 2:754-60.

120. Seventh Amphibious Force, Report of Balikpapan-Manggar-Borneo Operations, June-July 1945, September 5, 1945, Barbey Papers; Barbey, *MacArthur's Navy*, pp. 316-20.

121. King, *Official Reports*, p. 187.

122. James, *MacArthur*, 2:283-84.

123. Morison, *Breaking the Bismarck's Barrier*, p. 13.

124. Frazier Hunt, *MacArthur and the War against Japan* (New York, 1944), p. 139.

125. Courtney Whitney, *MacArthur: His Rendezvous with History* (New York, 1956), p. 103.

126. These comments have been extracted from the fitness reports written by these admirals on Barbey.

127. Mrs. Daniel E. Barbey to the author, May 28, 1986, author's collection.

MAPS

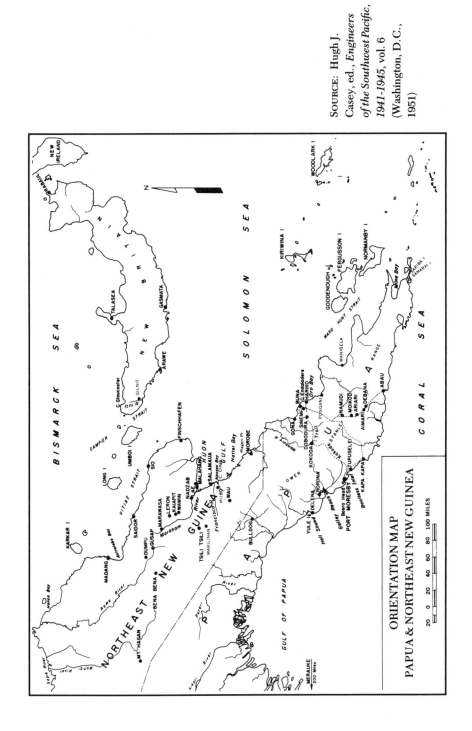

ORIENTATION MAP
PAPUA & NORTHEAST NEW GUINEA

SOURCE: Hugh J. Casey, ed., *Engineers of the Southwest Pacific, 1941-1945*, vol. 6 (Washington, D.C., 1951)

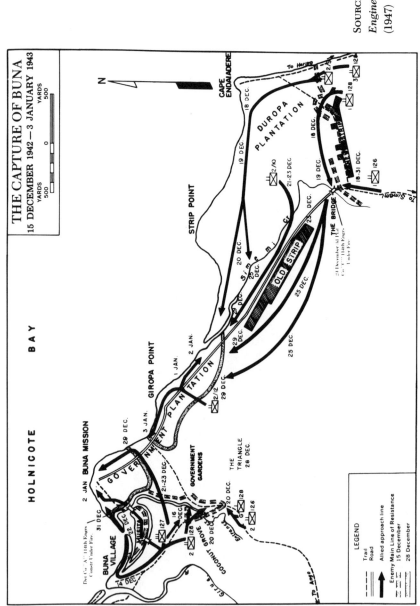

SOURCE: Casey,
Engineers, vol. 1
(1947)

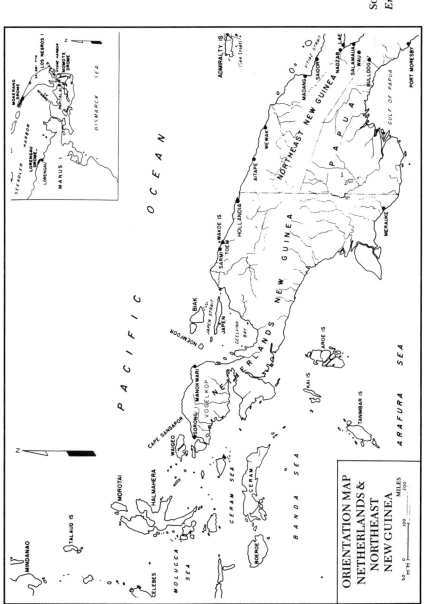

ORIENTATION MAP
NETHERLANDS &
NORTHEAST
NEW GUINEA

SOURCE: Casey,
Engineers, vol. 6

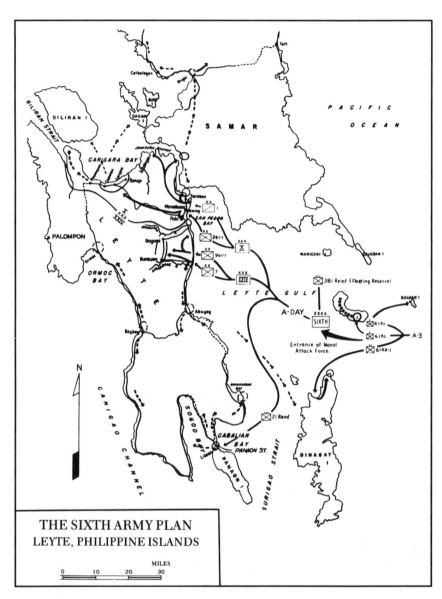

THE SIXTH ARMY PLAN
LEYTE, PHILIPPINE ISLANDS

MILES
0   10   20   30

SOURCE: Casey, *Engineers*, vol. 1

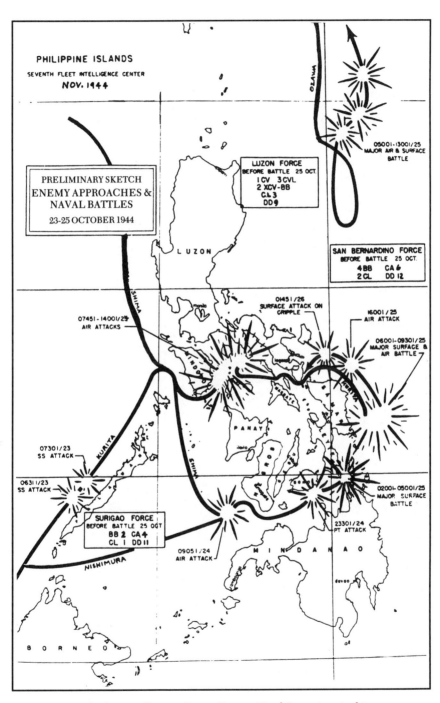

PHILIPPINE ISLANDS
SEVENTH FLEET INTELLIGENCE CENTER
NOV. 1944

PRELIMINARY SKETCH
ENEMY APPROACHES &
NAVAL BATTLES
23-25 OCTOBER 1944

LUZON FORCE
BEFORE BATTLE 25 OCT.
1 CV   3 CVL
2 XCV-BB
CL 3
DD 9

05001-13001/25
MAJOR AIR & SURFACE
BATTLE

SAN BERNARDINO FORCE
BEFORE BATTLE 25 OCT.
4 BB   CA 6
2 CL   DD 12

L U Z O N

01451/26
SURFACE ATTACK ON
CRIPPLE

07451-14001/25
AIR ATTACKS

16001/25
AIR ATTACK

06001-09301/25
MAJOR SURFACE &
AIR BATTLE

P A N A Y

07301/23
SS ATTACK

06311/23
SS ATTACK

02001-05001/25
MAJOR SURFACE
BATTLE

SURIGAO FORCE
BEFORE BATTLE 25 OCT
BB 2   CA 4
CL 1   DD 11

23301/24
PT ATTACK

09051/24
AIR ATTACK

M I N D A N A O

NISHIMURA

KURITA

SHIMA

B O R N E O

SOURCE: 7th Fleet Intelligence Center Report, Naval Operations Archives

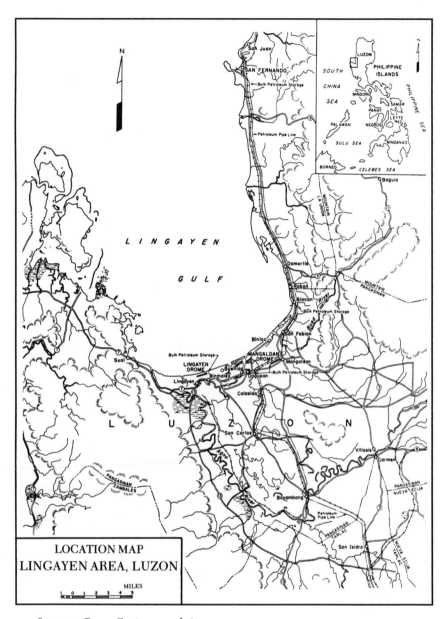

LOCATION MAP
LINGAYEN AREA, LUZON

MILES

SOURCE: Casey, *Engineers*, vol. 6

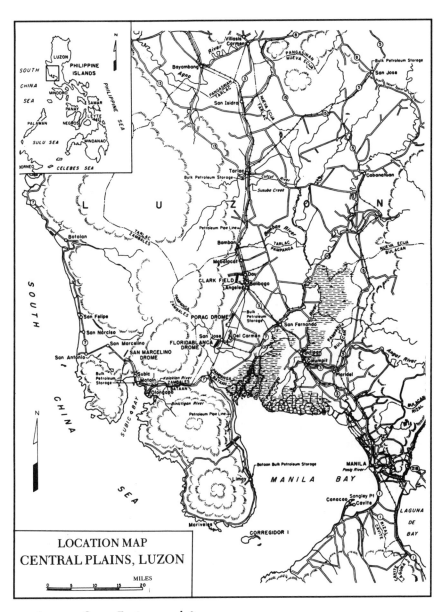

LOCATION MAP
CENTRAL PLAINS, LUZON

MILES

SOURCE: Casey, *Engineers*, vol. 6

BIBLIOGRAPHICAL ESSAY

THOMAS A. BLAMEY

The major primary source is the Blamey Papers held in the Australian War Memorial, Canberra. Written records and war diaries for the campaigns are also held in the War Memorial. Inasmuch as Curtin left no papers of his own on strategy, the Shedden Papers are crucial to an understanding of the relationship between MacArthur, Curtin, and Blamey; they are held in the Australian Archives, Canberra. The MacArthur Papers, in the MacArthur Memorial, Norfolk, Virginia, and the Sutherland Papers, in the National Archives, Washington, D.C., complement the Blamey and Shedden papers. The Rowell Papers in the Australian War Memorial and the Vasey Papers in the National Library of Australia are valuable for the command crisis of August-September 1942. The Berryman Papers in the Australian War Memorial are useful for strategic planning in 1944 and 1945.

John Hetherington, *Blamey, Controversial Soldier* (Canberra, 1973), an expanded and revised version of Hetherington's earlier biography of Blamey, which was published in 1954, is the best account of Blamey's life. It provides a good picture of Blamey's personality, but although it covers the main aspects of his military performance, the treatment is somewhat uncritical. Norman D. Carlyon, *I Remember Blamey* (Melbourne, 1980), was written by Blamey's aide-de-camp for the first half of the war and is naturally stronger for that period. It is an interesting personal account. The most detailed treatment of Australia's land campaigns in the Pacific is found in the official histories: D. McCarthy, *South-West Pacific Area, First Year* (Canberra, 1959); David Dexter, *The New Guinea Offensives* (Canberra, 1961); and Gavin Long, *The Final Campaigns* (Canberra, 1963).

D. Clayton James, *The Years of MacArthur, 1941-1945* 3 vols. (Boston, 1970-85), volume 2, gives a good outline of MacArthur's relations with the Australians, but it is not the strongest part of the book. Gavin Long, *MacArthur as Military Commander* (Sydney, 1969), is sound and balanced and provides an Australian perspective on the important strategic issues concerning Blamey and MacArthur. The most detailed treatment of the strategic questions, and further evidence for the arguments presented in this chapter, appear in D.M. Horner, *Crisis of Command: Australian Generalship and the Japanese Threat, 1941-1943* (Canberra, 1978), and in D.M. Horner, *High Command: Australia and Allied Strategy, 1939-1945* (Sydney, 1982).

Books which provide additional insight into Blamey's relationship with MacArthur include: S.F. Rowell, *Full Circle* (Melbourne, 1974), which deals with Rowell's relationship with Blamey in the Middle East and also with his argument with and dismissal by Blamey in New Guinea; Peter Charlton, *The Unnecessary War* (Melbourne, 1983), which discusses the campaigns in the last year of the war; Stuart Sayers, *Ned Herring: A Life of Sir Edmund Herring* (Melbourne, 1980), which provides Herring's perspective; and Lloyd Ross, *John Curtin: A Biography* (Melbourne, 1977), which describes Blamey's and MacArthur's relationship with the prime minister. Australian-American relations are covered more generally in Roger Bell, *Unequal Allies* (Melbourne, 1977); Christopher Thorne, *Allies of a Kind: The United States, Britain, and the War against Japan, 1941-1945* (London, 1978); and Paul Hasluck, *The Government and the People, 1942-1945* (Canberra, 1970).

WALTER KRUEGER

The extensive collection of Krueger Papers at the U.S. Military Academy Library, West Point, New York, is by far the most important source of material on his life. It is well organized and easy to use. The Papers of Fay W. Brabson, U.S. Army Military History Institute, Carlisle Barracks, Pennsylvania, contain a number of personal letters from Krueger that shed light on his early career. The Military History Institute also houses the papers of George H. Decker and Clyde D. Eddleman, together with extensive interviews with these two men who were closest to Krueger during World War II. Helpful material provided to the author by General Eddleman and Colonel Walter Krueger, Jr., will be deposited with the Krueger Papers at West Point.

Secondary sources on Krueger are woefully thin. Two wartime articles merit attention: Frank L. Kluckhorn, "Master of Amphibious Warfare," *New York Times Magazine,* December 31, 1944, and Gordon Walker, "General Walter Krueger: Mystery Man of the Pacific," *Christian Science Weekly Magazine,* June 9, 1945. The only noteworthy account to appear since the war is Arthur S. Collins, Jr., "Walter Krueger," *Infantry* (January-February 1983):15-19.

Material on Krueger's campaigns in the Southwest Pacific can be found in the papers of Douglas MacArthur, MacArthur Memorial, Norfolk, Virginia, and in the records of the headquarters of Alamo Force and Sixth Army, Washington National Records Center, Suitland, Maryland. The Papers of Thomas F. Hickey and Andrew D. Bruce at the Military History Institute are especially helpful for the Leyte campaign. The author also profited from Major General David W. Gray's lengthy critique of the fighting at Leyte.

The U.S. Army's superb official histories were heavily used for Krueger's wartime service: John Miller, jr., *CARTWHEEL: The Reduction of Rabaul* (Washington, D.C., 1959), Robert Ross Smith, *The Approach to the Philip-*

pines (Washington, D.C., 1953), M. Hamlin Cannon, *Leyte: The Return to the Philippines* (Washington, D.C., 1954), and Robert Ross Smith, *Triumph in the Philippines* (Washington, D.C., 1963). MacArthur's GHQ produced *Reports of General MacArthur*, 2 vols. in 4 parts (Washington, D.C., 1966), an important source of information that must be used with care. Hugh J. Casey, ed., *Engineers of the Southwest Pacific, 1941-1945,* 7 vols. (Washington, D.C., 1947-53), details the massive problems encountered—and overcome—by the engineers.

Krueger recounts his wartime experiences in *From Down Under to Nippon* (Washington, D.C., 1953), a carefully written volume that relies heavily on reports generated by Sixth Army headquarters. Other important memoirs include Douglas MacArthur, *Reminiscences* (New York, 1964), Robert L. Eichelberger, *Our Jungle Road to Tokyo* (New York, 1950), George C. Kenney, *General Kenney Reports* (New York, 1949), and Daniel E. Barbey, *MacArthur's Amphibious Navy* (Annapolis, 1969). For Eichelberger's candid comments on men and events, see Jay Luvaas, ed., *Dear Miss Em: General Eichelberger's War in the Pacific, 1942-1945* (Westport, Conn., 1972).

The second volume of D. Clayton James, *The Years of MacArthur*, 3 vols. (Boston, 1970-85), dominates the secondary literature. This model of lucid scholarship also contains a comprehensive bibliographical essay. Although the author judges Krueger too harshly, Ronald H. Spector, *Eagle against the Sun* (New York, 1985), is still the best single-volume treatment of the war in the Pacific. Edward J. Drea, *Defending the Driniumor* (Fort Leavenworth, Kans., 1984), uses recently declassified Ultra material to great advantage in analyzing the fighting on New Guinea. Stanley L. Falk, *Decision at Leyte* (New York, 1966) is a classic, while William B. Breuer, *Retaking the Philippines* (New York, 1986), adds little to our understanding of the subject.

GEORGE C. KENNEY

The primary source for understanding General Kenney's leadership of the Far East air forces in the Southwest Pacific during World War II is his eleven volumes of notebooks on file in the Office of Air Force History, Washington, D.C., and at the USAF Historical Research Center, Maxwell Air Force Base, Alabama. The Kenney notebooks are indispensable for the planning and conduct of the air war in the Pacific. Moreover, Kenney also discusses personalities and, characteristically, is almost never loath to express his opinion. These notebooks were used by General Kenney as the basic material for his book, *General Kenney Reports: A Personal History of the Pacific War* (New York, 1949). As readers of his book are aware, Kenney was an unusually deft writer.

The General George C. Kenney Papers, also available in Washington and at Maxwell Air Force Base, are especially relevant where Kenney's post-World War II career and the retirement years are concerned. There is some documentation relevant to the war, however, as well as the original type-scripts of General Kenney's books about Pappy Gunn and Dick Bong.

As noted, *General Kenney Reports* is one of the best memoirs to emerge from World War II, readable, in depth, and peppered with insight. Also see the official history of the army air forces in World War II, Wesley F. Craven and James L. Cate, eds., *The Army Air Forces in World War II*, 7 vols. (Chicago, 1948-58), especially volumes 4 and 5.

The official unit histories of the war are on file at the U.S. Air Force Historical Research Center, Maxwell Air Force Base, Alabama, and on microfilm in the Office of Air Force History, Washington, D.C. There are also a number of relevant official USAF numbered historical studies on file at Maxwell and in Washington, as follows: Richard L. Watson, Jr., Study 113, "The Fifth Air Force in the Huon Peninsula Campaign, January-October 1943" (1946); Richard L. Watson, Jr., Study 116, "The Fifth Air Force in the Huon Peninsula Campaign, October 1943-February 1944" (1947); Harris G. Warren, Study 43, "The Fifth Air Force in the Conquest of the Bismarck Archipelago, November 1943-March 1944" (1946); Joe G. Taylor, Study 86, "Close Air Support in the War against Japan" (1955); James C. Olson, Study 38, "Operational History of the Seventh Air Force, November 1943-July 1944" (1945); and Richard L. Watson, Jr., Study 17, "Air Action in the Papuan Campaign, July 1942-January 1943" (1944).

General Arnold's view is recorded in Henry H. Arnold, *Global Mission* (New York, 1949). General Kenney wrote several books: *The MacArthur I Know* (New York, 1951); *The Saga of Pappy Gunn* (New York, 1959); and *Dick Bong, Ace of Aces* (New York, 1960).

For an insightful consideration of the B-29 issue between Kenney and General Arnold, see Stanley L. Falk, "General Kenney, the Indirect Approach, and the B-29s," *Aerospace Historian* 27 (1981): 147-55.

Any number of official interviews, conducted by the Oral History Division of the USAF Historical Research Center, and on file at Maxwell Air Force Base and in the Office of Air Force History, touch upon General Kenney's career. The most comprehensive is an interview conducted with General Kenney by James G. Hasdorff in August 1974 at Bay Harbor Islands, Florida; this interview is particularly good on the World War II years. Other official interviews that pertain in some way to Kenney include those with Lieutenant Generals Ennis C. Whitehead and Barney Giles.

Many books touch on the air war in the Pacific during World War II. For the official summary report on air operations, see the U.S. Strategic Bombing Survey, *Summary Report Pacific War* (Washington, D.C., 1946). Also consult Louis Morton, *Strategy and Command: The First Two Years* (Washington, D.C., 1962).

Additional books relevant to the air war in the Pacific and of interest to the general reader include Steve Birdsall, *Flying Buccaneers: The Illustrated Story of Kenney's Fifth Air Force* (Garden City, 1977), and Vern Haughland, *The AAF against Japan* (New York, 1948). A recent addition to the literature of the Pacific war is Ronald H. Spector, *Eagle against the Sun: The American*

War with Japan (New York, 1985), a volume in the series *The Macmillan Wars of the United States*. Spector is highly critical of MacArthur and, although he gives Kenney his due, basically has little coverage of air operations in the Southwest Pacific.

THOMAS C. KINKAID

Research concerning Admiral Thomas Cassin Kinkaid, during the time he commanded the Seventh Fleet (November 26, 1943-November 19, 1945), properly begins with the collection of personal papers which he left to the Office of Naval History at the Naval Historical Center, Washington, D.C. The collection contains the admiral's official papers from his entry into the navy in 1904 until his death in 1972. While the documents are incomplete for his Seventh Fleet period, there is a substantial amount of official correspondence, dispatch files, reports, staff rosters, and operations orders. He kept no personal diary, but he did write almost daily to his wife, Helen Sherbourne Kinkaid, and these letters are available with the collection. Because of security regulations, Kinkaid did not write with any depth about operations, but the letters present a clear picture of his movements and insights into his relations with General Douglas MacArthur and other senior navy and army officers with whom he dealt. The Navy Operational Archives, a part of the Naval Historical Center, contain records of importance concerning Seventh Fleet operations. Dispatches, reports, correspondence, operations plans, action reports, command and unit war diaries, and histories can be found at the NOA. The deck logs of the vessels involved in Seventh Fleet operations are stored at the National Archives. Exceptionally valuable in documenting relations between the headquarters of the commander in chief, Pacific Fleet, Admiral Chester E. Nimitz, and the commander in chief, Southwest Pacific area, General Douglas MacArthur, as they related to the Seventh Fleet, is the "CINCPAC Command Summary and Running Estimate," which was maintained by Captain James M. Steele of Nimitz's staff. Dispatch traffic and vital correspondence are briefly summarized on a daily basis and the most important reproduced completely.

The personal papers of Fleet Admiral Ernest J. King and Fleet Admiral Chester W. Nimitz, both on deposit at the ONH, supplement the Kinkaid Papers. Both collections are large and carefully organized. An interesting and useful source concerning King and Nimitz is the file of minutes (on microfilm) from the regular meetings held between these two leaders throughout the war. Equally important, because of his participation in the Leyte and Lingayen Gulf operations, are the papers of Fleet Admiral William F. Halsey, located in the Manuscript Division of the Library of Congress. The collection is not as full as those for Nimitz and King. Because Kinkaid was also commander, Allied naval forces, Southwest Pacific, and served under MacArthur's command, it was important to use the General of the Army Douglas MacArthur Archives in Norfolk, Virginia. These records included dispatch files, official correspondence, operations plans and orders, and personal correspondence concerning Kinkaid and his command. The MacArthur papers are carefully organized and serviced.

Other manuscript collections that provided useful information concerning Admiral Kinkaid as Seventh Fleet commander were those of Vice Admiral Daniel E. Barbey (ONH), Rear Admiral Richard W. Bates (Naval War College, Newport, Rhode Island), General of the Army George C. Marshall (Marshall Library, Lexington, Virginia), Admiral Richmond Kelly Turner (ONH), and Vice Admiral Theodore S. Wilkinson (LCMD). The Hoover Institution, Stanford, California, houses the personal papers of Rear Admiral Clifford E. Van Hook, Kinkaid's deputy commander, and the papers of Vice Admiral Frank D. Wagner, who was commander, Fleet Aviation, Seventh Fleet.

The Oral History collections of Columbia University and of the U.S. Naval Institute (USNI) contain useful material. Admiral Kinkaid's oral history was published by Columbia University in 1961, but for this chapter the author preferred to use the rough "first draft" typescript available in the admiral's papers. Other oral histories used were: Admiral Richard L. Conolly (Columbia), a group commander in the Seventh Amphibious Force; Rear Admiral Arthur H. McCollum (USNI), the intelligence officer of the Seventh Fleet; Admiral Felix B. Stump (Columbia), a CVE group commander; and Rear Admiral Raymond D. Tarbuck (USNI), senior naval officer attached to General MacArthur's staff.

The author received a half dozen letters of great historical value written by Rear Admiral Valentine H. Schaeffer, who served as chief of staff to Admiral Kinkaid. Then a commodore, Schaeffer was with Kinkaid during the Leyte, Mindoro, and Lingayen operations. Other officers who served with Kinkaid and were willing to share their memories included: Admiral Russell S. Berkey, commander of the Seventh Fleet cruiser force; Vice Admiral Ralph W. Christie, commander, submarine force, Seventh Fleet; Vice Admiral George C. Dyer, who served on the COMINCH staff; Lieutenant Commander David Freeman, who served as Kinkaid's flag lieutenant and aide; Commodore Russell M. Ihrig, who served on Admiral Nimitz's staff; and Rear Admiral Charles J. Maguire, who was a plans officer on Kinkaid's staff. The author was able to interview Admiral Kinkaid's widow, Mrs. Helen S. Kinkaid, more than a dozen times before her death in December 1980. Also interviewed were Admiral Russell S. Berkey (Old Lyme, Conn., 1976), Lieutenant Commander David Freeman (Rumson, N.J., 1976), Captain Joseph H. Garvin (Berkeley, Calif., 1977), and Captain Thomas K. Kimmel, Admiral Kinkaid's nephew (Annapolis, Md., 1976).

For this study, the author found that the following memoirs/autobiographies were particularly useful. Daniel E. Barbey, *MacArthur's Amphibious Navy: Seventh Amphibious Force Operations, 1943-1945* (Annapolis, 1969); Robert L. Eichelberger, *Our Jungle Road to Tokyo* (New York, 1950); William F. Halsey and J. Bryan, *Admiral Halsey's Story* (New York, 1947); George C. Kenney, *General Kenney Reports* (New York, 1949); Ernest J. King and Walter

Muir Whitehill, *Fleet Admiral King: A Naval Record* (New York, 1952); Walter Krueger, *From Down Under to Nippon: The Story of Sixth Army in World War II* (Washington, D.C., 1953); Douglas MacArthur, *Reminiscences* (New York, 1964); Jesse B. Oldendorf, as told to Hawthorne Daniel, "The Battle of Surigao Strait," *Blue Book Magazine* (March 1949), and "Lingayen Landing," *Blue Book Magazine* (April 1949); Frederick C. Sherman, *Combat Command: The American Aircraft Carriers in the Pacific War* (New York, 1982). The published biographies of the principal army and navy leaders with whom Admiral Kinkaid dealt are uniformly excellent. These include: Thomas B. Buell, *Master of Sea Power: A Biography of Fleet Admiral Ernest J. King* (Boston, 1980); D. Clayton James, *The Years of MacArthur*, vol. 2: *1941-1945* (Boston, 1975); Forrest C. Pogue, *George C. Marshall: Organizer of Victory, 1943-1945* (New York, 1973); E.B. Potter, *Bull Halsey* (Annapolis, 1985) and *Nimitz* (Annapolis, 1976).

The two series of operations history, *The United States Army in World War II*, published by the Office of the Chief of Military History, and *The History of United States Naval Operations in World War II*, written by Samuel Eliot Morison, are indispensable.

As might be expected, literature on the Battle for Leyte Gulf usually tends to support either Kinkaid or Halsey, with the exception of two major authors. The Halsey memoir, *Admiral Halsey's Story*, presents the battle as he saw it. The problems that beset Taffy 3 were the result of Kinkaid's lack of attention to aerial searches and to the division of the command between Halsey and Kinkaid. Admiral Kinkaid believed that his point of view was best presented in C. Vann Woodward, *The Battle for Leyte Gulf* (New York, 1947), and in Hanson W. Baldwin's chapter, "The Sho Plan: The Battle for Leyte Gulf, 1944," in *Sea Fights and Shipwrecks* (Garden City, 1955). While Baldwin presented extensive comments by Halsey and Kinkaid, his narrative accepts Kinkaid's views. The biographies of Halsey and Nimitz by E.B. Potter, noted above, tell the story of Leyte Gulf in a straightforward manner, but the narrative tends to find Halsey derelict in leaving San Bernardino Strait unguarded. Finally, Edwin B. Hoyt, *The Battle of Leyte Gulf: The Death Knell of the Japanese Fleet* (New York, 1972), presents the fullest account in English of the Japanese side. As for the Halsey-Kinkaid quarrel, like Potter, Hoyt finds Halsey derelict, but he is also understanding about Halsey's reasons for saying that he would abandon San Bernardino Strait again.

ROBERT L. EICHELBERGER

The Papers of Robert L. Eichelberger, an extensive collection that includes his voluminous dictations, 1952-1960, are located at the William R. Perkins Library, Duke University, Durham, North Carolina. Also important for understanding his wartime career is the wealth of operational data that can be found in Record Group 407 at the Federal Research Center, Suitland, Maryland. Other helpful primary sources are on deposit at the U.S. Army Military History Institute, Carlisle Barracks, Pennsylvania, especially the Papers of Innis P. Swift and Kenneth S. Sweany (chief of staff, Forty-first Division).

Eichelberger's account of his wartime service, *Our Jungle Road to Tokyo* (New York, 1950), should be read in connection with Jay Luvaas, ed., *Dear Miss Em: General Eichelberger's War in the Pacific, 1942-1945* (Westport, Conn., 1972), a more candid view of men and events. John F. Shortal, *Forged in Fire: Robert L. Eichelberger's Pacific War* (Columbia, S.C., 1987), is the most detailed account of his wartime service.

Jay Luvaas, "Buna, 19 November 1942-January 1943: A 'Leavenworth Nightmare,' " in Charles E. Heller and William Stofft, eds., *America's First Battles, 1776-1965* (Lawrence, Kans., 1986), interprets that important campaign, but see also Leslie Anders, *Gentle Knight: The Life and Times of Major General Edwin Forrest Harding* (Kent, Ohio, 1985). Samuel Milner, *Victory in Papua* (Washington, D.C., 1957), ably presents the American side, while Lida Mayo, *Bloody Buna* (Garden City, 1974), summarizes the view of the army's official historians. Dudley McCarthy, *Southwest Pacific Area, First Year: Kokoda to Wau* (Canberra, 1959), is the Australian official history, but see also D.M. Horner, *High Command: Australia and Allied Strategy, 1939-1945* (Sydney, 1982), for a broader view of Australian-American relations.

Pertinent secondary sources for later actions in the Southwest Pacific are discussed in the bibliographical essay on Walter Krueger.

ENNIS C. WHITEHEAD

The Ennis C. Whitehead Papers, consisting of 187 folders stored in three file cabinets, can be found at the U.S. Air Force Historical Research Center, Maxwell Air Force Base, Alabama. They contain private correspondence, operational plans, speeches, flying records, photographs, and other material that document his career. In addition, Donald M. Goldstein has in his possession a number of letters by Whitehead to family and friends that are not in the Whitehead Papers. The Goldstein collection also contains correspondence, interviews, and other documents that supplement the material at Maxwell.

The Papers of Carl Spaatz, Henry H. Arnold, and Frank Andrews, at the Library of Congress, Washington, D.C., are valuable for the early part of Whitehead's career, as are the Papers of Laurence Kuter at the U.S. Air Force Academy Library, Colorado Springs, Colorado. Also at the Air Force Academy are the Papers of Jarred V. Crabb, one of Whitehead's chief assistants during World War II; this collection is an invaluable source of information on bombing operations in the Southwest Pacific.

The Central Decimal Files of the Army Air Forces at the National Archives, Washington, D.C., especially the personal letters that can be found in file 312.1.A and B, provide a wealth of information on various phases of Whitehead's career. Also helpful are the unit histories at Maxwell Air Force Base. The Papers of Douglas MacArthur, MacArthur Memorial, Norfolk, Virginia, contain essential background material but have little that relates directly to Whitehead.

Donald M. Goldstein, "Ennis C. Whitehead, Aerospace Commander and Pioneer" (Ph.D. diss., University of Denver, 1970), examines Whitehead's career in detail. There are no other biographical studies.

Pat Robinson, *Fight for New Guinea* (New York, 1942), and Hugh Buggy, *Pacific Victory: A Short History of Australia's Part in World War II* (Melbourne, 1943), are contemporaneous accounts of events that remain useful. For printed primary and secondary sources on the air war in the Southwest Pacific, see the bibliographical essay for George C. Kenney.

DANIEL E. BARBEY

The best and fullest documentation of Barbey's operations in SWPA is the collection of his papers in the Operational Archives Branch of the Naval Historical Center, Washington, D.C. Therein are his own reports and those of subordinate force, group, and ship commanders, some action reports for the Seventh Fleet and Third Amphibious Force, action reports and war diaries of the ships he rode and commanded, and his monthly war diary. In addition there are his command history, chronology, the command history of his administrative command, and Lieutenant Commander W. F. Jibb, "History of the Seventh Amphibious Force." Last, the collection contains the large correspondence he maintained with men who served him or with him. These data clearly formed the basis for his book, *MacArthur's Navy: Seventh Amphibious Force Operations, 1943-1945* (Annapolis, 1969).

Additional information about Barbey may be found in the Papers of Thomas C. Kinkaid and of Chester W. Nimitz, at the Operational Archives, and in the William F. Halsey and Ernest J. King Papers in the Manuscript Division of the Library of Congress. Copies of Barbey's fitness reports were kindly furnished by Lieutenant Commander Robert J. Schulz, Naval Military Personnel Command Liaison Officer, National Personnel Records Center, St. Louis, Missouri.

Character sketches of Barbey appear in Frazier Hunt, "Uncle Dan, the Amphibious Man," *Saturday Evening Post*, July 1, 1944, pp. 24, 58, 60; Robert Shaplen, "The Duck-Billed Admiral: Amphibious Daniel E. Barbey Sets MacArthur's Men Ashore," *Newsweek*, October 2, 1944, p. 31; and John Walker, "Uncle Dan Barbey; An Amphibious Admiral Moved MacArthur's Men," *Life*, November 20, 1944, pp. 16-18.

Three important official reports are: Fleet Admiral Ernest J. King, U.S. Navy, commander in chief, U.S. Fleet, and chief of naval operations, *U.S. Navy at War, 1941-1945: Official Report to the Secretary of the Navy* (Washington, D.C., 1946); Supreme Commander for the Allied Power, *Reports of General MacArthur: The Campaigns of MacArthur in the Pacific*, 2 vols. in 4 parts (Washington, D.C., 1966); and U.S. Strategic Bombing Survey (Pacific), *The Campaigns of the Pacific War* (Washington, D.C., 1946).

Useful transcripts of oral interviews were those of Admirals Richard L. Conolly, William M. Fechtler, and Thomas C. Kinkaid, all in the Columbia University Oral History Program; of Rear Admiral Schuyler N. Pyne, at the U.S. Naval Institute; and the "Discussion-Interview" of Barbey by Henry I. Shaw, Jr., at the History and Museums Division, U.S. Marine Corps headquarters, Washington, D.C.

The development of amphibious doctrine has been followed in George C. Dyer, *The Amphibians Came to Conquer: The Story of Admiral Richmond Kelly Turner*, 2 vols. (Washington, D.C., 1971); Jeter A. Isely and Philip A. Crowl, *The U.S. Marines and Amphibious War: Its Theory and Its Practice in the Pacific* (Princeton, 1951); W.D. Puleston, *The Dardanelles Expedition* (Annapolis, 1926); and Alfred Vagts, *Landing Operation* (Harrisburg, Pa., 1952). Various allied subjects may be studied in Walter C. Ansel, "Naval Gunfire in Support of a Landing," *Marine Corps Gazette* (May 1932): 23-36; William F. Coleman, "Amphibious Reconnaissance Patrols," *Marine Corps Gazette* (December 1945): 22-25; Thomas J. Colley, "The Aerial Photograph in Amphibious Intelligence," *Marine Corps Gazette* (October 1945): 32-35; George C. Dyer, "Naval Amphibious Landmarks," *U.S. Naval Institute Proceedings* 92 (1966):61-70; and a series of articles by H.M. Smith entitled "Amphibious Tactics" that ran in the *Marine Corps Gazette* from June 1946 through early 1947.

Useful for the development of landing craft are R. Baker and others, *British Warship Design in World War II: Selected Papers from the Transactions of the Royal Institution of Naval Architects* (Annapolis, 1983), and George Edwin Mowry, *Landing Craft and the War Production Board, April 1942 to May 1944* (Washington, D.C., 1946). See also Edward L. Cochrane, "From Rendova to Normandy: The Biography of the LST," *Shipmate* (June 1944):12, 65, and Mark Tuban, "Sea-Going Truck [the DUKW]," *Marine Corps Gazette* (October 1946): 27-29. "How Well Do You Know Your Landing Craft?" *Marine Corps Gazette* (March 1948): 26-30, tests the reader's ability to recognize amphibious craft. Special articles are Perry C. Hill, "Love Charlie Item," *U.S. Naval Institute Proceedings* 71 (June 1945):675-79, on the development of the LCI; W.F. Royal, "Capabilities of Landing Craft, Type LST," NOB Norfolk, Va., Amphibious Force, U.S. Atlantic Fleet, Administration Command, May 25, 1943; and L.S. Swindler, "Japanese Landing Craft," *Marine Corps Gazette* (October 1945):53-57. The development of bases in SWPA can be followed in U.S. Bureau of Yards and Docks, *Building the Navy's Bases in World War II: History of the Bureau of Yards and Docks and the Civil Engineer Corps, 1940-1946*, 2 vols. (Washington, D.C., 1947).

For memoirs and secondary sources on the naval war in the Southwest Pacific, see the bibliographical essay for Thomas C. Kinkaid.

CONTRIBUTORS

PAOLO E. COLETTA received his doctorate from the University of Missouri. After spending three years in the U.S. Navy during World War II, he joined the faculty of the U.S. Naval Academy in 1946, where he remained until his retirement in 1983. His major works include biographies of William Jennings Bryan, William Howard Taft, and Admirals French Ensor Chadwick, Bradley A. Fisk, and Bowman Hendry McCalla; a naval history text; a study of the navy and defense unification; and bibliographies of American naval and U.S. Marine Corps history. With Robert G. Albion and K. Jack Bauer, he served as contributing editor of *American Secretaries of the Navy* (2 vols., 1980) and with Bauer produced *United States Navy and Marine Corps Bases* (2 vols., 1985). His biography of Vice Admiral Patrick N.L. Bellinger, a pioneering naval aviator, appeared in 1987. His next study will focus on Admiral William Adger Moffett and the development of naval aviation.

STANLEY L FALK received his doctorate from Georgetown University in 1959. During a long career with the government, he was chief historian of the U.S. Air Force, deputy chief historian for Southeast Asia at the U.S. Army Center of Military History, and professor of international relations at the Industrial College of the Armed Forces. His major publications include *Bataan: The March of Death* (1962), *Decision at Leyte* (1966), and *Seventy Days to Singapore: The Malayan Campaign, 1941-1942* (1975). He is now an independent historical consultant and lecturer.

DONALD M. GOLDSTEIN, who received his B.A. from the University of Maryland and his doctorate from the University of Denver, is associate professor and associate dean of the Graduate School of Public and International Affairs of the University of Pittsburgh. A veteran of twenty-two years in the U.S. Air Force, he retired as a lieutenant colonel. He has recently collaborated with Katherine V. Dillon to publish a series of books based on the research of Gordon V. Prange: *At Dawn We Slept: The Untold Story of Pearl Harbor* (1981), *Miracle at Midway* (1982), *Target Tokyo: The Story of the Sorge Spy Ring* (1984), and *December 7* (1987). Current projects include a history of air intelligence during World War II and a study of the forgotten war in Alaska.

D.M. HORNER is a regular army officer in the Royal Australian infantry corps. After graduating from the Royal Military College, Duntroon, in 1969, he served as platoon commander in Vietnam in 1971 and has held a variety of regimental and staff appointments. He took his M.A. degree from the University of New South Wales in 1976 and in that year was awarded a Churchill fellowship to investigate the study of military history overseas. He completed his doctorate at the Australian National University in 1980, for which he received the J.G. Crawford prize, the university's most prestigious Ph.D. award. He is the author of *Crisis of Command: Australian Generalship and the Japanese Threat, 1941-1943* (1978) and *High Command: Australia and Allied Strategy, 1939-1945* (1982); editor and principal author of *The Commanders: Australian Military Leadership in the Twentieth Century* (1984); and coeditor with Robert O'Neill of *New Directions in Strategic Thinking* (1981) and *Australian Defence Policy for the 1980s* (1982). Lieutenant Colonel Horner is presently an honorary fellow at the Australian Defence Force Academy.

WILLIAM M. LEARY received his doctorate from Princeton University in 1966. Professor of history at the University of Georgia since 1973, he has served as Fulbright-Hays senior lecturer in Taiwan (1974-1975) and Thailand (1979-1980) and has received research awards from the U.S. Army Military History Institute and the U.S. Air Force Historical Research Center. His publications include *The Dragon's Wings: The China National Aviation Corporation and the Development of Commercial Aviation in China* (1976), *Perilous Missions: Civil Air Transport and CIA Covert Operations in Asia* (1984), and *The Central Intelligence Agency: History and Documents* (1984), of which he is the editor. He is working on a biography of Allen Dulles.

JAY LUVAAS received his B.A. degree from Allegheny College and his doctorate from Duke University. From 1957 to 1982 he was a member of the history department at Allegheny College. He has been visiting professor of military history at the U.S. Military Academy (1972-1973) and Harold Keith Johnson Visiting Professor of Military History at the U.S. Army Military History Institute and currently occupies the General Maxwell D. Taylor chair in the profession of arms at the U.S. Army War College. His publications include *The Military Legacy of the Civil War: The European Inheritance* (1959) and *The Education of an Army: British Military Thought, 1815-1940* (1964). He edited and translated *Frederick the Great on the Art of War* (1966) and edited *The Civil War: A Soldier's View* (1958) and *Dear Miss Em: General Eichelberger's War in the Pacific* (1972). Most recently he has coauthored Army War College guides to the Battles of Gettysburg and Antietam.

JOHN F. SHORTAL is an infantry officer in the U.S. Army. After graduating from the U.S. Military Academy in 1974, he served in a variety of command and staff assignments in the United States and the Republic of Korea. He completed his doctorate at Temple University in 1985 and taught military history at West Point. He recently published *Forged in Fire: Robert L. Eichelberger's Pacific War* (1987). Major Shortal is currently a student at the U.S. Army Command and General Staff College at Fort Leavenworth, Kansas.

GERALD E. WHEELER received his doctorate from the University of California at Berkeley in 1954. He served on the faculty of the U.S. Naval Academy (1952-1957) before becoming professor of history at San Jose State University (1957-1983). He has been Fulbright-Hays senior lecturer in the Philippines (1963-1964) and Ernest J. King professor of maritime history at the U.S. Naval War College (1968-1969). His publications include *Prelude to Pearl Harbor: The United States Navy and the Far East, 1921-1931* (1963), *Admiral William Veazie Pratt* (1974), and "Edwin Denby" and "Charles Francis Adams III" in Paolo Coletta, ed., *American Secretaries of the Navy* (1980). He is writing a biography of Admiral Kinkaid.

HERMAN S. WOLK is chief of the General Histories Branch and chairman of the Publications Committee in the Office of Air Force History. After receiving his B.A. and M.A. degrees from the American International College, he studied at the Far Eastern and Russian Institute of the University of Washington in 1958-1959. He was a historian at the headquarters of the Strategic Air Command in 1959-1966. A fellow of the Inter-University Seminar on Armed Forces and Society, he is the author of *Planning and Organizing the Postwar Air Force, 1943-1947* (1984) and *Strategic Bombing: The American Experience* (1981) and is contributing editor to *Evolution of the American Military Establishment since World War II* (1978). His study of General Kenney's entire career has been published by the Office of Air Force History in *Makers of the United States Air Force*, ed. John L. Frisbee (1987).

INDEX

References to photographs are in boldface type.

This book is printed on acid-free paper meeting
the requirements of the American National Standard
for Permanence of Paper for Printed Library Materials. ⊖

Library of Congress Cataloging-in-Publication Data

We shall return! : MacArthur's commanders and the defeat of Japan,
    1942-1945 / William M. Leary, editor.
      p.   cm.
    Bibliography: p.
    Includes index.
    ISBN 0-8131-1654-6
    1. World War, 1939-1945—Campaigns—Pacific Area. 2. MacArthur,
Douglas, 1880-1964. 3. United States—Armed Forces—Biography.
I. Leary, William M. (William Matthew), 1934-
D767.9.W42   1988
940.54'26'0924—dc19   88-2731